Soupçon II

more seasonal samplings from the junior league of chicago

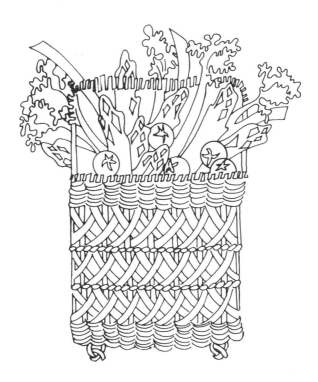

THE JUNIOR LEAGUE OF CHICAGO, INC.
CHICAGO, ILLINOIS
1982

The purpose of The Junior League is exclusively educational and charitable and is: to promote voluntarism; to develop the potential of its members for voluntary participation in community affairs; and to demonstrate the effectiveness of trained volunteers.

The proceeds from the sale of SOUPÇON II assist the community projects of The Junior League of Chicago, Inc.

FIRST EDITION

First Printing: 15,000 copies, June 1981
Second Printing: 25,000 copies, July 1982
Third Printing: 3,000 copies, July 2006

Additional copies may be obtained by addressing
Cookbook Committee Chair
The Junior League of Chicago, Inc.
1447 North Astor Street • Chicago, Illinois 60610
312-664-4462 ext. 109
E-mail: jlcsoupcon2@yahoo.com
Web site: www.jlchicago.org

Library of Congress
Catalog Card No. 2006927949
ISBN-10: 0-9611622-4-4
ISBN-13: 978-0-9611622-4-5

Cover Design By Mary Lois Hakewill

Printed by
Favorite Recipes® Press
an imprint of
FRP
P.O. Box 305142
Nashville, Tennessee 37230
1-800-358-0560

Printed in China

JUNIOR LEAGUE
of CHICAGO

The Junior League of Chicago, Inc.
1447 North Astor Street Chicago, Illinois 60610
Office: 312 664-4462 Facsimile: 312 664-1963
www.jlchi.org

Dear Friends:

Welcome back to Soupçon! The Junior League of Chicago is proud to make the extremely popular Soupçon II available to a new generation of chefs. Your purchase of this outstanding collection of recipes and cooking tips will help the JLC continue to provide our equally outstanding community projects focusing on mentoring, advocacy and education.

Thank you for your participation in our community service through which almost 2,000 women serve the Chicago community and its surrounding surburbs. Happy cooking and thank you again!

Best,

Elizabeth Hurley
President, 2004–2006

Michelle Kerr
President, 2006–2008

CONTRIBUTORS

Margarita Alexander
Sarah Allgyer
Joyce Aloy
Kathy Alspaugh
Mary Ann Amory
Judith Anderson
Pamela Anderson
Laurie Andrews
Helen Applegate
Leslie Attebery
Carol Audler
Valerie Ault
Diane Axton
Maria Bacinich
Deby Baker
Sue Ball
Linda Bartlett
Susan Bateman
Pamela Bayly
Mary Ann Beatty
Barbara Belt
Betty Bennett
Jean Bennett
Ann Berry
Jean Berghoff
Sandra Berris
Prudence Biedler
Pamela Bird
Susan Blankenship
Mary Ann Boggs
Susan Bowey
Nancy Brickman
Candy Bridgman
Carol Bryan
Heidi Buenger
Jeanne Burke
Ruth Burnell
Nan Burridge
Ann Burt
Lenore Cameron
Trevor Campbell
Anna Carmichael
Kathryn Carmichael
Crissy Cherry
Mary Ellen Christy

Sandra Clark
Candace Cleveland
Lynn Collins
Susan Craft
Pamela Cramer
Gwendolyn Cross
Peggy Crowe
Emily Cunningham
Sally Cunningham
Jan Curtiss
Edith Davies
Patty Delony
Joan DePree
Susan DePree
Susan Detchan
Nancy Dixon
Sharon Dixon
Janice Doty
Sherry Dubinsky
Madelaine Dugan
Katherine Egan
Anne Emmons
Kristine Engel
Patricia Ferguson
Gale Ferrone
Nan Ferry
Sally Fetzer
Cindy Fick
Mary Fields
Catherine Filippini
Beverly Fischer
Bonnie Folkerts
Suzanne Folland
Andrea Foote
Margaret Ann Fowler
Carolyn Fraker
Jaqueline Fuller
Eugenie Galbreath
Mary Jo Garre
Lolly Gepson
Wynella Gilbert
Laura Gilliam
Jayne Gilligan
Karen Gleason
Alice Goltra

Fredel Goodrich
Anne Goulding
Patricia Grant
Nancy Grimm
Janet Grisemer
Lynne Haarlow
Cynthia Haller
Bette Hansen
Nancy Harbottle
Brooks Hartley-
  Leonard
Rana Hatton
Rosalie Hawkins
Colleen Healy
Nancy Henderson
Theresa Hewitt
Celia Hilliard
Jean Hoagland
Claire Hodge
Constance Hodson
Judy Homeyer
Anne Hooker
Karen Howell
Martha Hoza
Carolyn Hughes
Sally Sue Hughes
Ann Ince
Jackie Jackson
Mary Lou Jenkins
Jean Jernstedt
Gloria Johnson
Vickie Johnson
Gail Kahn
Sydnie
  Kampschroeder
Joan Kasten
Suzanne Keating
Nancy Keenan
Suzan Kehoe
Joyce Kelly
Sally Kenaston
Susan Kimball
Emily King
Jeanne Kohn
Jan Ann Knight

CONTRIBUTORS

Katherine Krause
Judith Kreamer
Kristen Krider
Helen Kron
Susan Lamberson
Carolyn Lammers
Quin Lanning
Susan Larson
Susan Latta
Kitty Leatham
Barbara Ledinsky
Carol Lindsay
Anne Lockhart
Jenny Lord
Barbara Love
Sally Luedtke
Sharon Lytle
Pamela Luther
Virginia MacDonald
Ashley Maentz
Patricia Magner
Shirley Magner
Wendy Magnuson
Margaret Marshall
Peggy Martay
Joan Martin
Barbara Martin-Smith
Mary Mason
Parsla Mason
Mary Ann McDowell
Nancy Mead
Suzanne Menzel
Barbara Meyer
Carol Meyer
Phyllis Meyer
Martha Miceli
Gail Miller
Louise Mills
Nancy Mills
Meredith Moriarty
Joanne Morrow
Patricia Muir
Virginia Munson
Polly Naumann

Carolyn Neal
Brooke Nelson
Joan Nelson
Elizabeth Norton
Kathleen Nowlin
Jane Nyman
Maureen Oberdorf
Jennifer O'Brien
Marjorie O'Brien
Suzanne Oelman
Carol Olson
Nancy O'Mara
Jane O'Neil
Elizabeth O'Neill
Patricia Pace
Judith Patience
Mary Ann Peoples
Nancy Peterson
Suzanne Petkus
Mary Ann Pillman
Karen Price
Ruth Price
Happy Pross
Marcia Raborn
Pamela Ratchford
Claire-Ru Reid
Moira Rice
Christine Robb
Tish Robinson
Ann Rohlen
Cynthia Ross
Monique Rub
Judith Ryan
Kathleen Ryan
Wendy Sadler
Betty Scanlon
Alicia Schafer
Mary Schnieder
Deverie Schrieffer
Carol Schulz
Sandra Scott
Jan Sennott
Laura Shields
Pamela Shirley

Carol Shoop
Mary Smart
Chris Smith
Ellen Smith
Dee Dee Spence
Catherine
  Stephenson
Suzanne Stevens
Claire Stickney
Lisbeth Stiffel
Karen Stirling
Suzy Stout
Margaret Stowell
Cindy Stuhley
Helen Sutter
Beverly Sweeney
Joan Templeton
Jessica Tesarik
Gay Tews
Jill Theis
Jennifer Thompson
Patricia Titgemeyer
Judith Trees
Joan Trukenbrod
Anne Tuohy
Diane Vargas
Glenee Von Eschen
Karen Walton
Cynthia Ward
Jo Wayne
Patricia Weizer
Miriam Westin
Barbara Westover
Victoria Wheary
Jane Whitesides
Janice Whitsell
Judith Wilson
Mary Wolcott
Carol Woloson
Linda Wortman
Margaret Wright
Judith York
Barbara Young
Lee Youngstrom

TABLE OF CONTENTS

TABLE OF CONTENTS

INTRODUCTION

We take pleasure in presenting SOUPCON II, more seasonal samplings from the Junior League of Chicago. Soupcon, (sup'so^n, n. F.) is defined as a little bit, in this instance a culinary little bit of everything. SOUPCON II presents very simple, easy to prepare family meals to elegant, involved gourmet delights; unusual ethnic presentations to corn-fed beef, so dear to the midwestern heart. We have intended SOUPCON II as a companion edition to SOUPCON I carrying on the tradition of our successful first book. We feel that the seasonal format is very important. It is still true that seasonal produce gives better flavor at a lower cost. Since SOUPCON I was first printed seven years ago, life styles have changed in ways never imagined. Inflation, food processors, microwave ovens, more women in the work force, energy conservation — all have had a profound effect. In spite of needing speedy or frozen foods, we all enjoy an occasional elegant splurge.

In testing and selecting our recipes, we took into account cost, ease of preparation, recipe appeal, whether it could be made ahead, and if it could be frozen. In the final analysis, our main consideration and our basic criteria have been that the end result look and taste good. We have included recipes using ingredients readily available and have attempted to describe the most efficient method of preparation.

For many dishes we have found that by varying the selection of the sauce, you, the cook may create exciting, new variations from the same basic ingredient. We have included a wide selection of sauces and encourage you to use your imagination. We have also responded to requests for menus for large groups. Included are imaginative recipes and menu suggestions from our members and several of the Chicago area's best caterers.

Wine suggestions have been included for many recipes. You will notice that we have recommended a type rather than a specific wine. This allows greater flexibility in availability and cost.

We urge you to be creative. No recipe is sacrosanct; it is a guideline, a jumping off point for all sorts of taste experiences. In using recipes from SOUPCON II we strongly advise that you taste as you cook. Taste is subjective. When you read "season to taste" let your palate be the judge. Individual seasoning will increase your enjoyment of the final product.

Chicago is a food town: food is appreciated; food is an adventure; food is fun! Diets always have a way of waiting until Monday. Desserts materialize after every meal and chocolate is a staple. The Junior League of Chicago is an intrinsic part of this town and its atmosphere. We are confident that SOUPCON II will reflect the members' exuberance and the vitality of Chicago.

WINES — Selection and Serving

Wine — what a frustrating beverage it is to so many Americans! While we have the largest variety of wines to choose from in the United States, we often find this fact intimidating rather than gratifying. The French and Italians enjoy wine and they are not overly concerned with its mystique. Their secret is they don't take wine too seriously.

I have been asked to write about wine, my favorite subject, for SOUPCON II. I enjoy wine and I want you to share this enjoyment. Wine can be a wonderful, pleasure-giving beverage when treated properly. It needn't be complicated and it should always be fun.

Wine should not be thought of only for special occasions. On the contrary, the simpler the meal the more it can be enhanced by a glass of wine. Save the great wines for a particular celebration but consider serving at least a modest wine with dinner. A meal should be more than an inescapable refueling for the body. It should be a time of relaxation as well as nutrition. Wine can help it be just that.

There are many traditions, customs and folklores associated with the drinking of wine. The vast majority of these only serve to scare people away from the great pleasures of wine drinking. There are, however, a handful of hints that you might find helpful.

While wine may be drunk from any vessel, a good glass is essential in order to fully appreciate the wine's multifaceted, sensual characteristics. First of all, the glass should be crystal clear so that you can enjoy the wine's visual beauty. It should be a stemmed glass with a 6 to 12 ounce bowl gently curving to the lip. Regardless of the size of the glass, it should not be filled more than half way. This will enable you to swirl the wine in your glass and have its beautiful fragrances fill the air.

When serving more than one wine with a meal, use a different glass for each wine. If the glasses are of different sizes, use the larger for the red wine. It is perfectly acceptable and quite enjoyable to serve two different wines with the same course. It's a way of having a mini-wine tasting with your meal.

Different wines have different molecular structures and respond better at different temperatures. To serve a wine too cold will subdue its subtle characteristics. If you should own a bottle of wine that you don't like, however; serve it ice-cold and you'll probably find it quite palatable. If a wine is served to you too cold, you can always warm it by cupping your hands around the bowl as one does with a brandy snifter.

The flavor of most red wines is greatly enhanced when the bottle has been opened an hour or two before serving. This "breathing" allows the wine to come in contact with the air which will develop its flavors and take some of the sharp edges off a young wine. An older red wine (over 10 years) may require decanting to remove its natural sediment. Your wine merchant should be able to advise you on the necessity for breathing and decanting of the wine that he sells you.

You should be proud of the wine that you are serving so don't wrap the bottle in a towel as you are pouring it. A towel serves no purpose. If you give the bottle a slight twist as you complete pouring each glass, you can usually avoid any dripping. If you should spill red wine on your tablecloth or carpet, a little table salt or club soda poured onto the spill will inhibit the stain from setting.

Selecting the proper wine to serve is very subjective. One's taste in wine can be as diverse as one's taste in music. The place, the mood, the company, the weather, the budget are as important considerations as the food being served. When dining with your family, it can simply be a matter of serving the wine that you prefer. When selecting a wine to serve your guests, you are much safer to select a marriage of wine and food that has been tried, tested, and approved. There are certain wines that have been traditionally deemed classic companions to certain foods. When you hit upon the proper combination, the marriage enhances both, and the wine and food become greater than either would be by itself.

In general, light-bodied and flavored wines, regardless of color, go better with the lighter more delicate dishes. Robust and hearty wines will best complement richer, heavier, well-seasoned recipes. At no time should either the wine or the food be overpowering. There are certain foods and spices that do not go well with any wine. Vinegar, strong onion or garlic, hot mustard, curries, chili seasonings, and chocolate will kill the flavor of any wine. With dishes that contain these ingredients, it is best to serve either beer or a simple, inexpensive "beverage wine."

Bob Habermann and I have attempted to categorize wines into taste-types. Each type of wine has been coded and you will find a wine recommendation after many recipes in this book. These are based on personal experiences as well as those of the "experts" in the gastronomic sciences. Of course, this is intended only as a general guide and you are encouraged to experiment.

To your enjoyment and good health,
George J. Schaefer

As president of Schaefer's Wines & Spirits, George J. Schaefer has become recognized as one of the most knowledgeable wine merchants in the United States. Mr. Schaefer holds the title of "Master Connoisseur of French Gastronomy" and has been a member of many prestigious international gourmet fraternities.

Wine Tasting Party

SELECTION OF WINE

Establish a theme for the testing. You may wish to have a variety of wines from one geographical region, wines from the same grape from different regions (horizontal tasting), the same wine from different vintages (vertical tasting) or any number of other combinations. Your local wine merchant should be happy to assist you in making your selections.

AMOUNT NEEDED

Plan on serving 5 or 6 different wines. For each wine that you serve, allow one bottle (25 oz.) for every 8 to 10 guests. In addition, serve an aperitif wine so that early arrivals will have something to sip before the tasting begins.

GLASSWARE

Ideally you should use glass stemware. If you have enough, use a separate glass for each wine (6 wines x 12 guests = 72 glasses). If you are unable to arrange for that amount you may use 1 glass per guest. Then have some large bowls and pitchers of water available so that guests can pour out leftover wine and rinse their glasses before tasting the next wine.

FOOD

Cheese is a perfect accompaniment. Arrange wedges of several different types of mild-flavored varieties (Brie, Camembert, Gouda, Bel Passe, Muenster, or Mozzarella) and let each guest serve himself. Serve breadsticks, unsalted crackers and/or French bread. Excellent fresh fruit (grapes, pears, peaches) is also good. Blandness is the key. You want to cleanse the palate but not interfere with the taste of the wine.

SERVING THE WINE

The most practical method is to let each guest serve his own. Number the wines in the order that you wish your guests to taste them — whites before reds, dry before sweet and light-bodied before the more robust ones. Each wine should be accompanied with the necessary glassware and food. For a large group it is best to arrange the wines throughout a room or rooms rather than to cluster them in a central location. Provide each guest with a list of the wines, some information about each and space to write comments. After the tasting you may wish to conduct a poll to see which wines were most popular. If your guests are more experienced, you may try a blind tasting where the identity of each wine is concealed and participants are asked to guess which wine is which from the list you have provided.

A Guide To Dinner Wine Types And Us

Wine Type	Basic Characteristics
Light Dry White (Cool: 47°-52°F)	Clean, crisp, dry (lacking sweetness), subtle fruitiness and delicate flavor.
Full-Flavored Dry White (Cool: 47°-52°F)	Dry but with more hearty flavor than those listed above.
Medium-Dry White (Chilled: 45°-50°F)	A touch of sweetness with delicate grape fruitiness.
Sweet White (Cool: 42°-47°F)	Sweet, fuller-bodied, rich in fruitiness.
Light-Bodied Red (Slightly Cooled: 55°-60°F)	Light in body and color, fresh fruitiness.
Medium-Bodied Red (Cool Room Temp.: 62°-67°F)	Medium in body and color, dry and mellow (when mature).
Full-Bodied Red (Cool Room Temp.: 62°-67°F)	Full-bodied, deep color, robust and hearty flavor.
Rosé (Chilled: 45°-52°F)	Pink color, light-bodied, dry to medium-dry with slight fruitiness.
Sparkling Wine (Cold: 40°-45°F)	Carbonated, dry to medium-dry; white, pink or red in color.

Best-Known Examples	Favorite Uses
Chardonnay, Pinot Blanc, Dry Chenin Blanc, Sauvignon Blanc, Fumé Blanc, Muscadet, Pouilly-Fumé, Sancerre, Macon Blanc, Pouilly-Fuisse, Montrachet, French Chablis, Graves, Alsatian Riesling, Soave, Lugana and Verdicchio. For economy: California Chablis or White Table Wine.	Shellfish, fish, chicken, turkey, veal, ham, pork, cold meats, paté, quiche, hors d'oeuvres, snacks and pasta dishes with white sauce. Also as a cocktail or aperitif wine without food.
Gewurztraminer (dry), some California Chardonnay, Meursault, Corton-Charlemagne, or white Rhone wines.	More flavorful versions of above — highly seasoned or spiced dishes.
Most California rieslings, most Chenin Blancs, German Rhine or Mosel (QBA, kabinett or spatlese), Vouvray or Anjou Blanc. For economy: California Rhine.	Chicken, turkey, pork, delicate fish (trout, sole, etc.), Quiche Lorraine and most omelets. Also as a cocktail or aperitif wine without food.
California late-harvest riesling, French Sauternes and Barsac, German Rhine and Mosel (auslese or sweeter) or Hungarian Tokaji Aszu.	Most desserts and fresh fruits.
Gamay, Beaujolais, Valpolicella or Bardolino. For economy: California Claret.	Ham, turkey, stews, pot roasts, barbecued chicken, meat omelets, cold cuts and other casual meats.
Cabernet Sauvignon, Merlot, Barbera, some Zinfandel, Pinot Noir, Bordeaux, French Burgundy, Chianti Classico, Spanish Rioja or Penedes. For economy: California Burgundy or Red Table Wine.	Beef, lamb, veal, turkey, wild fowl (duck, pheasant etc.), spaghetti and most cheese.
Petite Sirah, Chateauneuf du Pape and most other French Rhones, Italian Barolo and Nebbiolo.	Beef, game (venison etc.), heavy stews or ragouts and most cheese.
Grenache rose, Gamay rose, Blanc de Noir, Tavel and Cabernet d'Anjou. For economy: California Vin Rosé.	Ham, pork, eggs, barbecued chicken and casual meals. Also as a cocktail wine without food.
Extra dry or brut (driest) Champagne from France, America or Spain; German Sekt or Italian Brut Spumante.	Festive celebrations, caviar or with just about any food or as a cocktail wine by itself.

1447

1447 N. Astor — A Brief History

Since 1954 the Junior League of Chicago has occupied a four-story townhouse at 1447 N. Astor. Located in the city's elegant Gold Coast community, this headquarters building is now part of the Astor Street Historic District.

It is hard to believe that a little over one hundred years ago the neighborhood was a sandy swamp at the edge of Lake Michigan where young boys shot ducks before daylight.

By 1875 the whole marsh had been drained, filled and named Lake Shore Drive, a fashionable roadway 200 feet wide and three quarters of a mile long. Astor Street (named in honor of John Jacob Astor, founder of the American Fur Company whose traders operated in the area during the early 19th century) was laid out one block to the west. It was divided into 25-foot lots and gradually developed, for the most part with townhouses that featured common walls and carefully arranged interior spaces. Prominent and wealthy families were drawn to the neighborhood.

In the late 1890's a four-story red brick house was built at 151 Astor (later renumbered "1447"). The design is an austere version of the Georgian Revival style, with a symmetrical facade, simple sash windows, and interesting geometric brickwork.

In 1899 the Chicago Blue Book lists the first occupants as a Mr. and Mrs. Charles D. Peacock, Jr. living at this address.

Charles D. Peacock, Jr. was the oldest son of C.D. Peacock, proprietor of a prestigious State Street jewelry store. At the age of 27 he moved his young family into the new townhouse at 151 Astor. There is no record that the Peacocks ever owned this house. In fact, it is quite probable that they rented it from their next door neighbor, Horatio N. May, a real estate speculator who owned the land on which it was built.

The interior had simple but elegant and well-proportioned spaces, a floor plan that would satisfy the domestic and social requirements of the typical affluent family. As was usual in houses of that time, the ground floor contained the kitchen, a series of dining and sleeping rooms for the help, a boiler room, laundry room, and various storage closets. On the first floor were the living room, library, and dining room, each with its own fireplace. There were also an elaborate dressing room and a grand staircase leading to the bedrooms upstairs — plenty of room for three young Peacock daughters to wander in.

The Astor Street house was empty during the summer months when the five Peacocks and their nurse Delia went to Sugar Loaf, the family peninsula on Green Lake.

In 1905 the Peacocks moved from the house on Astor Street to a bigger freestanding home on a large lot on Surf Street. Though the new location was only two miles to the north, at that time it meant leaving a fashionable "citified" dwelling for a rambling suburban estate.

Following the Peacocks' departure, a Dr. Phillips and his wife rented the townhouse for two years, and then in 1908 Wallace C. Winter, vice-president of a railway supply manufacturing company, bought it for $12,000. He lived there with his wife and three children until 1922, when he sold it to Lydia Thatcher Wheeler and moved to the suburb of Lake Forest.

Mrs. Wheeler was a wealthy and adventurous beauty who liked extravagant hats, fine food, and long journeys. She spoke fluent French and traveled on a steamer to Shanghai and Hong Kong at the age of 21. She was warm, outgoing, and deeply sympathetic. She was fascinated by psychoanalysis, and as a young volunteer at Children's Memorial Hospital, she recorded the case histories of Dr. Ralph Hamill's early psychiatric patients.

She and her husband Robert C. Wheeler, an investment banker, moved into 1447 Astor with their daughter Winifred and son Robert. On her many trips to Europe, Mrs. Wheeler began to collect antique furniture, paneling, and wallpaper, and gradually she transformed the simple interior of the townhouse into an elaborate French decor.

The 35-by-20-foot living room was paneled in light pine with a hand-carved fruit motif. The library was paneled in walnut, and a piece of stained glass was installed in the window overlooking the garden. The upstairs sitting room was decorated with eggshell moldings, and the dressing rooms were fitted with carved-in-Europe "built in" shelves. Mrs. Wheeler's bedroom was covered with a hand-done watercolored wallpaper, circa 1823, depicting a Frenchman's notion of scenes from daily life in China. The wallpaper was backed with old Paris newspapers, and a craftsman from the Art Institute was called over to see that it was properly hung.

Whenever the antique fixtures did not fit the proportions of the Astor Street house, local carpenters made up matching pieces. One of the home's most unusual features — a heavy molded door which doesn't open and leads to nowhere — was placed at the top of the entry stairs where every visitor would be certain to see it.

During World War II Mrs. Wheeler, then widowed for some time, moved to a Lake Shore Drive apartment. The house was put up for sale, but those who could afford to buy it wanted to divide it into apartments or otherwise alter the interior in a radical way. Mrs. Wheeler had invested too much of her time and resources in its decoration and had too many memories of family holidays, debuts, and wedding receptions in its gracious rooms to view such changes with equanimity.

Finally in 1953 Mrs. Wheeler donated the house to the Junior League of Chicago in memory of her husband. Her daughter Winifred was a member of the League, and aside from a general refurbishment, the original floor plan and her exquisite additions would be kept intact.

Prior to 1954 the Junior League of Chicago had occupied 14 different locations in its 41-year history, and it leased or borrowed additional space to operate ongoing activities like the Art Show and the Children's Theater. When Mrs. Wheeler first offered the house to the League, many members doubted that the League could afford to maintain it. A stronger faction felt that, even though a raise in dues would be necessary to support it, this 25-room house would give the League both a permanent home and a physical focus for its broadening activities. In June 1953 the membership voted to accept Mrs. Wheeler's gift.

Since the house had been empty for several years, it needed to be thoroughly cleaned and refurbished. The brickwork was washed with acid, the interior was completely repainted, and the woodwork was refinished — all for under $5,000. (To save money the chairman of the decorating committee painted the gold trim on the white French moldings herself.)

Mrs. Wheeler's daughter Winifred sent the original furnishings for the library from her home in California, and several other members donated antique furniture and paintings as well. The master bedroom (minus its watercolored wallpaper, which Mrs. Wheeler moved to the library in her Lake Shore Drive apartment) was now the Junior League board room. Winifred's suite became the guest quarters. Robert's bedroom, with its hand-painted French tile fireplace, became the office for the professional staff. The Junior League president modestly chose a small dressing room facing an air shaft for her own office.

The sustainers (members over the age of 40) assumed responsibility for the patio garden in the back. They landscaped it, planted the back wall with trees, and established a plan to serve an alfresco lunch during warm weather. However, the yard was too shady and the soil too rocky to encourage vegetation, the members were forced to use the fire escape to reach the tables, and the house was closed during July and August anyhow. After two years the idea of using the outdoor space for meals or other events was abandoned.

Today the Junior League of Chicago still occupies this landmark townhouse. Its long history and relaxed ambiance provide an engaging backdrop for the League's current civic activities and a sense of continuity with the past.

Celia Hilliard

SPRING MENUS

DO-AHEAD LUNCHEON FOR A SPRING MEETING

Fresh Strawberry Champagne Cup
Curried Crab Crepes
Spinach Mushroom Salad with Honey Russian Dressing
Texas Orange Muffins
Lemon-Nut-Berry Roll

MEDIEVAL BANQUET

Guests should come in costume, each bringing his own spoon and knife

Brie Tart
Jusselle Dates
Golden Apples
Ginger Beef
Braised Leeks and Mushrooms
Lemon Rice with Almonds
Parsley Bread

Lombardy Tart		Flower Cake
Ale	Mulled Wine	Cider

EASTER DINNER

Champagne Framboise
Gougere
Rack of Lamb with Madeira Sauce
Potato Baskets Filled with Petit Pois
Endive and Egg Salad
Ukranian Torte
Chocolate Easter Nests
Coffee

SPRING MENUS

KENTUCKY DERBY CELEBRATION DINNER

Rosebuds   Mint Juleps

Fresh Pea Soup
Chicken a la Crickets
Tangy Carrots
Potatoes Rosemary
Tossed Green Salad
Kentucky Pie

INFORMAL SUNDAY SUPPER

Pasta Primavera
Green Salad
Italian Bread
Lemon Surprise Meringues

ELEGANT DINNER FOR GOOD FRIENDS

Paté Maison with Cornichons
Seafood Supreme
Porc St. Hubert
Asparagus with Hazelnut Butter
Mixed Green Salad
Cheese
Extra Chocolate Chocolate Cake
Coffee
Brandied Apricot Truffles

LATE NIGHT JAPANESE SUPPER

Namasu
Tempura
Boiled Rice
Assorted Fresh Fruits with Sugar Cookies
Sake   Beer   Tea

BEVERAGES

CHAMPAGNE FRAMBOISE   8 Servings

3½ cups raspberries,
   pureed (fresh or frozen)
Superfine sugar to taste
6 oz. orange liqueur
2 bottles Champagne,
   chilled

Strain raspberry puree; add sugar and chill at least 2 hours until very cold. Stir in liqueur and chilled Champagne. Serve as aperitif in chilled, stemmed glasses.

CRANBERRY SLUSH   16-20 Servings
Before dinner cooler

1 bottle (46 oz.)
   cranapple juice
1 can (12 oz.) frozen
   lemonade, thawed
12 oz. vodka

Mix all ingredients together and freeze in 13 x 9-inch pan. Allow to soften in refrigerator about 20 to 30 minutes before serving. Serve in cocktail glasses with short wide straws.

LITTLE HARBOR CLUB HUMMER   2 Servings
Hmm . . . hmm

2 cups ice cream (vanilla
   or coffee)
1 oz. dark rum
1 oz. creme de cacao

Put ingredients in blender. Blend just until smooth. Pour into two 10-oz. glasses. Serve.

ROSEBUDS   2 Quarts
A lady's mint julep

32 oz. gin or vodka
20 oz. orange juice
Juice of 1 lemon
12 oz. grenadine
3 T. confectioners' sugar
Fresh mint

Combine all ingredients except mint. Stir well with plenty of cracked ice. Add crushed fresh mint. May be served in individual cocktail glasses with mint garnish or as a punch garnished with ice ring and sprigs of fresh mint.

BEVERAGES

RUM PUNCH

2 pkgs. (10 oz. each)
  frozen strawberries
1 can (6 oz.) frozen
  limeade
1 fifth light rum
1 or 2 bottles ginger ale
½ gallon orange sherbet
Sliced oranges and fresh
  whole strawberries

Put first 4 ingredients in punch bowl. Add sherbet. Garnish with orange slices and strawberries.

FRESH STRAWBERRY CHAMPAGNE CUP   4 Servings

1 pt. fresh strawberries
4 T. sugar
½ cup fresh orange juice
½ cup dry white wine
1 bottle Champagne on
  ice

Stem, wash, and cut strawberries in ½. One hour before serving combine strawberries, sugar, fresh orange juice, and dry white wine. Set in a cool place to macerate. To serve, divide mixture among 4 large glass goblets and fill each with chilled Champagne.

APPETIZERS

ASPARAGUS HORS D'OEUVRES

1 lb. loaf soft sandwich
   bread
1 can (15 oz.) asparagus
   spears
1 cup Yogurt Hollandaise
   Sauce
¼ cup grated Parmesan
   cheese
Melted butter

**YOGURT HOLLANDAISE
SAUCE:**

2 large egg yolks
1 cup plain yogurt
½ tsp. Dijon mustard
Salt, freshly ground white
   pepper, to taste

Trim crusts from bread. Flatten bread with rolling pin. Spread bread completely to edges with Hollandaise. Sprinkle with Parmesan cheese. Place 1 asparagus spear diagonally on each slice of bread. Roll up in bread. Place seam side down on baking sheet. Brush with melted butter. Bake at 400° for 12 minutes.

For sauce, thicken egg yolks, yogurt, and mustard in top of double boiler, until mixture coats a spoon. Season. This can be reheated slowly in a double boiler.

BACON-WATERCRESS PARTY ROLLS   Makes 30

1 cup chopped
   watercress or parsley,
   stems removed
16 slices bacon, cooked
   and crumbled
Few drops Worcestershire
   sauce
6 to 8 T. finely chopped
   walnuts (optional)
Mayonnaise
¼ lb. butter, softened
Garlic powder, to taste
15 slices white bread,
   crusts removed, rolled
   thin
Watercress, or parsley for
   garnish

Combine watercress, bacon, Worcestershire sauce, and walnuts, if desired, with just enough mayonnaise to bind. Combine butter and garlic powder; spread thinly on bread to cover each slice completely to the edges. Cover with watercress/bacon mixture; roll and place seam side down on freezing tray. Freeze. Remove from freezer just before serving, cut in ½ and garnish with a small sprig of watercress or parsley at the end of each roll. Dust with paprika. Rolls may be cut in ½, garnished and served immediately without freezing, if desired. At Christmas time, serve on tray with cherry tomatoes and bunches of watercress.

HORS D'OEUVRES

WARAK INIB MINSHEE (STUFFED GRAPE LEAVES)

Makes 50

Delicious appetizer or entree

50 grape leaves (1-qt. jar)
1 cup chopped onions
½ cup butter
1 lb. finely ground cooked
  lamb
½ cup white or golden
  raisins
¼ cup pine nuts
2 T. tomato paste
2 cloves garlic, finely
  chopped
½ cup chopped parsley
6 chicken wings
1 tsp. salt
Freshly ground pepper
Juice of 2 lemons

Rinse leaves and let drain. Make filling. Saute onions in butter until brown; add lamb, raisins, pine nuts, tomato paste, garlic, and parsley. Stir over medium heat 1 minute and adjust seasonings. Place leaf with shiny side down. Put 1 T. stuffing in center of leaf. Fold end of leaf like an envelope, tuck in the sides and continue to roll. Cut off stem. Place chicken wings in bottom of a large greased pan. Arrange stuffed leaves in rows in pan, alternating direction of each row. Sprinkle salt and pepper over leaves. Weight down leaves with a large plate or pot top. Add enough water to barely cover leaves. Cover pan with lid or aluminum foil. Cook over low heat for 35 minutes or until tender. Add lemon juice during the last 10 minutes of cooking.

JUSSELLE DATES

About 50

1 pkg. (1 lb.) pitted dates
1 cup brown bread
  crumbs
2 T. crushed dried sweet
  basil
½ tsp. salt
1 pkg. (8 oz.) cream
  cheese, softened
½ cup beef broth
3 hard-cooked eggs, well
  mashed

Make a lengthwise slit in dates; do not cut through. Cover with damp towel. Combine crumbs, basil, and salt. Beat cheese with broth; add spiced crumbs and eggs. (If too stiff, add small amount of broth.) Put mixture into pastry bag; pipe into dates. May be made day ahead and refrigerated.

APPETIZERS

PATE MAISON   16-20 Slices

1 cup minced onion
4 T. chicken fat or lard
½ lb. chicken livers
1½ lbs. boned cooked
    meat (chicken, turkey,
    pork or veal)
½ cup unsalted butter,
    softened
2 to 3 T. brandy or
    Cognac
1½ T. Pate Spice

PATE SPICE:

1 T. crushed bay leaf
1 T. dried thyme
1 T. powdered mace
1 T. dried rosemary
1 T. dried basil
2 T. ground cinnamon
½ tsp. cloves
½ tsp. allspice
1 tsp. ground white
    pepper
2 tsp. Spanish paprika
1 cup fine table salt

Saute onion in hot fat until limp and golden. Add livers; saute until last trace of pink disappears. Cool. Place livers and onion in food processor and puree. Add rest of meat and process until smooth. Blend in butter 1 T. at a time; process until fluffy. Add brandy and Pate Spice. Mix well. Adjust seasonings to taste. At this point you want it to be a little salty to taste because seasonings become less pronounced as pate chills. Turn into waxed paper-lined 9 x 5-inch loaf pan. Chill until firm (may easily be made a day or 2 ahead). To serve, turn onto platter and slice. Accompany with cornichons (small sour pickles) and crusty bread.

For pate spice, combine all ingredients except salt in food processor. Blend several minutes until all are fine and well combined. Add salt and process 2 to 3 minutes longer. Store in cool place in tightly covered jar. Makes 1½ cups.

MARVELOUS SHRIMP   25-30 Pieces

1 cup mayonnaise
¼ cup salad oil
3 T. chili sauce
1 tsp. celery seed
1 clove garlic, minced
1 T. minced onion
1 stalk celery with leaves,
    chopped
1 lb. shrimp, cleaned,
    cooked
2 strands fresh dill,
    separated

Put all ingredients except dill and shrimp in blender or food processor. Process "on-off" until just blended. Do not puree. Pour sauce over shrimp. Add dill and refrigerate. Serve well chilled.

26

HORS D'OEUVRES

STUFFED CLAMS

4-6 Servings

24 medium hard-shelled
  clams
4 slices bacon
1 small onion, chopped
½ lb. mushrooms,
  chopped
½ cup chopped celery
⅛ lb. Swiss cheese,
  grated
¾ cup fine, fresh bread
  crumbs
2 T. finely chopped
  parsley
1 small clove garlic,
  minced
¼ cup dry white wine
1 egg yolk
½ tsp. thyme
Salt and freshly ground
  black pepper
½ cup grated Parmesan
  cheese
Lemon wedges

Wash clams well; place in kettle and cover bottom of pan with ½ inch of water. Cover and steam until clams open. Drain; let cool. Remove clams from shells and chop. Reserve 24 clam shells. Cook bacon until crisp; crumble and set aside. Reserve fat. In 2 T. bacon fat, brown onion; then add mushrooms and celery. Cook until mushrooms wilt. Remove from heat. Add Swiss cheese, bread crumbs, parsley, garlic, wine, egg yolk, and thyme to mushroom mixture. Add salt and pepper to taste. Fill clam shells with mixture and sprinkle with Parmesan cheese. Place on cookie sheet and bake at 400° for 10 minutes or until golden brown and bubbly. Serve with lemon wedges on the side.

NOTE: May be made with ⅔ cup canned drained clams. Stuff mixture into medium to large mushroom caps which have been sauteed in 2 T. butter, 1 tsp. lemon juice, salt, and pepper until tender. Bake stuffed mushrooms at 400° for 10 minutes.

BRIE TART

10-12 Servings

1 unbaked 8-inch pastry
  shell
¾ lb. young Brie cheese
½ cup whipping cream or
  half and half
3 eggs, lightly beaten
½ tsp. brown sugar
¼ tsp. ginger
⅛ tsp. saffron
Salt and pepper to taste

Bake pastry shell at 425° for 10 minutes. Cool. Remove rind from Brie and discard. Combine cheese with rest of ingredients in blender; mix until smooth. Pour into pastry shell. Bake at 350° for 30 to 40 minutes, or until set and brown on top. Cut into squares or thin wedges to serve.

APPETIZERS

LIMPIA WITH SWEET AND SOUR SAUCE   Makes 50-60

1½ lbs. ground beef or
    pork
1 medium potato, minced
1 medium onion, minced
1 clove garlic, minced
1 stalk celery, minced
1 medium green pepper,
    minced
3 T. soy sauce
Dash salt
Won ton wrappers

For limpia, brown meat in saucepan, add rest of ingredients, except won ton wrappers. Cook slowly. Place 1 tsp. of mixture on each won ton wrapper; wrap as for egg roll. Fry in deep fat fryer for 2 minutes. Serve with sweet and sour sauce. For sweet and sour sauce, mix ingredients in a pan. Cook over medium heat, stirring until mixture thickens and becomes clear.

**SWEET AND SOUR
SAUCE:**

½ cup brown sugar
2 T. cornstarch
½ cup vinegar
1½ cups pineapple juice
2 T. soy sauce

CURRIED CHICKEN BALLS   5 Dozen

1 pkg. (8 oz.) cream
    cheese
¼ cup mayonnaise
2 cups cooked chicken,
    finely chopped
1½ cups blanched
    almonds, chopped
¼ cup chutney, chopped
2 tsp. curry powder
1 tsp. salt
1 cup grated coconut

Beat together cream cheese and mayonnaise. Add chicken, almonds, chutney, curry powder, and salt. Shape into 1-inch balls. Roll in the grated coconut. Chill until ready to serve. (May be made ahead of time and frozen.)

HORS D'OEUVRES

GINGER DIP
About 2½ Cups

1 cup mayonnaise
1 cup sour cream
¼ cup finely chopped
  onion
¼ cup minced parsley
¼ cup finely chopped
  water chestnuts
1 to 2 T. finely chopped
  candied ginger
2 cloves garlic, minced
1 T. soy sauce
Salt

Mix all ingredients; chill thoroughly. Serve on toasted rye bread strips.

TERIYAKI RIBS
12-16 Appetizer Servings

4 lbs. spareribs, cut in
  1½-inch pieces
⅔ cup brown sugar
⅔ cup soy sauce
¼ cup cider vinegar
2 cloves garlic, pressed
½ tsp. ground ginger
½ tsp. MSG
2 T. cornstarch

Simmer ribs in 1 cup water in covered pan for about 1 hour. Drain. In saucepan, mix brown sugar, soy sauce, vinegar, garlic, ginger, and MSG. Bring to a boil. Make a paste with cornstarch and ¼ cup water; add to mixture. Cook, stirring constantly, until smooth and glossy. Cool slightly. Dip ribs in mixture. Place in baking dish. Bake at 350° for 20 minutes.

CHEESE SPREAD
About 4 Cups

Marvelous accompaniment with soup, especially chicken bisque

1 lb. butter
½ lb. sharp Cheddar
  cheese, shredded
¼ lb. Romano cheese,
  grated
1 tsp. Worcestershire
  sauce
¼ tsp. garlic powder
½ tsp. paprika
Sourdough bread, sliced

Have ingredients at room temperature. Combine and whip until fluffy. Spread cheese mixture on bread, sprinkle with paprika and place under broiler until cheese begins to bubble and gets brown on edges. May also be used as a filling for grilled cheese sandwiches.

SOUPS

AVGOLEMONO SOUP

8 Servings

Greek egg and lemon soup

1 whole chicken breast, split
1 stalk celery, cut up
1 small onion, quartered
6 cups water
⅓ cup uncooked long-grain rice
1 tsp. salt
3 eggs
¼ cup fresh lemon juice
¼ cup chopped parsley
Thin lemon slices

Simmer chicken breasts, celery and small onion in water for 30 minutes. Skin and debone chicken, shred; using food processor, if desired. Strain stock; add enough water to measure 6 cups. Combine stock, rice, and salt in saucepan. Heat to boiling; cover, reduce heat and simmer 20 minutes. Beat eggs in bowl until frothy; slowly add lemon juice in a steady stream. Beat constantly to prevent eggs from curdling. Stir 2 cups hot stock and rice mixture into eggs, whisking constantly. Gradually pour back into soup. Cook slowly, stirring constantly, until slightly thickened. Stir in shredded chicken and parsley. Garnish each serving with a lemon slice.

CRAB BISQUE FLORENTINE

6 Servings

3 T. butter
1 T. grated onion
3 T. flour
2 cups half and half
1 tsp. Worcestershire sauce
3 cups cooked spinach
1 cup condensed beef bouillon
Salt to taste
Freshly ground pepper
½ cup crabmeat
½ cup sherry
¼ cup toasted almonds, chopped

Melt butter in heavy 2½-qt. saucepan. Stir in onion and flour; cook over low heat for 2 minutes. Do not brown. Heat half and half. Remove onion mixture from heat; whisk in hot cream and Worcestershire sauce. Blend thoroughly. Puree spinach in blender with bouillon. Stir spinach into cream; simmer for 10 minutes. Season with salt and pepper. Keep warm over simmering water until ready to serve. Just before serving, add crab and sherry. Simmer for 2 minutes to combine flavors. Thin with hot cream or bouillon, if necessary. Spoon into individual bowls and sprinkle with toasted almonds.

SOUPS

EASY CRAB VICHYSSOISE

6 Servings

2 cans (10 oz. each)
   cream of potato soup
2½ cups whipping cream
1 tsp. dill
5 tsp. chopped chives or
   2 T. grated onion
2 tsp. Worcestershire
   sauce
¼ tsp. garlic powder
Salt and pepper to taste
1 pkg. (6 oz.) frozen
   crabmeat, thawed and
   chilled

Combine soup and cream in blender or food processor. Add rest of ingredients, except crab. Chill. When ready to serve, add crab. Garnish with chives.

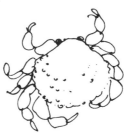

TURTLE SOUP

12 Servings

2 lbs. frozen turtle meat,
   defrosted
2 qts. water
1 small onion, quartered
1 bay leaf, crumbled
2 tsp. salt
¼ tsp. cayenne pepper
1½ cups finely chopped
   onions
8 T. butter, cut into ½-
   inch bits
½ cup flour
¼ cup canned tomato
   puree
¼ cup Worcestershire
   sauce
½ cup dry sherry
2 hard-cooked eggs,
   finely chopped
2 T. chopped fresh
   parsley
Lemon slices

Combine turtle and water; bring to boil. Skim off foam. Add quartered onion, bay leaf, salt, and cayenne pepper. Simmer, covered, for 2 hours. Cut meat into ½-inch cubes. Strain stock and reserve 4 cups. (May need to add water to make 4 cups.) Saute onions in butter until soft and golden brown. Stir in flour. Whisk in reserved stock. Cook, stirring constantly until thickened. Reduce to low heat; stir in tomato puree and Worcestershire sauce. Simmer 10 minutes. Add turtle, sherry, and eggs. Simmer 2 to 3 minutes. Garnish with parsley and lemon slices.

SOUPS

FRESH PEA SOUP

3-4 Servings

4 T. butter
1 leek, washed and sliced
6 outside lettuce leaves, shredded
1 lb. peas, fresh or frozen
1 tsp. salt
½ tsp. sugar
3⅛ cups water

Melt 3 T. of the butter in a saucepan over low heat. Add the leek, lettuce, peas, salt, and sugar. Stir to mix thoroughly with the butter; cover. Cook gently for 5 minutes. Add the water and simmer, covered, until tender, 10 to 15 minutes, depending on maturity of the peas. Reserve a few peas for garnish. Puree the soup. Return the pureed soup to the saucepan; reheat. Correct seasoning. Remove from heat; stir in the remaining butter. Serve garnished with the reserved peas.

CREAM OF BROCCOLI SOUP

About 4 Cups

½ pkg. (10 oz. size) frozen broccoli, cooked, drained
¼ cup butter
2 T. flour
2½ cups milk
½ cup half and half
1 vegetable bouillon cube
¼ cup sherry
Salt and pepper to taste

Process broccoli, butter, flour, and part of milk in food processor or blender. Put in saucepan; add rest of ingredients. Cook, stirring constantly, until thickened.

CREAM OF CARROT SOUP

8 Cups

1 small onion, chopped
2 T. butter
2 cans (13 oz. each) chicken broth
1 lb. carrots
2 T. uncooked rice
1 tsp. sugar
1 tsp. salt
¼ tsp. white pepper
2 cups half and half
Chopped parsley

Saute onion in butter until soft. Add broth, carrots, rice, and seasonings. Cover and simmer until carrots are tender and rice has puffed. Puree in blender until smooth; add half and half. Serve hot or cold with a sprinkle of chopped parsley.

SOUPS

CURRIED CREAM OF ZUCCHINI SOUP

4 Servings

Just the right amount of curry — delicious hot or cold

1 lb. young zucchini
2 T. butter
2 T. finely chopped
  shallots or onion
1 clove garlic, minced
1 tsp. curry powder
½ tsp. salt
½ cup half and half
1 can (13¾ oz.) chicken
  broth

Scrub zucchini and slice thin. Do not peel. Melt butter, add zucchini, shallots, and garlic. Cover tightly and simmer 10 minutes, shaking pan occasionally. Do not let vegetables brown. Put mixture in blender or processor; add remaining ingredients and blend. Serve hot with croutons or cold with chives.

To freeze, omit half and half. Add when defrosted. Freeze in 2 or 4-cup containers.

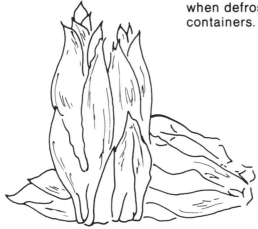

CREAM OF ENDIVE SOUP

6 Servings

6 heads of Belgian endive
4 T. butter
5 cups chicken broth
3 T. flour
1 cup whipping cream
Salt and freshly ground
  pepper to taste
¼ cup finely minced
  parsley
⅛ cup finely minced dill or
  chives (optional)

Trim and core out cone from bottom of each endive. Remove any discolored leaves. Heat butter and saute endive for about 5 minutes. Add 1 cup broth and simmer for about 15 minutes. Puree the mixture in food processor or blender. Return to stove and reheat. Add remaining broth. Combine ½ cup of heated mixture with the flour and mix well. Add to soup, whisking over low heat, until it thickens. Add cream; salt and pepper to taste. Heat thoroughly. Serve garnished with parsley and either dill or chives.

BREADS

GOUGERE PUFF

Fabulous

1 cup water
½ cup butter, cut into
   small pieces
1 cup flour
4 eggs
1½ cups (6 oz.) grated
   Gruyere cheese
1 tsp. Dijon mustard
1 tsp. salt
½ tsp. dry mustard
Dash of hot pepper sauce

Mix water and butter in saucepan, bring to boil. Boil until butter is melted. Add flour all at once and mix over medium high heat until mixture forms a ball and pulls away from sides of pan. Remove from heat and add eggs 1 at a time, beating thoroughly after each. Dough should be smooth and shiny after each addition. Blend in remaining ingredients. Outline an 8-inch circle on a buttered baking sheet. Place touching tablespoon-size drops of dough around this circle. Then form a second layer on top of the first. Bake 10 minutes at 450°. Reduce heat to 350° and bake 10 minutes. Reduce heat to 325° and bake until ring is puffed and brown, about 15 minutes more. Poke holes in ring to let steam escape. Place on serving plate and cut into wedges.

EASY BUTTERMILK PANCAKES

4 Servings

1½ cups flour, sifted
1 tsp. baking soda
½ tsp. salt
1 T. sugar
½ tsp. baking powder
2 eggs
2 cups buttermilk
6 T. vegetable oil
1 tsp. vanilla
Macadamia nuts, chopped
   (optional)

Sift the dry ingredients together. Beat the eggs. Add to the buttermilk and oil. Blend all ingredients together. Pour onto hot, oiled skillet. Turn once. Serve with syrup.

For a change, add macadamia nuts to batter. Serve with coconut syrup.

PARSLEY BREAD

1 Loaf

2 pkgs. active dry yeast
1¾ cups warm water
6 T. honey
7 to 8 cups unbleached
   white wheat bread flour
6 small eggs, plus 1 yolk
⅔ cup currants, softened
   in warm water to cover
1⅔ T. coarse salt
6 T. oil
1½ tsp. cinnamon
1½ tsp. rosemary
1½ tsp. basil
⅔ cup chopped parsley

Sprinkle yeast on ½ cup of warm water, stir in honey and proof 5 minutes. Add remaining water and beat in 3 cups flour until well combined. Cover with damp towel and let rise 30 to 45 minutes. Stir down and beat in 5 eggs and 1 yolk. Stir in currants. Add salt and oil. Mix cinnamon and herbs together; add to dough. At this point add enough flour so that dough comes away from sides of bowl. Knead for 10 to 12 minutes adding flour as needed. Cover and let rise until doubled. Punch down again and let rise 30 minutes. Punch down and let rest 5 minutes. Shape into free form. Brush with beaten whole egg and bake at 375° about 50 minutes.

BRAN MUFFINS

4 Dozen

1 qt. buttermilk
1 cup oil
4 eggs
1 cup honey
½ cup molasses
2½ cups bran flakes (in
   health food section, not
   with commercial
   cereals)
1 cup sesame seeds
1 cup wheat germ
1 cup brown sugar
5 cups whole wheat flour
5 tsp. soda
1 T. salt

Combine liquid ingredients; add to dry ingredients. Bake at 375° for 15 minutes in greased muffin tins. This recipe makes a gallon of batter, which you can keep refrigerated for a week or 2, taking out a little at a time. Decrease the size of container as batter is used so that there will not be a large air space at the top.

BREADS

STRAWBERRY BREAD
5 Small Loaves

Light textured — a tasty gift

1 cup butter
1½ cups sugar
1 tsp. vanilla
½ tsp. lemon extract
4 large eggs
3 cups sifted all-purpose flour
1 tsp. salt
1 tsp. cream of tartar
½ tsp. baking soda
1 cup strawberry jam or preserves
½ cup sour cream

Cream butter, sugar, vanilla and lemon extract until fluffy. Add eggs, 1 at a time, beating well after each addition. Sift together flour, salt, cream of tartar and soda. Combine jam and sour cream. Add jam mixture alternately with dry ingredients to creamed mixture, beating until well combined. Divide among 5 greased and floured 4½ x 2¾ x 2¼ loaf pans. Bake at 350° for 45 to 50 minutes or until tester comes out clean. Cool 10 minutes in pans. Remove and cool completely on wire racks. Serve with cream cheese for breakfast or as a snack.

BLUE CHEESE ROLLS
Makes 20

Easy and tasty

¼ cup butter
2 T. blue cheese
1 can (10 oz.) refrigerated biscuits

Melt butter in shallow pan in oven. Add blue cheese. Cut biscuits in ½. Roll in butter-cheese mixture. Bake according to instructions on biscuit package.

BISCUITS WALLY
12 Biscuits

Quick, light and delicious

½ pt. whipping cream
1¼ cups self-rising flour

Whip cream until it forms soft peaks. Mix in flour. Drop by tablespoonsful onto ungreased cookie sheet. Bake at 375° about 10 minutes, or until light brown.

BREADS

TEXAS ORANGE MUFFINS

72 Small Muffins

½ cup shortening
1 cup sugar
2 eggs
2 cups flour, sifted
¼ tsp. salt
1 tsp. baking soda
1 cup buttermilk
Grated rind of 2 oranges
½ cup white raisins,
　ground

SAUCE:

1 cup brown sugar
Juice of 1 orange

Cream shortening and sugar. Stir in eggs, 1 at a time. Sift together flour and salt. Add to shortening alternately with baking soda dissolved in buttermilk. Stir just until blended. Fold in orange rind and raisins. Spoon into buttered tiny muffin tins. Bake at 375° for 15 minutes.

For sauce, place sugar and orange juice in small saucepan. Cook over low heat until sugar dissolves. Dip warm muffins into sauce.

SOUR CREAM WAFFLES

4-6 Waffles

2 eggs
2 T. sugar
½ tsp. salt
1 tsp. baking soda
1 cup sour cream (no
　substitute)
1 cup milk
3 T. vegetable oil
1 tsp. vanilla
1½ cups all-purpose flour

Beat eggs until light and fluffy; add sugar, salt and baking soda. Beat in sour cream and mix well. Mix in milk, oil and vanilla; add flour and mix well. Waffles are better if mixture is allowed to stand for about 30 minutes. Delicious with fresh sliced fruit and almond butter.

ALMOND BUTTER

2 Cups

Delicious on waffles or pancakes

½ cup butter
½ cup sugar
1 cup (¼ lb.) blanched
　almonds, pulverized in
　blender
2 eggs
Grated rind of 1 lemon
¼ tsp. salt
¼ tsp. almond extract

Cream butter and sugar; add almonds. Mix at medium speed. Add eggs 1 at a time, beating continuously. Add lemon rind, salt and almond extract. Put into tightly covered container and chill. Before serving, whisk with fork to fluff. Keeps in refrigerator at least 1 week.

LUNCHEON DISHES

SPINACH-HAM-MUSHROOM ROLL   6 Servings
Delicious brunch dish

SPINACH ROLL:

6 eggs, separated
2 T. butter, melted
¾ tsp. salt
⅛ tsp. ground nutmeg
Dash pepper
⅓ cup fresh bread crumbs
⅓ cup milk
2 pkgs. (10 oz. each)
   frozen chopped
   spinach, thawed
2 T. grated Parmesan
   cheese
1 T. grated onion

FILLING:

12 oz. (4 cups) fresh
   mushrooms, sliced
½ cup chopped onion
3 T. butter
¼ tsp. salt
⅛ tsp. ground nutmeg
6 slices broiled ham
   (reserve)
6 fresh mushrooms,
   sliced (reserve)

**BLENDER HOLLANDAISE
SAUCE:**

3 egg yolks
1 T. water
1 tsp. prepared mustard
2 T. lemon juice
⅛ tsp. salt
Dash of cayenne pepper
¾ cup butter, melted

Light Dry White

For spinach roll, beat egg yolks until thick and pale yellow. Stir in butter, ½ tsp. of salt, nutmeg, and a dash of pepper. Soak bread crumbs in milk. Drain thawed spinach well; mix with moistened crumbs, cheese, onion, and egg yolks. Beat egg whites with ¼ tsp. of salt until stiff but not dry. Fold into the spinach mixture. Grease an 11 x 15-inch jelly roll pan. Line the bottom and sides smoothly with buttered waxed paper. Spread the spinach mixture evenly in the pan. Bake at 375° for 15 minutes or until the center feels barely firm when touched lightly. While roll is baking, prepare filling and sauce.

For filling, saute mushrooms and onions in butter over high heat until liquid is cooked away. Season with salt and nutmeg. Set aside. Keep warm.

For sauce, put all ingredients except butter into blender container. With blender turned on, pour in the hot butter in a slow steady stream. Blend about 30 seconds longer.

When roll is baked, place on buttered sheet of waxed paper. Invert onto a cookie sheet. Remove waxed paper. Lay reserved ham slices over the spinach in a single layer. Spread hot mushroom filling over ham. Roll up, starting with the long side. Ease roll onto a warmed serving platter, seam side down. Garnish top with reserved mushroom slices. Serve with warm sauce.

LUNCHEON DISHES

PASTA PRIMAVERA

6 Servings

Marvelous

½ cup unsalted butter
1 medium onion, chopped
1 large clove garlic, minced
1 lb. thin asparagus, thinly sliced
½ lb. mushrooms, sliced
6 oz. cauliflower in small pieces
1 medium zucchini, thinly sliced
1 carrot, halved lengthwise, thinly sliced
1 cup whipping cream
½ cup chicken broth
2 tsp. sweet basil
1 cup frozen tiny peas, thawed
5 green onions, chopped
Salt and pepper
1 lb. linguini, fettuccini, or spaghetti, cooked and drained
1 cup Parmesan cheese
Shrimp or diced ham (optional)

Light Dry White

Heat wok or large deep skillet over medium heat. Melt butter. Saute onion and garlic 2 minutes. Add vegetables except peas and onions; stir-fry 2 minutes. Increase heat to high. Add cream, broth, and basil; let boil 3 minutes. Stir in peas and onions last. Cook 1 minute. Adjust seasoning. Add pasta and Parmesan; toss thoroughly. You can toss in shrimp or ham or a few extra vegetables, if desired. Can be reheated by adding milk, half and half, or broth. This is delicious served with a fruit salad.

CHICKEN AND ORANGE SALAD

4 Servings

2½ cups chicken, cooked and cut in chunks
4 navel oranges, peeled and sectioned
12 ripe olives, sliced
1 red onion, thinly sliced
1 pinch rosemary
DRESSING:
½ cup lemon juice
¼ cup olive oil or salad oil
¾ tsp. salt
½ tsp. pepper

Combine salad ingredients and chill.

For dressing, combine all ingredients. Pour over chicken to marinate for several hours in refrigerator before serving.

39

LUNCHEON DISHES

NEW YORK CHICKEN LIVERS   2 Servings

½ lb. chicken livers
¼ cup butter
4 green onions with tops, minced
2 T. flour
1 tsp. prepared hot mustard
1 cup red or rose wine
Salt and pepper
Chopped parsley

Saute livers gently but quickly in butter; add onions. Combine flour, mustard, and wine. Add to livers and cook quickly over high heat. Season with salt and pepper. Serve over garlic bread or toast points. Sprinkle with chopped parsley.

CURRIED CRAB CREPES   12 Crepes
Great do-ahead

CREPES:

1 cup milk
¾ cup flour
¼ tsp. salt
2 eggs

FILLING:

5 T. butter
¼ cup flour
¾ tsp. salt
1½ cups milk
1 can (7½ oz.) crabmeat
1 tsp. minced shallots
½ cup dry white wine
1 tsp. curry powder
¼ tsp. Worcestershire sauce
⅛ tsp. pepper
Dash cayenne pepper

TOPPING:

1 egg yolk
⅛ tsp. salt
4 T. melted butter
2 tsp. lemon juice
¼ cup whipping cream, whipped
Grated Parmesan cheese

For crepes, put ingredients in blender; mix until combined. Cook crepes. Place between sheets of waxed paper. Set aside.

For filling, melt 4 T. butter; stir in flour and ½ tsp. salt. Gradually stir in milk. Cook, stirring constantly until white sauce thickens. Drain and flake crab. Saute shallots in 1 T. butter; add crab and simmer for 2 minutes. Add rest of filling ingredients. Simmer for 3 minutes. Add 1 cup of sauce. Fill crepes; arrange in shallow baking dish. Cover with foil and bake at 350° for 20 to 25 minutes.

For topping, beat egg yolk with salt until foamy; gradually beat in 2 T. melted butter. Mix remaining butter with lemon juice; add to egg yolk. Stir in remaining white sauce; fold in whipped cream. Spoon topping over crepes. Sprinkle with grated Parmesan cheese. Broil 4 to 6 inches from heat for about 3 minutes. (May be frozen before topping is added. To serve: defrost, make topping and cook.)

LUNCHEON DISHES

SALMON CREPES

1 can (16 oz.) salmon,
  cleaned, deboned, and
  flaked
1½ cups medium white
  sauce
1 T. finely chopped
  parsley
½ cup Parmesan cheese,
  grated
Salt and pepper to taste
Mayonnaise

CREPES:

1 cup flour
3 eggs
1½ cups milk
Dash of salt
Oil for frying

WHITE SAUCE:

6 T. butter
6 T. flour
1 cup milk
1 cup whipping cream
1 tsp. salt
⅛ tsp. white pepper

Light Dry White

Put salmon, white sauce, parsley, salt and pepper into a saucepan. Heat the mixture, but do not boil. Spoon part of the mixture onto each crepe so that the crepe can still be neatly folded. Now spread each filled and folded crepe with a light coating of mayonnaise. Then sprinkle each crepe with grated Parmesan cheese. Bake the crepes on a lightly greased cookie sheet at 400° for about 10 minutes or until top is lightly browned. Serve immediately.

For crepes, put flour, eggs, milk and salt into blender. Blend until smooth. Refrigerate 1 to 2 hours before frying. Make crepes in usual manner. Set aside 8 crepes. Stack any extra crepes between sheets of waxed paper; wrap stack tightly in foil and freeze for future use.

For sauce, melt butter; stir in flour. Gradually add milk and cream, whisking constantly. Cook over high heat stirring constantly. When sauce comes to a boil, reduce heat and simmer 5 minutes. Season with salt and pepper. Sauce will be thick.

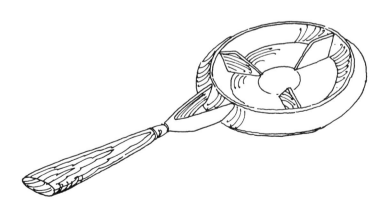

LUNCHEON DISHES

CRAB LUNCHEON SANDWICH   6 Servings

1 pkg. (8 oz.) cream
   cheese
2 T. mayonnaise
1 T. lemon juice
1 T. minced onion
1 tsp. horseradish
½ tsp. Worcestershire
   sauce
Dash hot pepper sauce
1 can (6 oz.) crabmeat
6 Holland rusks or thickly
   sliced toasted bakery
   bread
6 thick tomato slices
1 cup grated Cheddar
   cheese
Paprika

Combine cream cheese, mayonnaise, lemon juice, onion and seasonings. Add crab. Put rusks on cookie sheet. Top each with tomato slice. Spread generously with crab mixture. Top with cheese and sprinkle with paprika. Bake at 350° for 15 minutes or until bubbly.

DEVILED EGG AND HAM CASSEROLE   8 Servings

8 eggs, hard cooked
¼ cup butter, melted
½ tsp. prepared mustard
1 T. grated onion
½ T. Worcestershire
   sauce
1 tsp. minced parsley
1 cup ground or finely
   chopped ham

SAUCE:

¼ cup butter
5 T. flour
Salt, pepper, paprika to
   taste
1 cup hot beef broth
1 cup milk
1 cup grated cheese
Paprika

Cut eggs in ½. Reserve whites. Mash yolks. Add ¼ cup butter, mustard, onion, Worcestershire, parsley and ham to yolks. Fill reserved halves. Set aside in glass baking dish.

For sauce, combine butter with flour, salt, pepper, and paprika. Heat. Slowly blend in broth, milk, and cheese. Pour sauce over stuffed egg halves. Sprinkle with paprika. Bake at 325° for 20 minutes.

LUNCHEON DISHES

MUSHROOM-SPINACH PIE
6-8 Servings

Rich and satisfying

1 unbaked, deep-dish,
9-inch pastry shell
1 lb. fresh mushrooms,
sliced
1 medium onion, sliced
2 T. butter
½ lb. Swiss cheese,
grated
2 pkgs. (12 oz. each)
frozen spinach souffle,
defrosted

Saute mushrooms and onions in butter until mushrooms are brown and onions are soft. Place mushrooms and onion in pastry shell. Top with cheese, then with defrosted spinach souffle. Bake at 350° for 65 minutes. Let stand 15 minutes before serving. Variation: line shell with ¼ lb. thin slices of ham; then spinach mixture.

EGG AND ASPARAGUS CASSEROLE
6-8 Servings

3 to 4 cups homemade
croutons
1 cup butter
1 lb. mushrooms, sliced
12 hard-cooked eggs,
sliced
2 lbs. fresh asparagus,
cooked (reserve
cooking liquid)
2 bunches green onions,
chopped
Parmesan cheese
Paprika

SAUCE:
4 T. flour
4 T. butter
1 cup asparagus cooking
liquid
2 cups sour cream

Saute croutons in ¾ cup of butter. Line the bottom of a 3-qt. casserole with the croutons. Saute mushrooms in remaining butter. Layer eggs, asparagus, onions, and mushrooms in casserole. Pour sauce over the top. Sprinkle with cheese and paprika. Bake at 350° for 20 minutes.

For sauce, make a roux with butter and flour. Cook without coloring until flour is cooked. It will smell like nuts when cooked. Add the asparagus liquid and cook until thick. Add the sour cream. Be careful not to let the mixture curdle.

Full-Flavored Dry White

43

ENTREES: MEATS

FILLET OF BEEF WITH GREEN PEPPERCORNS

8-10 Servings

1 fillet of beef (4 lbs.)
2 T. oil
Salt and pepper
3 T. Cognac or brandy
1½ cups brown stock or
   beef broth
1 cup whipping cream
3 T. green peppercorns
1 T. lemon juice
Salt and pepper
3 T. butter, softened

Medium-Bodied Red

Trim and tie fillet. Heat oil in skillet; brown fillet all over at moderately high heat. Season fillet with salt and pepper; transfer to baking dish. Roast the fillet at 450° for 20 to 25 minutes for rare. Transfer to cutting board and let stand 10 minutes. Pour fat from pan. Add 3 T. heated Cognac; ignite it and shake pan until flames die down, stirring in all brown bits clinging to pan. Add 1½ cups brown stock and 1 cup whipping cream. Reduce sauce over moderately high heat to about 2 cups. Add green peppercorns, lemon juice, and salt and pepper to taste. Remove pan from heat and swirl in softened butter. Cut six ½-inch slices from fillet and arrange slices and remaining fillet on heated platter. Spoon some of sauce over fillet. Pass remaining sauce. Garnish with watercress or parsley and cherry tomatoes. Serve with homemade shoestring potatoes and a green vegetable.

SHERRIED BEEF TENDERLOIN

8-10 Servings

A do-ahead special

1 whole beef fillet, well
   trimmed (4 to 5 lbs.)
1 cup soy sauce
1 cup olive oil (or ½ olive
   oil, ½ peanut oil)
1 cup sherry
6 garlic cloves, chopped
1 tsp. hot pepper sauce
Salt and pepper to taste
Parsley sprigs and cherry
   tomatoes

Medium-Bodied Red

Combine all ingredients except parsley and tomatoes. Marinate meat in refrigerator for 24 hours, turning several times. Remove meat; dry on paper towels and place on roasting rack. Rub with a small amount of oil; roast at 475° for 25 minutes (very rare) or 30 minutes (rare), basting several times with marinade. Check for desired doneness. Keep at room temperature until serving time. Slice and reassemble in oval or rectangular dish. Decorate by placing large parsley sprigs and a few cherry tomatoes at each end.

44

ENTREES: MEATS

GINGER BEEF

A medieval beef dish

2 lbs. boneless beef
  chuck
1½ cups dry red wine
15 peppercorns, crushed
3 thin slices fresh ginger
  or ½ tsp. ground ginger
½ tsp. ground cloves
⅛ tsp. allspice
⅛ tsp. mace
⅛ tsp. saffron threads
  (optional)
Flour
Salt and pepper
2 T. oil
2 T. butter
1 large onion, minced
½ cup beef broth or water

Medium-Bodied Red

Cut beef into 1½-inch cubes. Put in non-metal dish. Add wine, peppercorns, ginger, cloves, allspice, mace and saffron. Cover and marinate in refrigerator overnight. Drain meat, reserving marinade; pat dry and dust with flour seasoned with salt and pepper. In Dutch oven, brown beef in hot oil and butter, adding more oil if necessary; remove meat cubes when browned. Saute onion in remaining fat until softened, adding more butter and oil if necessary. Deglaze pan with broth or water; add reserved marinade and bring to boil. Reduce to simmer; add meat and simmer for 1½ to 2 hours or until beef is tender. Before serving, adjust seasonings.

STEAK KEW

6 Servings

½ lb. steak (round, flank,
  sirloin) sliced thin
3 T. soy sauce
1 clove garlic, chopped
2 slices fresh ginger,
  finely chopped
1 T. chopped green
  onions
1 T. bottled oyster sauce
½ tsp. sugar
2 tsp. cornstarch
½ lb. fresh snow peas
3 T. peanut oil
8 to 10 mushrooms
  (preferably Chinese
  mushrooms), sliced
½ tsp. salt or to taste

Light-Bodied Red

Marinate sliced steak in 2 T. soy sauce. Mix garlic, ginger, green onions, oyster sauce, 1 T. soy sauce, sugar, and cornstarch. Drop snow peas into boiling water; when water returns to boil, drain peas and remove from heat. Heat oil and add mushrooms; stir-fry 1 minute. Stir in steak and garlic mixture. Stir-fry 1 to 2 minutes; add salt if desired. Serve hot with steamed rice.

ENTREES: MEATS

STEAK POLYNESIAN

6 Servings

1½ lbs. beef sirloin, cut in
1½-inch strips
Seasoned salt
2 T. oil
1 medium onion, thinly
sliced
1 green pepper, cut into
strips (optional)
½ cup sliced celery
1 T. finely chopped
candied ginger
1 cup brown sugar
⅓ cup soy sauce
1 can (16 oz.) bean
sprouts or 2 cups fresh
bean sprouts
1 can (8 oz.) bamboo
shoots, diced
1 can (5 oz.) water
chestnuts, sliced
2 T. cornstarch
2 T. water
1 can (20½ oz.)
pineapple chunks
Cooked rice

Season meat with salt; stir-fry in skillet in hot oil until barely brown. Set aside. Add onion; stir-fry until soft. Add green pepper, celery, ginger, sugar, and soy sauce. Simmer 2 minutes. Drain bean sprouts, bamboo shoots and water chestnuts; reserve liquid and add vegetables to skillet. Mix cornstarch with water; stir into mixture with ½ cup of reserved liquid. Cook, stirring constantly until thickened. Add meat and pineapple chunks; heat through. Serve over rice.

Light-Bodied Red

VEAL MARSALA

4 Servings

4 veal cutlets (about 4 oz.
each)
1 clove garlic, minced
2 T. butter
2 T. olive oil
¾ cup Marsala wine
4 very thin slices ham
4 slices baby Swiss
cheese
¼ cup freshly grated
Parmesan cheese

Pound veal cutlets until thin. Heat garlic in butter and oil until bubbly. Add veal; brown quickly on both sides. Add wine; simmer 2 minutes. Transfer cutlets to broiler pan. Top each with ham, then Swiss cheese. Sprinkle with Parmesan cheese. Broil just until lightly browned. Serve with Marsala sauce from pan.

Medium-Bodied Red

ENTREES: MEATS

VEAL PROVENCALE
4 Servings

5 green onions, thinly
   sliced
¼ cup olive oil
1 lb. thinly sliced veal
   cutlets (or turkey
   cutlets or beef cube
   steaks)
Flour
Seasoned salt
⅛ tsp. garlic powder
¼ cup dry vermouth
¼ cup sweet vermouth
¼ cup chicken broth
2 T. butter
6 fresh mushrooms,
   sliced
Lemon slices
Minced fresh parsley

Saute green onions in olive oil; set aside. Pound veal until thin. Dredge in flour. Saute in oil until brown and crisp on both sides. Sprinkle with seasoned salt to taste and garlic powder; set aside. Keep warm. To skillet, add green onions, vermouths, broth, butter, and mushrooms; carefully sprinkle in 1 tsp. flour. Cook, stirring constantly, for about 5 minutes. Pour sauce over veal. Place a lemon slice on each piece. Sprinkle with parsley.

Light-Bodied Red

LEMON VEAL OR CHICKEN
6 Servings

Quick and easy

2 lbs. veal scallops (or
   boneless chicken
   breasts)
½ cup flour
2 tsp. salt
½ tsp. freshly ground
   pepper
Dash cayenne pepper
   (optional)
8 T. butter
4 T. oil
1 T. fresh or ¼ tsp. dried
   tarragon (optional)
5 T. freshly squeezed
   lemon juice
5 T. chopped fresh
   parsley
1 lemon, thinly sliced

Flatten veal or chicken by pounding gently between layers of waxed paper. Combine flour, salt, pepper, and cayenne pepper in a plastic bag. Shake veal to coat evenly. Brown veal in 4 T. butter and 4 T. oil combined. Do not overcook. Remove veal; drain fat. Melt remaining 4 T. butter, add tarragon, if desired; lemon juice, parsley. Heat to simmering. Add veal to cover with sauce. Serve immediately, garnished with lemon slices and parsley.

Light Dry White

ENTREES: MEATS

RACK OF LAMB WITH MADEIRA SAUCE   4 Servings

1 rack of lamb
3 T. butter, softened
2 cloves garlic, chopped
4 tsp. thyme
2 tsp. rosemary
2 tsp. lemon juice
1 tsp. salt
¼ tsp. freshly ground
   pepper
2 cloves garlic, slivered
1 cup beef broth
¼ cup Madeira wine
2 T. flour mixed with 2 T.
   butter

Medium-Bodied Red

Remove the outer skin of lamb; trim the meat leaving a little fat. Combine next 7 ingredients. Make incisions in the meat; insert garlic slivers. Rub butter mixture over meat. Refrigerate about 4 hours. Put foil over bones and ends so they do not burn. Roast in 450° oven for 10 minutes, or until meat thermometer registers 160°. Turn down heat to 350° and cook 30 minutes more. Lamb should be served pink. Skim fat from pan. Add broth and Madeira. Boil, scraping up bits from pan. Add flour mixture; cook and stir until thickened. Put paper frills over bones.

DILLED LAMB WITH MUSHROOMS   6-8 Servings

2 lbs. lean lamb, cubed
2 T. butter
1 cup beef broth
2 T. dill seed
2 T. fresh dill weed
1 tsp. salt
1 bay leaf
3 T. flour
½ cup dry white wine
1 lb. fresh whole
   mushrooms
1 cup sour cream
Cooked rice

Medium-Bodied Red

Brown lamb cubes in butter. Add broth, dill seed, fresh dill, salt, and bay leaf. Cover and simmer 30 minutes. Mix flour with wine; stir into meat mixture. Add mushrooms. Cook 15 minutes, stirring occasionally. Stir in sour cream; heat through, but do not boil. Serve over rice.

ENTREES: MEATS

LAMB FILLETS ON ARTICHOKES

4 Servings

2 cups minced onions
Water
9 T. butter
¼ cup flour
¼ tsp. salt
¼ tsp. white pepper
¾ cup milk
2 egg yolks
8 rib lamb chops, at least
   1 inch thick, boned
½ cup Madeira wine
¾ cup chicken broth
8 cooked artichoke
   bottoms

Medium-Bodied Red

Cover onions with water; bring to a boil, reduce heat and simmer for 3 minutes. Drain. In a saucepan melt ¼ cup butter. Add onions and cook slowly for 10 minutes. Do not brown. Stir in 2 T. flour, salt and pepper. Add milk. Cook, stirring constantly, until thickened. Cover and cook over low heat for 20 minutes. Puree in blender or food processor. Combine 2 T. flour, 2 T. softened butter, and egg yolks. Beat in a little hot onion puree; stir this into remaining puree. Cook, stirring constantly, until thick. Do not boil. In a skillet, brown chops in 1 T. butter on high heat for 3 to 4 minutes on each side, or until medium rare. Remove from skillet; keep hot. Add Madeira and chicken broth to skillet. Cook over high heat until liquid is reduced by a third. Swirl in 2 T. butter; adjust seasonings. Keep warm.

Heat artichoke bottoms; arrange on a heatproof platter. Fill with onion sauce, reserving about ½ cup. Place a lamb fillet on each; top each with 1 T. onion sauce. Broil a few minutes, or until sauce is hot and tinged brown. Serve Madeira sauce on the side.

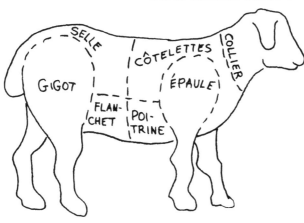

ENTREES: MEATS

ROGNONS DE VEAU AU VIN ROUGE   4 Servings

2 veal kidneys
4 to 6 T. butter
1 small onion, finely
   chopped
¾ cup sliced mushrooms
Salt and pepper to taste
1 T. flour
½ cup dry red wine
½ cup water
Cooked rice, molded into
   a ring

Wash kidneys. Remove all fat, skin, and hard center membrane. Cut kidneys into small pieces. Melt butter and add kidneys, onion, mushrooms and salt and pepper. Saute over high heat 2 to 3 minutes. Add flour and blend thoroughly. Add wine and water. Let mixture simmer down briefly and pour kidneys and sauce into rice ring. This works equally well with calves liver.

Medium-Bodied Red

FOIE DE VEAU GRILLE   4-6 Servings

1 lb. young calves liver
4 T. butter
2 cloves garlic, mashed
¼ cup tarragon wine
   vinegar
1 T. chopped fresh
   tarragon

Slice liver ¼ inch thick. Saute in butter over high heat, 2 minutes on each side. When liver is almost cooked, add garlic and continue cooking. Arrange liver on hot platter. Stir vinegar into pan juices. Add more butter if pan is dry. Pour sauce over liver and sprinkle with tarragon.

Medium-Bodied Red

ENTREES: MEATS

SWEETBREADS IN CHAMPAGNE SAUCE   4 Servings

1 pair (about 1 lb.) veal
   sweetbreads
Dash salt
1 T. lemon juice
¼ cup butter
¼ cup brandy, warmed
½ cup dry Champagne or
   dry white wine
2 green onions and tops,
   thinly sliced
2 T. minced parsley
¼ tsp. salt
⅛ tsp. pepper
¾ cup whipping cream
4 slices Canadian bacon,
   browned
2 English muffins, split,
   toasted

Medium-Bodied Red

Soak sweetbreads in cold water 1½ hours, changing water once or twice. Put in pan of water to cover with a dash of salt and 1 T. lemon juice for each qt. of water. Heat to boiling. Cover, reduce heat, and simmer 20 minutes. Drain; put in ice water. Carefully remove membranes, connecting tube, and discolored portions. Cut in small pieces and flour lightly. Saute sweetbreads in butter 8 to 10 minutes. Ignite brandy and pour into pan with sweetbreads. Shake pan until flames die. Add Champagne, onions, parsley, salt, and pepper. Simmer 2 to 3 minutes. Remove sweetbreads; keep warm. Whisk cream into sauce; gently boil 5 minutes to thicken slightly. Return sweetbreads to heat. Place a Canadian bacon slice on each English muffin half. Spoon sauce over.

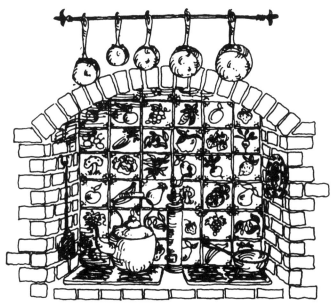

ENTREES: MEATS

GINGER PORK WITH ASPARAGUS   4 Servings

1 lb. boneless pork, cut in strips
6 medium fresh asparagus stalks
1 clove garlic, minced
1 T. fresh ginger, thinly julienned
3 T. oil
½ cup chicken broth
1 T. soy sauce
½ tsp. black pepper
1 T. cornstarch

Medium-Dry White

Slice asparagus on the diagonal, cutting pieces about ¾ inch long. In wok or frying pan, saute pork, asparagus, garlic, and ginger in oil until pork loses its pink color. Add chicken broth, soy sauce, pepper and cornstarch mixed with a little water. Cook and stir until thickened. Add salt to taste. Serve with rice.

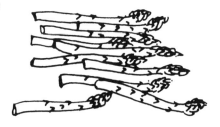

PORC ST. HUBERT   6 Servings

Deliciously different flavor

1 pork tenderloin (2 lbs.) or 6 pork chops
Salt and pepper
¼ cup salad oil
¼ cup Dijon mustard
¼ cup red wine vinegar
4 shallots, chopped
¼ cup butter
1 cup chicken broth
⅓ cup Bar-le-Duc preserves or currant jelly
1 T. honey
1 T. cornstarch
¼ cup Madeira wine

Medium-Dry White

Cut tenderloin into slices ½ inch thick. Season with salt and pepper. Mix oil, mustard and vinegar. Combine with pork. Marinate covered in refrigerator at least 2 hours or overnight. In large skillet, saute shallots in butter until tender. Drain marinade and reserve. Quickly brown meat about 3 to 4 minutes on each side. Remove meat and keep warm. Add chicken broth, jelly, honey, and marinade. Cook down by about ⅓. Add cornstarch which has been dissolved in Madeira. Bring to boiling, stirring constantly until sauce is clear. Spoon some of sauce over meat and serve immediately. Serve with French fried potatoes and a green vegetable.

ENTREES: MEATS

ROAST PORK TENDERLOIN WITH ORANGE SAUCE

6 Servings

½ cup bread crumbs
1 T. prepared Dijon
   mustard
Salt
Pepper
1 tsp. thyme
Orange juice to make
   paste
1 pork tenderloin (3 lbs.)

SAUCE:

2 oranges
1 cup water
½ cup sugar
1 T. Dijon mustard
1 cup beef broth
¼ cup raspberry vinegar
   or good red wine
   vinegar
1 T. cornstarch

Medium-Dry White

Combine bread crumbs, mustard, salt, pepper, and thyme. Add drops of orange juice to make a thick paste. Cover tenderloin with paste and cook at 350° for 35 minutes. Meanwhile, make sauce. Peel rind from oranges being careful not to include pith. Cut rind into thin strips and put in heavy pan with water and sugar, boiling slowly until rind is translucent and liquid is of syrupy consistency. Cut oranges into segments and remove any seeds. Off heat, carefully stir orange segments into syrup. Add mustard. Heat beef broth. When pork is done, remove to heated platter and keep warm. Deglaze pan with raspberry vinegar and pour juices into syrup. Stir cornstarch into beef broth and pour into syrup. Stir constantly over medium heat until cornstarch is clear and sauce has thickened. Correct seasonings. Slice pork into ¼-inch slices and arrange on platter. Pour some of the sauce over meat and pass remaining sauce. Serve with shoestring fried potatoes and green beans or julienned zucchini.

HAM WITH PORT WINE SAUCE

4 Servings

4 ham steaks, cut ½ inch
   thick (canned ham may
   be used)
4 T. butter
6 green onions, finely
   chopped
1 cup whipping cream
1 T. prepared mustard
2 tsp. cornstarch
¼ cup port wine

Light-Bodied Red

Trim ham steaks thoroughly and make small cuts around edges to prevent curling. Heat butter in large skillet; add green onions and ham. Cover and cook over low heat for 10 minutes being careful to keep butter from burning. Uncover; add cream. Stir in mustard. Dissolve cornstarch in wine; add to pan. Heat until thickened. Sauce may be made separately and served with thinly sliced baked ham.

53

ENTREES: POULTRY

CANTONESE LEMON CHICKEN   8 Servings

2 whole chicken breasts,
  skinned and boned
1 tsp. salt
1 T. light soy sauce

BATTER:

½ cup flour
2 T. cornstarch
⅛ tsp. baking powder
¼ tsp. salt
¼ tsp. sugar
½ cup water

COOKING OIL:

2 cups peanut oil

SAUCE:

1 T. warm peanut oil
1 green onion, cut in 2-
  inch lengths
2 large lemons, sliced
  thin
1 cup chicken broth
3 T. sugar
1 tsp. salt
1 T. cornstarch

Light Dry White

Cut chicken into bite-sized chunks. Marinate in salt and soy sauce for 15 minutes. Combine batter ingredients, mixing thoroughly. Coat chicken with batter and refrigerate for at least 1 hour to make batter adhere better. Heat 2 cups of peanut oil to 375° and deep-fry a few pieces of chicken at a time until golden brown. Keep warm in 200° oven. To make sauce, heat 1 T. peanut oil in wok or heavy skillet. Stir-fry green onion a few seconds; add lemon slices; stir-fry another 30 seconds. Combine chicken broth, sugar, salt and cornstarch and add to lemon, stirring until thickened. Keep warm. To serve, arrange chicken on platter lined with lettuce leaves, pour sauce over.

ENTREES: POULTRY

CHICKEN BREASTS EN PAPILLOTE   8 Servings

4 whole chicken breasts,
   halved, boned and
   skinned
½ cup flour
1 tsp. salt
½ tsp. pepper
1 tsp. curry powder
3 T. butter
2 T. sherry
⅓ cup orange marmalade
3 T. brown sugar
3 T. vinegar
1 can (11 oz.) mandarin
   oranges, drained
Parchment paper or foil

Dredge chicken in mixture of flour, salt, pepper and curry powder. Saute in butter about 3 minutes on each side. Combine sherry, marmalade, sugar, and vinegar. Cut parchment paper into 8 heart-shaped pieces. Place a breast half on each piece. Cover each with sauce and oranges. Crimp and roll paper around breast and twist end so each is leakproof. Place on cookie sheet and bake at 350° for 12 to 15 minutes until puffed. Slit top with knife to serve.

Medium-Dry White

CHICKEN SAN FRANCISCO   8 Servings

4 whole chicken breasts,
   split, boned
½ lemon
Salt, pepper, flour
¼ cup butter
3 green onions with tops,
   chopped
½ cup white wine
½ cup chicken broth
4 egg yolks
1 cup half and half, or
   whipping cream
1 T. minced parsley
1 T. minced chives
¼ tsp. nutmeg
⅛ tsp. cayenne pepper
⅛ tsp. tarragon or chervil
Few drops lemon juice

Rub chicken breasts with lemon. Dredge with mixture of salt, pepper, and flour. Heat butter in a heavy skillet; saute chicken until golden. Cover and simmer 10 minutes. Add onions; cover and cook 5 minutes longer. Remove cover. Shake pan. Add wine and chicken broth. Cover and simmer 10 minutes or until chicken is tender, shaking pan frequently. Remove chicken. Beat egg yolks with cream and spices. Cook over low heat, stirring constantly, until sauce is slightly thickened. Do not boil. Add a few drops of lemon juice. Adjust seasoning. Return chicken to sauce and coat. Serve at once.

Full-Flavored Dry White

ENTREES: POULTRY

CHICKEN NICOISE

8 Servings

4 whole chicken breasts, boned and split
½ cup butter
2 T. chopped black olives
1 T. minced chives
1 T. fresh or 1 tsp. dried sweet basil
2 cloves garlic, minced
Salt and pepper
Flour
2 eggs, beaten
2 cups fine dry bread crumbs
Oil
2 cups medium bechamel sauce
1 tsp. anchovy paste

Pound breasts between sheets of waxed paper to flatten. Be careful not to break flesh. (The resultant piece should be fan-shaped.) Blend butter with olives, chives, basil and garlic. Make small, tapered "fingers" of butter; chill in freezer for 15 minutes. Roll breasts around butter, tucking in ends of meat to make a neat package. Roll in flour seasoned with salt and pepper. Dip in beaten egg. Finally, roll in bread crumbs. Cook in oil to cover, heated to 360°, until golden brown. Drain on absorbent paper. Combine warm bechamel sauce with anchovy paste. Serve over chicken.

Full-Flavored Dry White

CHICKEN A LA CRICKETS

4-6 Servings

3 T. butter
3 T. flour
½ tsp. salt
¼ tsp. white pepper
2 cups milk
1 cup half and half
½ tsp. Worcestershire sauce
3 to 4 drops hot pepper sauce
¼ cup sherry
2 egg yolks, beaten
4 to 6 whole chicken breasts, skinned, boned, split, and cooked

Melt butter in small saucepan. Blend in flour, salt, and pepper with wooden spatula. Stir in milk and cream. Heat to boiling, stirring constantly. Boil 1 minute until sauce thickens. Stir in Worcestershire, hot pepper sauce, and sherry. Add a little of the sauce to egg yolks. Return all to saucepan.

Place cooked chicken breasts in shallow ovenproof serving dish. Pour sauce over chicken breasts. Put under broiler until browned and bubbly.

Recipe can be prepared hours in advance and warmed in 325° oven before broiling.

Light Dry White

ENTREES: SEAFOOD

SOLE EN PAPILLOTE

12 sole fillets (about 4 lbs.)
24 small mushroom caps
¾ cup butter, melted
½ cup chopped shallots (about 8)
1 tsp. salt
⅛ tsp. white pepper
12 slices carrots
1 split (6½ oz.) dry Champagne
1 cup canned chicken broth, skimmed
½ cup flour
Butcher paper or parchment
¼ cup whipping cream
2 T. lemon juice
2 T. chopped parsley
1 egg white, slightly beaten
12 lemon wedges

Light Dry White

Thaw fish, if frozen. Set aside the 12 best looking mushroom caps. Slice rest of caps; arrange on centers of fillets. Fold ends of fillets over mushrooms. Spread ¼ cup butter in baking pan; sprinkle with shallots, salt, and pepper. Then put in fillets, folded side down. Put 12 remaining mushroom caps and carrots in pan. Heat Champagne and broth to boiling; pour over fish. Cover pan with foil; immediately bake at 350° for 20 minutes. While fish is baking, prepare beurre manie by mixing remaining ½ cup butter with flour.

For the papillote, cut an oval from 1 large piece of the paper 20 inches long x 14 inches wide; from another cut an oval 1 inch longer. Butter smaller sheet within 1 inch of edge; place on ovenproof platter.

When fish is baked, carefully transfer fillets, mushrooms, and carrots to plate to drain. Cover with foil to keep warm. Raise oven temperature to 400°. Drain liquid from pan into saucepan. Place over medium heat; add beurre manie, a little at a time, stirring with a whisk until smooth and thick enough to coat whisk. (You may not need all of it.) Stir in cream and lemon juice. Arrange fillets, mushrooms, and carrots on buttered paper. Spoon sauce on top. Sprinkle with parsley. Keep rest of sauce warm. Brush edges of paper with egg white diluted with a little water. Place second piece of paper on top; fold bottom edge over top, rolling them together and crimping to seal. Brush edges and tops with egg whites. Bake at 400° for 10 minutes, or until paper gets crisp. Pass remaining sauce. Serve with lemon wedges, boiled potatoes, and broccoli.

ENTREES: SEAFOOD

TEMPURA (JAPANESE FONDUE)
6 Servings

A big hit with children and adults

BATTER:

6 large eggs
¾ cup cold water
1½ cups sifted flour
½ cup cornstarch

VEGETABLES AND SHRIMP:

3 small zucchini, cut into rounds
1 green pepper, cut in strips
1 large onion, cut in thick slices
6 large mushrooms, sliced
6 small carrots, cut in rounds
½ lb. fresh green beans
½ lb. fresh spinach
1½ lbs. uncooked shrimp, shelled, deveined, with tails left on

SAUCE:

½ cup soy sauce
⅓ cup sake or sherry
1 cup chicken broth

COOKING OIL:

2 to 3 cups peanut or sesame oil

Beer or Warm Sake

For batter, beat eggs until frothy; add water. Beat in flour and cornstarch. Mix until smooth. Chill. Meanwhile, prepare vegetables. Pat prepared shrimp and vegetables dry and arrange among 6 dinner plates. For sauce, combine all ingredients and simmer until heated. Heat cooking oil to 375° and put in fondue pot. Provide individual portions of batter and sauce. Each person should dip vegetables and shrimp into chilled batter and deep-fry for 1 to 2 minutes. When vegetables and shrimp are done, dip into sauce. Serve with steamed rice, warm sake or beer. The tempura may also be deep-fried in batches, kept warm and served cooked.

ENTREES: SEAFOOD

RED SNAPPER WITH TOMATO SAUCE　　6 Servings

Easily made at the last minute if everything is at hand

6 fresh red snapper fillets
Salt, pepper
Flour for dredging
4 T. olive oil
3 large shallots, finely
　minced
3 large garlic cloves,
　finely chopped
6 to 8 ripe tomatoes,
　peeled, seeded,
　chopped
2 T. finely chopped fresh
　mixed herbs: oregano,
　thyme, chervil or 2 tsp.
　dried
1 ripe avocado
1 to 2 tsp. lime juice
Dash hot pepper sauce
1 T. tomato paste
　(optional)
Avocado slices
Lime slices

Light Dry White

Season fish with salt and pepper and dredge in flour. Shake off excess flour. Heat olive oil in large skillet and saute fillets for 2 minutes on each side. Remove them to flameproof baking dish. In same oil, saute shallots and garlic. When lightly browned, add tomatoes and cook for 3 or 4 minutes. Pour the mixture over fish fillets, sprinkle with herbs. Cover dish with buttered waxed paper. Bake for 25 to 30 minutes in 350° oven.

Mash avocados in small bowl while the fish fillets are baking. Do not mash too fine. Add lime juice, salt, pepper, and hot pepper sauce.

When fish is done, lift out carefully and place on warm platter. Place baking dish over direct heat and reduce sauce by ⅓. Add tomato paste, if desired. Lower heat and add avocado mixture. Do not let this come to a boil. Correct seasoning and pour sauce over fish. Garnish with avocado and lime slices.

HERBED BAKED SCALLOPS　　6 Servings

Nice first course served in shells

2 lbs. fresh bay scallops
½ cup butter
3 T. minced parsley
1½ tsp. basil, crumbled
1 tsp. salt
¼ tsp. pepper

Light Dry White

Wash scallops in cold water, drain on paper towels. Put in single layer in shallow 1½-qt. baking dish. Dot with butter; sprinkle with parsley, basil, salt, and pepper. Bake at 350° for 5 minutes. Stir scallops to coat with butter mixture. Bake about 20 minutes more or just until tender.

59

ENTREES: SEAFOOD

SEAFOOD SUPREME

6-8 Servings

8 T. butter
1 clove garlic, minced
1 shallot, minced
8 jumbo shrimp
1 lb. bay scallops or large
  sea scallops, cut into
  quarters
½ lb. white crabmeat
1 T. chopped parsley
1 cup Vouvray or other
  white wine
1 cup whipping cream
Paprika

Melt butter in heavy skillet; add garlic and shallot. Cook, stirring 1 minute. Add shrimp and scallops. Cook several minutes until heated through. Do not overcook. Stir in crabmeat; continue cooking 1 minute. Add parsley, wine, and whipping cream, stirring after each addition. Adjust seasonings. This should be served in shallow soup dishes and eaten with a spoon. Dust each serving with paprika and serve with French bread.

Medium-Dry White

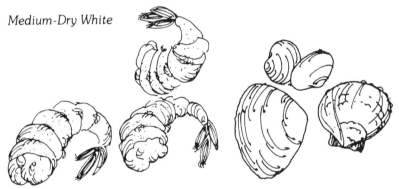

ALMEJAS PESCADORES

6 Servings

Fisherman's clams

1 can (10 oz.) baby clams
1 pkg. (6 oz.) frozen
  cooked shrimp, thawed
  (optional)
1 cup dry white wine
1 tsp. marjoram
1 tsp. paprika
1 small onion, minced
1 clove garlic, minced
¼ cup butter
2 T. oil
Salt and pepper
Grated cheese

Drain clams; rinse to remove any sand. Place clams, shrimp, wine, marjoram, and paprika in heavy pan to marinate while you prepare sauce. In heavy skillet, saute onion and garlic in butter and oil until onion is tender. Do not let onion brown. Add clam mixture; cook down by about ⅓. May be served as a first course or served over buttered vermicelli as an entree. Pass grated cheese, if desired.

Light Dry White

ENTREES: SEAFOOD

SHRIMP WITH LOBSTER SAUCE 4-6 Servings

No lobster — sauce is made with pork

1 lb. fresh shrimp in shells
2 T. mashed black beans
2 cloves garlic, minced
1 medium slice fresh ginger, minced
½ tsp. salt
¼ cup heavy soy sauce
1½ T. sherry
1 tsp. sugar
2 T. cornstarch
¼ cup peanut oil
½ lb. ground pork
2 cups rich chicken broth
2 eggs
2 T. chicken broth
4 green onions with tops, sliced lengthwise

Medium-Dry White

Shell and devein shrimp. Slit backs of shrimp, but do not cut in half. Mix beans, garlic, ginger, and salt; set aside. Mix 2 T. soy sauce, sherry, and sugar; set aside. Mix other 2 T. soy sauce with cornstarch. Heat 2 T. peanut oil in pan; add bean mixture. Stir-fry 15 seconds. Add pork; stir-fry 2 minutes. Add shrimp and soy-sherry mixture. Stir 1 minute. Add 2 cups broth. Cover and simmer 5 to 7 minutes. Slowly add cornstarch mixture; stir and cook until thick. Beat eggs with 2 T. broth; stir into shrimp mixture. Let sit 30 seconds. Put on serving dish. Heat 2 T. peanut oil until smoking. Pour oil over shrimp and garnish with sliced scallions. Serve with steamed rice.

WHITEFISH IN WHITE WINE AND ROQUEFORT SAUCE 2 Servings

2 fillets (6 oz. each) whitefish, or other firm-fleshed fish
1 T. finely minced shallots
2 cups dry white wine
1 cup whipping cream
Salt, pepper
4 oz. Roquefort cheese
¼ tsp. lemon juice
Parsley and cherry tomatoes for garnish

Light Dry White

Place fish, shallots, wine, and cream in shallow, buttered baking dish. Cover with buttered brown or waxed paper and poach 8 to 12 minutes in 350° oven. (Do not overcook; keep liquid at a simmer. Fish is done when fork pierces flesh easily.) When done, drain liquid into heavy saucepan. Keep fish covered and warm over hot water. Reduce liquid by ½ and add Roquefort cheese, stirring until completely melted. Add lemon juice. Arrange fish on plates and season to taste with salt and pepper. Divide sauce between fillets. Garnish with parsley and cherry tomatoes. Serve with green salad and good French bread.

ENTREES: SEAFOOD

SOLE BONNE FEMME

6 Servings

6 fillets of sole (6 oz. each)
2 cups milk
2 cups water
1 tsp. salt
Dash of white pepper
2 T. honey
2 T. sherry

BONNE FEMME SAUCE:

4 T. butter
4 T. flour
2 cups chicken broth
½ tsp. salt
⅛ tsp. white pepper
½ tsp. sugar
2 egg yolks
3 T. creme fraiche
¼ cup sour cream
1 T. lemon juice

Light Dry White

Combine milk, water, salt, pepper, honey, and sherry in large skillet. Heat to a boil. Add fish fillets. Bring to a boil and then reduce heat to a simmer. Poach about 8 minutes. Liquid should not be saved. Keep fish warm until sauce is ready.

For sauce, melt butter, stir in flour and cook over moderate heat, stirring 2 to 3 minutes. Add broth and cook, stirring constantly until thickened. Add salt, pepper, and sugar. Combine egg yolks with creme fraiche, sour cream and lemon juice. Stir ½ cup of hot sauce into creme mixture, then combine both mixtures. Do not boil. Serve immediately with poached sole.

SHRIMP CASSEROLE

4 Servings

2 T. chopped shallots or onions
2 T. butter
1 lb. raw shrimp, shelled (or 14 oz. pkg. frozen shrimp)
¼ lb. fresh mushrooms, sliced
1 tsp. salt
1 tsp. paprika
1 cup medium white sauce
1 cup sour cream
2 tsp. soy sauce
½ cup Sauterne wine
Parmesan cheese

Light Dry White

Saute shallots in butter; add raw shrimp and mushrooms. Cook for 5 minutes. Add seasonings, the white sauce, sour cream, soy sauce and wine. Heat thoroughly. Turn into a casserole and bake at 350° for 10 minutes. Top with Parmesan cheese. Serve with rice.

VEGETABLES

ASPARAGUS IN HAZELNUT BUTTER
4 Servings

1 lb. fresh asparagus
2 T. butter
2 T. chopped hazelnuts

Cook asparagus in boiling salted water until tender but still firm. Drain and place in serving dish. Melt butter in small skillet; add hazelnuts. Saute slowly until butter turns golden brown. Watch carefully, do not let butter burn. Remove from heat and spoon evenly over asparagus.

BROCCOLI SOUFFLE RESTAURANTEUR
6 Servings

Very elegant

¼ cup butter
¼ cup flour
½ cup whipping cream, scalded
½ cup rich chicken broth
3 egg yolks
1 tsp. grated onion
1 tsp. chopped parsley
1 tsp. Worcestershire sauce
1 tsp. finely chopped chives
Salt, pepper, nutmeg
1½ cups cooked chopped broccoli
⅓ cup grated Cheddar cheese
4 egg whites, stiffly beaten

Melt butter; stir in flour. Gradually stir in scalded cream mixed with chicken broth. Cook, stirring constantly, until mixture thickens. Remove from heat. Beat egg yolks with onion, parsley, Worcestershire sauce, and chives. Add salt, pepper, and nutmeg to taste. Stir a little hot mixture into the egg yolks; combine with remainder. Add broccoli and cheese. Fold in egg whites. Turn into 2-qt. buttered souffle dish. Bake at 400° for 25 minutes.

TANGY CARROTS
4 Servings

Good with ham

5 to 6 carrots, finely grated
4 T. butter
2 T. prepared brown mustard
1 T. brown sugar
1 T. lemon juice
2 T. raisins (optional)

Saute carrots in 2 T. butter for 5 minutes. In saucepan, combine remaining 2 T. butter, mustard, brown sugar, and lemon juice. Heat. Pour over carrots; toss. If desired, stir in raisins.

VEGETABLES

BRAISED CELERY IN CREAM SAUCE   6-8 Servings

Excellent taste; unique way to serve celery

1 cup sliced or chopped, fresh mushrooms
¼ cup minced green onions with tops
1 clove garlic, minced
3 T. butter
3 T. flour
¼ cup white wine
1 cup milk
1 cup half and half
½ tsp. salt
Dash white pepper
Dash nutmeg
1 T. Madeira wine
2 T. brandy
1 bunch celery
½ cup chicken broth
¼ cup bread crumbs

Saute mushrooms, onions, and garlic in butter. Stir in flour and wine; stir and simmer for 3 minutes. Gradually stir in milk and cream. Add salt, pepper, and nutmeg. Cook, stirring constantly, until thickened. Add brandy and Madeira. Meanwhile, cut celery in 3 to 4-inch lengths. Place in another pan with chicken broth. Simmer, covered, for 10 minutes or until tender. Coat bottom of a 13 x 9-inch baking dish with a little sauce. Add celery; coat with remaining sauce. Sprinkle with bread crumbs. Bake at 350° for 15 to 20 minutes, or until heated through.

CUCUMBERS WITH HOLLANDAISE   4 Servings

Delicious with ham

4 cucumbers
2 T. butter
Lemon juice
Salt and pepper to taste
½ cup whipping cream
½ cup hollandaise sauce

Peel, cut in ½ lengthwise and seed the cucumbers. Cut into 1¾ x ½-inch strips. Blanch in salted boiling water to cover for 1 minute. Drain. In a skillet cook the cucumbers in 2 T. butter over moderately low heat, tossing them occasionally, for 7 minutes. Do not let them color. Transfer to buttered 12 x 7½-inch baking dish. Add lemon juice, salt and pepper to taste. Whip the cream until it holds very soft peaks. Combine with hollandaise sauce. Top cucumbers with sauce. Put dish under a preheated broiler for 1 to 2 minutes, or until the sauce is glazed.

ACCOMPANIMENTS

HARICOTS VERTS PROVINCAL   6 Servings

1½ lbs. fresh green beans, whole or French cut
3 T. olive oil
1 clove garlic, peeled and crushed
2 anchovy fillets, minced
1 T. minced parsley
1 T. minced shallots
1 T. white vinegar
Salt and pepper to taste

Cook beans in salted, boiling water until tender-crisp. Rinse with cold water and drain. In heavy saucepan, heat oil and garlic; add anchovies, parsley, and shallots. Stir, cooking over low heat, 5 minutes. Add beans and cook for 3 minutes. Pour into serving dish; deglaze pan with vinegar and pour juices over beans. Season to taste with salt and pepper.

LIMA BEAN PUREE   6 Servings

Delicious served with lamb

1 pkg. (10 oz.) baby lima beans
1 medium boiling potato, peeled and cut into eighths
2 tsp. minced shallots
2 T. butter
½ cup whipping cream
¼ cup sour cream
Salt and pepper to taste
Parsley

Place lima beans and potato in salted boiling water and cook over medium heat 30 to 40 minutes or until very tender. Saute shallots in butter until limp but not brown. Add whipping cream to shallots and heat. Do not boil. Drain beans and potato. Puree in food processor or put through food mill. Mix in sour cream and shallot mixture. Adjust seasonings. Pour into 1-qt. souffle dish or individual ramekins. Sprinkle with chopped parsley.

PUREE OF PEAS   4 Servings

1½ cups peas
1 small potato, peeled and diced
2 T. butter, softened
2 T. mayonnaise
¼ tsp. salt
¼ tsp. sugar
2 T. finely chopped sweet gherkins

Cook peas and potato in salted, boiling water to cover until tender. Drain. Put peas, potato, butter, mayonnaise, salt and sugar in food processor or blender and puree. Spoon into small dish and stir in gherkins. May be served in individual ramekins.

VEGETABLES

PETIT POIS

6 to 10 lettuce leaves
   (outside leaves from
   head lettuce
   preferable)
1½ lbs. small peas (frozen
   work well)
1 large onion, chopped
   fine (or ½ lb. pearl
   onions)
4 T. butter
½ tsp. salt
1 T. sugar
½ cup water
3 sprigs parsley
1 slice bacon, cooked,
   drained, crumbled

Place lettuce, peas, onion, 2 T. butter, salt, sugar, parsley, and water to cover in a heavy saucepan. Mix gently and cover. Simmer until peas are tender, about 25 minutes. Remove from heat; remove parsley. Add remaining butter and return to heat shaking pan until butter is melted and almost all liquid has evaporated. To serve, sprinkle with crumbled bacon.

CHINESE SNOW PEAS

¼ cup chopped green
   onions
1 T. oil
1 lb. snow peas
½ cup sliced mushrooms
¼ cup chicken broth
½ tsp. salt
1 tsp. cornstarch
1 tsp. cold water
2 T. soy sauce
2 tsp. sugar

Saute onions in oil; add snow peas and mushrooms. Stir-fry 1 minute. Stir in broth and salt. Combine cornstarch and water; add to peas. Cook until thick. Stir in soy sauce and sugar. Serve with Chinese meat dish, steak or chicken.

ACCOMPANIMENTS

POTATO BASKETS

4 Baskets

4 medium potatoes,
   grated
Ice water
Oil for deep frying
Salt

To make baskets, you may use either a Bird's Nest Fryer or 2 strainers, 1 about 3 inches in diameter and a second one about ⅜ inch smaller. Preheat oil to 375°. Peel potatoes and grate; this may be done in food processor. Soak grated potatoes for 30 minutes in ice water. Drain and dry well between layers of paper towels. Before filling strainers, dip them in oil to keep potatoes from sticking. This must be done before making each basket. Line the larger strainer with 2 layers of potatoes; press smaller strainer into larger one. Fry basket for 3 to 4 minutes or until golden brown. Remove potatoes from strainers; a sharp rap on a table should loosen the basket. Salt as desired. These are best made ahead, drained, cooled, and tightly wrapped in foil. They may be frozen. Before using, return to room temperature and fry 1 minute more at 375° to 390°. Fill with vegetables or garnishes such as: ratatouille, tomato pudding, or sauteed mushrooms.

POTATOES ROSEMARY

2-3 Servings

3 T. butter
2 T. olive oil
10 small new potatoes,
   peeled
1 tsp. salt
1 tsp. dried rosemary,
   crushed
⅛ tsp. pepper

Melt butter; combine with olive oil in shallow baking dish. Add potatoes; coat well. Sprinkle with seasonings. Bake, uncovered, at 400° for 45 minutes, or until crisp and browned.

VEGETABLES

LEMON RICE WITH ALMONDS

4-6 Servings

1 large lemon
1 cup uncooked rice
1¾ cups chicken broth
½ tsp. salt
½ tsp. cinnamon
¼ tsp. nutmeg
1 T. butter
⅔ cup coarsely ground almonds
½ cup currants
1 cup dry white wine
1 cup cooked peas (fresh or frozen)
4 T. honey

Grate rind of lemon and reserve. Squeeze juice and pulp from lemon and reserve. Place lemon rind, lemon juice, rice, broth, salt, cinnamon, nutmeg and butter in top of double boiler. Cover and set over simmering water and steam for 30 minutes or until liquid is absorbed. In a small saucepan, simmer almonds and currants in white wine for 10 minutes. Add almonds, currants and peas to rice. Stir over low heat, about 5 minutes. Transfer to serving dish. Drizzle honey over top.

VEGETABLE CURRY

4-6 Servings

2 cups brown rice
4 cups water
1 T. butter
1½ tsp. salt
2 to 3 onions, thinly sliced
2 T. butter
1 T. curry powder or more
¼ cup flour
1½ cups water
1 lb. carrots, cut in rounds and cooked
1 cup raisins
1 cup raw or toasted cashews
3 T. mango chutney or more
1 T. sugar

Simmer rice in 4 cups water with 1 T. butter and salt about 75 minutes or until done. Set aside and keep warm. Saute onions in 2 T. butter. Add curry powder and flour. Stir and cook 1 minute. Whisk in 1½ cups water. Add cooked carrots, raisins, cashews, chutney, and sugar. May need additional water. Simmer 10 minutes. Serve over rice.

ACCOMPANIMENTS

GOLDEN "APPLES"

10 Servings

Medieval dish that creates the illusion of apples

1 lb. ground pork
¾ lb. ground beef
½ lb. bulk pork sausage
¾ tsp. salt
¾ tsp. nutmeg
½ tsp. ground cloves
2 eggs
¾ cup currants
6 egg yolks
¼ tsp. saffron
6 to 8 T. flour
2 apples, peeled, sliced
2 T. butter
Cinnamon
4 to 6 T. honey

For meatballs, combine pork, beef, sausage, salt, nutmeg, cloves, eggs and currants. Mix well. Shape into balls about 1¼ inches in diameter. Bake on a rack at 350° for 20 minutes. Cool and refrigerate 30 minutes. Blend yolks, saffron and flour. Paste should be thick but not dry. Paint paste on meatballs with a pastry brush. Bake at 350° for 15 minutes, or until meatballs are warmed. Saute apple slices in butter until tender. Sprinkle with cinnamon. Remove meatballs to platter. Garnish with apple slices. Drizzle all with honey.

CHEESE AND SPINACH TIMBALES

6 Servings

3 eggs, separated
⅔ cup milk
2 T. butter, melted
½ lb. grated Swiss cheese
½ tsp. salt
Few grains red pepper
2 cups cooked spinach, finely chopped

Beat egg yolks; add milk, melted butter, cheese, and seasoning. Stir while heating. Mix ½ of cheese sauce with spinach and fold in stiffly beaten egg whites. Fill buttered timbale molds (may use ramekins or custard cups) with the mixture and place in a pan of hot water. Bake at 325° until firm, about 20 minutes. Turn out on a hot platter, garnish with slices of hard-boiled egg. Pour remaining cheese sauce around the timbales.

SALADS, DRESSINGS & SAUCES

ARTICHOKE-PEA SALAD

4 Servings

1 pkg. (10 oz.) frozen
  peas with mushrooms,
  cooked
2 hard-cooked eggs,
  chopped
¼ cup sweet pickle relish
2 T. chopped onion
1½ cups mayonnaise
2 T. lemon juice
1 tsp. salt
½ tsp. pepper
½ tsp. dill
¼ tsp. oregano
¼ tsp. dry mustard
4 artichokes, cooked,
  chilled, chokes
  removed
Pimiento strips

Combine peas and mushrooms with eggs, pickle relish and onion. Combine mayonnaise, lemon juice, salt, pepper, dill, oregano, and dry mustard; blend well. Add about ½ cup mayonnaise mixture to pea mixture or enough to moisten. Stuff the artichokes with the pea mixture. Chill until ready to serve. Garnish with pimiento strips. Serve with the remaining dressing.

ARTICHOKE BOTTOMS FILLED WITH SHRIMP

6-8 Servings

8 to 12 canned artichoke
  bottoms
½ cup mayonnaise
2 T. chopped parsley
1 T. capers
1 T. olive oil
2 T. finely chopped green
  onions
1 tsp. anchovy paste
½ lb. shrimp, cooked and
  diced
½ cucumber, peeled and
  thinly sliced
Salt and pepper to taste

Gently toss all ingredients together except the artichoke bottoms. Place mixture in artichoke bottoms and serve on a bed of lettuce. Garnish with parsley or pimiento, if desired.

70

SALADS, DRESSINGS & SAUCES

ENDIVE AND EGG SALAD
4-6 Servings

A different way to use Easter eggs

½ lb. Belgian endive
4 to 6 T. homemade
  mayonnaise
1 tsp. Dijon mustard
2 to 3 hard-cooked eggs,
  sliced
Salt and pepper

Core endive and remove any discolored leaves. Separate leaves. Leaves may be left whole or cut into halves or quarters if large. Combine mayonnaise with mustard and toss with endive. Gently fold in egg slices. Salt and pepper to taste.

BROCCOLI SALAD
10-12 Servings

3 lbs. fresh broccoli,
  cooked, chopped
1 jar (6 oz.) olives,
  chopped
2 stalks celery, chopped
1 cup chopped green
  onions with tops
6 hard-cooked eggs,
  chopped
1 cup mayonnaise
⅛ tsp. salt

Cook broccoli until tender-crisp. Drain; cool and chop. Add olives, celery, onions, and eggs. Stir in mayonnaise and salt to taste. Chill. Can be made day ahead. If desired, substitute 4 pkgs. (10 oz. each) frozen chopped broccoli.

NAMASU
4 Servings

Serve with Tempura

2 medium cucumbers
½ tsp. salt
½ cup Japanese rice
  vinegar
2 T. sugar
1 tsp. finely chopped
  fresh ginger
¼ tsp. MSG
Thinly sliced carrots

Partly pare cucumbers leaving strips of green. Slice thin. Sprinkle with salt and let stand for 15 minutes. Press to remove excess liquid. Combine remaining ingredients and stir into cucumbers. Chill. Add thinly sliced carrots for color.

SALADS, DRESSINGS & SAUCES

PAMPLEMOUSSE AU CHAMPAGNE   8 Servings

4 whole grapefruit
1 ripe honeydew melon
2 cups seedless green
   grapes
Sugar
Fifth of Champagne
Chopped mint leaves

Cut grapefruit in ½. Spoon out sections. Remove membranes from grapefruit halves. Slice melon in ½; remove seeds. Make melon balls or cut into 1-inch cubes. Combine grapefruit sections, melon balls and grapes. Sprinkle with sugar to taste. Stir in 1 cup Champagne. Chill. To serve, fill grapefruit shells with fruit mixture; pour some Champagne over each. Garnish with mint leaves.

DEVILED EGG SALAD   4-6 Servings

1 envelope unflavored
   gelatin
½ cup water
1 tsp. salt
¼ tsp. Worcestershire
   sauce
2 T. lemon juice
Dash hot pepper sauce
Dash mustard
¾ cup mayonnaise
½ cup diced celery
6 hard-cooked eggs,
   chopped
Grated onion to taste

SHRIMP SAUCE:

1 cup mayonnaise
2 T. chili sauce
1 T. catsup
1 T. each: vinegar,
   chopped chives, green
   pepper, pimiento
1 tsp. paprika
1 T. lemon juice
1 can (7½ oz.) shrimp,
   drained

Sprinkle gelatin over water. Heat slightly to dissolve. Add spices. Cool. Stir in mayonnaise. Fold in remaining ingredients. Pour into well-oiled mold or individual molds. Chill until set. Unmold on bed of lettuce. Serve with shrimp sauce.

For sauce, combine ingredients. Blend well.

SALADS, DRESSINGS & SAUCES

DAY-AHEAD SPINACH SALAD　　　　4 Servings

½ to ¾ lb. fresh spinach torn into bite-sized pieces
½ medium cucumber, thinly sliced
½ cup thinly sliced radishes
¼ cup thinly sliced green onions
2 hard-cooked eggs, sliced
¾ to 1 cup thick blue cheese dressing
5 slices bacon, cooked, crumbled
½ cup salted Spanish peanuts

Arrange spinach evenly in shallow salad bowl. Layer with cucumber, radish, onion, and eggs. Spread dressing over all. Cover and chill 24 hours. Before serving, sprinkle with bacon and peanuts.

RICE AND ARTICHOKE SALAD　　　　6 Servings

Easy, delicious and different

1 pkg. (6 oz.) chicken flavored rice or Rice-a-Roni
12 large black olives, sliced
4 green onions, thinly sliced
1 small green pepper, chopped
⅓ cup real mayonnaise
2 jars (5½ oz. each) marinated artichoke hearts, cut in halves
⅓ cup artichoke marinade
¾ tsp. curry powder
1 pkg. (10½ oz.) frozen peas, cooked and cooled (optional)
1 cup chopped, cooked chicken (optional)

Cook rice according to directions on package omitting butter. Mix mayonnaise and marinade with curry powder. Add other ingredients. Add peas or chicken, if desired. Toss and chill. Serve in glass bowl lined with leaf lettuce.

SALADS, DRESSINGS & SAUCES

CRABMEAT AND SNOW PEAS
12 Servings

Serve as a first course or a simple spring luncheon

6 oz. fresh snow peas
6 oz. frozen or canned
  crabmeat
¼ tsp. curry powder
1 T. lemon juice
4 T. mayonnaise

Clean snow peas and take out back vein. Mix together other ingredients and toss with fresh snow peas. Chill until serving. Serve on a lettuce leaf.

WESTERN SALAD
8 Servings

Colorful and tasty

½ cup salad oil
¼ cup lemon juice
3 T. tarragon vinegar
2 T. sugar
2 T. minced onion
1 clove garlic, crushed
1 tsp. salt
½ tsp. dry mustard
Freshly ground pepper
1 can hearts of palm,
  sliced
1 avocado, sliced
½ bunch radishes, sliced
2 small heads Boston
  lettuce
Croutons

In jar or shaker, place oil, lemon juice, vinegar, sugar, onion, and seasonings. Shake thoroughly. Pour over hearts of palm, avocado, and radishes. Mix lightly. Chill. Just before serving, arrange lettuce leaves on salad plates. Spoon vegetable mixture on lettuce. Serve sprinkled with croutons.

MINT SAUCE
¾ Cup

½ cup sugar
¼ cup wine vinegar
1 cup chopped fresh mint
  leaves, save 1 sprig

Combine sugar and vinegar in a saucepan and gently boil for 5 minutes. Pour over mint leaves, cover and let stand 1 to 2 hours. Strain into sterilized bottle with sprig of fresh mint. Recipe may be doubled. Serve with lamb.

SALADS, DRESSINGS & SAUCES

RASPBERRY VINEGAR   1 Pint

12 raspberries
1 pt. red or white wine
   vinegar

Place berries in a non-metal container with tightly fitting lid. Pour vinegar over berries, cover and store in cool dark place 2 to 4 weeks; shake gently occasionally. May be strained at this point. Vinegar will continue to improve with age as it mellows.

RASPBERRY VINEGAR DRESSING FOR ASPARAGUS

4 T. light salad oil
4 T. raspberry vinegar
1 tsp. salt
1 T. sugar
Few grindings fresh white
   pepper
1 clove garlic, peeled
¼ tsp. basil

Combine all ingredients. Shake well. Let stand 1 hour before serving. Pour over asparagus.

GREEN MAYONNAISE   About 1½ Cups

Delicious with eggs, chicken, or green vegetables

½ cup boiling water
¼ of 10-oz. pkg. frozen
   spinach
¼ cup parsley
¼ cup watercress leaves
1 T. chives
½ tsp. dried tarragon
1 egg
2 egg yolks
½ tsp. salt
Dash pepper
Grated rind and juice of 1
   lemon
¾ cup salad oil

Add spinach to boiling water; cover and cook until thawed, about 3 minutes. Add parsley, watercress, chives, and tarragon. Simmer 2 more minutes. Drain; pat dry. Place in blender or food processor. Add egg and yolks, salt, pepper, lemon rind and juice. Puree. Add oil in slow steady stream until all oil is absorbed.

SALADS, DRESSINGS & SAUCES

GARLIC DRESSING
About 1⅓ Cups

For garlic lovers only

2 to 4 cloves garlic
1 tsp. dry mustard
½ tsp. salt
½ tsp. freshly ground
pepper
⅓ cup white wine vinegar
⅓ cup water
⅔ cup oil

Chop garlic in food processor. Add dry ingredients, vinegar, and water. While processing, add oil. (Crumbled blue cheese makes a tasty addition.)

HONEY-RUSSIAN DRESSING
2½ Cups

Great for spinach salad

1 cup oil
½ cup honey
½ cup cider vinegar
½ cup minced onion
⅓ cup chili sauce
1 T. Worcestershire
sauce
½ tsp. salt

Place all ingredients in covered jar. Shake well.

LOW-CALORIE YOGURT DRESSING
1½ Cups

Tangy and good

1 carton (8 oz.) plain low-
fat yogurt
¼ cup vinegar
¼ cup lemon juice
1 T. each: dried chives,
basil, dill, parsley
flakes
1 clove garlic, mashed

Combine all ingredients; mix well. Chill.

DESSERTS & SWEETS

LEMON SURPRISE MERINGUES

A perfect dessert for spring!

MERINGUES:

3 egg whites, at room
   temperature
1 tsp. vanilla
½ tsp. cream of tartar
¼ tsp. salt
¾ cup sugar

LEMON FILLING:

3 egg yolks
1 cup sugar
¼ cup cornstarch
⅛ tsp. salt
1 cup water
1 T. grated lemon rind
¼ cup lemon juice
2 cups whipping cream
2 T. confectioners' sugar
10 to 12 fresh whole
   strawberries

For meringues, beat egg whites until frothy. Beat in vanilla, cream of tartar, and salt. Gradually add sugar, continue beating until very stiff peaks form. Cover cookie sheet with unglazed paper. Drop beaten egg whites from spoon into 10 to 12 mounds, 2 inches apart. Hollow out centers. Bake at 250° for 1 hour, or until dry to touch. Turn upside down on same paper. Bake 5 minutes more. Cool on rack. Cover lightly with plastic wrap until needed. To make filling, combine in top of double boiler egg yolks, sugar, cornstarch, and salt. Stir in water, lemon rind, and lemon juice. Cook over hot water, stirring constantly, until thi kened and clear. Cool. Whip 1 cup whipping cream. Fold into lemon filling. Spoon into meringue shells. Chill several hours. Just before serving, whip remaining 1 cup whipping cream with confectioners' sugar. Spoon onto lemon filling. Decorate each with a strawberry.

KENTUCKY PIE

Pecan pie with a difference

¾ cup maple syrup
¾ cup sugar
⅓ cup butter, softened
3 eggs, beaten
1 to 2 T. bourbon
⅓ cup semisweet
   chocolate pieces
¾ cup chopped pecans
1 unbaked 9-inch pastry
   shell
Whipped cream (optional)

Mix syrup, sugar, butter, eggs, and bourbon in bowl until smooth. Stir in chocolate pieces and pecans. Pour mixture into pastry shell. Bake at 350° for 40 to 45 minutes. Serve warm with whipped cream if desired.

DESSERTS & SWEETS

ROSY RHUBARB DESSERT
6-8 Servings

Nice anytime you can get fresh rhubarb

CRUST:

1 cup flour
2 T. sugar
½ cup butter
¼ cup chopped walnuts
(optional)

FILLING:

¾ cup sugar
3 T. flour
¾ lb. fresh rhubarb, cut in
1-inch pieces (about 3
cups)
3 egg yolks, slightly
beaten
⅓ cup milk
½ tsp. vanilla

MERINGUE:

3 egg whites
⅓ cup sugar

For crust, combine flour and 2 T. sugar. Cut in butter. Stir in walnuts. Press into 9-inch square baking pan. Bake at 350° for 20 minutes.

For filling, combine sugar and flour. Stir in rhubarb. Combine egg yolks, milk, and vanilla. Add to rhubarb. Spoon over hot crust. Bake 40 minutes more.

For meringue, beat egg whites until foamy; gradually add ⅓ cup sugar, continue beating until stiff peaks form. Spread over hot rhubarb. Bake 12 to 15 minutes, or until lightly browned. Cool and refrigerate.

LOMBARDY FRUIT TART
6-8 Servings

10 pitted prunes
10 dried figs
10 pitted dates
1 cooked 9-inch pate
brisee shell
3 T. minced raw bone
marrow
1 cup whipping cream
3 eggs, lightly beaten
3 T. minced parsley
2 T. brown sugar
1 tsp. cinnamon
¾ tsp. grated orange rind
½ tsp. salt
Pinch of mace or nutmeg

Mince prunes, figs and dates and distribute evenly in bottom of pastry shell. Sprinkle bone marrow on top. Combine cream, eggs, parsley, brown sugar, cinnamon, orange rind, salt and mace. Pour over fruit and bake in upper ⅓ of 375° oven for 30 minutes or until custard is set and top is golden. Let sit 5 minutes before serving.

DESSERTS & SWEETS

STRAWBERRY-RHUBARB COBBLER   6-8 Servings

1 cup plus 1 T. flour
2 T. sugar
1½ tsp. baking powder
¼ tsp. salt
¼ cup cold unsalted
  butter
½ cup half and half
2½ cups sliced fresh
  rhubarb or frozen
  unsweetened rhubarb,
  thawed, drained
⅔ cup sugar
1½ T. quick cooking
  tapioca
2 tsp. lemon juice
2½ cups halved fresh
  strawberries
2 T. kirsch
Whipping cream

Sift flour, 2 T. sugar, baking powder and salt in a large bowl. Cut in butter until mixture resembles coarse crumbs. Make a well in center. Pour half and half into well, stir until moistened and dough cleans side of bowl. Combine rhubarb, ⅔ cup sugar, tapioca, and lemon juice in medium-sized saucepan. Heat to boiling; reduce heat; simmer, stirring constantly 2 minutes. Remove from heat; add strawberries and kirsch. Pour into buttered 6-cup baking dish. Gently spread dough over hot filling. Place dish on baking sheet. Bake at 425° until top is golden brown, 25 to 30 minutes. Cool 30 minutes. Serve with cream.

STRAWBERRY PIE   6-8 Servings

1 baked 9-inch pastry
  shell (use pate brisee)
1 qt. fresh strawberries
1 cup sugar
1½ T. cornstarch
1 tsp. lemon juice
2 T. strawberry liqueur
  (optional)
1 cup whipping cream

Sort through strawberries; reserve about 6 of the best for the topping; then pick out enough of the next best to fill the pastry shell. If strawberries are very large, slice in ½ lengthwise. Put remainder in food processor or blender with sugar and process until pulpy, not liquid. Put strawberry-sugar mixture into a heavy pan; add cornstarch and lemon juice. Stir until the cornstarch has been completely dissolved. Cook over medium high heat, stirring constantly, until mixture is clear and thickened. Remove from heat and stir in liqueur. Pour over berries that have been arranged in pastry shell. Whip cream until it stands in stiff peaks. Spoon over pie; top with reserved berries.

DESSERTS & SWEETS

LEMON-NUT-BERRY ROLL
Delicious and beautiful

6-8 Servings

4 eggs, separated
¾ cup sugar
1 T. grated lemon rind
1 T. lemon juice
½ cup flour
¾ tsp. baking powder
½ cup finely chopped pecans
1 cup whipping cream, whipped
2 T. confectioners' sugar
1 pt. fresh strawberries, sliced (or other fruit)

Beat egg whites until foamy; gradually add ½ cup of the sugar. Continue beating until stiff peaks form. In a small bowl, beat egg yolks until light. Gradually add remaining ¼ cup sugar, beating until mixture is thick and creamy. Mix in lemon rind and lemon juice. Stir together flour and baking powder; fold into egg yolk mixture. Fold egg whites, chopped nuts, and egg yolk mixture together — just until blended. Spread in a 15 x 10-inch pan which has been greased, lined with waxed paper, and again greased. Bake at 375° for 13 to 15 minutes, or until the top springs back when touched lightly. Immediately turn onto a towel that has been sprinkled with confectioners' sugar. Remove paper, roll up from the narrow end. Cool completely.

Fold 2 T. confectioners' sugar into whipped cream. Carefully unroll cake; spread with whipped cream. Scatter berries on top; roll up. Place on serving platter; chill up to 2 hours. Sprinkle with confectioners' sugar and a few whole berries. Slice and serve.

RHUBARB CRUNCH

8 Servings

1 cup rolled oats
1 cup brown sugar
½ cup flour
½ cup butter
½ cup granulated sugar
1 T. flour
1 tsp. cinnamon
⅛ tsp. salt
3 cups diced fresh rhubarb
1 T. water

Combine oats, brown sugar, ½ cup flour, and butter. Sprinkle ½ of mixture in an 8-inch square baking pan. Combine granulated sugar, 1 T. flour, cinnamon, and salt; combine with rhubarb and water. Spoon onto oat mixture in pan. Cover with remaining oat mixture. Bake at 350° for 45 minutes.

DESSERTS & SWEETS

FLOWER CAKE
Dramatic finale for medieval banquet

ALMOND MILK:

1½ cups blanched
   almonds
3 to 4 T. ice water
3 cups boiling water
1½ T. honey
Dash of salt

ROSEE:

½ cup dried, crushed rose
   petals, violets,
   primroses or hawthorn
   flowers or 1½ cups
   fresh petals
3 cups almond milk
1½ tsp. cinnamon
½ tsp. ginger
1 cup sugar
½ cup flour
1½ cups minced dates
⅓ cup pine nuts
1½ cups whipping cream,
   whipped

CAKE:

1 (13 x 9-inch) white
   cake, cooled
Fresh flower petals

For milk, grind almonds in blender adding ic water until they re finely ground. Add honey and salt to boiling water and dissolve. Add almonds. Soak 15 minutes stirring occasionally. May be made up to 3 days ahead and refrigerated.

For rosee, soak petals in 2 cups almond milk for 15 minutes. Add cinnamon, ginger, and sugar. Cook over medium heat until sugar is dissolved. Combine reserved 1 cup almond milk and flour. Mix or shake until smooth. Add to rest of almond mixture and cook until thick, stirring constantly. Add dates and nuts. Chill. Fold in whipped cream.

Put cake on platter. Smooth rosee over top and sides of cake. Decorate cake with fresh flower petals.

MELTAWAYS   10 Dozen

1 cup butter, softened
1¼ cups confectioners'
   sugar
1 tsp. vanilla
1 cup sifted flour
2 T. cornstarch
¼ tsp. salt
1 cup chopped nuts
10 oz. milk chocolate,
   melted, cooled

Cream butter and sugar; add vanilla. Sift together flour, cornstarch, and salt. Add to butter. Fold in nuts and chocolate. Shape into small balls, 1 rounded tsp. each. Place on ungreased cookie sheets, allowing room for spreading. Bake on middle rack at 250° for 40 minutes. Store in airtight container.

DESSERTS & SWEETS

CHEESECAKE WITH HOT RASPBERRY SAUCE

Graham cracker crust
mixture to line 9-inch
spring-form pan
(optional)
3 pkgs. (8 oz. each)
cream cheese
4 large eggs
1 cup sugar
1 tsp. vanilla
1 pt. sour cream
¾ cup superfine sugar
1 pkg. (10 oz.) frozen
raspberries, thawed
2 T. Grand Marnier
1 to 1½ T. cornstarch

Combine cream cheese, eggs, sugar, and vanilla in large mixing bowl and beat at medium speed 25 minutes. Place in 9-inch spring-form pan (pan can be slightly greased or have graham cracker crust lining it). Bake at 355° for 40 minutes. Cool for 35 minutes. Meanwhile, beat sour cream and sugar together for 10 minutes. Pour over cake. Return to oven and bake at 400° for 10 to 15 minutes until barely browned. Do not let it burn or boil. Cool overnight. Before serving, heat berries to boiling, add Grand Marnier which has been mixed with cornstarch. Cook until thickened. Serve in separate bowl to ladle onto cheesecake.

CHEESECAKE BARS

16   2-inch Squares

¼ cup butter
⅓ cup brown sugar
1 cup flour
½ cup chopped pecans
¼ cup currant jelly

FILLING:

1 pkg. (8 oz.) cream
cheese
¼ cup sugar
1 egg
2 T. milk
2 T. lemon juice
½ tsp. vanilla

Cream butter. Add brown sugar and flour. Blend until mixture resembles cornmeal. Add pecans. Reserve 1 cup mixture for topping. Press remaining in an 8-inch square pan. Bake 15 minutes at 350°. Cool. Spread crust with jelly. For filling, beat cream cheese and sugar. Beat in egg and milk. Add lemon juice and vanilla. Turn onto cooled crust and sprinkle with reserved topping. Bake 30 minutes at 350°. Cool before cutting.

DESSERTS & SWEETS

UKRANIAN TORTE

16-20 Servings

Make ahead and refrigerate or freeze

BATTER:

13 large eggs, separated
1½ cups confectioners'
   sugar
2½ cups grated walnuts

FILLING:

1⅓ cups sugar
6 T. water
2 whole eggs
6 egg yolks
1 lb. unsalted butter,
   softened
2 tsp. vanilla
¾ cup seedless raspberry
   jam
1 to 2 tsp. instant coffee
   powder

For batter, beat egg yolks until light and fluffy; add confectioners' sugar and continue beating until batter forms thick ribbons when beater is lifted. Fold in grated walnuts. Beat egg whites until stiff. Stir ½ cup of egg whites into batter, then fold in remaining egg whites. Pour into 3 well-buttered and floured 9-inch cake pans. Bake in 300° oven for 1 hour. Cool.

For filling, bring sugar and water to a boil over high heat. When liquid is clear, cover for 1 minute. Remove cover and boil to soft-ball stage. Combine eggs and yolks in saucepan and immediately drizzle hot syrup onto eggs, beating constantly. Set over simmering water. Beat slowly until mixture is very hot and forms thick ribbons. Remove from heat; beat over cold water until cool. Beat in butter about 2 T. at a time. Add vanilla. Add raspberry jam to ½ of filling and spread between layers. Add instant coffee powder to remaining filling; adjust amount to taste. Frost sides and top. Chill.

SHREDDED WHEAT BASKETS

16 Baskets

Add your choice of fillings for a festive dessert

5 large shredded wheat
   biscuits
¾ cup shredded coconut
¼ cup sugar
½ cup butter, melted

Crumble shredded wheat; add coconut, sugar, and butter. Press into 16 custard cups. Bake at 350° for about 10 minutes. Cool. Loosen with knife. Fill with ice cream, fresh fruit, or cooked custard.

DESSERTS & SWEETS

VANILLA BAVARIAN CREAM WITH RASPBERRY SAUCE
6-8 Servings

BAVARIAN CREAM:

1 envelope (1 T.)
   unflavored gelatin
½ cup sugar
⅛ tsp. salt
1¼ cups milk
2 eggs, separated
1 tsp. vanilla
1 cup whipping cream,
   whipped

RASPBERRY SAUCE:

1 pkg. (10 oz.) frozen
   raspberries
¼ cup sugar
¼ cup port wine
1 T. cornstarch
1 T. lemon juice
⅛ tsp. salt
2 T. butter

For bavarian cream, mix gelatin, ¼ cup sugar, and salt in top of double boiler. Beat egg yolks with milk; add to gelatin mixture. Cook over hot water, stirring constantly, until gelatin is dissolved, about 6 minutes. Remove from heat, add vanilla. Chill until mixture mounds slightly when dropped from a spoon. Beat egg whites until stiff but not dry. Gradually add remaining ¼ cup sugar and continue beating until stiff. Fold the gelatin mixture into the egg whites. Carefully fold in whipped cream. Turn into oiled 5-cup mold. Chill until set. Unmold onto serving plate; serve with raspberry sauce. For sauce, combine all ingredients except butter and cook over low heat, stirring frequently, until thickened and clear. Remove from heat and stir in butter. Strain, if desired. Serve warm.

ANGEL PECAN DELIGHT
6-8 Servings

Delicious with fresh fruit

3 egg whites
½ cup sugar
1 cup Ritz cracker
   crumbs
1 cup chopped pecans
2 tsp. vanilla
1 tsp. almond flavoring
1 cup whipping cream

Beat egg whites until foamy; gradually add sugar, continuing to beat until stiff peaks form. Fold in cracker crumbs, pecans, 1 tsp. vanilla, and almond flavoring. Spoon into a greased and floured 9-inch springform pan; bake at 350° for 25 to 30 minutes. While still warm, poke holes in top with fork. Spoon ½ cup whipping cream over dessert. Chill. Whip remaining cream; fold in 1 tsp. vanilla. Spoon on top for garnish.

DESSERTS & SWEETS

EXTRA CHOCOLATE CHOCOLATE CAKE   12 Servings

3 to 4 tsp. unsweetened
   cocoa
½ cup butter, softened
½ cup (4 oz.) cream
   cheese, softened
1¼ cups sugar
2 eggs
1 tsp. vanilla
3 cups flour
2 tsp. baking soda
1 tsp. salt
2 cups milk
4 squares (1 oz. each)
   unsweetened
   chocolate, melted
1 pkg. (6 oz.) semisweet
   chocolate pieces

CREAMY CHOCOLATE FROSTING:

1 pkg. (6 oz.) semisweet
   chocolate pieces
6 T. butter
4 oz. cream cheese,
   softened
4 cups confectioners'
   sugar, sifted
1 tsp. vanilla
1 egg
Milk

For cake, butter three 8-inch cake pans and dust with cocoa. Cream butter, cream cheese, and sugar until fluffy, about 5 minutes. Beat in eggs, 1 at a time. Blend in vanilla. Mix flour, soda, and salt. Alternately blend flour and milk into cheese mixture beginning and ending with flour. Mix in melted unsweetened chocolate. Divide ½ of batter evenly among 3 pans; sprinkle all of semisweet pieces equally on top of batter. Pour remaining batter on top of each. Bake at 350° for 20 to 25 minutes or until cake tester comes out clean. Cool 10 minutes. Remove from pans. Cool thoroughly.

For frosting, melt chocolate pieces with 1 T. butter in top of double boiler. Beat cream cheese and 5 T. butter until fluffy. Gradually blend in sugar and vanilla; stir in melted chocolate. Beat in egg. Add milk, 1 tsp. at a time until spreading consistency. Decorate cake with shaved chocolate, if desired.

RHUBARB-STRAWBERRY DESSERT SAUCE

A microwave method for an old favorite

1 lb. fresh rhubarb, cut in
   1-inch pieces (3 cups)
1 cup sugar
1 T. cornstarch
½ cup water
1 cup halved fresh
   strawberries

Combine rhubarb, sugar, and cornstarch in a 1½-qt. glass casserole. Stir in water. Cover. Microcook on high 8 minutes, stirring once. Add strawberries. Cover and continue cooking 2 minutes or until mixture is thickened and bubbling. Chill. Serve over vanilla ice cream.

EASTER

EASTER BREAD

Prepared by both the Swiss and Italians, this Easter coffeecake appears to have eggs resting in a nest

2¼ to 3¼ cups sifted flour
¼ cup sugar
1 tsp. salt
1 pkg. dry yeast
⅔ cup milk
2 T. butter
2 eggs, at room temperature
½ cup mixed candied fruits
¼ cup chopped blanched almonds
½ tsp. anise seed
2 T. butter, melted (about)
5 uncooked eggs, dyed
Basic confectioners' icing
Colored sprinkles

In a large bowl, mix 1 cup flour, sugar, salt and dry yeast. Set aside. In a saucepan, combine milk and 2 T. butter. Heat over low heat until liquid is warm. (Butter does not have to melt.) Gradually add this mixture to dry ingredients and beat 2 minutes at medium speed of electric mixer, scraping bowl occasionally. Add eggs and ½ cup flour, or enough flour to make a thick batter. Beat at high speed 2 minutes scraping bowl occasionally. Stir in enough additional flour to make a soft dough. Turn out onto lightly floured board; knead until smooth and elastic, about 8 to 10 minutes. Place in greased bowl; turn to grease top. Cover; let rise in warm place, free from drafts, until doubled in bulk, about 1 hour.

Combine fruits, nuts, and anise seed. Punch dough down; turn out onto lightly floured board. Knead in fruit mixture. Divide dough in ½. Roll each ½ into a 24-inch rope. Twist ropes together loosely and form into ring on greased baking sheet. Brush with melted butter. Place uncooked dyed eggs into spaces in the twist. Cover; let rise in warm place, free from drafts, until doubled in bulk, about 1 hour.

Bake at 350° about 30 to 35 minutes, or until done. Remove from baking sheet and cool on wire rack. Drizzle icing over coffeecake and decorate with colored sprinkles.

EASTER

CHOCOLATE EASTER NESTS

Makes 20 Nests

1 bar (9¾ oz.) milk
chocolate
1 pkg. (4 oz.) sweet
baking chocolate
1 pkg. (4 oz.) shredded
coconut
2 cups cornflakes,
crushed
Jelly beans

Melt milk chocolate and baking chocolate in top of a double boiler. Stir in coconut and cornflakes. Spoon onto waxed paper and form into nest shapes. Cool. Fill with jelly beans.

BROWN BUNNY EGGS

An old German Easter custom

Save the brown outside peels from your onions until Easter time. Soak the peels in a large pot (not aluminum) until limp. Fit as many raw eggs in shells as desired in the pot, arranging so the peels surround the eggs. Bring just to boil and simmer until hard boiled, about 45 minutes, with enough water in pot to cover eggs. The shells will be a light brown to dark brown depending on how long or hard you boil the eggs. Onion water may be used for more than one batch of eggs. When done, cool the eggs and lightly grease them for shine.

LOLLYPOPS

2 Dozen

A great children's project, with supervision

2 cups sugar
⅔ cup corn syrup
½ cup water
2 T. strawberry or orange
extract
Few drops red or orange
food coloring
24 lollypop sticks

In large saucepan, combine sugar, corn syrup, and water. Heat to boiling. Cover and boil 3 minutes, so steam can wash down any crystals on sides. Uncover. Boil, without stirring, to 300° on candy thermometer (hard crack stage). Carefully stir in extract and coloring. Quickly pour over lollypop sticks which have been laid out on foil. May be poured in any size or shape desired. Cools in 30 minutes.

1447

SUMMER MENUS

GROOM'S DINNER

Grilled Mustard Shrimp on Skewers
Cold Fillet of Beef Japonais
Shoestring Potatoes
Herbed Green Beans
Biscuits Wally
Mixed Greens with Creamy Salad Dressing
Prince of Wales Cake

SUMMER BRUNCH

Cold Two-Melon Soup
Dilled Spinach, Ham and Mushroom Crepes
Molded Gazpacho Salad with Avocado Dressing
Rose Geranium Cake
Assorted Teas

TERRACE SUPPER FOR A SIZZLING EVENING

Frozen Watermelon Daiquiris
Mock Vitello Tonnato
Cold Rice Salad
French Bread
Peches Supremes

SCHOOL'S OUT CHILDREN'S LUNCHEON

Watermelon Punch
Tostadas
Double Chocolate Ice Cream Cake

SUMMER MENUS

FIRECRACKER FEAST

Henry's Manhattan Clam Chowder
Charcoal Grilled Hamburgers
on Cheddar-Onion Hamburger Buns
Beans for Barbecue
Tomatoes and Cucumbers with Fresh Herbs
Blueberry Cream Cake

BASTILLE DINNER

French Fresh Tomato Soup
Mousse de Crevettes with Sauce Bercy
Steak Piquante
Microwave Fresh Vegetable Platter
Fresh Peach and Blueberry Tart

MEDITERRANEAN DINNER

Lemon Sangria
Armenian Appetizer
Leg of Lamb with Avgolemono Sauce
Colache
Rice or Barley
Galactobouriko

BEVERAGES

MOONLIGHT PUNCH

Refreshing party punch for children

6 cups sugar
4 cups water
1 cup or more mint leaves
4 cups lemon juice
8 qts. ice water
4 qts. ginger ale

Mix sugar and 4 cups water; boil 3 minutes. Add mint leaves and cool. Add lemon juice and strain into punch bowl over ice. Add ice water. Add ginger ale just before serving.

PEACH CHABLIS

16-20 Servings

½ cup sugar
½ cup water
2 ripe peaches, peeled, pitted and chopped
½ cup orange-flavored liqueur
1 T. lemon juice
1 qt. Chablis, chilled
1 qt. club soda, chilled
Mint leaves

Place sugar and water in pan; cook over medium heat until sugar is completely dissolved. Pour syrup over peaches; stir in liqueur and lemon juice. Cover and refrigerate overnight. When ready to serve, pour peach mixture into punch bowl and stir in Chablis and club soda. Add cracked ice and mint leaves for garnish.

WATERMELON PUNCH

About 1 Gallon

Wonderful fun for a children's party

1 large watermelon (about 25 lbs.)
1 can (12 oz.) frozen lemonade, thawed
2 cups water
¼ cup grenadine syrup
1 to 2 (32 oz.) bottles lemon-lime carbonated beverage, chilled
Straws

Select a melon about 20 inches long with a flat base. Day before serving, cut (sawtooth) an 8-inch oval section out of top and reserve. Scoop out pulp and remove seeds. Puree pulp in blender or processor. Strain and put into melon. Stir in undiluted lemonade, water, and grenadine. Replace "lid." Refrigerate overnight. Before serving, stir in lemon-lime beverage until ¾ full. Use a skewer to poke holes in melon for straws. Serve with "lid" on. For adults you may spike the watermelon with vodka.

BEVERAGES

FROZEN WATERMELON DAIQUIRIS 4 Servings

3 cups seeded, cubed
  watermelon
⅓ cup sugar
⅓ cup freshly squeezed
  lime juice
½ cup light rum
Mint leaves for garnish

Put watermelon, sugar, lime juice, and rum in food processor or blender. Process until slushy. Freeze about 2 hours, until very thick and slushy. Spoon into glasses. Garnish with mint leaves. Rum may be omitted, if you like.

LEMON SANGRIA 1½ Quarts

4 cups dry white wine,
  chilled
2 unpeeled lemons,
  sliced (seeds removed)
1 unpeeled orange, sliced
1 green apple, peeled,
  cored and cut into
  wedges
½ cup Cognac
¼ cup sugar
10 oz. club soda, chilled
Ice cubes

Combine wine, lemons, orange, apple, Cognac, and sugar in a large pitcher and chill overnight. Just before serving, add soda and ice cubes; stir lightly.

FRUIT FREEZE 6-8 Servings

Great summer popsicle treat

1 pt. fresh strawberries
2 cups fresh watermelon
  cubes
Sugar to taste

Combine berries, melon, and sugar in food processor. Blend well. Turn into individual molds such as small paper cups with a stick inserted. Freeze until firm.

APPETIZERS

ARMENIAN APPETIZER

1 cup chopped onions
¼ cup pignola (pine) nuts
1 cup uncooked white rice
¼ cup fresh parsley, stems removed
¼ cup (or less) currants
½ cup fresh dill
Salt and pepper
Juice of 1 lemon
¼ cup tomato paste
1 lb. or more grape leaves, rinsed and drained, stem end removed

Saute onions and pine nuts in a little oil. Add remaining ingredients to onions (except grape leaves). Mix and cook 5 minutes. Add 1 cup water and cook 15 minutes. Line a pot with a few grape leaves, fill remaining grape leaves with shiny side down. Place some of the onion-pine nut mixture near the stem end. Fold stem end up to cover mixture. Fold in sides, then roll up. Place in leaf-lined pot. Pour ½ cup oil, a little lemon juice and 1 cup water over rolled leaves. Weight leaves with small plate. Cover and simmer 30 to 40 minutes. Let cool before removing from pot. Chill in refrigerator. Serve cold with lemon wedges.

SAN FRANCISCO WINNER AVOCADO LAYERED DIP

2 avocados, peeled and pitted
Dash salt
Lemon juice
1 cup sour cream
½ pkg. (1¼ oz.) taco seasoning mix
1 cup grated Monterey Jack cheese
1 cup grated sharp Cheddar cheese
1 cup finely chopped tomatoes
Dash hot pepper sauce
¼ cup chopped green onions
¼ cup chopped black olives

Mash avocados with salt and lemon juice. Spread on bottom of round platter. Combine sour cream and taco mix; spread on top of avocado. Top with layers of grated cheese and pat down. Add tomatoes next and sprinkle with hot pepper sauce. Top with green onions and black olives. Serve with corn chips.

HORS D'OEUVRES

FRESH HERB TERRINE

4-6 Servings

1 lb. boneless pork
½ lb. boneless veal
4 oz. pork fat
¾ cup chopped onion
2 cloves garlic, minced
1 T. butter
1½ cups packed chopped
  fresh spinach
3 T. brandy
1 egg, slightly beaten
1½ T. fresh basil or 1 tsp.
  dried basil leaves
1½ T. snipped fresh
  rosemary or 1 tsp. dried
  rosemary leaves
1 T. fresh thyme or ½ tsp.
  dried thyme leaves
1 tsp. salt
½ tsp. crushed fennel
  seeds
½ tsp. freshly ground
  black pepper
6 oz. sliced bacon
3 hard-cooked eggs
Fresh thyme sprig

Cut pork, veal, and pork fat into small pieces. Pass mixture twice through metal blade of food processor. Saute onion and garlic in butter in small skillet about 5 minutes. Add spinach; cook, stirring about 1 minute. Transfer to bowl. Stir meat mixture into onion mixture. Stir in remaining ingredients except bacon, hard-cooked eggs, and thyme sprig. Arrange bacon slices across bottom and up sides of 8½ x 4½-inch loaf pan, letting alternate slices overhang each side of pan. Place ½ of meat mixture in loaf pan. Arrange hard-cooked eggs lengthwise in a row in center of meat, pressing down lightly. Cover with remaining meat mixture. Wrap bacon over top. Place thyme sprig on top.

Heat oven to 350°. Cover loaf pan with aluminum foil. Set in baking pan with enough hot water to reach ⅓ of the way up sides of pan. Bake 1¼ hours, or until meat juices run clear. Let stand uncovered 20 minutes. Pour off fat. Cover; place weight on top of loaf; refrigerate at least 24 hours. To serve, run spatula around edge of pan and unmold. Trim fat. Cut into ½-inch slices.

Fresh Herb Terrine can be stored in freezer, wrapped in freezer wrap up to 1 month.

APPETIZERS

INDONESIAN SATE

2 cups chicken, cut into
   ¾-inch cubes
10 to 12 bamboo skewers
1 T. lemon juice
1 T. minced fresh ginger
½ tsp. grated lemon rind
¼ tsp. cayenne pepper
1 clove garlic, minced

SAUCE:
¼ cup chopped onion
1 T. ground ginger
½ tsp. red pepper, ground
   or flakes
¼ tsp. ground cardamon
2 T. oil
1 cup coconut milk or
   whipping cream
Juice of ½ lemon
2 T. brown sugar
3 T. soy sauce
½ cup peanut butter

Put 5 cubes of chicken on each skewer. Mix lemon juice, ginger, lemon rind, cayenne, and garlic in shallow dish. Add meat. Marinate for at least 1 hour. Grill over charcoal or on top of stove in a heavy skillet with enough oil to cover bottom of pan. Turn until done.

For sauce, crush onion, ginger, red pepper, and cardamon in mortar or food processor. Saute mixture in oil, stirring constantly. Add coconut milk, lemon, brown sugar, and soy sauce. Simmer 5 to 10 minutes. Add peanut butter; stir and simmer until well mixed. Thin with water as desired. Serve warm with meat.

PICKLED SHRIMP
12 Appetizer Servings

Marvelous on greens for luncheon salad

1½ lbs. cooked, shelled
   shrimp
Sliced onions, soaked in
   cold water

DRESSING:
1 cup salad oil
⅓ cup vinegar
2 T. Worcestershire
   sauce
2 tsp. sugar
1 tsp. salt
½ tsp. dry mustard
Dash hot pepper sauce

Put a layer of shrimp in a 2-qt. jar, then a layer of sliced onions. Repeat layers of shrimp and onion, until all shrimp is used. Combine dressing ingredients; pour over shrimp. Refrigerate at least 12 hours. Drain shrimp before serving.

HORS D'OEUVRES

TOMATO CHEESE SAVORIES
4 Servings

Serve with petit filet mignon for brunch

1 pkg. (8 oz.) cream cheese
1 egg yolk
1 T. chopped chives
1 T. chopped fresh basil (optional)
Salt to taste
4 rounds bread, cut to fit tomato slices
4 thick slices tomato

Mix cream cheese, egg yolk, chives, basil, and salt thoroughly. Toast bread; place tomato slices on bread and spread with cheese mixture. Bake at 400° for 5 to 8 minutes. Watch carefully; cheese should be brown on top. For finger hors d'oeuvres cut bread into 1 to 1½-inch rounds; top with thick slices of cherry tomatoes and a heaping tsp. of cheese spread. Bake as above.

CHEESE AND SHRIMP STUFFED CHERRY TOMATOES
Makes About 40

1 basket large cherry tomatoes
1 pkg. (8 oz.) cream cheese, room temperature
¼ cup catsup
1 tsp. dill
1 pkg. (6 oz.) frozen, cleaned shrimp, cooked

Wash and stem tomatoes, cut each in ½; scoop out seed pockets. Drain tomatoes, cut side down, for 30 minutes. In a small bowl combine cheese, catsup, and dill. Fill tomatoes and top each with 1 small shrimp. Tomatoes can be scooped out and filled 1 day ahead of serving.

BRANDADE
6-8 Servings

Delightful first course

12 oz. cod fillet poached, all skin and bones removed
4 oz. bread crumbs
½ cup real mayonnaise
8 cloves garlic
1 T. salt
Ground black pepper
Juice of ½ lemon
Watercress for garnish

Poach cod. Mash garlic to paste with salt. Add garlic mixture and remaining ingredients except watercress to food processor fitted with metal blade and process until smooth. Place in rectangular cake pan and refrigerate for 2 days. Serve with hot toast and garnish with watercress.

APPETIZERS

DILLED CRAB DIP
3 Cups

1 pkg. (8 oz.) cream
  cheese, softened
1 cup mayonnaise
3 shallots, minced
¼ cup fresh dill, or 1 to 2
  T. dried dill
1 beef bouillon cube,
  crushed
1 tsp. hot pepper sauce
1 can (7½ oz.) crabmeat,
  drained, flaked

Mix all ingredients together except crab. Stir in crab. Serve with fresh vegetables or crackers.

TACO DIP
3-4 Cups

Also makes a good relish for a Mexican dinner

2 large fresh tomatoes,
  chopped
About 4 to 5 oz. black
  olives, chopped
2 mild pickled peppers,
  chopped
3 green onions with tops,
  chopped
1 tsp. garlic salt
3 T. olive oil
Salt and pepper

Combine chopped ingredients, garlic salt, and oil; mix. Salt and pepper to taste. Chill overnight. Serve with nacho cheese chips or regular tortilla chips. May have to pour juices off before serving.

CUCUMBER-ONION SPREAD
2 Cups

Tasty and refreshing

1 cucumber, peeled,
  seeded, and chopped
1 small onion, chopped
1 pkg. (8 oz.) cream
  cheese, softened
½ tsp. celery salt
Dash hot pepper sauce
Mayonnaise to taste

Squeeze as much moisture out of the chopped cucumber and onion as possible in the corner of a towel. Mix all ingredients together. Serve on rye bread rounds decorated with watercress or chopped parsley.

HORS D'OEUVRES

HOT CHEESE HORS D'OEUVRES   Makes About 80

½ lb. sharp Cheddar
  cheese, grated
½ lb. bacon, fried and
  crumbled
1 medium onion, grated
1 pkg. (4 oz.) chopped
  almonds (optional)
1 cup good quality
  mayonnaise
1 tsp. Worcestershire
  sauce
Salt and pepper
1 loaf firm sandwich
  bread

Mix all ingredients together except bread. Cut crusts off bread and spread with cheese mixture. Cut in quarters. Can be frozen at this point. Freeze quarters on cookie sheets and when frozen, place in bags. When ready to serve, take amount needed and place under broiler until bubbly and slightly brown, or bake at 450° for 10 minutes.

KÖRÖZÖT (HUNGARIAN CHEESE SPREAD)   2 Cups

1 pkg. (8 oz.) cream
  cheese, softened
½ cup softened butter, not
  margarine
3 T. sour cream
2 tsp. paprika
1 tsp. prepared mustard
½ small onion, grated very
  fine

Combine all ingredients. Make early in the day or night before. Chill. Bring to room temperature before serving. Goes well with plain crackers or party rye.

HERRING APPLE APPETIZER   2 Cups

1 jar (8 oz.) herring in
  wine sauce
1 large red apple,
  unpeeled, diced
½ cup sliced Spanish
  onion
½ cup sour cream
Party rye or pumpernickel
  bread

Drain herring and cut into bite-sized pieces. Combine herring with apple and onion. Add sour cream and mix well. Chill. Serve in bowl surrounded by bread.

APPETIZERS

SPINACH DIP   About 3 Cups

½ cup chopped green
   onion
1 cup mayonnaise
1 pkg. (10 oz.) frozen
   chopped spinach,
   thawed and squeezed
   dry
1 cup sour cream
½ tsp. oregano
½ tsp. lemon juice
½ cup chopped fresh
   parsley
1 tsp. salt
½ tsp. pepper
1 tsp. seasoned salt

Combine all ingredients and beat until well blended. Cover and chill 2 days to let flavors blend. Serve with raw vegetables.

SMOKED OYSTER DIP   3 Cups

2 cans (3.6 oz. each)
   smoked oysters,
   minced
2 pkgs. (8 oz. each)
   cream cheese
¼ cup evaporated milk
1 T. lemon juice
1 T. Worcestershire
   sauce
Dash hot pepper sauce
Salt

Combine all but oysters. Add oysters to mixture. Refrigerate. Serve cold with crackers.

DILL-CURRY DIP   2 Cups

Delicious over hot vegetables

1 cup mayonnaise
1 cup sour cream
1 T. grated onion
1 T. minced parsley
2 tsp. dill
2 tsp. curry powder
1 tsp. seasoned salt

Blend ingredients. Store in covered bowl in refrigerator. Serve as dip with assorted crisp vegetables. Keeps well in refrigerator for 1 to 2 weeks.

HORS D'OEUVRES

ROQUEFORT DIP FOR RAW VEGETABLES   3 Cups

1 cup mayonnaise
8 oz. sour cream
½ cup chives
⅓ cup minced green
    onions with tops
Worcestershire sauce
Lemon juice
Salt and pepper to taste
2 Roquefort wedges (may
    use blue cheese, 2 oz.
    weight)

Mix thoroughly in blender or food processor. Refrigerate overnight. Do not freeze. Serve with asparagus, celery, carrots, cauliflower, green beans, zucchini or other raw vegetables.

COLD BLUE CHEESE SOUFFLE   12 Servings

1 envelope unflavored
    gelatin
2 T. cool water
4 T. butter, softened
4 oz. cream cheese,
    softened
4 oz. blue cheese,
    softened
1 egg, separated
1 tsp. Dijon mustard
½ cup whipping cream,
    whipped

Soften gelatin in cool water, then gently stir over low heat to dissolve. Using a food processor, beat together butter and cheeses adding egg yolk, mustard, and gelatin. In separate bowl beat egg white until stiff but not dry. Gently fold into cheese mixture by hand. Then fold in whipped cream. Prepare a 1-qt. souffle dish with a collar of oiled waxed paper or foil. Tie to the dish with string. Spoon mixture into the dish so that it comes up over the sides and up to the top of the collar. Chill for several hours or overnight. Remove collar and serve with crackers.

PERT'S CHEESE CURDS   Makes 40-50 Pieces

1 pkg. (8 oz.) Monterey
    Jack cheese

Cut cheese in ½ lengthwise. Put in food processor tube with slicing disc. Place cheese slices in non-stick pan and bake at 350° for 8 to 10 minutes or until very light golden brown. Cool. Can be made ahead and stored in airtight container. If processor not available, can be thinly sliced by hand.

APPETIZERS

MARINATED BAKED EGGPLANT
4 Cups

Good addition to antipasto platter

2 cloves garlic, mashed
1 tsp. crumbled rosemary
¼ cup olive oil
1 eggplant (about 1½ lbs.), cubed
2 large ripe tomatoes, thinly sliced
6 T. wine vinegar
3 T. salad oil
2 T. grated onion
2 tsp. sugar
1 tsp. salt
Pinch crushed red pepper

Mix garlic, rosemary, and olive oil; stir into eggplant. Put in shallow 3-qt. baking dish; top with slices of tomatoes. Bake at 300° for 30 minutes. Lower heat to 225° and bake 20 minutes longer. Remove from oven. Mix rest of ingredients; pour over eggplant. Add more salt and pepper, if necessary. Marinate in refrigerator at least 2 hours. Stir before serving. Keeps refrigerated about 10 days.

HAM WHEELS
Makes 100

Men love these

2 pkgs. (8 oz. each) cream cheese, softened
10 slices of boiled ham, not too thinly sliced
10 green onions, cleaned and trimmed

Spread softened cheese on a slice of ham, out to edges. Place green onion across short end; roll up. Trim ends of onions and pack ham roll with extra cheese if necessary. Repeat with each ham slice. Refrigerate to firm up cream cheese, about 1 hour. Cut each roll into slices about ½ inch thick. Arrange on platter with parsley sprigs. These can be frozen.

HOMEMADE BOURSIN CHEESE

Best made a day ahead

8 oz. cream cheese, softened
1 clove garlic, crushed
2 tsp. fresh minced parsley
½ tsp. basil leaves
2 T. chopped chives
1 T. dry white vermouth
Pinch of lemon pepper

Blend cream cheese with garlic. Add remaining ingredients. Chill and serve with stoned wheat thins or other crackers. To make a dip for crudites, add ½ cup sour cream.

HORS D'OEUVRES

GOUDA PARTY SPREAD

8 oz. Gouda cheese, room
  temperature
¼ cup sour cream
½ tsp. prepared mustard
¼ tsp. Worcestershire
  sauce
Dash hot pepper sauce
⅛ tsp. garlic salt
1 T. pickle relish
1 T. minced pimiento
1 pkg. (3 oz.) smoked,
  sliced beef, chopped

Cut thin slice from top of Gouda shell; scoop out cheese, leaving shell intact. Mix with sour cream, mustard, sauces, and garlic salt until smooth. Add relish, pimiento, and beef; blend. Fill reserved shell. Serve on bed of greens with crackers.

ZUCCHINI CAVIAR GEMS WITH VODKA ASPIC

VODKA ASPIC:

3½ cups chicken broth
1 egg white
1 egg shell, broken
1 cup white wine
1 T. vodka
2 envelopes unflavored
  gelatin
1 cup cold water

ZUCCHINI:

1 pkg. (8 oz.) cream
  cheese, softened
⅓ cup sour cream
2 T. finely chopped onion
1½ tsp. fresh dill
1½ tsp. lemon juice
⅛ tsp. white pepper
4 small zucchini, 1½
  inches in diameter
2 T. red lumpfish caviar
2 T. black caviar
Chopped parsley
1 hard-cooked egg,
  sieved

For aspic, beat together chicken broth, egg white and shell. Simmer 10 minutes. Set aside for ½ hour. Strain through cheesecloth. Add white wine and vodka. Sprinkle gelatin on water to soften. Dissolve over low heat. Add gelatin to chicken broth. Pour into a 15 x 10-inch jelly roll pan. Chill until set. Cut into ¼-inch cubes. Refrigerate.

For zucchini, beat cream cheese. Add sour cream and mix. Add seasonings. Cut zucchini into 1-inch pieces and core out center. Pipe on cream cheese mixture and swirl on top like a dome. Sprinkle some with black caviar and egg and some with red caviar and parsley. Place on a tray and place vodka aspic cubes all around. May be made ahead and refrigerated.

SOUPS

YOGURT, RADISH AND CUCUMBER SOUP

6-8 Servings

2 cucumbers, peeled,
    seeded, coarsely
    ground
2 cartons (8 oz. each)
    plain yogurt
1 cup chicken broth
¼ cup ground radishes
2 T. olive oil
1 T. white wine vinegar or
    to taste
Salt and pepper to taste
1 T. finely chopped mint
Mint sprigs, sliced radish
    for garnish

Blend all ingredients; chill. Garnish with mint and sliced radish.

CURRIED BROCCOLI BISQUE

10-12 Servings

2 pkgs. (10 oz. each)
    frozen, chopped
    broccoli
2 qts. chicken broth
¼ cup butter
2 medium onions,
    quartered
1 T. curry powder
Salt and pepper to taste
2 to 4 T. lime juice
Sour cream

In a large pan combine broccoli, broth, butter, onion, and seasonings. Cover and cook 9 minutes, or just until broccoli is soft. (Do not overcook to retain good green color.) Process in blender in 3 or 4 batches until all has been blended. Add lime juice to taste. Refrigerate at least 6 hours. Skim off fat. Serve cold with a dollop of sour cream.

ZUCCHINI SOUP

6 Servings

½ cup butter
1 cup chopped onion
2½ cups chicken broth
1½ lbs. small zucchini,
    shredded
2 tsp. basil
1 tsp. salt
½ tsp. nutmeg
¼ tsp. white pepper

Saute onion in butter until tender. Stir in chicken broth, zucchini, and seasonings. Heat to boiling. Puree a portion at a time in blender or food processor; leave slightly lumpy. Serve hot or cold.

SOUPS

FRENCH FRESH TOMATO SOUP
8 Servings

Best with homegrown tomatoes

8 large, overripe,
  tomatoes
8 T. butter
1 small onion, chopped
2 cloves garlic
1 tsp. Maggi sauce
1 drop hot pepper sauce
1 T. paprika
1 tsp. dry mustard
2 T. parsley
1 T. basil
3 T. arrowroot
2 T. chicken stock base
2 cups water
2 cups whipping cream
Nutmeg, salt, sugar to
  taste
½ cup dry sherry

Peel tomatoes. Melt butter and saute onion. Combine tomatoes and sauteed onion with all remaining ingredients except cream, nutmeg, salt, sugar, and sherry. Bring to a boil and simmer 15 to 20 minutes, or until tomatoes collapse. Puree in blender or food processor. Return to pot. Add remaining ingredients. Bring just to boiling point, whisking constantly. Do not boil.

CHILLED FRESH PEA SOUP
10-12 Servings

2 pkgs. (10 oz. each)
  frozen green peas
1 onion, sliced
2 cups chicken broth (1
  cup white wine,
  optional)
2 lettuce leaves, torn
Salt and pepper to taste
Pinch sugar
4 T. butter
4 T. flour
2 cups milk
1 cup whipping cream
1 can (10½ oz.) cream of
  tomato soup, thinned
  with cream
Paprika

Cook peas and onion in broth (and optional wine) with lettuce and seasonings. Puree in blender or processor. Melt butter. Add flour. Cook a few minutes. Stir in milk; cook and stir 5 minutes. Add puree; thin with cream to proper consistency. Chill 2 hours. To serve, add 1 T. tomato soup to each bowl and swirl it around. Sprinkle each serving with paprika.

SOUPS

COLD TWO-MELON SOUP

8 Cups

Delightful for ladies' luncheon

3 cups coarsely chopped cantaloupe
3 cups coarsely chopped honeydew melon
⅓ cup fresh lime juice
2 cups fresh orange juice
¼ cup honey
2 cups dry Champagne
1 cup whipping cream, whipped
8 strawberries

Chop finely 1½ cups of both cantaloupe and honeydew melons. Set aside. Place remaining melon in blender with lime juice, orange juice, and honey. Puree mixture a few seconds. Pour into large bowl; stir in reserved melon and Champagne. Cover and refrigerate until ready to serve. Pour into iced sherbet dishes. Garnish with whipped cream and strawberries.

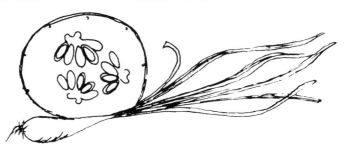

COLD SPINACH-CUCUMBER SOUP

10-12 Cups

1½ lbs. spinach, chopped, stems removed (or 2 boxes (10 oz. each) frozen chopped spinach, thawed)
3 T. butter
2 bunches green onions, chopped
3 medium potatoes, thinly sliced
4 cups chicken broth
4 medium cucumbers, peeled, seeds removed, diced
1 T. salt, plus salt to taste
Pepper
Juice of ½ lemon
¾ cup milk
¾ cup whipping cream

Boil spinach in a large pot of salted boiling water (for 3 to 4 minutes). Drain and set aside. Melt butter in large saucepan. Add green onions and cook gently for 3 minutes. Add potatoes, broth, and cucumbers. Cover and bring to a boil. Reduce heat and simmer over low heat for about 10 minutes or until potatoes are soft. Add spinach, salt, pepper, and lemon juice. Add milk and cream and puree in blender or food processor. Chill. To serve, garnish with chopped chives or thinly sliced cucumber.

SOUPS

HENRY'S MANHATTAN CLAM CHOWDER 8-10 Servings

Best made with Quahogs

1 dozen Quahogs or 3
   dozen medium clams
6 slices bacon, fried,
   drained and crumbled,
   fat reserved
2 large onions, chopped
4 cups chopped tomatoes
2 potatoes, chopped
1 cup diced celery
½ cup diced carrots
½ cup peas
½ cup green beans, cut
   into ½-inch pieces
½ cup fresh corn, cut from
   cob
1 tsp. thyme leaves or to
   taste
Salt, pepper to taste

Place well-scrubbed clams in large pot with ½ inch of water. Steam until clams begin to open. Remove clams from shells. Strain juices from clams and reserve. Chop clams into bite-sized pieces. Saute onion in reserved bacon fat until tender but not browned. In a large stockpot put clams, reserved clam juice, onion, tomatoes, bacon, potatoes, celery, carrots, peas, beans, corn, thyme, salt and pepper. Add 1 qt. of boiling water; bring mixture to a boil. Then lower heat and simmer 3 to 4 hours. Correct seasonings. With crusty bread and salad makes a complete meal.

SUMMER HERBED TOMATO SOUP   About 12 Cups

1 large carrot
1 stalk celery
1 leek, white part only
1 clove garlic
1 T. olive oil
2 cans (28 oz. each) plum
   tomatoes, seeded
4 cups chicken broth
1 T. fresh basil or 1 tsp.
   dried basil
1½ tsp. fresh thyme or ½
   tsp. dried thyme
1 bay leaf
Salt and pepper
½ cup sour cream
Minced fresh basil leaves
   for garnish

In large saucepan, cook carrot, celery, leek, and garlic in olive oil until tender. Add plum tomatoes, chicken broth, and a cheesecloth bag containing basil, thyme, and bay leaf. Add salt and pepper to taste. Bring the liquid to a boil; reduce heat and simmer, covered for 25 minutes. Cool slightly; discard the cheesecloth bag. Puree the mixture in batches in food processor fitted with steel blade or in blender. Chill. Adjust seasonings. Whisk in sour cream, 1 T. at a time. Garnish with fresh basil leaves.

BREADS

BLUEBERRY CREAM CAKE   8 Servings
Nice flavor

1 cup whipping cream, whipped
2 eggs
1 tsp. almond extract
1½ cups flour
1 cup sugar
2 tsp. baking powder
⅛ tsp. salt
1 cup blueberries, preferably fresh, tossed with 1 T. flour
½ cup confectioners' sugar

Beat eggs 1 at a time into whipped cream. Add extract. Sift together flour, sugar, baking powder and salt. Stir into cream. Add blueberries tossed with flour. Pour into an 8-inch round, buttered and floured spring-form pan. Bake at 350° for 35 minutes or until lightly browned. Cool on rack for 10 minutes. Remove from pan. When completely cool, sift confectioners' sugar on top.

ZUCCHINI PANCAKES   8-10 Pancakes

2 large zucchini
3 eggs
¼ cup flour
½ tsp. sugar
1 tsp. salt
¼ cup grated Parmesan cheese
½ tsp. garlic powder
½ tsp. oregano
2 tsp. chives

Coarsely grate zucchini and dry well between paper towels. Beat eggs; stir in all ingredients. Heat some oil and fry ½ cup of mixture per pancake. Brown lightly on both sides.

ZUCCHINI GEMS   8 Muffins
These are delicious and freeze well

¾ cup flour
¼ tsp. baking soda
¼ tsp. baking powder
¼ tsp. salt
¼ tsp. cinnamon
1 egg
½ cup sugar
¼ cup salad oil
1 cup grated unpared zucchini
½ cup raisins and nuts combined

Mix flour, baking soda, baking powder, salt and cinnamon; set aside. Beat egg, sugar and oil until blended. Add flour mixture, zucchini, raisins and nuts, stir just until dry ingredients are moistened. Fill buttered muffin cups ⅔ full. Bake at 350° for 25 minutes. Loosen edges to remove. Raw zucchini can be grated ahead and frozen so muffins can be made all year. Recipe may be doubled.

BREADS

ORANGE-RAISIN BREAD   1 Loaf

A food processor special

DOUGH:

1 pkg. active dry yeast
¼ cup warm water
3 T. sugar
2½ cups flour
1 tsp. salt
3 T. butter, cut in 3 or
  more pieces
⅔ cup orange juice at
  room temperature

FILLING:

1 T. sugar
1 tsp. cinnamon
½ cup raisins

Dissolve yeast in warm water with 1 T. sugar. Let stand about 5 minutes. Put flour, 2 T. sugar, and salt in bowl of food processor fitted with metal blade. Add butter; process until butter is cut in, about 20 seconds. Add yeast mixture; process 5 seconds. With machine running, add half of orange juice through feed tube, then dribble enough of remaining juice to form a ball of dough. Let machine run 20 seconds to knead dough. Place dough in greased bowl turning to coat all sides. Cover and let rise in warm place until double in bulk, 1 to 2 hours. Punch down and roll out dough to form a rectangle 10 x 18 inches. Sprinkle sugar, cinnamon, and raisins over dough. Starting with the narrow end, roll up dough and pinch ends to form loaf. Place in greased 5-cup loaf pan. Cover and let rise until doubled, about 1 hour. Bake at 375° for 25 to 30 minutes.

CHEDDAR-ONION HAMBURGER BUNS   Makes 20

5¾ to 6¾ cups unsifted
  flour
3 T. sugar
1½ tsp. salt
2 pkgs. dry yeast
2 T. butter, softened
2 cups hot water
1½ cups grated sharp
  cheese
¼ cup finely chopped
  onion

Combine 2 cups flour, sugar, salt and dry yeast in a mixing bowl. Add softened butter. Gradually add hot water and beat 2 minutes at medium speed. Add 1 cup flour. Beat on high 2 minutes. Stir in cheese, onion and enough flour for a soft dough. Knead on floured board 8 to 10 minutes. Place in greased bowl, turning once. Cover. Let rise 1 hour. Punch down. On floured board, divide into 20 pieces and form into slightly flattened balls. Place on greased sheets. Cover and let rise until doubled, about 45 minutes. Bake at 400° for 15 to 20 minutes.

LUNCHEON DISHES

SWEDISH MEAT SALAD

4 Servings

Great for a picnic

2 cups cooked medium-
  rare roast beef, cut into
  bite-sized pieces
1 small onion, minced
1 apple, diced
2 stalks celery, chopped
1 to 2 T. pickled beets,
  minced
2 tsp. liquid from beets
¼ cup mayonnaise

Combine all ingredients and chill.
Serve on lettuce leaves.

DILLED SPINACH, HAM
AND MUSHROOM CREPES

6-8 Servings

CREPES:

1 cup flour
1½ cups milk
3 eggs
Salt to taste
Freshly ground white
  pepper (optional)
2 T. melted butter, cooled
1 T. dill

FILLING:

1 bunch green onions,
  minced
½ lb. mushrooms,
  chopped
3 T. butter
2 pkgs. (10 oz. each)
  frozen chopped
  spinach, cooked briefly
  and squeezed dry
½ lb. ham, diced
  (prosciutto, preferred)
½ cup sour cream
Salt, pepper to taste
Melted butter
Freshly grated Parmesan
  cheese

For crepes, combine ingredients in
food processor or blender for 5
seconds. Let stand at room temperature several hours or refrigerate
overnight. Prepare crepes.

For filling, saute green onions and
mushrooms in 3 T. butter until lightly
golden. Add spinach, ham, and sour
cream. Season to taste. Mix well.
Place 2 T. filling in each crepe; roll up.
Place in shallow greased casserole.
Brush with melted butter and sprinkle
with Parmesan cheese. Cover with
foil. Bake at 350° for 20 minutes, or
until heated through and cheese is
melted. (Crepes and filling may be
frozen separately).

LUNCHEON DISHES

HAM-CHEESE-ZUCCHINI PIE

6 Servings

1 large onion, thinly
  sliced
3 small zucchini, thinly
  sliced (about ¾ lb.)
1 large clove garlic,
  crushed
⅓ cup olive oil or cooking
  oil, or mixture
2 cups cooked slivered
  ham (⅔ lb.)
1 cup shredded Swiss
  cheese (4 oz.)
1¼ cups sour cream
1 tsp. dill
1 tsp. salt
¼ tsp. pepper
1 baked 10-inch pastry
  shell
½ cup packaged bread
  crumbs
¼ cup grated Parmesan
  cheese
2 T. butter, melted
Tomato wedges
Parsley

Saute onion, zucchini and garlic in oil in a large skillet, about 5 minutes, or until zucchini is tender crisp. Add ham, Swiss cheese, sour cream, dill, salt and pepper; mix thoroughly. Spoon into baked pastry shell. Toss together bread crumbs, Parmesan cheese and melted butter. Sprinkle in a 2-inch bank around edge of pie, leaving center open. Bake at 350° for 35 minutes or until bubbly. Let stand 10 minutes before serving. Garnish with tomato wedges and parsley, if desired.

TURTLE BEACH CHICKEN SALAD

6-8 Servings

2 cans (11 oz. each)
  mandarin oranges,
  drained
½ cup slivered blanched
  almonds, toasted
2 cups julienned turkey or
  chicken
2 cups bean sprouts,
  drained
2 hard-cooked eggs,
  chopped
¾ cup mayonnaise
1½ tsp. chives
½ tsp. curry powder, or to
  taste
Salt to taste

Combine first 5 ingredients. Chill. Add mayonnaise, chives, curry powder and salt shortly before serving.

LUNCHEON DISHES

CRAB-TOPPED SALAD TOWERS   8 Servings

Quick luncheon

CRAB DRESSING:

2 cups mayonnaise
1 green pepper, finely chopped
4 T. finely chopped onion
4 T. chili sauce
2 T. catsup
2 tsp. Worcestershire sauce
Salt and paprika to taste
1 can (7½ oz.) crabmeat, flaked
2 hard-cooked eggs, chopped

SALAD:

2 to 3 large bunches watercress
8 pieces of toast, crusts removed
2 avocados, cut in 8 slices
8 tomato slices
8 deviled egg halves, sliced

For dressing, combine all ingredients except crab and eggs. Mix thoroughly. Fold in crabmeat and eggs. Chill. To assemble salads, place a mound of watercress (or chopped lettuce) on each of 8 luncheon plates. Add toast, avocado slices, tomato slices, and deviled eggs. Top with crab dressing.

PASTEL PARADISE   1 Serving

Delicious luncheon salad from a Florida restaurant

3 leaves lettuce
1 scoop fruit-flavored frozen yogurt, softened
2 T. sliced orange
2 T. sliced strawberries
2 T. sliced grapefruit
2 T. sliced apples
2 T. sliced grapes
2 T. sliced bananas
2 T. blueberries
1 T. coconut
1 T. chopped pecans

Arrange lettuce on luncheon plate. Place frozen yogurt in center; top with fruit. Sprinkle with coconut and nuts. Serve immediately.

LUNCHEON DISHES

SPINACH SOUFFLE ROLL   8 Servings

4 T. butter
½ cup flour
½ tsp. white pepper
2 cups milk
5 eggs, separated
2 T. butter
1 T. finely chopped
   shallots
½ cup chopped
   mushrooms
1 pkg. (10 oz.) frozen
   chopped spinach
1 T. Dijon mustard
¼ tsp. ground nutmeg
Paprika
Fresh parsley

Grease a 15 x 10 x 2-inch jelly roll pan, line with waxed paper, grease again, lightly dust with flour. In saucepan, melt 4 T. butter; blend in flour, salt, and pepper. Add milk; stir until thick and bubbly. Remove from heat. Beat egg yolks until thick and lemon colored. Gradually add white sauce to beaten yolks, stirring constantly; cool. Beat egg whites until stiff, but not dry. Fold into cooled sauce. Spread evenly over prepared pan. Bake at 400° for 25 to 30 minutes or until puffed and brown. While souffle bakes, melt 2 T. butter; saute shallots until tender. Add mushrooms; cook 3 minutes. Cook spinach according to package directions; drain very well. Add to mushrooms, then add mustard and nutmeg. When souffle is done, turn out immediately onto a clean towel, spread with spinach filling. Roll up jelly roll style, beginning with a long edge by lifting edge of towel. Transfer to serving plate seam side down; garnish with paprika and fresh parsley sprigs. To serve, slice like a jelly roll.

SUMMER PITA SANDWICH   6 Small or 3 Large Sandwiches

1 medium-sized ripe
   avocado
1 T. lemon juice
1 medium tomato,
   coarsely chopped
3 green onions with tops,
   coarsely chopped
1 to 2 T. olive oil
3 slices bacon, cooked,
   drained and crumbled
2 to 3 T. alfalfa sprouts
Salt and pepper
Pita bread

Peel and dice avocado; sprinkle with lemon juice. Combine avocado with tomatoes, green onions and olive oil; toss lightly. Season to taste. Toast bread 3 to 5 minutes at 400° or until crisp and hot. Cut bread in half so that pocket forms. Add bacon and alfalfa sprouts to filling; spoon into heated bread. Serve at once.

LUNCHEON DISHES

CALIFORNIA HAM AND FRUIT SALAD   6 Servings

1¼ lbs. cooked
    Westphalian or other
    good quality ham, cut in
    thin strips
½ cup blueberries
½ medium honeydew
    melon, cut into chunks
4 plums, quartered
3 nectarines, quartered
1 cup seedless green
    grapes
2 oranges, peeled and
    sectioned
Lettuce leaves, bibb or
    red leaf

Combine ham, blueberries, melon, plums, nectarines, grapes, and oranges. Set aside while making dressing. For dressing, mix apricots with lime juice; add mayonnaise. Fold into whipped cream. Fold ½ of the dressing into the ham-fruit mixture. Chill until ready to serve. Just before serving, line serving plates with lettuce leaves, arrange salad over leaves. Garnish with pistachios or mint leaves. Pass extra dressing.

APRICOT DRESSING:

½ cup apricots put
    through food mill (if
    using canned, drain)
Juice of 1 fresh lime
2 T. mayonnaise
1 cup whipping cream,
    whipped
Chopped pistachios or
    mint leaves for garnish

SHRIMP SALAD   12 Servings

Good summer main dish

4 lbs. cooked, cleaned
    shrimp
2 cups sliced water
    chestnuts
2 cups diced celery
2 cups mayonnaise
½ cup minced green
    onions
2 T. soy sauce
2 T. lemon juice
1 T. curry powder
1 can (16 oz.) pineapple
    chunks, drained
2 cups toasted almonds

Toss all ingredients together except almonds. Chill thoroughly. Garnish with toasted almonds. Recipe may be doubled or cut in ½.

LUNCHEON DISHES

SEAFOOD-MACARONI SALAD WITH HOMEMADE DRESSING

10-12 Servings

1 lb. fresh shrimp,
   cooked, shelled,
   coarsely chopped
1 can (7½ oz.) crabmeat
   or 1 pkg. (8 oz.) frozen
   crabmeat, flaked
1 can (6½ oz.) white tuna
   in water, drained and
   flaked
2 cups chopped celery
1 cup chopped cucumber
1 cup chopped green
   pepper
1 box (7 oz.) tiny
   macaroni (bowknots,
   curly, or small shells),
   cooked

THOUSAND ISLAND DRESSING:

2 cups mayonnaise
Dash Worcestershire
   sauce
¼ tsp. prepared mustard
¼ cup chili sauce
4 green onions with tops,
   chopped
Pickle relish to taste

Place salad ingredients in large bowl. Thoroughly mix dressing ingredients; pour over salad. Toss lightly. Chill. Serve on lettuce leaves. (Dressing can be made in food processor.)

LES OEUFS VOL AU VENT

6 Servings

2 tomatoes, coarsely
   chopped in food
   processor or blender
2 T. finely chopped onion
Dash of garlic powder
1½ T. parsley
6 poached eggs
6 cooked pattie shells
Hollandaise sauce

Simmer first 4 ingredients for 5 minutes. Put an equal amount of the mixture in the bottom of each pattie shell. Place a poached egg on top. Spoon Hollandaise over top of egg.

115

ENTREES: MEATS

COLD FILLET OF BEEF JAPONAIS   8-10 Servings

1 fillet of beef, trimmed
  (about 4 lbs.)
1 cup Japanese soy
  sauce
1 cup olive or peanut oil
1 cup sherry
6 garlic cloves, minced
1 tsp. hot pepper sauce
Few grindings of pepper

Medium-Bodied Red

Marinate fillet in rest of ingredients for 24 hours, turning several times. Remove and dry. Rub with oil. Place on rack in roasting pan. Roast at 475° for 25 minutes for very rare, 28 to 30 minutes for rare. Baste with marinade 3 to 4 times during roasting. Cool. Arrange on platter with watercress and cherry tomatoes. Serve with marinated vegetables.

STEAK PIQUANTE   4-6 Servings

4 to 6 individual beef
  steaks (rib, strip, T-
  bone)
1 cup crumbled blue
  cheese
½ cup Madeira
3 T. butter
2 T. grated onion
Juice of 1 lemon
Dash hot pepper sauce
Salt and pepper to taste

Medium-Bodied Red

Mix all ingredients except steaks, beating until fluffy. Broil steaks to desired doneness. Spread cheese mixture over each steak. Broil 10 seconds more. Serve immediately.

STIR-FRIED STEAK WITH   3-4 Servings
MUSHROOMS AND WATERCRESS

1 lb. flank steak
2 T. cornstarch
2 T. soy sauce
5 T. peanut oil
¾ lb. fresh mushrooms,
  thinly sliced
1 bunch watercress
6 green onions with tops,
  thinly sliced

Light-Bodied Red

Cut steak in strips across grain. Toss in bowl with cornstarch, soy sauce and 2 T. peanut oil. Marinate 1 hour. Add 2 T. oil to wok and heat until very hot. Add mushrooms. Stir-fry 2 minutes. Remove. Add 1 T. oil to wok. Heat. Stir in beef and green onions and cook for 1 minute. Add watercress and mushrooms. Stir-fry 30 seconds. Serve immediately.

ENTREES: MEATS

CHINESE GRILLED FLANK STEAK   4-6 Servings

1 beef flank steak (about
    1½ lbs.)
½ cup dark soy sauce
¼ cup sugar
¼ cup sherry
2 cloves garlic, slivered
Few drops hot pepper
    sauce

Medium-Bodied Red

Score both sides of steak; place in glass dish. Combine remaining ingredients in saucepan. Heat, stirring, until sugar is dissolved. Cool; pour over meat. Marinate in refrigerator for 4 to 6 hours, turning occasionally. Grill over hot coals or broil quickly, (3 to 4 minutes on each side for rare), brushing with marinade. Slice thinly on diagonal. Serve as main course with snow peas, steamed rice, and hot mustard or chutney. Or thread sliced meat on skewers and serve as hors d'oeuvres, keeping warm in hot marinade.

BRAZILIAN BEEF ROAST   3 Servings per Pound

1 high-quality beef rump
    roast or sirloin tip (4-6
    lbs.)
2 cups uncooked rice
1 clove garlic, peeled
2 T. olive oil
4 cups beef broth

SAUCE:

1 onion, chopped
1 green onion, top only,
    chopped
10 sprigs parsley,
    chopped
2 tomatoes, very ripe,
    chopped
1½ T. olive oil
¼ cup vinegar
1 clove garlic, crushed
Salt and pepper to taste

Beer

Roast meat at 325°, allowing 25 minutes per pound for rare. Fry rice and garlic in oil. Add broth; cover and simmer until liquid is absorbed. For sauce, combine chopped onion, green onions, parsley, tomato, oil, vinegar, garlic, salt and pepper. Mash onion, parsley and tomato slightly against side of bowl. To serve, slice beef thinly; spoon sauce over meat and serve with rice and extra sauce.

117

ENTREES: MEATS

CARNE ASADA

6 to 8 boneless skirt
  steaks
⅓ cup red wine vinegar
⅓ cup olive oil
1 tsp. oregano
½ tsp. coarsely ground
  pepper

SALSA FRESCA:

4 medium tomatoes
1 large onion, finely
  chopped
½ green pepper, chopped
2 T. butter
Salt
Pepper or hot sauce

Beer

Place skirt steaks (unrolled) in shallow glass dish. Combine vinegar, oil, oregano and pepper. Pour over meat. Marinate in refrigerator at least 4 hours, turning occasionally. Grill steaks 4 to 5 inches above hot coals or in broiler, brushing with marinade. Allow 4 to 5 minutes per side for medium rare. Serve with Salsa Fresca. For Salsa Fresca, peel and seed tomatoes, cut in large chunks. Saute onion and green pepper in butter in pan set on grill. Add tomato chunks; heat through. Season with salt and pepper to taste.

TOSTADAS

2 lbs. ground beef,
  browned, drained
2 cans (16 oz. each)
  refried beans
2 cans (10 oz. each)
  enchilada sauce
12 corn tortillas
Cooking oil
3 avocados, chopped
1 carton (16 oz.) sour
  cream
Salt, pepper, lemon juice
1 head lettuce, shredded
4 tomatoes, peeled,
  chopped
2 bunches green onions,
  thinly sliced with tops
¾ cup sliced ripe olives
12 oz. Monterey Jack
  cheese, grated

Beer

Combine browned meat, beans and sauce; simmer 10 to 15 minutes. Fry tortillas in hot oil until crisp. Combine avocados with sour cream; season to taste with salt, pepper, and lemon juice. To serve, place ingredients on table. Let each guest assemble a tostada as follows: Place tortilla on plate. Add some meat mixture, then lettuce and a choice of vegetables. Top with avocado mixture and a sprinkling of cheese.

ENTREES: MEATS

BEEF WITH DILL SAUCE

6 Servings

2½ lbs. beef stew meat
1 onion, minced
1 garlic clove, minced
3 T. butter
3 T. flour
2½ cups hot beef broth
½ cup red wine
½ cup canned tomatoes, chopped
2 T. minced parsley
1 tsp. dill
⅓ cup chopped dill pickles
Salt and pepper to taste

Medium-Bodied Red

Brown meat. Saute onion and garlic in butter. Stir in flour; add broth, wine, tomatoes, parsley, dill, pickles, and meat. Cover and simmer 2 hours or until tender. Season to taste. Thicken sauce if necessary. Serve with rice.

BAKED CORNED BEEF

10 Servings

1 corned beef brisket (4 to 5 lbs.)
2 cloves garlic
4 bay leaves
Whole cloves
⅓ cup brown sugar
⅓ cup catsup
3 T. vinegar
1 T. prepared mustard

Medium-Bodied Red

Roll and tie beef. Place in Dutch oven; cover with cold water. Add garlic and bay leaves. Cover and simmer for 3 hours, or until tender. Cool in liquid. Drain. Stud fat side with cloves. Blend remaining ingredients; spread on meat. Bake, uncovered, at 275° about 1 hour, basting occasionally. (Or, place 6 to 8 inches above charcoal burned until covered with gray ash. Grill, turning and basting occasionally, for 30 to 40 minutes.)

ENTREES: MEATS

LEG OF LAMB WITH AVGOLEMONO SAUCE

12 Servings

1 leg of lamb (6 to 7 lbs.)

MARINADE:

1 cup thinly sliced onion
⅔ cup olive oil
3 T. lemon juice
2 T. minced parsley
½ tsp. pepper
1 tsp. salt
1 tsp. oregano
3 bay leaves, crumbled
3 cloves garlic, minced

AVGOLEMONO SAUCE:

3 egg yolks
1 T. cornstarch
1 T. minced parsley
1 T. lemon juice
1 tsp. salt
Dash hot pepper sauce
3 cloves garlic, minced

Medium-Bodied Red

Have leg of lamb boned, if desired. Combine all marinade ingredients in a large bowl or pan. Marinate lamb 12 to 24 hours, turning occasionally. Place lamb on rack in open roasting pan. Roast at 325° until meat thermometer reaches 160° to 170°, basting with marinade. Allow 25 to 30 minutes per pound. Let rest for 10 to 15 minutes.

To prepare sauce, combine all ingredients in processor or blender. Add juices from roasting pan, adding water if needed. Cook, stirring constantly, until sauce coats a spoon.

RIO GRANDE PORK ROAST

8 Servings

1 boneless rolled pork loin roast (about 3 lbs.)
1 tsp. chili powder
½ tsp. garlic salt
½ tsp. salt
½ cup catsup
½ cup apple jelly
1 T. vinegar
1 cup crushed corn chips (optional)

Light Dry White

Place pork, fat side up, on rack in shallow roasting pan. Combine ½ tsp. chili powder, garlic salt, and salt; rub into roast. Roast uncovered at 325° for 2 to 2¼ hours, or until meat thermometer registers 170°. Brush meat with glaze 10 to 15 minutes before roast is done. (Sprinkle with crushed corn chips, if desired.) To prepare glaze, combine catsup, jelly, vinegar, and ½ tsp. chili powder in saucepan; simmer for 5 minutes. Remove roast from oven when done. Let stand for 10 minutes. Measure pan drippings. Add water to make 1 cup. Heat. Pass sauce with meat.

ENTREES: MEATS

WHOLE BONELESS PORK LOIN ROAST 20-24 Servings

1 whole pork loin (about 16 lbs.)

MARINADE:

1 cup vinegar
Juice of 1 lemon
1½ tsp. salt
Pepper
2 bay leaves
1 large clove garlic, mashed
½ tsp. rosemary (optional)

Light Dry White

Have butcher bone and tie roast. (Bones are suitable for barbecued ribs.) Combine all marinade ingredients and marinate meat at least 24 hours, turning occasionally. Roast at 275° in marinade for 1 hour. Drain marinade. Raise oven to 325° and continue roasting, basting occasionally with marinade, about 20 minutes per pound or until thermometer registers 170°. Or, after initial oven roasting, cook on grill allowing 20 minutes per pound, basting occasionally. Let stand 20 minutes before serving. Serve hot or cold with horseradish applesauce or mustard mayonnaise.

CHINESE BARBECUED PORK TENDERLOIN 4 Servings
Exotic picnic supper

1 lb. pork tenderloin
½ tsp. salt
¼ tsp. pepper
¼ tsp. Chinese five spice powder
1 tsp. sherry
2 T. soy sauce
3 T. hoison sauce
¼ tsp. red food coloring
Roasted sesame seeds

MUSTARD SAUCE:

2 oz. dry mustard
½ tsp. salt
2 oz. boiling water
2 tsp. oil

Medium-Dry White

Cut meat to make it 1½ inches thick, ½ inch wide, and 7 inches long. Combine rest of ingredients except sesame seeds; rub into pork. Marinate at least 2 hours. Roast on broiling rack at 325° for 40 minutes total, turning once. Slice and serve hot or cold, sprinkled with sesame seeds. Serve with mustard or soy sauce. For mustard sauce, combine ingredients and work into a smooth paste.

ENTREES: POULTRY

SALAD OLIVER
6 Servings

A chicken salad for men

2 chicken breasts (¾ lb. each)
1 large onion, peeled and quartered
2 tsp. salt
½ cup coarsely chopped and drained sour dill pickles
4 new potatoes, peeled, cooked, cooled, and thinly sliced
3 hard-cooked eggs, thinly sliced
⅛ tsp. white pepper or to taste
¾ cup mayonnaise
¾ cup sour cream
2 T. capers
1 T. finely cut fresh dill
1 small head Boston lettuce
6 green olives
1 medium tomato, peeled and cut into wedges

Simmer chicken breasts with onion and 2 tsp. salt in water to cover until tender. Cut meat in ½-inch wide strips. Combine with the pickles, potatoes, and eggs. Sprinkle with salt and white pepper to taste. In a small bowl, beat together mayonnaise and sour cream; stir ½ of it into chicken mixture. To serve in the traditional Russian manner, shape salad in a pyramid in the center of a serving platter. Spread remaining mayonnaise/sour cream dressing over the salad; sprinkle with capers and dill. Circle edge of platter with lettuce leaves, olives, and tomato wedges.

Medium-Dry White

ENTREES: POULTRY

OVEN TO GRILL BARBECUED CHICKEN   8 Servings

4 to 5 lbs. chicken parts
1 cup vegetable oil
⅓ cup tarragon wine
   vinegar
¼ cup sugar
¼ cup catsup
2 T. grated onion
1 T. Worcestershire
   sauce
1½ tsp. dry mustard
1 tsp. salt
1 tsp. garlic powder
½ tsp. hot pepper sauce
⅛ tsp. pepper

Combine all ingredients except chicken in large ovenproof baking pan with high sides. Add chicken, turning to coat well. Marinate chicken overnight, or at least 6 hours, turning occasionally. Bake chicken in marinade at 350° for 25 to 30 minutes, or until nearly done. Transfer to hot charcoal grill. Cook, turning and basting with sauce, frequently, until nicely browned and completely cooked.

Medium-Dry White

CHICKEN-PEACH PARMESAN   8 Servings

4 whole chicken breasts,
   split (preferably with
   wings attached)
¼ cup butter
1 tsp. salt
⅛ tsp. pepper
3 green onions with tops,
   thinly sliced
1 pkg. (2¼ oz.) slivered
   almonds (½ cup)
½ tsp. tarragon
½ cup chopped fresh
   parsley
8 cling peach halves; or 4
   fresh peaches, peeled,
   halved
½ cup grated Parmesan
   cheese

Brown chicken lightly in butter. Sprinkle with salt and pepper. Place chicken in shallow baking dish. To pan drippings, add onions, almonds, tarragon, and parsley. Saute for 1 minute; distribute evenly over chicken breasts. (Could be held at this point.) Cover and bake at 350° for 20 minutes. Uncover; arrange peaches around chicken. (With fresh peaches, add at beginning.) Sprinkle peaches and chicken with cheese. Bake, uncovered, for 15 minutes longer, or until chicken is done.

Medium-Dry White

ENTREES: POULTRY

CHICKEN WITH TOMATOES AND TARRAGON

4 Servings

1 chicken, cut up; or 4
  chicken breasts
2 T. butter or oil
Salt, pepper
½ lb. fresh mushrooms,
  sliced
1 large onion, cut up
1 garlic clove, minced
1 can (16 oz.) stewed
  tomatoes
½ cup dry white wine or
  vermouth
1 tsp. tarragon
1 tsp. sugar
1 bay leaf

Medium-Dry White

Brown chicken in butter or oil. Remove to a greased casserole dish. Sprinkle with salt and pepper to taste. In same skillet, gently saute mushrooms, onion, and garlic clove. Add stewed tomatoes (reserve some liquid), wine, tarragon, sugar, and bay leaf. Simmer a few minutes to blend flavors. Pour mixture over browned chicken. Cover and bake at 350° for 45 minutes, until tender. Serve sauce over chicken and rice or noodles.

CHICKEN-SHRIMP CASSEROLE

8 Servings

1½ lbs. shrimp
1 cup uncooked rice
3 T. oil
4 whole chicken breasts,
  split, skinned and
  boned
½ cup chopped onion
1 lb. fresh mushrooms,
  sliced

SAUCE:

1 can (15 oz.) tomato
  sauce
2 cups whipping cream
½ cup dry sherry
1 tsp. salt
1 T. Worcestershire
  sauce
¼ tsp. pepper
¼ tsp. thyme

Light Dry White

Cook shrimp according to package directions. Drain and set aside. Cook rice. Put in bottom of a 9 x 13-inch baking dish. Heat oil in skillet. Gently saute chicken breasts. Set aside.

Reserve 2 T. drippings from browning chicken. Saute onion in drippings. Remove onion and saute mushrooms in same pan after adding 3 T. butter to pan. Stir in onion and sauce ingredients until well blended. Put shrimp on top of rice in baking dish, then chicken breasts, then sauce. Bake, covered, for 60 minutes at 350°. Sprinkle with minced parsley to serve. Recipe may be doubled.

ENTREES: POULTRY

PASTA WITH CHICKEN

6 Servings

Different and very easy

1 lb. green spinach
noodles
4 T. olive oil
8 T. butter
1 cup finely chopped
onion
1 tsp. minced garlic
4 whole chicken breasts,
cubed
½ lb. zucchini, cubed
4 cups cherry tomatoes
2 tsp. salt
Few grindings pepper
1 tsp. basil
1 tsp. oregano
2 cups shredded Swiss
cheese

While pasta is cooking, heat oil and 4 T. butter in skillet over high heat. Add onion and garlic and cook until onion is golden. Turn down heat and add chicken. Cook until chicken is white, about 5 minutes. Add zucchini, tomatoes, salt, pepper, basil and oregano. Mix hot, drained pasta with remaining butter. Add chicken mixture and toss gently. Sprinkle with cheese and serve.

Full-Flavored Dry White

MOCK VITELLO TONNATO

10-12 Servings

1 turkey breast (4 to
5 lbs.)
1 can (7 oz.) tuna,
drained
1 can (2 oz.) anchovies
1 to 2 cups homemade
mayonnaise, with no
spices
Juice of 1 or 2 lemons
3 T. capers
½ cup chopped parsley

Light Dry White

Cook turkey breast according to package directions. Chill completely. Meanwhile, make sauce. Combine tuna, anchovies, mayonnaise, lemon juice, and 1 T. capers. Blend until smooth. Remove the whole breast from the bone in 2 pieces. Cut across the grain into medallions. Lay on platter, overlapping slices. Pour sauce over the meat. Cover with foil and chill for 12 hours. At serving time, sprinkle with parsley and remaining 2 T. capers. Serve with cold rice salad.

COLD RICE SALAD

10-12 Servings

4 to 5 cups cooked rice
1 cup tomatoes, chopped
1 stalk celery, chopped
½ cup chopped parsley

Combine ingredients and chill.

ENTREES: SEAFOOD

MOUSSE DE CREVETTES WITH SAUCE BERCY

8 Servings

A first course or main course with boiled potatoes and green salad

1 lb. frozen medium
  shrimp, shelled,
  deveined, thawed
5 egg whites
Salt
Freshly ground white
  pepper
1¾ cups whipping cream,
  well chilled

SAUCE BERCY:

2 cups clam juice (1-pt.
  bottle)
4 to 5 shallots or green
  onions, minced
12 parsley sprigs, minced
Salt
Freshly ground white
  pepper
½ cup dry white wine
6 T. butter
4 T. flour

Light Dry White

Cut up the shrimp. Place ½ of the shrimp and 3 egg whites in electric blender adding a dash of salt and white pepper. Blend for 1 minute or until it is a firm-textured, smooth paste. Transfer to a large bowl. Blend remaining shrimp and egg whites the same way. Combine the 2 mixtures. (Or process shrimp and egg whites all at once in food processor.) Place the bowl over a bowl of ice. Working quickly with a flat wooden spatula, add the chilled cream very slowly, almost drop by drop, as you would in making mayonnaise. When all the cream is incorporated and you have a smooth, firm-textured mixture, season with salt and pepper to taste. Spoon into a buttered, round 1½-qt. mold. Place a round piece of waxed paper on top of the mold. May be prepared ahead to this point and refrigerated. Set the mold in a pan of hot water. Water should reach to about ½ the depth of the mold. Bake at 425° for 1 hour. Unmold on a heated platter. Spoon Sauce Bercy over mousse. Pass remaining sauce on the side.

For sauce, combine the clam juice, shallots, 1 T. of the parsley, salt, pepper, and wine in an enameled saucepan. Place over high heat; boil down by about ⅓. In another pan, melt 4 T. of the butter, stir in flour, and cook for 1 or 2 minutes, stirring constantly. Stir the reduced broth into roux and cook, whipping occasionally with a wire whisk, for about 10 minutes. Can be prepared ahead to this point. Seal with plastic wrap and set aside. When ready to serve, reheat and add remaining melted butter and parsley.

ENTREES: SEAFOOD

DOOR COUNTY FISH BOIL

Chicagoans who vacation in Door County, Wisconsin, enjoy the special fish boils with big pots cooking over open fires. Cole slaw, cherry pie, and beer complete the traditional menu

Cheesecloth
2 to 3 small new potatoes
   per person
2 to 3 small white onions
   per person
½ lb. whitefish or lake
   trout per person, cut in
   steaks with skin left on
½ cup table salt per gallon
   of water
1 cup kerosene

Beer

Prepare 3 cheesecloth bags: 1 containing potatoes, 1 containing onions, and 1 containing fish. Fill a very large pot ¾ full with water. A 30-qt. canning pot can be used and can cook enough for 10 people. Put in ½ the salt. Bring to a boil over hot charcoal fire. Add potatoes (wrapped in cheesecloth). Boil 20 minutes. Add onions (wrapped in cheesecloth). Bring back to boil; boil 10 minutes. Add remainder of salt. Add fish (wrapped in cheesecloth). Boil 15 minutes. Add more water if necessary to keep water level up. Flash the fire with kerosene to cause water to boil over pot. (This gets rid of scum and salt.) Remove cheesecloth bags; open and arrange on plates.

EASY SHRIMP SCAMPI   5-6 Servings

A sure hit!

½ cup butter
½ cup olive oil
1½ T. lemon juice
¼ cup chopped shallots
   (or green onions)
1 T. minced garlic
1 tsp. salt
Pinch pepper
2 lbs. large shrimp,
   shelled
¼ cup minced parsley

Light Dry White

Melt butter, add oil, then stir in other ingredients except shrimp and minced parsley. Stir to combine well and heat through. Remove from heat. Add shrimp and turn to coat shrimp all over. Put into broiling pan, making sure shrimp is in single layer. Pour sauce all over. Can refrigerate at this point, covered, all day. When ready to cook, uncover and broil 3 to 4 inches from heat for 5 minutes. Turn shrimp and broil other side 5 to 10 minutes, depending on shrimp size. Transfer to serving dish, sprinkle with parsley. Serve over rice.

ENTREES: SEAFOOD

MICROWAVE SOLE AMANDINE   3-4 Servings

⅔ cup unsalted butter
1 T. cornstarch
Juice and grated rind of 1
   lemon
1 lb. sole fillets
Salt and pepper to taste
⅓ cup slivered almonds
Finely chopped parsley

Light Dry White

In glass measuring cup, melt ⅓ cup butter; add cornstarch. Mix thoroughly. Add lemon juice and rind. Place fillets on roast rack and pour sauce over them. Cover with waxed paper; cook 5 minutes on high. Rotate dish after 2 minutes, if necessary. Let stand 2 to 3 minutes. Add salt and pepper to taste. While fish is standing, saute almonds in remaining ⅓ cup butter on high for 4 to 6 minutes, stirring every minute. Sprinkle over fish; garnish with chopped parsley.

WALNUT SHRIMP   4 Servings

1 lb. raw shrimp, cleaned
1 T. soy sauce
4½ T. vegetable oil
2 tsp. sherry
1 tsp. cornstarch
¼ tsp. white pepper
2 green onions
½ cup bamboo shoots
½ cup coarsely chopped
   walnuts
Slice fresh ginger or 1
   clove garlic
1 tsp. salt
½ tsp. sesame oil
¼ tsp. MSG (optional)

Full-Flavored Dry White

Cut shrimp into thirds and place in bowl. Sprinkle with soy sauce, 1 T. of vegetable oil, sherry, cornstarch, and pepper. Toss to coat. Cut green onions diagonally into 1-inch pieces and set aside. In preheated wok or skillet, heat 1½ T. vegetable oil. Toss in bamboo shoots and walnuts. Stir-fry for 1 minute. Remove and set aside in a bowl. Clean and dry wok. Heat 2 T. vegetable oil. Add ginger or garlic clove and swirl for a few seconds to flavor oil. Discard ginger or garlic. Add green onions and shrimp; stir-fry for 2 minutes. Add bamboo shoots and walnuts. Stir well to heat. Add salt, sesame oil and MSG. Stir well. Serve over hot rice.

ENTREES: SEAFOOD

GRILLED MUSTARD SHRIMP ON SKEWERS

5-6 Entree Servings; 8 Appetizer Servings

1 lb. medium or large
  shelled shrimp
3 T. dry mustard
1 tsp. brown sugar
1 tsp. horseradish
  powder
½ tsp. salt
½ tsp. pepper
1 can (12 oz.) beer
  (about)
Butter

Beer

Select medium shrimp for appetizer servings, large for main course. Mix seasonings; add enough beer to make a thin sauce. Refrigerate 2 hours; if thick, add more beer. Coat shrimp with sauce ½ hour before cooking. Arrange shrimp on skewers. Grill 4 inches from glowing coals for 4 to 5 minutes, basting with butter and sauce.

CRAB IMPERIAL

4 Servings

1 lb. fresh crabmeat
1 whole egg, beaten
3 T. mayonnaise
2 tsp. flour
1 tsp. parsley
¼ tsp. dry mustard
Dash Worcestershire
  sauce
Salt, pepper to taste
2 egg yolks, blended
1 T. butter, melted
Paprika

Light Dry White

Remove bone from crab; flake crab. Blend whole egg, 2 T. mayonnaise, flour, and seasonings. Pour over crab; mix lightly. Place in shell ramekins. Combine egg yolks, butter, 1 T. mayonnaise, and a dash of salt. Pour over crabmeat. Sprinkle with paprika. Bake at 375° for 12 to 15 minutes, or until lightly browned.

VEGETABLES

BEANS FOR BARBECUE   8-10 Servings

Great with ribs and green salad

2 pkgs. (10 oz. each)
  frozen lima beans
2 cloves garlic, peeled
2 tsp. salt
6 T. butter
3 cups grated sharp
  Cheddar cheese
½ cup Sauterne wine

Cover beans with cold water; add garlic cloves. Cover pot and bring to boil. Reduce heat and simmer 40 minutes. Add salt. Raise heat; boil uncovered about 15 minutes to reduce liquid. Reduce heat; add butter, cheese and Sauterne. Simmer uncovered over very low heat until cheese melts. Stir very gently so it does not become mushy. Turn into serving dish.

HERBED GREEN BEANS   4 Servings

1 lb. fresh green beans
3 to 4 qts. rapidly boiling
  water
4 T. butter
½ cup minced onion
½ clove garlic, minced
¼ cup minced celery
½ cup minced parsley
1 tsp. fresh rosemary or
  ¼ tsp. dried
¼ tsp. dried basil
¾ tsp. salt

Trim ends from beans, then cut them diagonally into 2-inch pieces. Boil for 6 to 8 minutes or until tender-crisp. Drain and rinse in cold water. Melt butter in a skillet. Saute onion, garlic, and celery, cooking for about 5 minutes. Add parsley, rosemary, basil and salt; cover and simmer for 10 minutes. Before serving, toss and warm the green beans with herb-flavored butter.

DILLED CARROTS WITH CREME FRAICHE   6 Servings

Fresh and delightful

1 lb. carrots, quartered
  and cut into ½-inch
  sticks
¼ cup butter
2 tsp. sugar
½ cup dry white wine
¾ cup creme fraiche
¼ cup snipped fresh dill
Salt and pepper

Place carrots in large pan of boiling salted water and boil 2 minutes. Drain carrots and rinse with cold water. Saute carrots in butter and sugar for 2 minutes. Add salt and pepper to taste. Stir in ½ cup wine; bring liquid to boil. Cook over moderately high heat until tender. Remove from heat; stir in creme fraiche and cook stirring until heated through and slightly thickened. Stir in dill. Correct seasonings.

ACCOMPANIMENTS

COLACHE
6-8 Servings

A peppery Spanish vegetable stew

4 small summer squash
  or zucchini
4 T. butter and bacon fat,
  mixed
1 large onion, thinly
  sliced
2 green peppers, seeded
  and quartered
4 tomatoes, peeled and
  chopped
Salt
Freshly ground black
  pepper
Cayenne pepper
3 ears fresh corn or 1
  pkg. (10 oz.) frozen
  corn

Cut squash into ½-inch cubes. Melt butter and bacon fat in heavy skillet; fry squash until partly brown. Pour off liquid and reserve. Add onion and pepper; fry 3 to 4 minutes. Add tomatoes, salt, pepper and cayenne to taste; remove corn from cob and add to mixture. Cover and cook over slow heat ½ hour. Reserved liquid may be added as necessary. Before serving, correct seasonings; it should be peppery and hot. Goes well with chicken.

STUFFED CUCUMBERS
4 Servings

Different first course or summer vegetable

2 cucumbers, unpeeled
1 cup green beans, diced
  and cooked
1 cup petite peas, cooked
Salt and pepper to taste
¾ to 1 cup green
  mayonnaise
2 T. minced chives or to
  taste

Cut cucumbers in ½ lengthwise. Boil for 2 minutes. Rinse under cold water, drain and dry thoroughly. Chill. Combine beans, peas, salt, pepper and enough mayonnaise to bind. Chill. When ready to serve, hollow out cucumbers to within ¼ inch of skin, fill with chilled bean mixture and pipe on remaining mayonnaise. Sprinkle with chives.

MAIS FRIT
6-8 Servings

Breakfast or dinner dish

1 dozen ears young corn
Salt and pepper to taste
1 T. butter
1 small onion, minced

Cut corn from cobs; squeeze all juice from cobs. Mix with salt and pepper. Melt butter in heavy skillet; add onion and saute until it starts to brown. Add corn and more butter as necessary. Cook stirring constantly until corn is cooked, about 15 to 20 minutes.

VEGETABLES

FRESH CORN SOUFFLE

6-8 Servings

2 cups fresh corn or 1
   pkg. (10 oz.) frozen
   corn, fully thawed
1 cup milk
4 T. butter
4 T. flour
1 vegetable bouillon cube
Pinch of cayenne pepper
Generous pinch of nutmeg
¾ tsp. salt
4 eggs, separated
½ tsp. cream of tartar

Combine corn and milk in blender and whirl at medium speed about 15 seconds or until smooth. In saucepan, melt butter. Stir in flour, cooking a few minutes. Stir in seasonings. Beat corn mixture into hot roux stirring constantly until thick and smooth. Remove from heat and beat in egg yolks 1 at a time. Beat egg whites until foamy, add cream of tartar and beat until stiff but not dry. Fold egg whites into corn mixture. Pour into buttered 2-qt. souffle dish and bake 30 minutes at 350° or until puffed and golden.

FETTUCINE ALLA COUSTEAU

4 Servings

Blue and green like the ocean

½ lb. fresh spinach leaves
1 cup whipping cream
2 oz. Gorgonzola cheese
4 T. butter
1 oz. vodka
4 oz. ricotta cheese
1 oz. blue cheese
1 oz. blue Curacao
Salt, pepper to taste
1 lb. fettucine
3 oz. Parmesan cheese,
   grated

Light-Bodied Red

Wash spinach. Shake off excess water. Cook only in water still clinging to leaves. Stir on high heat until barely cooked. Drain and chop. In a skillet, bring cream to a simmer. Add Gorgonzola, butter and vodka. Blend well. Season with salt and pepper. Add spinach, ricotta, blue cheese, and Curacao. Simmer and stir until well blended. Keep warm over low heat. Cook fettucine according to package directions, drain and toss with warm sauce. Sprinkle with grated Parmesan cheese and toss again. Serve at once.

ACCOMPANIMENTS

JOHN WAYNE'S CHEESE CASSEROLE

10-12 Servings

Add zip to your barbecue

1 lb. Monterey Jack cheese, grated
1 lb. Cheddar cheese, grated
2 cans (4 oz. each) green chilies, drained, diced
4 eggs, separated
⅔ cup evaporated milk
1 T. flour
½ tsp. salt
⅛ tsp. pepper
2 medium tomatoes, sliced

Combine cheeses and chilies in a buttered 3-qt. casserole. Beat egg whites until stiff, but not dry. Beat together yolks, milk, flour, and seasonings. Fold wh tes into yolk mixture. Fold eggs into cheese. Bake at 325° for 30 minutes. Arrange sliced tomatoes on top and bake 30 minutes more. Garnish with chopped chilies.

PASTA ALLA CAPRESE

6 Servings

12 plum or 4 large tomatoes, thinly sliced lengthwise
3 to 4 cloves garlic, crushed
1 long thin yellow-red sweet pepper, sliced thin
20 leaves fresh basil, torn in ½
½ cup olive oil
1 tsp. salt
5 to 6 twists of pepper mill
1 lb. pasta
1 pkg. (8 oz.) mozzarella cheese, cubed
Freshly grated Parmesan cheese

At least 1½ hours before serving, combine tomatoes, garlic, sweet pepper, basil, oil, salt, and pepper in a bowl large enough to contain both sauce and cooked pasta. Let stand without refrigerating. When pasta is cooked and well drained, toss in bowl with mozzarella and sauce. Mix quickly but well. Serve immediately. Pass Parmesan cheese at table.

Light Dry White

133

VEGETABLES

PESTO GENOVESE

4 Servings

Razzle, dazzle, basil

1 cup loosely packed
  fresh basil
⅓ cup natural pistachio
  nuts, shelled
2 cloves garlic, peeled
¾ cup freshly grated
  Parmesan cheese
½ cup olive oil, finest
  quality
1 lb. spaghetti or
  homemade fettuccini
  noodles, cooked
3 T. butter

Light Dry White

Place the basil in a blender or food processor. Add pistachio nuts and garlic. Blend or process, stirring down carefully with rubber spatula, when necessary. When well blended, add the cheese. Gradually add the olive oil while blending on low speed. When spaghetti is cooked, drain quickly, pour into hot serving dish. Toss with butter, add pesto sauce, toss well.

RED ONIONS

8-10 Servings

Side dish for barbecue

8 to 10 red onions,
  peeled and sliced or
  chopped
2 cups sugar
2 cups homemade
  mayonnaise

Cover onions with cold water mixed with 1 cup of sugar. Let stand covered overnight. Drain, and repeat process for at least another 4 hours adding second cup of sugar. Drain again leaving sugar in bottom of bowl. Mix mayonnaise with onions.

BAKED POTATO SKINS

2 Servings

2 medium baking
  potatoes
1 T. butter, melted
½ cup grated Cheddar
  cheese
4 slices bacon, cooked,
  crumbled
Sour cream

Rinse and scrub potatoes. Pierce with fork. Bake at 425° for 1 hour or until soft and cooked. Remove from oven. Cover with damp paper towel to cool without drying out skins. Cut potatoes in ½ lengthwise. Scoop out insides (and use for another meal) leaving about ¼-inch of potato next to the skin. Brush outsides with melted butter. Sprinkle insides with cheese and bacon. Bake on cookie sheet at 350° for about 30 minutes or until crisp. Serve with sour cream. You may wish to substitute 1 tsp. Parmesan cheese for the Cheddar cheese, bacon, and sour cream.

ACCOMPANIMENTS

BAKED HERBED SUMMER SQUASH   6 Servings

2 cups bread cubes made from good-quality, day-old bread
1 cup creme fraiche (sour cream or whipped cream is an acceptable substitute)
1½ lbs. summer squash, sliced
1 large onion, chopped
3 T. butter
½ cup butter, melted
Thyme
Sage
Rosemary (ground)
1 cup Veloute sauce

VELOUTE SAUCE:

2 T. butter
2 T. flour
1 cup chicken broth
Salt
White pepper

Toast bread cubes in oven at a low temperature. Make the Veloute sauce by melting 2 T. butter in top of double boiler and blending in flour. Slowly add chicken broth blending until thick and smooth. Season to taste with salt and white pepper. Take 1 cup Veloute sauce and blend with 1 cup creme fraiche. Set aside.

Saute squash and onion in 3 T. butter for 3 to 5 minutes. (If squash is not cooking as you saute, put a lid on the pan and let it steam for a few minutes.) When you are through, the squash should still be firm and the onions should be translucent, not burned. Toss bread cubes in ½ cup melted butter.

Grease a large baking dish. Layer the bottom with some bread cubes, then some squash and onions, then some sauce, then thyme, sage, and rosemary to taste. Repeat layers until all ingredients are used up, saving some bread cubes for the top Bake in a moderate oven (350° to 375°) for 25 to 30 minutes.

COLD STUFFED TOMATOES   8-10 Servings

8 to 10 medium tomatoes
½ lb. fresh mushrooms
2 jars (6 oz. each) marinated artichoke hearts
¾ cup mayonnaise
¾ cup sour cream
2 T. minced onion
2 tsp. curry powder
2 tsp. lemon juice
Paprika

Scoop out each tomato leaving a ¼-inch shell. Reserve meat of tomatoes for another use. Coarsely chop mushrooms and then artichoke hearts. Combine with remaining ingredients. Fill each tomato with mixture. Refrigerate. Before serving sprinkle with a dash of paprika. These may be made a day ahead; do not fill until ready to serve.

VEGETABLES

MICROWAVE FRESH VEGETABLE PLATTER

10-12 Servings

Beautiful and nutritious

1 lb. broccoli, cut into stalks
1 small head cauliflower, cut in flowerettes
1 large yellow squash, sliced ¼ inch thick
1 large zucchini, sliced ¼ inch thick
½ lb. fresh mushrooms, cut in ½
1 small sweet red pepper, cut in strips
1 small green pepper, cut in strips
½ cup butter, melted (unsalted, preferred)
¼ tsp. garlic salt
Dash pepper

On large round serving dish, arrange broccoli around edge. Next, arrange cauliflower; in center place yellow squash and zucchini. Arrange mushrooms and peppers decoratively on top. Combine butter, garlic salt, and pepper; drizzle over vegetables (save a little butter). Cover tightly with plastic wrap. Microcook on "High" for 14 to 18 minutes, turning dish ¼ turn every 5 minutes. Let stand covered 5 minutes before serving. Drizzle with remaining butter.

SIMPLE SAUTEED ZUCCHINI

6 Servings

3 to 4 medium zucchini
½ tsp. salt
1 small onion, chopped
1 clove garlic, minced
¼ cup chopped green pepper
⅓ cup butter

Grate zucchini. Place in a colander. Toss with ½ tsp. salt. Let drain for ½ hour. Pat dry on paper towels. Saute onion, garlic, and green pepper in butter until soft. Add zucchini and saute over medium heat for 3 to 4 minutes, stirring frequently.

ACCOMPANIMENTS

STUFFED ZUCCHINI GORDON   2 Servings

1 (10 oz.) zucchini
Salt
Parmesan cheese, freshly
   grated
1 cup fresh bread crumbs
½ cup finely grated
   Gruyere cheese
½ cup finely grated Gouda
   cheese
2 large shallots, thinly
   sliced
1 jalapeno pepper,
   seeded and chopped
¼ tsp. dill
¼ tsp. basil
¼ tsp. oregano
½ tsp. garlic salt
¼ tsp. parsley
Salt to taste
Pepper to taste
2 tsp. butter
1 tsp. olive oil
Paprika

Wash zucchini, cut off stem and drop squash into small amount of boiling water; cover, cook 10 minutes. Drain and cool. Cut squash in ½ lengthwise; remove and discard seeds leaving a firm shell. Sprinkle with salt and Parmesan cheese; set aside. In a bowl, combine next 12 ingredients. Divide the stuffing between the halves pressing it firmly and mounding it. Dot the zucchini with butter and sprinkle ½ tsp. olive oil over each ½. Sprinkle each ½ with freshly grated Parmesan cheese and a dusting of paprika. Place in a shallow dish and cook at 350° for 15 minutes.

TOMATO WEDGES PROVENCAL   4 Servings

2 T. fine dry bread
   crumbs
¼ cup minced onion
¼ cup minced parsley
½ clove garlic, minced
2 T. softened butter or
   olive oil
½ tsp. salt
¼ tsp. dried basil
⅛ tsp. pepper
4 tomatoes

In small bowl, mix bread crumbs, onion, parsley, garlic, butter and seasonings. Cut each tomato into wedges. Place in a greased shallow baking dish. Sprinkle with mixed ingredients. Bake at 425° for 5 to 8 minutes or until tomatoes are tender.

LOW-FAT, LOW-CHOLESTEROL POTATO SALAD

8-10 Servings

7 to 10 potatoes (about 3 lbs.)
2 stalks celery, diced
1 medium onion, diced
½ green pepper, diced
4 to 5 slices sweet or dill pickle, diced
7 eggs, hard cooked
1 pt. reduced calorie mayonnaise (about)
½ cup prepared mustard
2 T. mustard seed, soaked in 3 T. vinegar
Salt, pepper
Fresh chives, minced (optional)

Boil potatoes in jackets in salted water until tender; peel and dice. Add to vegetables in large bowl. Dice whites only of eggs; add to bowl. (Yolks are not used.) Mix mayonnaise, mustard, mustard seed, salt and pepper to taste and chives. Toss with ingredients in bowl. Chill.

BRAZILIAN SALAD

4 Servings

Unusual combination

2 bunches fresh spinach
1½ lbs. shrimp, cooked and cleaned
1¼ cups thinly sliced celery
1¼ cups julienne cut green pepper
6 green onions, thinly sliced
¼ cup finely chopped parsley
¾ cup olive oil
¼ cup lime juice
¾ tsp. grated lime rind
1 tsp. sugar
¾ tsp. ground cumin
⅛ tsp. cayenne pepper
Salt to taste
3 bananas, cut in pieces
¼ cup chopped salted peanuts
¼ cup shredded fresh coconut

Clean spinach and break into pieces. Combine shrimp, celery, green pepper, green onions, and parsley. In another bowl, mix oil, lime juice and rind, sugar, cumin, cayenne pepper, and salt. Pour over shrimp mixture. Toss. Cover and chill 1 hour. Line plates with spinach. Mound with shrimp. Surround with bananas. Sprinkle with peanuts and coconut.

STEAK SALAD

6 Servings

DRESSING:

1 cup mayonnaise
¼ cup chopped dill pickle
2½ T. minced onion
1½ T. Rhine wine
1 T. finely chopped
   cooked spinach
1½ tsp. prepared mustard
1 tsp. lemon juice
½ tsp. sugar
½ tsp. Worcestershire
   sauce
1 egg yolk

SALAD:

1 lb. beef sirloin or
   tenderloin, cut into 1-
   inch cubes
½ tsp. basil
1 tsp. salt
½ tsp. oregano
½ tsp. MSG
½ tsp. black pepper
½ tsp. thyme
⅛ tsp. garlic powder
2 T. butter
2 heads Boston lettuce
Watercress, curly or
   Belgian endive
1 avocado, sliced
12 pitted black olives for
   garnish

Combine dressing ingredients; season to taste with salt and pepper. Chill. For salad, put seasonings in plastic bag; add meat and shake to coat evenly. Quickly brown meat in hot butter in skillet to degree of doneness you prefer. Cool for 2 minutes. Divide lettuce, watercress, endive, and avocado slices among 6 plates. Divide steak cubes among salads. Garnish with black olives. Serve dressings on the side.

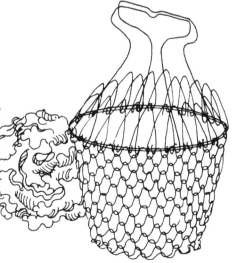

SALADS, DRESSINGS & SAUCES

MOLDED GAZPACHO SALAD
6-8 Servings

2 envelopes unflavored
   gelatin
1¼ cups tomato juice
⅓ cup red wine vinegar
1 tsp. salt
Dash hot pepper sauce
2 small tomatoes, peeled
   and diced
1 medium cucumber,
   pared and diced
½ green pepper, seeded
   and diced
¼ cup chopped onion
1 T. chopped chives

In a medium saucepan, sprinkle gelatin over ¾ cup tomato juice to soften for 3 minutes. Stir constantly over low heat until gelatin is dissolved. Remove from heat. Stir in remaining tomato juice, vinegar, salt, and hot pepper sauce. Set in bowl of ice, stirring occasionally, until mixture is the consistency of lightly beaten egg whites, about 15 minutes. Fold in tomatoes, cucumber, green pepper, onion, and chives. Pour into 1½-qt. mold that has been rinsed with cold water. Cover and refrigerate until firm, at least 6 hours. Serve with generous amounts of Avocado Dressing.

AVOCADO DRESSING
2 Cups

1 large ripe avocado
½ cup sour cream
½ cup half and half
1 T. grated onion
Dash cayenne pepper
1½ tsp. salt
⅛ tsp. sugar
1 garlic clove, crushed
1 T. lemon juice

For dressing, peel avocado. Cut into chunks and place in food processor or blender. Add remaining ingredients and blend until smooth. Refrigerate.

ZUCCHINI SALAD
6 Servings

4 to 5 medium zucchini
3 T. lemon juice
½ cup olive oil
2 to 3 T. sour cream
1 tsp. Dijon mustard
1 small clove garlic,
   mashed
Salt, white pepper
1 small red onion, thinly
   sliced
3 T. finely grated
   radishes
1 T. minced parsley

Drop zucchini in boiling water for 5 minutes. Drain thoroughly. While still warm, slice in ½ lengthwise and then in ¼-inch slices. Sprinkle with 1 T. lemon juice and 2 T. olive oil. Combine remaining lemon juice and olive oil with sour cream, mustard, and garlic. Whisk until perfectly blended. Add salt and pepper to taste. Pour dressing over zucchini. Add onion and toss. Chill 2 or 3 hours or overnight. Before serving, toss again and sprinkle with grated radishes and parsley.

SALADS, DRESSINGS & SAUCES

VERMICELLI SALAD

1 pkg. (14 oz.) thin
  vermicelli
2 T. olive oil
1 cup French dressing
  (vinaigrette)
¼ cup chopped parsley
¼ cup chopped green
  onion
¼ tsp. dried basil
¼ tsp. oregano
1¼ cups mayonnaise
2 T. red wine tarragon
  vinegar
Garlic, seasoned salt,
  coarse black pepper to
  taste
Shredded chicken or
  pieces of shrimp
  (optional)

Drop vermicelli into boiling, salted water to which you have added the olive oil. Boil, stirring frequently, just until tender, 10 to 12 minutes. Rinse in cold water, drain thoroughly. Toss gently with French dressing. Add herbs, mayonnaise, and vinegar; toss again. Season to taste. Chill thoroughly, preferably overnight. Serve on a bed of lettuce garnished with cherry tomatoes.

SALADE DE POMMES DE TERRE

Potato salad

3 lbs. red potatoes
2 T. dry vermouth
¼ cup chicken broth
2 green onions, minced
¼ cup wine vinegar
½ cup oil
1 T. sugar
2 tsp. salt or to taste
1 tsp. Dijon mustard
Freshly ground white
  pepper
¼ cup chopped parsley

Cook potatoes in boiling water until just tender (about 20 minutes); do not overcook. Drain and rinse in cold water. When cool enough to handle, peel and slice. Gently combine potatoes with vermouth, broth, and green onions. Let stand for several minutes. Combine vinegar, oil, sugar, salt, mustard, and pepper. Stir into potatoes. Adjust seasonings. Fold in chopped parsley. May be eaten either chilled or at room temperature. Keeps well in refrigerator.

SALADS, DRESSINGS & SAUCES

SALMON MOUSSE WITH CUCUMBER-DILL SAUCE

**6 Entree Servings;
10 Appetizer Servings**

Lovely on a buffet table

2 envelopes unflavored
  gelatin
½ cup dry white wine
2 thick slices onion
2 T. lemon juice
1 can (16 oz.) red salmon,
  undrained
½ cup catsup
2 cups whipping cream
1 T. parsley
1 tsp. dill
½ tsp. chervil
Cucumber-Dill Sauce

Dissolve gelatin in wine; heat until dissolved. Pour into blender or food processor. Add onion and lemon juice; blend. Add salmon and catsup; blend. Keeping motor on, pour in 1 cup whipping cream. Add seasonings. Add remaining 1 cup whipping cream; blend. Pour into 6-cup fish mold. Serve with sauce.

CUCUMBER-DILL SAUCE

1¾ Cups

1 medium cucumber,
  peeled and seeded
1 cup sour cream
1 T. lemon juice
1 tsp. dill
1 tsp. chopped chives
¼ tsp. white pepper

Shred cucumber and sprinkle with salt; let stand 1 hour. Drain; combine with sour cream, lemon juice, dill, chives and pepper. Chill.

FRUIT SALAD WITH POMEGRANATE SEEDS

6-8 Servings

1 large pomegranate
2 avocados
3 oranges, peeled, sliced
2 bananas, sliced
½ cup golden raisins
½ carton (4 oz.) orange
  yogurt
½ carton (4 oz.) lemon
  yogurt
¼ lb. cashews
Lettuce leaves

To prepare pomegranates, peel off outside skin; remove juicy red seeds that are inside. These are what you eat. One hour before serving, slice avocados in chunks about the same size as sliced bananas. Put in bowl with the other fruits; toss gently with orange and lemon yogurts. Refrigerate for 1 hour. Just before serving, toss with pomegranate seeds and nuts. Serve on lettuce leaves. If desired, decorate with more nuts.

SALADS, DRESSINGS & SAUCES

SOUTH PACIFIC FRUIT SALAD
6 Servings

Wonderful at brunch

1 cup cubed guava
2 cups cubed fresh
  pineapple
1 cup orange slices
1 cup cubed papaya
1 cup cubed mango
1 cup strawberry halves
1 cup pitted cherries
1 cup banana slices
¼ cup macadamia nuts,
  halved
½ cup Cognac
½ cup Cointreau
2 T. sugar
Mint sprigs

Combine fruits and nuts. Mix Cognac, Cointreau and sugar. Pour over salad. Cover and chill. Garnish with mint.

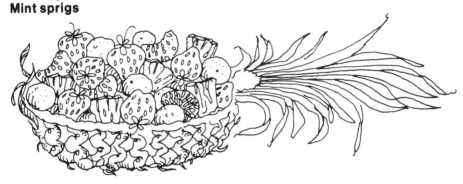

LEMON PAPAYA SALAD
4-6 Servings

1 pkg. (3 oz.) lemon
  gelatin
1 cup boiling water
1 pkg. (3 oz.) cream
  cheese, softened
1 egg yolk
⅛ tsp. salt
½ cup sour cream
¼ tsp. grated lemon peel
1½ tsp. lemon juice
1 egg white, stiffly beaten
1 papaya, seeded,
  peeled, and diced
1 pt. blueberries
Mint leaves

Dissolve gelatin in water. Cool. Combine cheese, egg yolk, and salt. Stir sour cream, lemon peel and juice into cheese mixture. Add gelatin. Chill until partially set. Fold in egg white and papaya. Pour into 4-cup, oiled ring mold. Chill 4 hours or overnight. To serve, unmold and fill center with blueberries and garnish with mint leaves.

SALADS, DRESSINGS & SAUCES

SALAD DRESSING WITH VARIATIONS

4 T. cider vinegar
6 T. vegetable oil
2 tsp. sugar
1 tsp. salt
Freshly ground pepper
1 clove garlic, peeled and
left whole

Put all ingredients in a jar with cover and shake well. Refrigerate until ready to use; remove garlic before pouring over salad. May be made 1 day in advance; may be doubled.

TOMATOES AND CUCUMBERS WITH FRESH HERBS
4-6 Servings

6 ripe tomatoes, cut into
eighths
2 T. finely chopped
chives
2 T. finely chopped
parsley
1 cucumber, sliced thin

Mix tomatoes and herbs with salad dressing and allow to marinate in refrigerator several hours before serving. Slice cucumbers and soak in lightly salted water; refrigerate. When ready to serve, drain cucumbers and stir into tomatoes. Serve chilled.

MARINATED MUSHROOMS
4 Servings

Use as hors d'oeuvre or salad

1 lb. small button
mushrooms (if using
large ones, cut into
halves or quarters
depending on size)
½ cup water
1 tsp. lemon juice
1 tsp. salt
Freshly ground pepper
1 tsp. thyme leaves
1 tsp. rosemary
1 medium onion, chopped
fine

Clean and trim mushrooms. In a heavy covered skillet, simmer mushrooms until just tender with water, lemon juice, salt, and pepper. Drain. Place mushrooms, herbs and onion into ceramic or glass dish; stir in a doubled recipe of salad dressing, cover and allow to marinate in refrigerator at least overnight. May be kept about a week in refrigerator without noticeable deterioration.

SALADS, DRESSINGS & SAUCES

MARINATED BROCCOLI
4-6 Servings

1½ to 2 lbs. fresh
   broccoli, trimmed
1 T. finely chopped
   shallots
3 T. sour cream

Place trimmed broccoli, heads up, in about 1 inch of lightly salted boiling water. Water should just cover bottom of stems. Cover and cook no more than 10 minutes; broccoli should still be crisp. Drain and cool. To the prepared salad dressing, add shallots and sour cream. Pour over broccoli and refrigerate. May be made several hours ahead.

DILLY SALAD
8-10 Servings

Refreshing with cold chicken or turkey

2 pkgs. (3 oz. each)
   lemon gelatin
½ cup boiling water
½ cup dill-shallot vinegar
½ cup sugar
2 tsp. fresh dill
2 cups thinly sliced
   cucumbers
1 cup finely chopped
   celery
¼ cup finely chopped
   green pepper
3 T. minced chives
2 tsp. salt
1 cup mayonnaise

Dissolve gelatin in boiling water. Add vinegar, sugar and dill. Pour into 2-qt. mold. Chill until slightly thickened. (Do not let it begin to set.) Add cucumbers, celery, green pepper, chives, salt, and mayonnaise. Chill until firm.

DILL-SHALLOT VINEGAR
1 Cup

2 large cloves shallots
6 to 8 sprigs fresh dill
1 cup white vinegar (5%
   acidity)

Do not peel shallots. Cut shallots into quarters and place in 8 oz. bottle that has tight fitting cap. Place dill in bottle and pour white vinegar in to cover. Cap tightly and put in cool dark place for about 4 to 6 weeks. May be strained; ready to use.

SALADS, DRESSINGS & SAUCES

GOURMET'S VINEGAR
1 Quart

Best made with herbs fresh from the garden

¼ cup chopped marjoram
¼ cup chopped basil
1 tsp. rosemary leaves
¼ cup fresh mint
¼ cup chopped dill
1 bay leaf, crumbled
¼ tsp. whole allspice
¼ tsp. black pepper
3 whole cloves
3 cups good quality red
wine vinegar

Put all ingredients in 1-qt. non-metal container. Cover tightly. Let stand 4 to 6 weeks in cool, dark spot. Then strain through coffee filter and bottle as desired. An 8 oz. decorative bottle makes a lovely gift. Use in salad dressings and to deglaze roasting pans.

CREME FRAICHE I

1 cup whipping cream
1 tsp. buttermilk

Combine ingredients in a jar. Cover tightly and store in warm place away from drafts 36 to 48 hours. Stir occasionally. Refrigerate in covered jar. Keeps 2 to 3 weeks.

CREME FRAICHE II

½ pt. sour cream
1 pt. whipping cream

Put sour cream into a saucepan and gradually stir in whipping cream. Heat gently over low heat to start the fermenting action. Be careful not to go over 85°. Set, partially covered, in a warm place overnight, until the cream has thickened. Stir up, cover and refrigerate.

NOTE: Creme fraiche is used often in France. It will not curdle when boiled. It may be used in any recipe that calls for sour cream. Also 2 T. of Grand Marnier or other liqueur may be added to 1 cup of creme fraiche for spooning over fresh fruit.

146

SALADS, DRESSINGS & SAUCES

CREAMY SALAD DRESSING   About 1½ Cups

1 egg
⅓ cup tarragon vinegar
1½ tsp. salt
1 tsp. pepper
2 tsp. sugar
1 tsp. lemon juice
1 tsp. Dijon mustard
½ tsp. dry mustard
1 large clove garlic,
  minced
⅔ cup salad oil
½ cup half and half
  (about)

Put whole egg in blender or food processor; blend. Stop blender; add 2 T. vinegar, salt, sugar, pepper, lemon juice, mustards, and garlic. Blend again, gradually add oil through top until it is absorbed by egg mixture. Add remaining vinegar and enough half and half to reach the desired consistency. Adjust seasonings. Crumbled blue cheese may be added, if desired.

NO-OIL FRENCH DRESSING   2½ Cups

1 can (10¾ oz.)
  condensed tomato soup
1 cup red wine vinegar
¼ cup sugar
1 T. Worcestershire
  sauce
1 tsp. prepared
  horseradish
1 tsp. salt
1 tsp. paprika
1 tsp. grated onion
1 tsp. freshly ground
  black pepper
1 to 2 cloves garlic,
  mashed

Mix all ingredients together. This may be done in food processor. Pour into bottle. Cover and store in cool place. Keeps well for weeks. Shake before using.

CREAM DRESSING FOR FRUIT SALAD   About 1 Quart

1 pkg. (3 oz.) cream
  cheese, softened
1 cup sour cream
1 egg yolk
2 tsp. sugar
1 cup whipping cream,
  whipped

Beat together cream cheese, sour cream, egg yolk, and sugar. Chill. Just before serving, fold in whipped cream. (Can be held up to 2 days.) To make a dessert sauce for fruit, add more sugar.

SALADS, DRESSINGS & SAUCES

DRUNKEN SALMON MARINADE   2 Cups

Can be used on chicken also

Salmon fillets or salmon
   steaks
1 cup dry vermouth
¾ cup vegetable oil
⅓ cup lemon juice
2 T. chopped chives
2 tsp. salt
1 clove garlic, crushed
¼ tsp. marjoram
¼ tsp. pepper
¼ tsp. sage
¼ tsp. thyme
⅛ tsp. hot pepper sauce

Combine all ingredients except salmon. Pour over salmon. Cover and marinate in refrigerator at least 4 hours. Remove and grill, brushing with marinade.

TZAIZAKI (SUMMER BREAD TOPPING)   About 4 Cups

Delicious on gyros sandwiches

1½ large cucumbers,
   peeled
2 cups sour cream
4 cloves garlic, pressed
½ tsp. salt
2 T. olive oil
2 T. tarragon vinegar

Grate cucumbers; put in colander. Put sour cream, pressed garlic, and salt in a bowl. Squeeze water out of cucumbers and add to sour cream mixture. Add olive oil and vinegar; stir. Refrigerate for several hours before serving to allow flavors to blend.

MARINADE FOR SHISHKEBOB   3 Cups

1½ cups salad oil
¾ cup soy sauce
¼ cup Worcestershire
   sauce
½ cup red wine vinegar
⅓ cup lemon juice
2 T. dry mustard
1 T. coarsely ground
   pepper
2¼ tsp. salt
1½ tsp. minced parsley
2 cloves garlic, crushed

Combine all ingredients and mix well. Cover and store in refrigerator or freeze. Use as marinade for meat.

SALADS, DRESSINGS & SAUCES

FOOLPROOF BEARNAISE
2 Cups

Serve on hamburgers for a gourmet touch

6 T. melted butter
¼ cup flour
2 cups hot water
2 tsp. lemon juice
1 tsp. salt
Few grains paprika
Dash white pepper
4 egg yolks
½ cup white wine vinegar
½ cup dry white wine or
  vermouth
1 T. instant minced
  onions
1 T. dried tarragon
¼ tsp. pepper
Pinch salt
1 T. parsley

Cook first 7 ingredients in double boiler until sauce thickens. Stir continuously using whisk. Add egg yolks at last minute. In a saucepan, boil vinegar, wine, onions, tarragon and seasonings over moderate heat until the liquid has been reduced to ¼ cup. Let cool slightly. Combine the 2 mixtures. Add 1 T. parsley. Keep warm over hot water.

SPICY BARBECUE SAUCE
3 Quarts

1 large onion, chopped
  (1½ cups)
2 cloves garlic, minced
Cooking oil
2 bottles (28 oz. each)
  barbecue sauce
2 cans (6 oz. each)
  tomato paste
1½ cups water
¼ cup brown sugar
¼ cup red wine vinegar
1 T. Worcestershire
  sauce
1 tsp. oregano
¾ tsp. red pepper flakes

Saute onion and garlic in small amount of oil; drain. Put in large pot with remaining ingredients. Bring to boil; reduce heat and simmer, uncovered, 3 hours.

DESSERTS & SWEETS

PEACH ALMOND CREPES WITH CARAMEL SAUCE

6-8 Servings

CREPES:

1½ cups milk
4 eggs
1 cup sifted flour
2 T. brandy
1 T. sugar
4 T. butter, melted

FILLING:

3 egg yolks
½ cup sugar
2 T. cornstarch
1 cup milk, hot
4 T. butter
¼ tsp. almond extract
1 T. brandy
¼ cup ground blanched
  almonds
3 to 4 peaches, peeled,
  pitted, halved, poached

CARAMEL SAUCE:

½ cup firmly packed dark
  brown sugar
½ cup dark corn syrup
1 T. butter

Combine crepe ingredients in blender. Blend until smooth. Let batter rest for at least 1 hour. Cook crepes. Set aside.

For filling, combine yolks, sugar, cornstarch and whisk until light. Slowly add hot milk. Place over medium heat and whisk until thick and creamy. Stir in butter, almond extract and brandy. Add almonds. Mix lightly. Remove from heat. Set aside. Cut up peaches. Spread lighter side of each crepe with filling and top with peaches. Roll crepes. Place in baking dish. Bake at 375° for 8 to 10 minutes or until heated through. Serve with caramel sauce.

For sauce, place sugar, corn syrup and butter in saucepan. Cook, stirring over medium heat until sugar is dissolved and sauce is warm. To serve, arrange crepes on plates and spoon on sauce.

TORTONI CAFETTA

8 Servings

1 egg white, beaten stiff
1 T. instant coffee
⅛ tsp. salt
6 T. sugar
1 cup whipping cream
1 tsp. vanilla
⅛ tsp. almond extract
¼ cup almond slivers,
  toasted with a pinch of
  salt
Chocolate shavings and
  almonds (optional)

Beat egg white with instant coffee and salt until stiff, but not dry. Beat in 2 T. of sugar, 1 T. at a time. Beat the cream with remaining ¼ cup sugar until stiff. Add vanilla and almond extract. Fold into meringue mixture. Add almonds. Fill individual cups or ice tray. Freeze for at least 2 hours. Decorate top of each cup with almonds and shaved chocolate.

DESSERTS & SWEETS

SOLANGE'S FLAN DE QUESO CREMA　　　6-8 Servings

Perfect ending for Spanish or Mexican dinner

½ cup sugar
¼ cup water
1 can (13 oz.) evaporated milk
4 eggs
1 cup sugar
2 pkgs. (8 oz. each) cream cheese
2 tsp. vanilla

Place ½ cup sugar and water in heavy saucepan. Bring to boil over high heat, shaking pan occasionally until sugar is dissolved. Cover pan for 1 minute. Remove cover and cook until syrup begins to caramelize. It should be light brown. Immediately pour caramel into 1½-qt. oiled mold, coating sides and bottom. Let cool. Mix evaporated milk, eggs, sugar, cream cheese, and vanilla until smooth. This may be done in food processor. Pour cheese mixture into caramelized mold. Set mold in another pan. Pour enough hot water in outer pan to come ½ way up sides of mold. Bake in 350° oven for about 1 hour. Custard is done when knife inserted into custard comes out clean. Cool on rack for ½ hour. Refrigerate. Unmold to serve.

CHOCOLATE SQUARES　　　40 Squares

1 cup shortening
½ cup white sugar
1½ cups brown sugar
2 eggs, separated
1 T. water
1 tsp. vanilla
2 cups sifted flour
1 tsp. baking soda
½ tsp. salt
1 cup semisweet chocolate pieces
1 cup shredded coconut or chopped peanuts

Cream shortening. Gradually add white sugar and ½ cup of brown sugar. Add egg yolks, water and vanilla; beat thoroughly. Sift flour with soda and salt. Add to creamed mixture. Blend. Spread evenly in greased 15 x 10-inch jelly roll pan. Press chocolate pieces into batter. Beat egg whites to soft peaks, gradually add remaining brown sugar and beat to stiff peaks. Spread meringue over batter. Sprinkle with coconut or peanuts. Bake at 375° for 20 minutes. Let stand several hours before serving.

DESSERTS & SWEETS

PEACH CRISP WITH MAPLE SAUCE
6-8 Servings

Wonderful taste

PEACH CRISP:

1 cup flour
½ cup packed brown sugar
½ cup granulated sugar
½ tsp. cinnamon
¼ tsp. nutmeg
¼ tsp. salt
½ cup butter
8 medium, fresh peaches, peeled, sliced (5 to 6 cups)
2 T. maple syrup
Juice and rind of ½ lemon

CREAMY MAPLE SAUCE:

1½ cups whipping cream
⅓ cup maple syrup
3 T. light corn syrup

For peach crisp, combine flour, sugars, cinnamon, nutmeg, and salt. Cut into butter with pastry blender or fork until crumbly. Combine peaches with maple syrup, lemon juice, and rind. Place in 9-inch square baking pan. Sprinkle with crumb mixture. Cover with foil. Bake at 375° for 30 minutes. Remove foil. Bake 15 minutes more, or until crisp on top. Serve warm or cold with creamy maple sauce.

For sauce, combine ingredients and simmer about 30 minutes or until thickened and reduced. Chill.

DOUBLE CHOCOLATE ICE CREAM CAKE
12 Servings

3 cups almond macaroon crumbs
½ cup chopped pecans
1 pkg. (6 oz.) semisweet chocolate pieces, chopped
½ cup melted butter
1 pt. chocolate ice cream, softened
1 pt. vanilla ice cream, softened
1 pt. whipping cream, whipped
Slivered almonds

Combine macaroon crumbs, pecans, and chocolate pieces with melted butter. Spread ⅓ of mixture in bottom of spring-form pan. Add softened chocolate ice cream, then ⅓ of macaroon mixture, softened vanilla ice cream, last of macaroon mixture. Freeze. Before serving, place frozen cake on platter. Frost with whipped cream; top with almonds.

DESSERTS & SWEETS

FRESH FRUIT TARTS

Makes 2 Pastry Shells

Simple French tarts, use best fruit available

PASTRY:

1 cup flour
½ cup sugar
¼ lb. butter, preferably
sweet, cut into small
pieces
1 egg yolk

Combine flour and sugar. Work in butter until well combined. Add egg yolk and mix with hands until dough forms a firm ball. Roll out ½ the dough and fit into 9-inch pie tin, weight it and bake 5 minutes at 425°. Remove weight and continue baking another 3 to 4 minutes until golden. Remove from oven and cool completely before filling. Pastry may be made well in advance.

FRESH PEACH AND BLUEBERRY TART

6-8 Servings

4 to 5 large, ripe but firm
peaches
½ tsp. lemon juice or to
taste
½ cup sugar
2 T. cornstarch
½ pt. blueberries
¼ cup apricot brandy
1 cooked 9-inch pastry
shell

Peel and slice peaches. Sprinkle with lemon juice. Stir in sugar. Let stand until sugar is dissolved and juices form. Drain juice into heavy saucepan. Add cornstarch. Stir until cornstarch is dissolved. Add 2 T. of blueberries. Cook over medium high heat until mixture thickens and becomes clear. Remove from heat and add brandy, sliced peaches, and rest of blueberries. This mixture may then be refrigerated. When ready to serve, spoon fruit mixture into cooled pastry shell.

SAUTEED APPLE TART

6-8 Servings

2 T. butter
1 cup sugar
Pinch of salt
¾ tsp. cinnamon
½ tsp. nutmeg
¼ tsp. cloves
½ tsp. lemon juice
6 to 8 apples, peeled,
cored, and sliced thin
½ cup Calvados or apple-
jack
1 cooked 9-inch pastry
shell

In a heavy skillet melt butter. Add sugar, stirring until it dissolves. Toss spices and lemon juice with apples. Add to skillet stirring constantly until apples are thoroughly coated with sugar mixture. Add Calvados. Stir over medium high heat until Calvados has evaporated and apples are tender. More Calvados may be added if necessary. Spoon into prepared shell and serve warm.

DESSERTS & SWEETS

STRAWBERRY MOUSSE

8-10 Servings

2 to 3 pts. fresh
  strawberries (4½ cups
  sliced)
1⅓ cups sugar
1½ T. cornstarch
2 T. unflavored gelatin
⅓ cup Grand Marnier or
  kirsch
2 cups whipping cream

SAUCE:

1 pt. fresh strawberries
2 T. sugar
1 pkg. (10 oz.) frozen
  raspberries, defrosted
¼ cup Grand Marnier or
  kirsch
Grated orange peel

Put the sliced strawberries in a skillet with 1 cup of sugar. Bring to a boil. Cook, stirring over low heat, until sugar dissolves. Blend cornstarch with gelatin and Grand Marnier. Stir until gelatin is melted. Add to berries. Stir until gelatin mixture is dissolved and well blended. Cool until mixture is syrupy. Do not let mixture become cold or it will be too firm. Beat the cream. When it begins to stiffen, slowly beat in the remaining sugar. Continue beating until stiff. Fold into strawberry mixture. Spoon the mousse into a lightly oiled 2-qt. mold. Cover and chill overnight. Unmold mousse and serve with sauce. For sauce, slice strawberries. Stir in sugar, defrosted raspberries, Grand Marnier or kirsch. Add grated orange peel to taste.

FROZEN CHOCOLATE CHEESECAKE

8-10 Servings

CRUST:

1½ cups chocolate wafer
  crumbs
⅓ cup butter, melted

CAKE:

8 oz. cream cheese,
  softened
¼ cup sugar
1 tsp. vanilla
1 pkg. (6 oz.) chocolate
  pieces, melted
2 egg yolks, beaten
2 egg whites, beaten until
  stiff with ¼ cup sugar
1 cup whipping cream,
  whipped
¾ cup chopped nuts

For crust, combine crumbs and butter; press in bottom of a 9-inch spring-form pan.

For cake, combine cream cheese, sugar, vanilla, and melted chocolate. Fold egg yolks, egg whites, and whipping cream in order given into chocolate mixture. Add nuts. Pour into crust and freeze. Remove from freezer a few minutes before serving.

DESSERTS & SWEETS

CASSATA IMPERIALE

A deliciously different meringue dessert

6 egg whites, at room
  temperature
Pinch of salt
¼ tsp. cream of tartar
1½ cups sugar
1 tsp. white vinegar

FILLING:

1 cup whipping cream
1 envelope unflavored
  gelatin
⅓ cup almond liqueur or
  rum
2 squares (1 oz. each)
  semisweet chocolate
1½ cups green seedless
  grapes, halved
1½ cups grapes (red or
  black), halved and
  seeded
½ cup broken walnuts
12 walnut halves

Beat egg whites until foamy; add salt and cream of tartar. Continue beating until egg whites hold their shape. Add sugar, 1 T. at a time; add vinegar. Beat until egg whites are stiff, but not dry. Pour meringue into buttered and floured 9-inch spring-form pan; smooth top. Place in 300° oven for about 1 hour. Let cool on rack 10 minutes, then gently loosen sides of meringue from pan. Remove meringue from pan; set on rack and carefully fit ring of pan back around meringue. Let cool completely before removing ring. Top will fall.

For filling, whip cream until stiff; dissolve gelatin in liqueur or rum and fold into cream. Grind 1 square chocolate into powder and make chocolate curls with the other. Combine chocolate powder, grapes and broken walnuts; gently fold into cream. Spoon mixture onto meringue. Decorate with walnut halves and chocolate curls. Serve immediately or refrigerate until ready to serve.

DESSERTS & SWEETS

LEMON MOUSSE "CHEZ MADELAINE" 6-8 Servings

2 oz. unsalted butter
⅓ cup whipping cream
4 medium eggs
1 cup sugar
¾ cup freshly squeezed
   lemon juice
Grated rind of 2 lemons
½ cup egg whites, at room
   temperature
⅛ tsp. cream of tartar
4 T. sugar
½ lemon, sliced thin

Heat butter and cream together over low heat until butter melts. In a small bowl, vigorously beat 4 eggs, 1 cup sugar, lemon juice and rind together. Remove butter and cream from heat; add lemon mixture. Return saucepan to low heat. Stir constantly until custard thickens noticeably. Do not let it boil. Strain custard through a sieve into a clean bowl. Cover with a round of buttered waxed paper to prevent a skin from forming. Let cool to room temperature. When cool, refrigerate until well chilled, at least 1 hour. Beat egg whites until frothy. Add cream of tartar; continue beating until soft peaks form. Begin adding sugar, 1 T. at a time, beating well after each addition. Whites will be stiff and meringue-like after absorbing all the sugar. Remove the waxed paper from the chilled custard and add ⅓ of the beaten whites. Stir them into the custard. Lift another ⅓ of the whites onto the custard. This time fold in the whites. Repeat with last ⅓ of whites. Transfer to a decorative bowl or individual serving dishes. Chill thoroughly or freeze. When serving, garnish with lemon slices.

POTATO CHIP COOKIES 4 Dozen

1 cup butter, softened
½ cup sugar
1½ cups flour, sifted
½ cup crushed potato
   chips
½ cup chopped pecans
Confectioners' sugar

Cream butter and sugar; add sifted flour, potato chips and pecans. Chill. Form into small balls, 1 heaping tsp. each. Bake on ungreased cookie sheets at 350° for 18 to 20 minutes. Roll in confectioners' sugar.

DESSERTS & SWEETS

PAPAYA MERINGUE SURPRISE
4 Servings

3 egg whites
3 T. sugar
2 ripe papayas
1 pt. ice cream (coconut, pineapple, or vanilla)
1 egg yolk, lightly beaten
1 T. brown sugar

Beat whites until fluffy. Gradually add sugar; continue beating until stiff peaks form. Cut papayas in ½; seed. Arrange on baking sheet covered with brown paper. Place large scoop of ice cream in each shell. Cover with meringue; seal edges well. With a small brush, lightly paint swirls with egg yolk; sprinkle with brown sugar. Bake at 450° for 3 to 5 minutes, or until lightly browned. Serve at once.

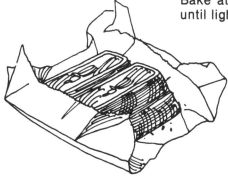

MARVELOUS MOCHA PIE
8 Servings

20 chocolate Oreo cookies, crushed
¼ cup butter, melted
1 qt. coffee ice cream

CHOCOLATE SAUCE:

3 squares (3 oz.) unsweetened chocolate, melted
¼ cup butter
⅔ cup sugar
⅔ cup evaporated milk
1 tsp. vanilla

TOPPING:

1 cup whipping cream, whipped
Almonds (toasted, sliced or slivered)

Melt butter. Mix well with crushed cookies and press into pie plate. Spread 1 full qt. ice cream over crust and freeze. For sauce, bring chocolate, butter and sugar to a boil. Gradually add evaporated milk. Cook until thickened. Let cool; add vanilla. Spread over ice cream and return to freezer until sauce sets. Before serving, top with whipped cream; garnish with nuts. A small amount of Kahlua may be spooned over whipped cream before serving.

DESSERTS & SWEETS

ROSE GERANIUM CAKE

1 cup sweet butter
Rose Geranium leaves,
  number depends on leaf
  size
3 cups granulated sugar
3 cups unsifted cake
  flour (5 cups sifted)
3 tsp. baking powder
1 cup milk
1 tsp. almond extract
6 egg whites

FILLING:

1 cup sugar
½ cup water
3 egg whites, stiffly
  beaten
½ tsp. almond extract
  (scant)

ICING:

2 T. Geranium-flavored
  butter
1 cup confectioners'
  sugar
Whipping cream

Smother sweet butter in freshly gathered and well-rinsed rose geranium leaves. Wrap in damp cloth and tin foil; store in refrigerator overnight. Remove leaves from butter. Reserve. Brush three 9-inch cake pans with a little additional butter and flour; lay 1 large reserved leaf on bottom of each pan. Cream flavored butter; add sugar gradually and beat thoroughly. Sift flour with baking powder 3 times. Fold flour into butter mixture alternating with milk and almond extract, beginning and ending with flour. Beat thoroughly. Whip egg whites until stiff but not dry. Gently fold egg whites into cake batter. Carefully spoon batter into prepared pans. Bake at 350° until light brown, about 30 minutes. Do not overbake. Cool in pans for 10 minutes and turn on wire racks. Carefully remove leaves. When cool, fill and frost cake.

For filling, boil sugar and water to fine thread stage (236°). Pour slowly over stiffly beaten egg whites and beat continuously until almost cold. Add almond extract a few drops at a time making sure flavor isn't too strong. Pile between cake layers.

For icing, cream butter and sugar adding a little cream. Whip until very light. Spread on top of cake.

STRAWBERRIES TANGO

1 qt. fresh strawberries
1½ cups sour cream
1 cup brown sugar
½ cup Amaretto liqueur

Halve any large strawberries. Combine sour cream, brown sugar, and liqueur. Stir in all but 6 strawberries. Chill. Place in 6 sherbet glasses. Garnish with reserved strawberries. Also good served on cake or in meringue shells.

DESSERTS & SWEETS

CHOCOLATE CAKE WITH CREAM FILLING

10-12 Servings

2 cups boiling water
1 cup unsifted unsweetened cocoa
2¾ cups sifted all-purpose flour
2 tsp. baking soda
½ tsp. salt
½ tsp. baking powder
1 cup butter
2½ cups granulated sugar
4 eggs
1½ tsp. vanilla

FROSTING:

1 pkg. (6 oz.) semisweet chocolate pieces
½ cup half and half
1 cup butter
2½ cups unsifted confectioners' sugar

FILLING:

1 cup whipping cream, chilled
¼ cup unsifted confectioners' sugar
1 tsp. vanilla

In a medium bowl, combine water and cocoa mixing with a whisk until smooth. Cool completely. Sift flour with soda, salt, and baking powder. Grease well and lightly dust with flour or cocoa three 9 x 1½-inch layer cake pans. In a large bowl at high speed, beat butter, sugar, eggs, and vanilla; scraping bowl occasionally, until light, about 5 minutes. At low speed, beat in flour mixture (in thirds), beginning and ending with flour mixture. Don't overbeat. Divide evenly into pans. Bake at 350° about 25 minutes. Cool in pans 10 minutes. Remove carefully and cool on racks.

For frosting, in medium saucepan, combine chocolate pieces, half and half, and butter. Stir over medium heat until smooth. Remove from heat and blend in confectioners' sugar. In a bowl set over ice, beat until it holds its shape.

For filling, whip cream with sugar and vanilla; refrigerate.

To assemble, on a plate place 1 layer top side down. Spread with ½ of the filling. Place second layer, top side down and spread with remaining filling. Put third layer on, top side up. Frost sides first, covering whipped cream. Cover rest of cake and refrigerate at least 1 hour.

DESSERTS & SWEETS

PRINCE OF WALES CAKE
Often served as the groom's cake

CAKE:

⅓ cup butter
1½ cups sugar
3 eggs, well beaten
2 T. molasses
1½ tsp. baking soda
1½ tsp. cinnamon
¾ tsp. ground cloves
¾ tsp. nutmeg
3 cups sifted cake flour
1½ tsp. baking powder
1½ cups buttermilk
Finely grated rind of 1
    lemon

LEMON FILLING:

¾ cup sugar
3 T. cornstarch
¼ tsp. salt
1 egg yolk
Grated rind and juice of 1
    lemon
1 T. butter

BOILED ICING:

1 cup sugar
½ tsp. cream of tartar
⅓ cup hot water
2 egg whites
¼ tsp. vanilla
¼ tsp. almond extract

For the cake, cream butter and sugar until fluffy. Add eggs, then molasses. Beat well. Sift dry ingredients together 3 times. Add to butter mixture alternately with the buttermlk and lemon rind. Pour batter into 2 well-buttered and floured 9-inch cake pans. Bake at 350° for 20 to 25 minutes.

For the filling, combine sugar, cornstarch and salt in a saucepan. Stir in yolk and rind. Add enough water to the lemon juice to make 1 cup. Stir into sugar mixture and cook, stirring constantly until thick. Stir in butter. Cool to room temperature. Spread between the cake layers.

For the icing, beat sugar, cream of tartar and water in a saucepan. Cook to soft ball stage (236° on a candy thermometer). Beat egg whites until stiff but not dry. Pour hot syrup over whites in a fine stream beating constantly. Continue beating until icing forms stiff peaks. Beat in flavorings. Ice the cake.

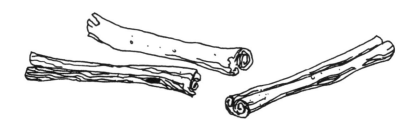

DESSERTS & SWEETS

ZUCCHINI CAKE

Freezes well

3 cups sifted flour
1 tsp. cinnamon
1¼ tsp. salt
1½ tsp. baking soda
1 tsp. baking powder
1 cup salad oil
2 cups sugar
3 eggs
2 tsp. vanilla
2 T. sherry
1 cup grated zucchini
1 tsp. grated lemon peel
1½ cups chopped nuts
1 cup seedless raisins

GLAZE:

1½ cups sifted
   confectioners' sugar
⅛ tsp. salt
1 T. butter
2 T. cream or sherry

Combine flour, cinnamon, salt, soda, and baking powder. Mix well and set aside. Beat together salad oil and sugar; add eggs 1 at a time, beating well after each. Add vanilla, sherry, zucchini, and lemon peel. Add flour mixture; stir to blend. Fold in nuts and raisins. Turn into buttered 10-inch angel food cake pan or 9-inch bundt pan. Bake at 325° for 75 minutes. Cool 5 minutes in pan; turn out onto rack to cool. Drizzle with glaze, if desired, before serving.

For glaze, cream sugar, salt, and butter. Add cream or sherry.

LEMONADE COOKIES

About 6 Dozen

Good for children to make

1 cup butter
1 cup sugar
2 eggs
3 cups flour
2 tsp. grated lemon rind
1 tsp. baking soda
1 can (6 oz.) frozen
   lemonade concentrate,
   thawed
Additional sugar

Cream butter and sugar until fluffy. Add eggs one at a time, beating between each addition. Add flour, lemon rind, and baking soda gradually. Stir in ½ cup of concentrate. (Reserve ¼ cup lemonade concentrate for glaze.) Drop dough 2 inches apart onto ungreased cookie sheet. Bake at 375° for 8 to 10 minutes, or until lightly browned. Brush with reserved lemonade concentrate and sprinkle with sugar.

DESSERTS & SWEETS

WINE JELLY WITH FRUIT
4 Servings

1 envelope unflavored
   gelatin
½ cup cold water
½ cup sugar
1½ cups rose or port wine
Rind of ½ lemon
¼ cup cherries or
   strawberries, halved
¾ cup sliced peaches
¾ cup sliced bananas
½ cup whipping cream,
   whipped and
   sweetened with sugar
   and vanilla

Soak gelatin in water. Boil ¼ cup sugar, wine and lemon rind over moderate heat until sugar dissolves. Simmer 5 minutes. Add gelatin; dissolve. Remove lemon rind. Pour ½-inch layer into oiled and chilled 1-qt. mold. Chill until set. Arrange cherries, cut side up, on set gelatin. Sprinkle with some of the remaining sugar. Pour into ½-inch gelatin. Chill until set. Continue layering with fruit, sugar, and gelatin ending with gelatin. Cover and chill until set. Unmold and serve with whipped cream.

PÊCHES SUPREMES
8 Servings

A great way to use overripe or bruised peaches

4 to 5 large peaches,
   peeled, pitted, cut into
   small cubes
2 cups sugar
4 cups orange juice
¼ cup lemon juice
¾ cup apricot brandy

Combine peaches and sugar, let stand ½ hour. Then stir well. Stir in orange juice and lemon juice, then add brandy. Mix all ingredients well and freeze. Before serving, remove from freezer and let stand until soft enough to spoon into serving glasses. Serve each portion with 1 or more T.'s apricot brandy. This can be taken frozen in an ice chest to a picnic.

OKLAHOMA LEMON ICE CREAM
About 4 Quarts

8 cups milk
3 cups sugar
4 lemons, halved,
   washed, stemmed, and
   seeded
Pinch of salt
½ pt. whipping cream,
   whipped

Scald milk. (Do not boil.) Add sugar; continue stirring. Put lemons in to float. Add pinch of salt. Cool and then put in refrigerator overnight (covered). When ready to freeze, squeeze lemons (with your hands) into milk mixture. Discard lemons. Put mixture in freezer container of a hand or electric ice cream freezer. Add whipped cream. Freeze following your ice cream freezer's directions.

JAMS, JELLIES

PEACH CONSERVE
6 Pints

Delicious on ice cream

8 cups peaches, peeled, pitted and coarsely chopped
4 cups sugar
½ lb. raisins
2 oranges
1 lemon
½ lb. chopped nuts

Place peaches, sugar and raisins in a heavy 4-qt. saucepan. Squeeze pulp and juice from oranges and lemon; combine with peaches. Stir constantly over medium high heat until mixture comes to boil. Reduce heat to simmer and continue cooking until mixture thickens, about 1 hour. Grate rind from 1 orange and 2 tsp. rind from lemon. When mixture has thickened, add grated rind and nuts; simmer 10 minutes longer. Pour into hot, clean jars.

BLACKBERRY JAM WITH ORANGE 8-10 Jars (8 oz. each)

2 lbs. blackberries
1½ cups orange juice
3 T. lemon juice
1 T. grated orange peel
4 cups superfine granulated sugar

Cook blackberries in ¾ cup of orange juice in a large, heavy pan over low heat, until heated through. Puree ½ of cooked berries. Return pureed berries to the other berries in the pan. (If you do not want any seeds, strain all the fruit through cheesecloth or very fine strainer — a tedious task, so you may opt for seeds!)

Add lemon juice, grated orange peel, and remaining orange juice; stir over high heat until it comes to a rolling boil. Stir in sugar; return to boil. Continue cooking over medium heat, stirring until thick, about 15 to 30 minutes. (You can speed up the thickening process by adding a packet of liquid pectin and stirring off heat after jam has boiled a few minutes.)

Remove from heat and stir several minutes to prevent fruit from floating. Pour into sterilized jars and seal.

JAMS, JELLIES

ANTIPASTO PLATTER

SQUASH PICKLES

4 Quarts or 8 Pints

8 cups squash, sliced or
  chopped
2 cups chopped onions
2 bell peppers, seeded
  and chopped
2 red peppers
½ cup pickling salt
2 cups vinegar
3 cups sugar
2 tsp. mustard seed
2 tsp. celery seed

Combine squash, onions, and peppers in glass bowl; pour salt over. Let stand 2 hours. Drain. Bring vinegar, sugar, mustard and celery seed to boil. Add squash mixture. Return to boil. Immediately pack in clean jars leaving ½ inch at the top. Seal and process in water bath canner for 10 minutes.

GREEN TOMATO PICKLES

5 Quarts or 10 Pints

1 gallon green tomatoes,
  diced
1 cup pickling salt
1 qt. white vinegar
3 cups sugar
2 tsp. black pepper
1 qt. onions, diced
1 qt. bell peppers, diced
10 hot green chili peppers

Pour salt over tomatoes in large glass bowl and let stand 3 hours. Drain. Bring vinegar, sugar and black pepper to boil. Add chopped onion and bell peppers; cook 15 minutes, lifting and stirring from bottom of pot. Pack in clean hot jars, leaving a 1-inch space. Place 1 whole chili pepper in each pt. Seal and process in water bath canner for 15 minutes.

PICKLED CARROTS

4 Pints

36 to 48 baby carrots
12 small white onions
½ cup pickling salt
8 hot green chili peppers
4 tsp. dried tarragon
20 peppercorns
2 bay leaves
1 pt. white wine tarragon
  vinegar

Wash carrots and peel onions. Place in glass bowl with pickling salt and let stand for 24 hours. Drain carrots and onions; pack in clean jars with 2 hot peppers in each jar. To each jar add 1 tsp. tarragon, 5 peppercorns, ½ bay leaf and fill with boiling white wine tarragon vinegar. Let stand overnight. Drain vinegar into saucepan and bring to boil. Pour over carrots leaving ½-inch space at the top. Seal and process in a water bath canner for 30 minutes.

PRESERVES & PICKLES

PICKLED BEETS
4 Pints

4 lbs. beets
8 hot green chili peppers
1¼ cups sugar
1½ cups white vinegar
½ cup water
1 T. whole allspice

Wash deep red beets. Leave 2 inches of stems and the top roots. Boil until skins can be slipped. Remove skins; trim beets. Peel and slice or leave the small ones whole. Pack into clean, hot jars leaving 1 inch at the top. Place 2 whole peppers in each jar.

While beets are cooking, combine sugar, vinegar, water, and allspice in a saucepan. Bring to boiling point and simmer 10 minutes. Pour hot liquid over the beets and peppers leaving 1 inch at the top. Seal and process in a water bath canner 30 minutes. The water needs to cover tops of jars 1 or 2 inches without boiling over.

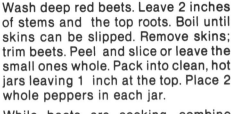

LIME PICKLES
4-5 Quarts

2 cups pickling lime
2 gallons water
1 gallon sliced small
   cucumbers
2 qts. cider vinegar
11 cups sugar
1 T. pickling salt
1 T. celery seed
1 T. whole allspice
1 T. mixed spices

Combine pickling lime and water in crock or enamelware — not aluminum. Soak cucumbers overnight in the lime water. Stir occasionally. In the morning remove cucumbers and rinse 3 times in cool water. Soak 3 hours in ice water. Drain. Bring the rest of the ingredients to a boil. Pour over the pickles. Let stand 3 hours. Boil pickles in juice 35 minutes. A little green food coloring can be added, if desired. Spoon into hot, sterilized jars, leaving ⅛-inch headspace and seal.

JAMS, JELLIES

CORNICHONS MAINTENON
About 1 Quart

A crisp, sour pickle, delicious with pates

2 lbs. cornichons
(smallest cucumber
pickles)
1¼ cups coarse salt (sel
de mer or kosher)
6 medium cloves garlic,
peeled
¼ lb. small white onions,
peeled
6 medium shallots,
peeled
2 sprigs fresh tarragon or
1 tsp. dried tarragon
6 peppercorns
1½ qts. white vinegar

Brush cornichons to get off all residue; cut off tails. Put in bowl with a handful of salt and rub vigorously. Dry each pickle. Put in crock; cover with rest of salt and let stand 24 hours. Drain and dry pickles. Put back in clean crock with garlic, onions, shallots, tarragon and pepper. Pour in enough cold vinegar to cover. Cover crock and allow to stand in cool place for 3 weeks. Drain and replace with new vinegar to cover. Let stand 3 more weeks. Repeat process 1 more time. Keep in crock in cool place.

DIVINE PICKLED ONIONS
4 Pints

Keep for one year: they get better

½ oz. pickling spices with
chilies removed
6 oz. white sugar
1¼ pts. tarragon wine
vinegar
2 qts. small onions,
peeled

Place spices, sugar, and vinegar into a large pot. Bring to a boil and boil 5 to 7 minutes. Add onions and return to boil. Boil 1 minute. Drain onions, reserving liquid. Pack onions in hot sterilized jars. Reheat liquid to a boil, then pour over onions to cover. Seal jars when completely cooled.

GRANNY BOEHM'S DILL PICKLES
1 Quart

The secret of crisp pickles is pickling them the day they are harvested

2 to 3 heads of dill
7 to 8 washed cucumbers
(2 to 3 inches long)
2 cloves garlic
1 T. pickling salt
1 T. sugar
½ cup white vinegar

Sterilize a qt. jar and place all ingredients in jar. Fill to the top with cold water. Process 10 minutes in hot water bath. This recipe may be increased as desired.

PRESERVES & PICKLES

MANGO CHUTNEY

4 Quarts

About the closest to Major Grey's

6 lbs. fruit (chopped mangoes with some apricots)
1 lb. raisins
1 lb. currants
⅛ cup salt
2 lbs. sugar
¼ lb. fresh ginger (boiled until soft and finely chopped)
4 cloves garlic, chopped fine
3 red chili peppers, chopped
1 qt. cider vinegar
½ tsp. cinnamon
½ tsp. allspice
½ tsp. ground cloves
2 onions, minced

Place all ingredients in a large pot. Simmer, stirring occasionally until thoroughly cooked, about 1½ to 2 hours. It should be of a thick consistency, but not too dry. Spoon into hot sterilized jars leaving ¼-inch headspace. Seal.

PEACH CHUTNEY

Eight ½-Pint Jars

Hot and peppery

1½ cups sugar
1½ cups vinegar
½ cup lemon juice
½ cup currant jelly
1 T. salt
1 tsp. ground ginger
¼ tsp. cayenne pepper
4 lbs. peaches, peeled, pitted and chopped (8 cups)
2 green peppers, chopped
2 red peppers, chopped (may substitute canned Italian red peppers)
1 cup golden raisins

In a 5-qt. Dutch oven, combine sugar, vinegar, lemon juice, jelly, salt, ginger, and cayenne. Mix well. Heat to boiling. Stir in peaches, peppers and raisins. Boil gently, stirring occasionally, until mixture thickens, about 45 minutes. Spoon into clean hot ½-pt. jars, leaving ¼-inch headspace. Adjust lids. Process in boiling water bath for 15 minutes, counting after water returns to boil.

FALL MENUS

HEARTY BREAKFAST

Bloody Mary's Deluxe
Hangtown Fry
Perfect Whole Wheat Pancakes
Scrambled Eggs
Super Apple Cake

ELECTION NIGHT SUPPER

Spicy Beef Bones
Boston Baked Beans
No-Yeast Raisin Bread
Cherry-Apple Pie

THANKSGIVING ELEGANCE

Apple-Almond Punch
Oyster Bisque
Breast of Capon with Artichoke Hearts and Mushrooms
Southern Sweet Potatoes
Baked Stuffed Onions
Pumpkin Ice Cream Pie
Brandied Peanuts
Coffee

GAMING TABLE

Potent Punch
Stuffed Mushrooms
Pheasants in Brandy and Cream
Honey Glazed Chestnuts
Red Cabbage
Cranberry Ice
Assorted Cheeses
Poached Peaches in Raspberry Sauce

FALL MENUS

A CHINESE DINNER FOR THE CONNOISSEUR

Sugared Walnuts
Home-Style Egg Rolls
Hot and Sour Soup
Steamed Sole with Black Bean Sauce
Sweet and Sour Chicken Savoy
Fried Rice
Spiced Orange Slices
Tea

ANNIVERSARY DINNER

Champagne Punch
Leeks in Armagnac
Coquilles St. Jacques Au Vin D'Ail
Tournedos Rossini
Carrots Flambe
Hearts of Palm with Garlic Dressing
Luscious Orange Baked Alaska

SOUP BUFFET

Each guest ladles his own from the simmering pots

Antipasto Platter
French Bread
Polish Fresh Mushroom Soup
Pistou Soupe
Seafood Gumbo
Nick's Mocha Torte
Gateau Fromage de Normande with Sauteed Apples with Calvados

BEVERAGES

APPLE-ALMOND PUNCH
16-20 Servings

Delightful before lunch

½ gallon apple cider
1 cup Amaretto liqueur
Juice of 1 lemon
Juice of 2 oranges
20 toasted whole almonds

Combine all liquid ingredients and chill. Serve with ice in punch glasses. Float a toasted almond in each glass.

APRICOT BRANDY

Wonderful over fresh peaches

8 oz. dried apricots
2 cups sugar
2 cups vodka

Combine all ingredients in a bottle that is square or has flat areas for turning. Bottle must get ¼ turn every day for 30 days. Then let it stand for 60 days. Serve each glass of brandy with an apricot.

BLOODY MARY DELUXE
8-10 Servings

1 can (46 oz.) tomato juice
½ cup beef broth
6 T. fresh lime juice
¼ cup Worcestershire sauce
2 tsp. sea salt or coarse salt
1 tsp. ground pepper
1 tsp. celery salt
1 tsp. dill
½ to 1 tsp. hot pepper sauce
1 tsp. prepared horseradish
1 to 2 cups vodka

Put all ingredients except vodka in pitcher; mix well. Fill 12-oz. glasses with ice. Add 1 to 2 oz. vodka to each glass. Add tomato mixture. Garnish with celery sticks, cucumber sticks or slices, and lime.

BEVERAGES

CHAMPAGNE PUNCH

25 Servings (4 oz. each)

1 fifth dry Champagne,
    chilled
2 bottles (1 qt. each)
    chilled ginger ale
1 cup bourbon or rye
½ cup Cointreau or other
    orange liqueur
Ice

Combine ingredients in punch bowl. Add ice. Increase recipe as desired.

SPIKED CIDER

2 Quarts

Strictly adult

2 qts. cider
1 tsp. whole allspice
12 to 16 whole cloves
2 sticks cinnamon
Ground nutmeg
1 to 2 cups rum

Combine cider, allspice, cloves, and cinnamon. Heat and simmer 10 minutes. Add rum. Serve piping hot in mugs, with dash of nutmeg or a whole cinnamon stick in each.

UNDER-THE-SINK COFFEE LIQUEUR

4 cups water
3½ cups sugar
9 tsp. instant coffee
13 oz. grain alcohol
1 T. vanilla

Boil 2 cups of water with sugar until sugar is dissolved and liquid is clear. Cool completely. Add instant coffee to 2 cups boiling water. Cool. Combine syrup, coffee, grain alcohol and vanilla. Put in bottles, cork and let stand for 30 days.

POTENT PUNCH

1 fifth of bourbon
1 can (12 oz.) frozen
    lemonade concentrate
2 oz. Cointreau
1 qt. soda water
Sliced oranges for garnish

Mix and pour over ice. Garnish with sliced oranges.

APPETIZERS

ARTICHOKE NIBBLES

6 Dozen

2 jars (6 oz. each)
  marinated artichoke
  hearts, reserve
  marinade from 1 jar
1 small onion, finely
  chopped
1 clove garlic, minced
4 eggs
¼ cup bread crumbs
¼ tsp. salt
⅛ tsp. pepper
⅛ tsp. oregano
⅛ tsp. hot pepper sauce
½ lb. shredded Cheddar
  cheese
2 T. minced parsley

Place reserved marinade in skillet. Chop artichokes. Add onion and garlic to marinade. Cook about 5 minutes or until onion is soft. Beat eggs with fork, add bread crumbs and seasonings. Stir in cheese, parsley, artichokes, and onion mixture. Turn into greased 7 x 11-inch pan. Bake 30 to 35 minutes at 325°. Cool 5 minutes. Cut into small squares.

HOT CRABMEAT SPREAD

2 Cups

1 pkg. (8 oz.) cream
  cheese, softened
1 can (7½ oz.) crabmeat,
  diced and well drained
  (do not use frozen
  crabmeat)
2 T. finely chopped green
  onion
1 T. whipping cream
½ tsp. cream-style
  horseradish
¼ tsp. salt
Dash pepper
⅓ cup toasted, sliced
  almonds

Mix all ingredients. Place in buttered baking dish. Bake at 375° for 15 minutes. If made ahead and refrigerated, heat for 20 minutes. Serve with assorted crackers and let guests spread their own.

HORS D'OEUVRES

HANKY PANKY

40 Servings

Great meat and cheese appetizer!

1 lb. ground beef
1 lb. hot pork sausage
1 lb. Velveeta cheese, cubed
1 can (4 oz.) mushroom pieces, drained, chopped
½ tsp. oregano
½ tsp. garlic and/or onion powder
2 loaves party rye bread

Brown beef and sausage. Drain. Add cheese; stir until melted. Add remaining ingredients. Spread on cocktail rye. Place on cookie sheet and freeze. When frozen, put in plastic bag for freezer storage. To serve, put on cookie sheet and broil until done.

EASY PATE MOLD

4 Cups

1 envelope unflavored gelatin
2½ cups beef consomme
2 pkgs. (3 oz. each) cream cheese
2 T. whipping cream
¼ tsp. minced garlic
½ tsp. Beau Monde seasoning
½ cup pate de foie gras

Soften gelatin in ¼ cup consomme. Heat remaining consomme to boiling. Add gelatin mixture, stirring until dissolved. Soften cream cheese with cream; blend in garlic and Beau Monde seasoning. Set aside. Pour ½ of gelatin mixture into 4-cup spring mold. Chill until it starts to set. Add pate de foie gras; chill until set. Spread softened cream cheese over pate. Pour rest of gelatin mixture (may need to be reheated to pouring consistency) into mold. Chill until set. Unmold and serve with toast points.

TEXAS CRABGRASS

3 Cups

⅓ cup butter
½ cup finely chopped onion
1 can (7½ oz.) crabmeat, drained
¾ cup Parmesan cheese
1 pkg. (10 oz.) frozen chopped spinach, cooked and drained

Melt butter; add onion and saute until soft. Add crab, cheese, and spinach. Heat through. Serve hot with melba toast or crackers.

APPETIZERS

HOME-STYLE EGG ROLLS

16-18 Rolls

2 T. oil
¾ lb. Chinese barbecued pork or fresh pork shoulder, shredded
½ lb. raw shrimp, cleaned and shredded
1 oz. Chinese dried black mushrooms, shredded
4 oz. water chestnuts, shredded
4 oz. bamboo shoots, shredded
3 tsp. salt
1 tsp. black pepper
1 tsp. sugar
2 T. dark soy sauce
3 whole green onions, shredded
1 tsp. five spice powder
1 to 2 tsp. cornstarch
½ lb. bok choy or napa, shredded
¼ lb. snow peas, shredded
½ lb. bean sprouts, shredded
1 tsp. MSG
1 lb. egg roll wrappers
1 egg, well beaten
2 to 4 cups oil

Heat 2 T. oil in wok; stir-fry pork 2 minutes. Add shrimp, mushrooms, water chestnuts, bamboo shoots, 1½ tsp. salt, ½ tsp. pepper and ½ tsp. sugar. Stir-fry 3 minutes. Add soy sauce, green onions, and five spice powder. Add just enough cornstarch to lightly thicken. Stir until clear; remove from heat. Cool to room temperature. Blanch bok choy, snow peas and bean sprouts in water to cover 1 to 2 minutes. Drain and squeeze out as much water as possible. Combine 1½ tsp. salt, ½ tsp. pepper, ½ tsp. sugar and MSG; stir into vegetables. Combine vegetables with pork mixture. To wrap egg rolls, place wrapper with 1 corner pointing towards you. Squeeze a handful of filling to compact and place in corner nearest you. Roll wrapper away from you until 2½ inches of unrolled wrapper remain. Tuck in left and right sides; brush inner area with egg and continue rolling to seal. Deep-fry in oil heated to 375° for several minutes until golden brown. Turn constantly for even cooking. Serve with sweet and sour sauce or hot mustard.

BACON AND CHUTNEY APPETIZER

Makes 24

8 slices white bread
10 to 12 slices bacon
1 cup well-drained chutney, chopped fine

Toast bread and remove crusts. Cut each slice of bread into 2 pieces. Cut bacon in ½. Fry over low heat until half done (not brown). Spread chutney on toast fingers and top each with ½ slice of bacon. Broil 5 inches from heat until bacon is crisp. Serve hot.

HORS D'OEUVRES

CHEESE FONDUE

8 Servings

Use as main course or hors d'oeuvre

4 T. butter
¼ cup flour
1 clove garlic
1½ cups white wine
(Moselle, Rhine)
2 lbs. Swiss cheese,
grated
¼ tsp. nutmeg
1 T. Dijon mustard

Medium-Dry White

Melt butter; add flour, cook over low heat, stirring for 3 minutes. Add garlic and wine. Bring to a boil over moderate heat, stirring until thick and smooth. Add cheese ½ cup at a time, stirring and letting all cheese melt before adding next portion. When all cheese has been added and mixture is smooth, add nutmeg and mustard. Pour mixture into fondue pot.

Serve with platter of thinly sliced salami, pepperoni, Westphalian ham, garlic sausage — 1½ to 2 lbs. of any 1 or combination of all. French bread and a selection of parboiled vegetables such as cauliflower, broccoli, carrots, green peppers, red peppers or green beans may also be dipped into fondue.

HERBED CHEESE SPREAD

1 Cup

¼ lb. butter, softened
1 pkg. (8 oz.) cream
cheese
¼ tsp. garlic powder
½ tsp. marjoram
½ tsp. thyme
½ tsp. oregano
⅛ tsp. dill
⅛ tsp. pepper
⅛ tsp. basil
1 tsp. chopped chives
1 tsp. chopped parsley
¼ tsp. salt
Freshly ground pepper to
taste, to cover top
(optional)

Place butter and cream cheese in food processor (or blender). Blend until well combined; add all other ingredients except pepper. Blend well. Place in bowl, cover with pepper, if desired. Serve only slightly chilled.

APPETIZERS

LAYERED CRABMEAT APPETIZER

4 pkgs. (3 oz. each)
  cream cheese
2 T. Worcestershire
  sauce
2 T. lemon juice
2 T. grated onion
1 cup chili sauce
2 tsp. prepared
  horseradish (optional)
1 can (7½ oz.) crabmeat
¼ cup chopped parsley

Combine cream cheese, Worcestershire, lemon juice, and onion. Shape cheese mixture into flat rectangle; top with a layer of chili sauce mixed with horseradish, if desired, and a layer of crabmeat. Sprinkle with parsley. Serve with crackers.

CHEESE CRISPIES

7-8 Dozen

4 oz. butter
8 oz. grated sharp cheese
1 cup flour
Cayenne pepper to taste
1½ cups corn flakes,
  crumbled

Cream butter and cheese; add flour, pepper and cornflakes. Form into 2 rolls. Refrigerate until firm. Slice. Dip fork into cold water to press down. Bake at 300° for 20 minutes. Let cool.

HOT PEPPERED PORK DIP

2 lbs. diced pork shoulder
1 onion, chopped
1 tsp. salt
¼ tsp. pepper
2 cloves garlic
1 can (15 oz.) tomato
  sauce with bits
2 cans (4 oz. each) green
  chilies, chopped, with
  juice
3 to 6 jalapeno peppers,
  finely chopped
  (optional)

In a large skillet brown pork in small amount of oil. Remove and drain on paper towels. Drain fat from skillet; add 1 cup water, pork, onion, salt, pepper, and garlic. Simmer 30 minutes. Add tomato sauce, chilies, and jalapeno peppers (if desired). Simmer 1½ hours. Serve with nacho or corn chips.

HORS D'OEUVRES

BLUE CHEESE FONDUE

½ cup butter
½ cup blue cheese
1½ T. lemon juice
2 cans (14 oz. each) artichoke hearts, drained

Heat butter, cheese, and lemon juice, stirring constantly with whisk. Put in cheese fondue pot; place over candle. Surround with halved artichoke hearts. Provide fondue forks or bamboo skewers for dipping.

STUFFED MUSHROOMS   4-6 Servings

1 lb. large mushrooms
½ lb. mild or hot Italian sausage
1 small onion, chopped fine
2 T. butter
½ cup bread crumbs
1 tsp. garlic powder
1 tsp. salt
¼ cup Parmesan cheese

Remove stems from mushrooms; finely chop ½ of them. Remaining stems may be discarded. Place mushroom caps on cookie sheet. Saute stems, sausage, and onion in butter until sausage is brown. Drain fat. Add bread crumbs, garlic powder, salt, and cheese. Stuff caps with mixture. Broil 2 to 5 minutes.

BRAUNSCHWEIGER CAVIAR PATE

1 lb. braunschweiger, broken up
1 pkg. (8 oz.) cream cheese, at room temperature
2 T. milk
1 T. grated onion
1 tsp. sugar
1 tsp. chili powder
⅛ tsp. hot pepper sauce
1 jar (2 to 3 oz.) black caviar, washed and drained
Parsley
Party rye

Combine braunschweiger, ½ of cream cheese, 1 T. milk, grated onion, sugar, and chili powder. Beat until smooth. Form into an igloo shape on a serving plate. Cover and chill. Whip remaining cream cheese, milk, and hot pepper sauce until smooth. Spread evenly over braunschweiger. Cover with black caviar as evenly as possible and chill. Garnish with snipped parsley. Serve with party rye.

APPETIZERS

HOT CHEESE AND CHILI SPREAD

8 oz. sharp Cheddar
  cheese, shredded
2 cans (4½ oz. each)
  roasted chilies,
  drained, chopped
1 egg
2 T. milk

Put ½ of cheese in 9-inch greased pie plate. Add chilies, then remaining cheese. Mix egg and milk; pour over cheese. Bake at 350° for 30 minutes. Serve with tortilla chips or crackers.

APPETIZER PIE

About 40 Servings

1 pkg. (8 oz.) cream
  cheese, softened
2 T. milk
1 jar (2½ oz.) dried beef,
  finely snipped (¾ cup)
½ cup minced raw onion
  or 2 T. instant minced
  onion
2 T. finely chopped green
  pepper
⅛ tsp. ground pepper
½ cup sour cream
¼ cup coarsely chopped
  walnuts

Blend cream cheese and milk. Stir in beef, onion, green pepper, pepper, and sour cream. Spoon into 8-inch pie plate or small baking dish. Sprinkle walnuts on top. Bake at 350° for 15 to 20 minutes. Serve with crackers.

BASIC BLACK AND GOLD

3 Cups

1 cup ripe olives,
  coarsely chopped
8 oz. Cheddar cheese,
  grated
¼ cup mayonnaise
2 T. chopped onion
1 tsp. curry powder
½ tsp. garlic salt

Mix all ingredients. To serve hot, spread mixture on toast rounds; broil for 10 minutes. To serve cold, form into balls and roll in chopped parsley or sesame seeds. To serve as a dip, mix with an equal amount of sour cream.

MOTHER'S VEGETABLE SOUP

About 10 Cups

1 lb. ground beef
2 cans (16 oz. each)
  stewed tomatoes, plus
  1 can water
1 cup chopped onion
1 cup cubed potatoes
1 cup cut carrots
1 cup sliced mushrooms
½ cup diced celery
¼ cup long grain rice
1 bay leaf
½ tsp. thyme
¼ tsp. basil
¼ tsp. oregano
Salt and pepper to taste
Grated cheese

Brown ground beef in large saucepan. Pour off drippings. Add remaining ingredients, except cheese. Cover and cook until rice and vegetables are done. Serve topped with grated cheese.

POLISH FRESH MUSHROOM SOUP

6 Servings

½ lb. fresh mushrooms
3 T. butter
¼ tsp. caraway seeds
½ tsp. paprika
1 T. flour
4 cups chicken broth
1 egg yolk
1 cup sour cream
2 T. chopped fresh dill

Slice mushrooms. Saute in butter with caraway and paprika for 1 minute. Sprinkle with flour. Blend well. Add the chicken broth a little at a time. Simmer covered 30 minutes. Meanwhile, whip egg yolk with fork until creamy. Add sour cream and dill. Mix well. Pour hot soup into this mixture. Whisk it to mix thoroughly. Serve immediately.

SOUPS

CORN CHOWDER

About 8 Cups

Great use for leftover fresh corn

1 cup diced, pared
  potatoes
1 cup diced carrots
6 slices bacon
⅓ cup chopped onion
4 T. flour
1 tsp. salt
Dash pepper
3 cups milk
1 cup half and half
2 cups cooked fresh
  corn, cut from cob
Chopped parsley
  (optional)

Combine potatoes, carrots, and ½ cup water in saucepan. Cover and cook until tender, about 15 minutes. Cook bacon until crisp. Reserve drippings. Crumble bacon; set aside. Saute onion in 3 T. bacon drippings. Blend in flour, salt, and pepper. Blend in milk and half and half. Add potatoes, carrots, and their liquid. Cook and stir until smooth and slightly thickened. Add corn; heat through. Adjust seasonings. Serve in bowls with bacon and parsley sprinkled on top, if desired.

NO-FAT VEGETABLE SOUP

2 qts. water
8 pkgs. instant chicken
  bouillon
1 can (28 oz.) tomatoes
  with liquid
1 pkg. (10 oz.) frozen
  mixed vegetables
6 to 7 fresh or frozen
  okra, sliced
2 potatoes, peeled, diced
1 medium onion, chopped
¼ cup barley
1 bay leaf
1 tsp. salt
¼ tsp. pepper
Dash of hot pepper or
  sherry pepper sauce

Boil water and add bouillon. Add other ingredients, including any other vegetables desired. Cover and simmer 1 to 2 hours. Serve with additional pepper sauce, if desired.

SOUPS

OYSTER BISQUE

2 cans (10 oz. each)
  chicken and rice soup
½ cup soft bread crumbs
2 stalks celery
1 small onion, quartered
½ tsp. parsley flakes
1 bay leaf
2 tsp. salt
¼ tsp. pepper
2 cups oysters
  (measured without
  juice)
1 to 2 T. butter
2 T. flour
2 cups whole milk,
  scalded

Simmer undiluted chicken soup, bread crumbs, celery, onion, parsley flakes, bay leaf, salt, and pepper. If liquid is needed, rinse out can with clean water or oyster liquor. Put oysters in pan with 1 or 2 T. butter. Simmer 5 minutes, or until they are plump. Do not overcook. Remove bay leaf. Put all of the above through small blade grinder. Mix 2 T. flour with a little milk. Add to ground mixture. Add scalded milk to mixture and simmer 10 minutes longer. Do not boil.

HOT AND SOUR SOUP

6-8 Servings

4 cups chicken broth
½ cup water
¼ lb. pork shreds
1 T. soy sauce
4 Chinese dried
  mushrooms, soaked,
  sliced
½ cup bamboo shoot
  shreds
½ medium onion, sliced
  thin
Pepper
½ cup cider vinegar
1 tsp. hot oil
½ tsp. salt
3 T. cornstarch,
  dissolved in 3 T. water
1 egg, slightly beaten
½ tsp. sesame oil

Combine broth, water, pork, soy, mushrooms, bamboo shoots and onion. Boil. Reduce heat to low; skim off fat. Cover, simmer 3 minutes. Add pepper, vinegar, hot oil and salt; boil again. Gradually stir in cornstarch mixture; gently boil until soup is clear. Remove from heat and slowly beat in egg. Ladle into a preheated bowl and stir in sesame oil.

SOUPS

ITALIAN POTATO AND ONION SOUP   8-10 Servings

Best made ahead and reheated

2 lbs. boiling potatoes, pared, roughly chopped
1 small onion, chopped, (about ¼ cup)
¼ cup vegetable oil
3 T. butter
¼ cup finely chopped carrot
¼ cup finely chopped celery
2 cups milk or half and half
1 can (13 oz.) chicken broth
½ cup freshly grated Parmesan cheese
1 tsp. salt
3 T. chopped parsley

Put potatoes in large kettle with just enough water to cover. Bring to boiling. Lower heat; cover and cook until tender, about 20 minutes. Mash potatoes with their liquid through a food mill. Set aside. Saute onion in oil and butter until golden. Add carrot and celery; cook 2 to 3 minutes. Do not overcook; vegetables should remain crunchy. Add milk, broth, cheese, salt, and potatoes. Bring to boil; lower heat and cook 2 to 3 minutes, stirring constantly. Remove from heat; stir in chopped parsley. Serve with additional grated Parmesan cheese on the side. A food processor simplifies preparation.

CHICKEN AND KOHLRABI SOUP   6-8 Servings

1 frying chicken (3 lbs.)
2 onions, quartered
6 cups chicken broth
2 cups water
2 cups kohlrabi, cut into ½-inch cubes
2 T. butter
2 T. flour
Salt
2 T. finely chopped parsley
1 cup half and half

Combine chicken, onions, broth and water in soup kettle. Bring to boil. Cover, reduce heat, simmer for 40 minutes. Remove chicken and strain soup. Skim off fat. Add kohlrabi to soup and simmer 20 minutes until kohlrabi are tender. Meanwhile, remove chicken skin and bones. Dice chicken; return to soup. Melt butter in pan, whisk in flour and brown slightly. Slowly add ½ cup broth from soup. Cook to thicken, then whisk into pot. Simmer 10 minutes. Slowly add half and half and beat until warm. (Do not boil.) Sprinkle with chopped parsley.

PISTOU SOUPE

SOUP:

¾ cup dried navy beans
1 cup chopped onions
¼ cup olive oil
1 lb. fresh tomatoes, chopped
2 cans (10½ oz. each) beef broth
1½ cups diced carrots
1½ cups diced red potatoes
1 cup coarsely chopped leeks
½ cup coarsely chopped celery leaves
1 T. salt
Pepper
1½ cups sliced fresh green beans
1½ cups diced unpeeled zucchini
½ cup broken pieces spaghetti
2 pinches crumbled saffron thread
¾ to 1 lb. shredded corned beef or ham

PISTOU:

5 cloves garlic
5 T. dried basil
2 T. tomato paste
½ cup grated Parmesan cheese
6 T. olive oil

Bring navy beans and 3 cups water to boil; boil 2 minutes. Remove from heat; let beans soak 1 hour. Return to heat and simmer covered for 1 to 1½ hours, or until tender. Drain, reserving liquid. In soup pot, saute onions in olive oil until golden. Add tomatoes with liquid; cook 3 or 4 minutes. Add 3 qts. water, beef broth, carrots, potatoes, leeks, celery leaves, salt, and a few grindings of pepper. Heat to boiling; reduce heat and simmer, uncovered for 15 minutes. Stir in navy beans, their liquid, green beans, zucchini, spaghetti, and saffron. Simmer for 15 minutes or until vegetables are tender. Add meat. Prepare the pistou. In food processor chop garlic; add basil, tomato paste and cheese. Blend together. Slowly blend in olive oil. Thin pistou with 1 cup soup stock, then stir it into soup. Serve with additional grated Parmesan cheese.

BREADS

YEAST ROLLS

3 2 Dinner Rolls

Very buttery flavor

1 ¼ cups milk
2 pkgs. dry yeast
½ tsp. sugar
8 T. butter, melted
3 eggs, slightly beaten
½ cup sugar
6 to 7 cups flour, sifted
1 ½ tsp. salt

In a small saucepan, scald ¼ cup of milk and cool to lukewarm. Sprinkle yeast and ½ tsp. sugar over milk. Dissolve and let stand until mixture is foamy. Mix butter, eggs, milk and sugar. Add yeast mixture. Sift flour and salt. Add 6 cups to liquid mixture and mix well. Add additional flour as needed until dough is still soft but not sticky. Place in large bowl; cover with plastic wrap and dish towel. Secure with rubber band. Refrigerate overnight. Divide into quarters. On well-floured board, roll each quarter into 12-inch circle. Brush with melted butter. Cut into eighths. Starting at large end, roll into crescent-shaped rolls. Place on ungreased cookie sheet; leave several inches between each roll to allow for rising. Let rise 3 to 4 hours. Bake at 425° for 5 to 7 minutes. Remove to racks. Serve warm. May be frozen.

PERFECT WHOLE WHEAT PANCAKES

6 Medium Pancakes

1 cup whole wheat flour
1 tsp. baking powder
½ tsp. salt
1 egg
2 T. oil
2 T. honey
¾ cup milk

Combine whole wheat flour, baking powder and salt. Blend egg, oil, honey and milk. Add to flour mixture just before cooking. More milk may be added if a thinner batter is desired. Bake on hot griddle, turning once. Beware of burning.

BREADS

SWEET POTATO MUFFINS

From Christiana Campbell's Tavern in Williamsburg

1¼ cups sugar
1¼ cups cooked mashed
    sweet potatoes (can
    use canned)
½ cup butter, at room
    temperature
2 large eggs, at room
    temperature
1½ cups flour
2 tsp. baking powder
1 tsp. cinnamon
1 tsp. allspice
¼ tsp. nutmeg
¼ tsp. salt
1 cup milk
½ cup chopped raisins
¼ cup chopped pecans
2 T. sugar mixed with ¼
    tsp. cinnamon

Grease 24 muffin cups. Beat sugar, sweet potatoes and butter together until smooth; add eggs and blend well. Sift together flour, baking powder, spices and salt. Add alternately with milk to sweet potato mixture, stirring only until blended. Do not overwork. Fold in raisins and nuts. Spoon into muffin tins and sprinkle with cinnamon/sugar mixture. Bake at 400° for 25 to 30 minutes or until done.

FRESH APPLE POUND CAKE

3 cups flour
1 tsp. soda
1 tsp. salt
1½ cups corn oil
2 cups sugar
3 eggs
2 tsp. vanilla
2 cups finely chopped
    pared apple
1 cup chopped nuts

GLAZE:

½ cup butter
½ cup brown sugar
2 tsp. milk

Grease and flour 10-inch bundt pan. Stir together flour, soda and salt. In large bowl, beat together oil, sugar, eggs and vanilla until combined. Gradually beat flour mixture into oil mixture until smooth. Fold in apples and nuts. Turn into prepared pan. Bake at 350° for 60 to 80 minutes. Place pan on rack to cool. Place butter, sugar and milk in small pan. Bring to boil; stir constantly for 2 minutes. Place slightly warm cake on plate and spoon on glaze. Store in tightly covered container.

BREADS

PRETZELS WITH PERSONALITY

About 2 Dozen

½ cup warm water
1 pkg. dry yeast
1 cup milk
¼ cup honey or sugar
¼ cup butter, softened
1 egg, separated
1 tsp. table salt
5 cups flour
Coarse salt

Place warm water in a bowl. Sprinkle on yeast; stir until dissolved. Add milk, honey, butter, and egg yolk to yeast. Add table salt and enough flour to make stiff dough. Knead on a floured surface for 5 minutes. Let rise in warm place about 1 hour. Then cut into strips about 1 inch wide and 4 to 6 inches long. Fold each strip in ½ and roll into a rope. Shape ropes into pretzels, letters, or other shapes. Beat 1 T. water into egg white, brush over pretzels. Sprinkle each with coarse salt. Bake at 425°, about 15 to 20 minutes, or until golden brown.

APPLETTES

1 Dozen

⅓ cup butter
½ cup sugar
1 egg
1½ cups flour
2 tsp. baking powder
½ tsp. nutmeg
½ tsp. salt
⅓ cup milk
1½ cups peeled, shredded
   tart apples

Cream butter and sugar. Add egg and beat well. Sift flour, baking powder, nutmeg and salt. Add sifted ingredients to creamed mixture alternately with milk. Stir in shredded apples. Bake at 400° for 20 to 25 minutes in well-greased muffin tins. Cool on rack for 10 minutes. Dip muffin tops in melted butter, then cinnamon/sugar mixture.

TOPPING:

6 T. butter, melted
¾ cup sugar combined
   with 1 heaping tsp.
   cinnamon

3-2-1 BREAD

1 Loaf

Best when fresh from oven

3 cups self-rising flour,
   sifted
2 T. sugar
1 can (12 oz.) beer, room
   temperature

Mix ingredients for 1 minute. Place in buttered loaf pan. Bake at 350° for about 65 to 75 minutes.

BREADS

APRICOT-BANANA NUT BREAD   1 Loaf

2 cups flour
1 tsp. baking powder
½ tsp. baking soda
½ tsp. salt
½ cup dried apricots,
  chopped
½ cup chopped walnuts
¼ cup butter, softened
1 cup sugar
1 egg
¾ cup mashed bananas
  (1½ large)
½ cup milk

Sift together flour, baking powder, baking soda and salt. Stir in apricots and nuts. Set aside. Cream butter and sugar. Beat in egg. Add mashed bananas. Add dry ingredients alternately with milk to butter mixture, stirring just until blended. Place dough in a greased 9 x 5-inch loaf pan. Bake at 350° for about 1¼ hours. Cool before slicing.

CARROT PECAN BREAD   1 Loaf

1 cup sugar
¾ cup oil
1½ cups flour
1 tsp. soda
¼ tsp. salt
1 tsp. baking powder
1 tsp. cinnamon
2 eggs
1 cup grated carrots
½ cup chopped pecans

Blend sugar and oil. Add sifted dry ingredients. Add eggs 1 at a time. Fold in carrots and pecans. Grease and flour a loaf pan or line with waxed paper. Bake at 350° for 50 minutes. Remove from pan immediately.

FOOD PROCESSOR BANANA WALNUT BREAD   1 Loaf
Quick version of old favorite

¾ tsp. baking powder
1 tsp. baking soda
¼ tsp. salt
1 cup walnut meats
1⅓ cups flour
⅔ cup sugar
1 tsp. lemon juice
6 T. butter, cut into 6
  pieces
2 eggs
1¼ cups peeled bananas,
  about 3 large

Using metal blade, process baking powder, baking soda, salt, nuts and flour until nuts are coarsely chopped. Set aside. Process sugar, lemon juice, butter and eggs with metal blade for about 20 seconds. Scrape down sides of bowl. Add banana, process for 5 seconds. Add flour mixture. Turn machine on and off 4 to 5 times, just until flour is incorporated. Do not overmix. Bake in a buttered 9 x 5 loaf pan at 350° for 1 hour or until cake tester comes out clean.

LUNCHEON DISHES

MACARONI PIE WITH SHRIMP SAUCE 6 Servings

For ladies' luncheon

2 cups hot milk
1 cup soft bread cubes
¼ cup butter
1 cup cooked tiny macaroni rings (½ cup uncooked)
½ tsp. salt
Pepper to taste
1 T. chopped parsley
1 T. sliced green onions
2 T. finely chopped green pepper
2 T. chopped pimiento (optional)
1 T. grated horseradish
1 cup shredded Cheddar cheese
3 eggs, beaten

SHRIMP SAUCE:

¼ cup butter
5 T. flour
1½ cups milk
2 cups cooked shrimp

Pour milk over bread and butter; stir until butter is melted. Add macaroni, salt, pepper, parsley, onion, green pepper, pimiento, horseradish, cheese, and eggs. Pour in 8 x 8-inch baking dish and bake at 350° for 45 minutes. Cut into squares.

For sauce, melt butter in saucepan; add flour, stir to blend. Add milk; cook and stir until thickened. Add shrimp. Heat through; season to taste. Pour sauce over each serving.

MONTE CRISTO SANDWICHES

Good with a spiced peach salad

Sliced turkey
Sliced Swiss cheese
Sliced ham
Bread
2 eggs, beaten
1⅓ cups water
1½ cups flour
1 T. baking powder
¼ tsp. salt

Make sandwiches with turkey, Swiss cheese, and ham layered. Cut into fourths. Secure with toothpicks. Combine eggs and water. Sift dry ingredients; add to egg mixture. Mix well. Flip sandwiches into batter, coating completely. Deep fry in oil (360-375°) until golden. Sprinkle with confectioners' sugar, if desired. Serve immediately.

LUNCHEON DISHES

DUCK SALAD

3 cups julienned roast
  duck
1 small Bermuda onion,
  thinly sliced
½ cup Lemon Dressing
Grated rind of 1 orange
1 T. butter
¼ tsp. garlic salt
¼ cup coarsely chopped
  walnuts
3 medium oranges,
  peeled and thinly sliced
Lettuce leaves

LEMON DRESSING:

½ tsp. dry mustard
3 T. lemon juice
¼ tsp. salt
Pepper
6 T. olive oil

Combine duck and onion. Pour dressing and orange rind over duck; toss. Cover and refrigerate 2 hours. Heat butter in skillet over moderate heat. Add garlic salt and walnuts. Saute until golden brown. Combine oranges and duck; toss gently. Serve on bed of lettuce and sprinkle with nuts.

For dressing, combine all ingredients and mix in blender.

HOT CHICKEN SALAD

Colorful luncheon entree

3 cups diced cooked
  chicken
2 cups sliced celery
½ cup slivered almonds,
  toasted
½ cup sliced water
  chestnuts
¼ cup chopped pimiento
1 cup mayonnaise
½ cup sour cream
3 T. lemon juice
2 T. grated onion
½ tsp. salt
¼ tsp. pepper
1 cup Chinese noodles or
  French fried onion rings
½ cup grated Cheddar
  cheese

Mix chicken, celery, almonds, water chestnuts, and pimiento. In separate bowl, blend mayonnaise, sour cream, lemon juice, onion, salt and pepper. Mix with chicken mixture. Adjust seasonings. Pour into buttered 2-qt. casserole; top with noodles and cheese. Bake at 350° for 30 minutes.

LUNCHEON DISHES

CHAMPIGNONS EN COCOTTE   6 Servings
Delicious brunch dish

6 T. butter
1½ lbs. mushrooms, finely
    chopped
Salt
Freshly ground black
    pepper
Juice of ½ lemon
2 T. flour
1 cup milk
Freshly ground nutmeg
3 whole eggs
1 cup grated Swiss
    cheese
6 T. dry bread crumbs

Medium-Dry White

Melt 4 T. butter in a heavy skillet; add mushrooms, salt and pepper to taste and lemon juice. Cook over medium heat, stirring occasionally, until liquid has evaporated. Spoon into 6 individual ramekins. Melt remaining butter; stir in flour and add milk. Beat until smooth; season with salt, pepper and nutmeg. Simmer for 10 minutes. Beat eggs slightly. Add a bit of the hot white sauce to the eggs; combine, beating well. (It may be prepared in advance to this point. Cover the sauce tightly.) When ready to serve, heat sauce over medium heat and stir in ¾ cup of grated Swiss cheese. Spoon equal amounts of sauce into each ramekin. Sprinkle bread crumbs on the top of each and the remaining grated cheese. Place on a baking sheet in a 400° oven for about 15 minutes or until golden and bubbling. Serve immediately.

SUPER SANDWICHES   6 Servings

6 slices each: white,
    whole wheat, and
    pumpernickel bread
Softened butter
12 thin slices salami
⅔ cup coleslaw
6 slices bologna
12 thin slices of tomato
2 cups shredded Cheddar
    cheese
1 egg, beaten
¼ cup mayonnaise
2 T. pickle relish, drained
1 T. prepared mustard

Rose

Toast bread. Lightly butter 1 side of each slice of bread. On whole wheat place 2 slices salami, top with coleslaw. Cover with white toast buttered side up. Top with 1 slice of bologna and 2 tomato slices. Top with pumpernickel toast, buttered side down. Combine cheese, egg, mayonnaise, pickle relish, and mustard. Spread mixture on top of sandwiches. Heat under broiler until bubbly and golden brown. Let stand 1 to 2 minutes before serving.

LUNCHEON DISHES

CHICKEN LIVERS IN ONION CREPES   6-8 Crepes

CREPES:
1½ cups flour
½ tsp. salt
2 cups milk
3 eggs
1 T. butter, melted
¼ cup grated onion

CHICKEN LIVER FILLING:
4 to 6 T. butter
1 lb. chicken livers
1 T. finely chopped onion
2 T. dry sherry
Juice of ½ lemon
Salt to taste
1 cup bearnaise sauce

Medium-Bodied Red

To make crepes, blend flour, salt, milk, eggs, and butter in blender until smooth. Let rest 1 hour, then stir in onion. Cook crepes. Leftover batter can be frozen.

To make filling, melt butter in skillet. Saute livers and onions; add sherry and lemon juice. Cook for 5 minutes, stirring frequently. Season with salt. Chop liver into smaller pieces. Spread crepes with liver mixture and place in buttered baking dish. Pour bearnaise sauce over them and place under broiler until golden.

CURRIED EGG CASSEROLE   9 Servings

2 medium onions, minced
1 clove garlic, minced
1 piece fresh ginger, sliced
3 T. butter
1 T. curry powder
3 T. flour
2 cups chicken broth
3 cups milk
1 cup seedless raisins, soaked in tepid water, drained
1 small apple, peeled, cored and chopped
Juice of ½ lemon
1 strip lemon peel
18 hard-cooked eggs, peeled, sliced
1 pkg. English muffins
Chopped parsley

Medium-Dry White

Saute onions, garlic and ginger in butter until lightly browned. Stir in curry powder (use more, if you like a hotter curry); cook for a minute or two. Mix in flour; cook for a minute longer. Gradually add chicken broth and milk, which have been heated together. Stir and simmer until smooth. Strain into a double boiler. Add raisins, apple, lemon juice, and peel. Cook slowly over hot water for 10 minutes; then add seasoning to taste. Add eggs to curry sauce. Serve on English muffins. Sprinkle with parsley.

LUNCHEON DISHES

ARMENIAN PINWHEEL SANDWICHES   4-6 Servings

Tailgate picnic fare

1 round (14-inch) cracker bread for each sandwich, (available at specialty stores)

Medium-Dry White or Beer

Moisten bread by holding it under a gentle spray of cold water for about 10 seconds on each side or until well moistened. Place between clean damp towels (rounds may be stacked). Let stand until soft and pliable, about 1 hour. Check often; if bread still seems crisp in spots, sprinkle with additional water. Use 1 or more of the following fillings. Fill as directed, then roll up tightly and cover with damp paper towels. Wrap tightly in plastic wrap and chill until serving time. To serve, cut with a serrated knife into 12 slices. These may be made up to 2 hours ahead.

ROAST BEEF WITH HORSERADISH FILLING

1 pkg. (3 oz.) cream cheese
1 T. prepared horseradish
¼ tsp. pepper
1 T. milk (about)
⅓ to ½ lb. thinly sliced roast beef
1 cup alfalfa sprouts
2 medium tomatoes, cut in paper-thin slices

Beat cream cheese until light and fluffy. Stir in horseradish, pepper and enough milk for cheese to spread easily. Spread prepared cracker bread with the cheese; top with roast beef, alfalfa sprouts, and tomato slices. Roll and store as directed.

SMOKED SALMON WITH HORSERADISH FILLING

1 pkg. (3 oz.) cream cheese
1 T. prepared horseradish
¼ tsp. pepper
1 T. milk or cream
⅓ lb. thinly sliced smoked salmon
1 tsp. dill
1 cup loosely packed watercress leaves

Beat cream cheese until light and fluffy. Stir in horseradish, pepper and enough milk for cheese to spread easily. Spread prepared cracker bread with the cheese; top with smoked salmon. Sprinkle with dill and top with watercress. Roll and store as directed.

LUNCHEON DISHES

CURRIED CHICKEN FILLING

¾ lb. cooked, boned chicken
½ cup thinly sliced green onions
½ cup chopped green pepper
½ cup mayonnaise
1 T. lemon juice
1 tsp. curry powder
½ cup chopped peanuts
1 cup alfalfa sprouts or shredded lettuce

Chop chicken; combine with onions, pepper, mayonnaise, lemon juice, and curry. Spread mixture on prepared cracker bread. Sprinkle with peanuts and alfalfa sprouts. Roll and store as directed.

EGG SALAD FILLING

6 to 8 slices bacon, cooked
6 hard-cooked eggs
½ cup thinly sliced green onion
1 T. Dijon mustard
1 T. white vinegar
½ tsp. pepper
⅓ cup mayonnaise
Salt to taste
1 cup watercress leaves

Cook bacon; drain, crumble and set aside. Chop eggs and combine with onion, mustard, vinegar, pepper and mayonnaise. Season with salt. Spread egg salad on prepared cracker bread; top with watercress. Roll and store as directed.

TUNA FILLING

1 can (9¼ oz.) tuna, drained
⅓ cup thinly sliced green onions
⅓ cup thinly sliced green pepper (optional)
⅓ cup mayonnaise
⅓ cup chutney
1 cup shredded lettuce or alfalfa sprouts

Combine all ingredients except lettuce. Spread on prepared cracker bread. Top with lettuce. Roll and store as directed.

LUNCHEON DISHES

HANGTOWN FRY

4 Servings

Originated in California during the gold rush

½ pt. shucked oysters, reserve liquid
6 T. butter
2 T. Wondra flour
1 egg, beaten with 1 tsp. water
½ to ¾ cup fresh bread crumbs
2 tsp. freshly minced parsley
4 to 6 eggs, lightly beaten
1 T. milk or cream per egg
4 lettuce leaves, washed and dried
4 strips crisp bacon
¾ cup Super Chili Sauce

Dry oysters on paper towels. Melt butter in skillet. Dip oysters in flour, egg, then bread crumbs mixed with the parsley. Saute coated oysters in melted butter for a minute or 2 over medium heat until crust forms. Mix beaten eggs, oyster liquid, and milk or cream together. When oysters are crispy on both sides, add 3 T. more butter and allow to sizzle. Pour in egg mixture — scramble with the oysters. Salt and pepper to taste. Turn onto a lettuce-lined plate. Serve with bacon and chili sauce. This dish is often served with fried onions.

Light Dry White

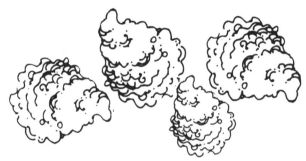

SUPER CHILI SAUCE

¾ Cup

1 T. minced celery
½ T. minced shallots or green onions
1 tsp. Worcestershire sauce
½ tsp. hot mustard
½ tsp. lemon juice
Dash hot pepper sauce, celery salt, garlic salt
½ cup chili sauce
2 tsp. minced fresh parsley

Mix together and refrigerate for at least 30 minutes.

LUNCHEON DISHES

BOSTON BAKED BEANS   6-8 Servings

1 lb. dried pea beans or
   navy beans
1 celery stalk, cut in ½
1 bay leaf
1 sprig parsley
½ tsp. thyme
¼ lb. salt pork
⅔ cup unsulphured
   molasses
¼ cup brown sugar
2 tsp. dry mustard
2 tsp. salt
¼ tsp. black pepper
1 medium onion, coarsely
   chopped
1 cup sherry

Soak beans overnight in cold water to cover. Drain beans, then cover with fresh water. Tie celery, bay leaf, parsley, and thyme in a bundle. Add to kettle. Bring to a boil; reduce heat and simmer slowly 30 to 60 minutes, or until bean skins burst when blown upon lightly. Drain beans, reserving cooking liquid. Slice salt pork into ¼-inch slices. Arrange beans and ½ the sliced pork in alternate layers in a 2-qt. pot or casserole. Score remaining pork; and place in center of the top layer of beans. Combine molasses, brown sugar, mustard, salt, pepper, onion, and 2 cups of cooking liquid. Pour over the beans. Bake, covered, at 300° for 6 to 8 hours, adding reserved cooking liquid as needed. One hour before beans are done. Pour sherry over them. Cover and bake 1 hour longer. Serve with No-Yeast Raisin Bread.

NO-YEAST RAISIN BREAD   2 Loaves

Enjoy this spread with cream cheese

2 cups seedless raisins
2 tsp. baking soda
2 cups boiling water
1½ cups brown sugar
2 T. vegetable shortening
2 eggs
¾ tsp. salt
3¼ cups sifted flour

Toss raisins and soda in a bowl. Cover with boiling water. Cool. Cream sugar, shortening, eggs and salt until fluffy. Add flour, combining well. Add cooled raisin mixture, mix until well blended. Place in 2 buttered loaf pans. Bake at 350° for 50 to 60 minutes or until toothpick comes out clean. Cool on rack.

197

ENTREES: MEATS

TOURNEDOS ROSSINI

2 Servings

2 tournedos of beef (filet mignons; 5 oz. each)
3 T. butter
Salt, pepper
½ cup Madeira wine
½ cup brown sauce
1 oz. truffles, chopped
2 fresh mushroom caps
2 oz. puree of foie gras
2 slices (½-inch thick) French bread, buttered, toasted

Saute tournedos in butter about 4 minutes on each side, longer if preferred medium. Remove meat; season to taste and keep warm. Add Madeira, brown sauce, truffles, and mushroom caps. Cook and stir 3 minutes. Spread foie gras on buttered French bread; place tournedos on bread; top with mushroom caps. Pour brown sauce over all. To prepare brown sauce, use standard French recipe.

Medium-Bodied Red

ELEGANT BEEF ROLLS

4 Servings

½ lb. ground pork
1 small onion, finely chopped
⅓ cup sliced mushrooms
Pinch rosemary
½ tsp. salt
¼ tsp. pepper
1 lb. round steak, ½ inch thick
Flour
2 T. oil
2 carrots, cut into 1-inch pieces
1 onion, stuck with 2 cloves
¾ cup Italian salad dressing plus ¼ cup rose wine
½ cup whipping cream
Cooked buttered noodles

Combine pork, onion, mushrooms, rosemary, salt, and pepper. Pound round steak to ¼-inch thickness and divide into four pieces. Place equal amounts of pork mixture on each piece. Roll up, tie with string, or secure with skewers. Coat each beef roll or "bird" with flour. In large skillet brown birds in hot oil. Add carrots, onion, and ½ cup of salad dressing mixture. Cover and simmer about 1½ hours, or until meat is tender. Place birds on platter, remove strings or skewers and keep warm. Strain cooking liquid; skim excess fat. Pour into skillet, add remaining dressing and cream. Heat through. Toss with hot buttered noodles. Place birds on top and serve.

Medium-Bodied Red

ENTREES: MEATS

VIENNA STEAKS

6 Servings

4 slices bacon, chopped
2 lbs. beef top round
  steak, about ½ inch
  thick
Flour, salt, pepper
1½ cups chopped onion
½ cup chopped carrot
1 clove garlic, minced
3 T. flour
3 cups beef broth
¼ cup white wine vinegar
2 T. minced parsley
3 bay leaves
⅛ tsp. thyme
⅛ tsp. allspice
1 thin strip lemon peel
¾ cup whipping cream
1 tsp. lemon juice

Saute bacon in large heavy skillet until cooked but not browned. Remove bacon and set aside. Cut beef into 6 serving pieces. Dredge in mixture of flour, salt, and pepper to taste. Brown meat in bacon fat on both sides. Remove meat. Add onion, carrot, and garlic. Saute, adding oil if needed. Stir in 3 T. flour. Add bacon and remaining ingredients, except cream and lemon juice. Return meat to skillet. Cover and simmer for 1 to 1½ hours, or until tender. Transfer meat to platter; keep warm. Strain liquid in skillet; add cream and lemon juice. Adjust seasonings. Serve over meat and accompanying potatoes or noodles.

Full-Bodied Red

STEAK TACOS

6 Tacos

1 lb. boneless beef
  (chuck, round, sirloin)
1 onion, chopped
2 T. olive oil
1 clove garlic, minced
½ green pepper, diced
⅛ tsp. ground cumin
½ tsp. salt
½ tsp. chili powder
5 T. tomato sauce
2 T. golden raisins
  (optional)
6 taco shells
½ cup shredded lettuce
½ cup shredded Cheddar
  cheese
1 container frozen
  guacamole, thawed (or
  homemade)

Cut meat in very thin strips, diagonal to the grain. Saute onions in oil. Add meat, garlic, green pepper, seasonings, tomato sauce and raisins. Simmer for ½ hour. Heat taco shells for 5 minutes. Grate lettuce and cheese. Stuff shells with meat mixture. Garnish with lettuce, cheese, and a spoonful of guacamole.

Light-Bodied Red

ENTREES: MEATS

SWEDISH MEATBALLS IN SOUR CREAM SAUCE

8 Servings

2 lbs. ground beef (or mixture of pork and beef)
2 cups soft white bread crumbs
3 T. finely chopped onion
2 tsp. salt
1 tsp. nutmeg
2 T. butter, softened
2 cups beef broth
1 lb. fresh mushrooms, quartered, sauteed
1 cup red wine
1 carton (16 oz.) sour cream
Buttered noodles

Mix beef, bread crumbs, onions, salt, nutmeg, and softened butter. Form into balls about 1½ inches in diameter. Bake at 350° about 15 to 20 minutes, until browned. Add beef broth, cover pan tightly with foil. Continue baking about 30 minutes, or until done. Remove meatballs and keep warm. Skim off fat; boil liquid to reduce by ½. Add mushrooms, wine, and meatballs. Simmer 5 minutes. Stir in sour cream. Heat through, but do not boil. Adjust seasonings. Serve over buttered noodles.

Light-Bodied Red

STIFADO (GREEK STEW WITH ONIONS)

6-8 Servings

¼ cup butter, melted
3 lbs. lean beef stew meat, cut in 1½-inch pieces
Salt and pepper to taste
1 to 2 bay leaves
3 lbs. pearl onions, peeled (or frozen onions, thawed)
2 T. allspice
1 stick cinnamon
1 can (6 oz.) tomato paste
2 T. brown sugar
2 T. vinegar
2 T. water

Melt butter in large casserole. Add beef. Sprinkle with salt and pepper. Place bay leaves on top of beef; top with onions. Tie allspice and cinnamon in cheesecloth. Bury in center of meat. Mix tomato paste, brown sugar, vinegar, and water. Pour over meat and onions. Cover and bake at 300° for about 3 hours. Serve with rice and Greek salad. Best made a day ahead and reheated. Do not freeze.

Full-Bodied Red

ENTREES: MEATS

RUSSIAN KULEBIAKA

Satisfies hearty appetites

BREAD:

2 pkgs. (13¼ oz. each) hot roll mix
1 cup lukewarm water
5 eggs

MEAT FILLING:

2 lbs. ground beef
1 cup chopped onion
½ lb. fresh mushrooms, sliced
Butter
4 cups cooked rice
1½ cups thick white sauce
4 eggs, hard cooked, chopped
½ cup chopped parsley
Salt, pepper

SAUCE:

½ cup butter
½ lb. fresh mushrooms, sliced
½ cup flour
3 cups milk
1 pt. (16 oz.) sour cream (2 cups)
2 T. tomato paste (optional)
1 T. dill
Salt, pepper

Medium-Bodied Red

For bread, mix yeast from roll mix with the water. Stir in 4 eggs, beaten. Stir in flour mixture. Turn out onto floured surface; knead for 5 minutes. Place in greased bowl. Cover and let rise in warm place until doubled in bulk.

For filling, brown ground beef and onion; pour off drippings. Saute mushrooms in butter. Combine beef, onion, mushrooms, rice, white sauce, chopped eggs, parsley, salt and pepper to taste.

To assemble, roll dough into a rectangle about 18 x 14 inches, reserving a piece the size of a small apple. Place rectangle of dough on cookie sheet. Pile filling down center of dough lengthwise. Fold over 1 long side. Beat remaining egg; brush a little on dough. Fold over other side, stretching to cover top and side. Tuck ends under. Brush all with egg. Decorate as desired with reserved dough; brush with egg. Let rise 30 minutes. Bake at 350° about 1 hour, or until golden brown.

For sauce, melt butter; saute mushrooms. Stir in flour. Gradually stir in milk. Cook, stirring constantly, until very thick and bubbly. Stir in sour cream, tomato paste, dill, and salt and pepper to taste. Heat through, but do not boil. Place Kulebiaka on large platter; garnish with parsley. Cut in thick slices at the table; serve with sauce.

ENTREES: MEAT

SPICY BEEF RIBS

4 Servings

6 T. butter, softened
1 T. Worcestershire
  sauce
2 tsp. curry powder
1 tsp. dry mustard
½ to 1 tsp. freshly ground
  pepper
¼ tsp. cayenne pepper
1 tsp. salt
2½ to 3 lbs. lean beef
  back ribs
½ cup flour

Light-Bodied Red

Coat roasting pan with 2 T. butter. Cream remaining butter; slowly add Worcestershire sauce, curry, mustard, black pepper, cayenne, and ½ tsp. of salt. Coat ribs with flour; shake off excess. Sprinkle with remaining salt. Arrange, fat side up, in pan. Roast at 450° for 10 minutes. With pastry brush, coat ribs with butter mixture. Reduce heat to 400° and cook for 30 to 35 minutes, until tender.

BEEF BARCELONA

18 Servings

9 medium onions, sliced
6 green peppers,
  chopped
3 cloves garlic, minced
6 lbs. boneless beef
  round, cut in 1½-inch
  pieces
Flour, salt, and pepper
3 cans (28 oz. each)
  tomatoes
1½ tsp. sugar
1½ cups red wine
11 oz. stuffed olives

Light-Bodied Red

In large skillet, saute onions, green peppers, and garlic in oil; set aside. Dredge beef in mixture of flour, salt, and pepper to taste. Brown in same skillet, adding more oil, if needed. Place meat and onion mixture in large roasting pan with lid. Add liquid from tomatoes and sugar. Cover and bake at 350° for 1 hour. Add wine and tomatoes, broken up. Cover and bake 1 hour more, or until tender. Stir in olives. Thicken liquid, if desired. Serve over rice. May be made the day before and reheated.

ENTREES: MEAT

REUBEN, REUBEN

12 Servings

12 slices medium thick
  rye bread
½ cup butter
1 T. horseradish
½ tsp. dry mustard
1 lb. cooked corned beef
1 large dill pickle
½ lb. Swiss cheese
1½ cups sauerkraut
2 tsp. sugar
6 eggs
3 cups milk
2 T. prepared mustard
Pinch of cayenne pepper

Beer

Butter a 9 x 13 baking dish. Cut crusts from bread. Cream butter, horseradish and dry mustard; spread generously on both sides of bread. Chop corned beef and pickle; grate cheese. Combine sauerkraut and sugar. Layer baking dish with ½ each of the bread, beef, pickles, cheese and sauerkraut. Repeat. Mix eggs, milk, prepared mustard and cayenne. Pour over beef mixture to cover. Let stand 3 to 4 hours or overnight. Bring to room temperature and bake in 350° oven 30 to 45 minutes. Cut and serve. This may be doubled, cooked, frozen and reheated.

SPAGHETTI PIES

12 Servings

12 oz. spaghetti
½ cup butter
1 cup freshly grated
  Parmesan cheese
3 eggs, well beaten
2½ lbs. ground beef
1 cup finely chopped
  onion
2 cans (15 oz. each)
  tomato sauce
2 cans (6 oz. each)
  tomato paste
2 tsp. sugar
⅓ cup water
1 T. oregano
Garlic salt
Basil
Salt
2 cups sour cream
8 oz. shredded
  mozzarella cheese

Light-Bodied Red

Cook spaghetti al dente, drain. Stir in butter, Parmesan cheese, and eggs. Chop well with knife and fork; form into a "crust" in 2 buttered 10-inch pie tins. Let cool.

Cook ground beef and onion; drain off fat. Stir in tomato sauce and paste, sugar, water, and other seasonings. Heat through. Spread sour cream on bottom of spaghetti "crusts." Fill pies with meat sauce. Cover with mozzarella. Bake at 350° for 30 minutes. May be frozen.

ENTREES: MEAT

VEAL PARMESAN

VEAL:

6 to 8 slices veal (about 4 oz. each)
3 eggs, beaten
1 cup fine bread crumbs
¼ cup butter
12 oz. Mozzarella cheese, sliced
½ cup grated Parmesan cheese

TOMATO SAUCE:

½ cup chopped onion
1 clove garlic, minced
2 T. butter
1 can (29 oz.) Italian-style tomatoes
2 T. sugar
½ tsp. basil
½ tsp. oregano
½ tsp. salt
¼ tsp. pepper

Medium-Bodied Red

Pound veal slices very thin. Dip veal in egg, then in crumbs to coat. Brown on both sides in hot butter. Place in large shallow casserole. Spread with a scant ½ of sauce. Top with ½ of cheese slices. Spread with remaining sauce, after setting aside a little. Top with remaining cheese slices. Spoon on the reserved sauce. Sprinkle with Parmesan cheese. Bake at 350° for 20 minutes, or until bubbly and cheese is melting. For tomato sauce, saute onion and garlic in butter. Add remaining ingredients; mash tomatoes with fork. Heat to boiling; reduce heat and simmer for 10 minutes.

PORK ROAST WITH CURRANT SAUCE

½ cup soy sauce
½ cup sherry
2 cloves garlic, minced
1 T. dry mustard
1 tsp. ground ginger
1 tsp. dried thyme, crushed
4 to 5 lb. pork roast, boned, rolled and tied

CURRANT SAUCE:

1 jar (10 oz.) currant jelly
2 T. sherry
1 T. soy sauce

Medium-Dry White

Marinate pork roast in first 6 ingredients by placing in a plastic bag for 24 hours. Roast, uncovered, at 325° for 2½ to 3 hours or until meat thermometer registers 170°. For sauce, heat currant jelly until melted. Add sherry and soy sauce. Serve over pork roast.

ENTREES: MEAT

ROAST LOIN OF PORK ST. CLOUD

8-10 Servings

1 center-cut pork loin
   roast (4 to 5 lbs.)
2 cloves garlic, slivered
Salt, pepper
2 T. butter, melted
1 cup dry white wine
1 cup chunky applesauce
2 medium apples,
   unpeeled, thinly sliced
¼ cup brown sugar
½ cup whipping cream

Light Dry White

Cut small gashes in meat; insert a garlic sliver in each gash. Rub meat with salt and pepper. Place, fat side up, in roasting pan. Roast at 450° for 30 minutes. Mix butter and wine with pan juices. Continue roasting for 30 minutes, basting 2 or 3 times. Reduce heat to 350°. Roast and baste for 1 hour or until meat thermometer registers 170°. Allow 30 to 35 minutes per pound. When meat is almost done, remove from oven. Pour off ¾ of fat. Spread meat with applesauce. Mix apple slices with brown sugar; arrange around meat. Continue baking until apples are tender. Transfer meat to platter. Add cream to roasting pan; cook with apples and pan juices for 5 minutes. Pour sauce over slices of roast.

CARAWAY PORK WITH SAUERKRAUT

6-7 Servings

Casual supper for a cold evening

1 lb. boneless pork
   shoulder, cubed
1 T. cooking oil
1 medium onion, sliced
2 cans (16 oz. each)
   sauerkraut, rinsed,
   drained
1 can (16 oz.) tomatoes,
   undrained, broken up
3 medium potatoes, cut in
   chunks
½ lb. Polish sausage,
   sliced on diagonal
¼ cup Madeira or sherry
2 tsp. caraway seeds
½ tsp. salt
¼ tsp. pepper
1 T. cornstarch

Beer

Brown pork cubes in oil; add onion slices. Cook slowly until softened. Add remaining ingredients except cornstarch. Cover and simmer for 2 hours, or until potatoes are tender. Transfer to serving dish with slotted spoon. Thicken cooking liquid with cornstarch mixed with a little water. Stir into meat-kraut mixture.

ENTREES: MEAT

PORK TENDERLOIN SCALOPPINE　　　4-6 Servings

1½ lbs. pork tenderloin,
  thinly sliced
½ cup flour
2 T. oil
2 T. butter
½ cup sherry
½ cup water
½ cup chopped green
  onion
1 clove garlic, minced or
  mashed
1 tsp. salt
¼ tsp. thyme
¼ tsp. rosemary
¼ tsp. oregano
⅛ tsp. pepper
½ lb. fresh mushrooms,
  sliced

Pound meat thin; dredge in flour. Quickly brown in oil and butter. Stir in sherry and water. Add remaining ingredients except mushrooms. Cook, covered, over low heat for 30 minutes. Add more liquid if necessary. Add mushrooms; cook, covered, for 15 minutes. Serve immediately.

Light Dry White

PUERCO Y FRIJOLES　　　12 Servings

Mexican pork and beans

3 to 4 lbs. boneless pork
  shoulder, cubed
1 lb. dried pinto beans,
  soaked overnight
  according to package
  directions
1 can (6 oz.) tomato
  paste
1 can (4 oz.) chopped
  green chilies
1 medium onion, chopped
2 T. chili powder
1 T. salt
½ to 1 T. cumin
1 tsp. oregano
2 cloves garlic, minced
7 cups water
Cooked rice

Place all ingredients except rice in large pot or Dutch oven. Heat to boiling. Cover, reduce heat, and simmer for 5 to 5½ hours. Uncover; cook about 30 minutes to thicken. Serve over rice or corn chips. Pass lettuce, onion, tomato, avocado, sour cream, chopped olives, and cheese as condiments, if desired.

Light-Bodied Red

APRICOT-STUFFED HAM GLACE

20-28 Servings

1 fully cooked whole ham (10 to 14 lbs.)
1 cup uncooked white rice
1 can (29 oz.) apricot halves
1 cup diced celery
2 T. butter
½ cup thinly sliced green onions with tops
½ cup chopped walnuts
1 tsp. grated lemon rind
1 tsp. rosemary, crushed
Salt, pepper
½ cup sugar
¼ cup lemon juice
1 clove garlic, crushed
½ tsp. salt

Medium-Dry White

Have butcher bone ham. To prepare stuffing, cook rice according to package directions until tender. Drain apricots, reserving liquid; chop. Saute celery in butter until tender. Add green onions; cook until translucent. Combine cooked rice, celery, scallions, apricots, nuts, lemon rind, ¾ tsp. rosemary, and salt and pepper to taste. Stuff pocket left by removing ham bone. Bake at 350° for 2 hours.

Meanwhile, prepare glaze by combining in a saucepan 1 cup reserved apricot liquid, 1 cup drippings from roasting pan, sugar, lemon juice, garlic, ¼ tsp. rosemary, and salt. Simmer 5 minutes. Brush over ham. Continue baking 30 to 60 minutes longer, basting occasionally. Meat thermometer should register 130°.

ENTREES: POULTRY

CHICKEN CORDON BLEU

8 Servings

4 whole chicken breasts,
  boned, split and
  skinned
8 thin slices prosciutto
  ham
8 thin slices Swiss
  cheese
¼ cup flour
1 egg, beaten
2 T. milk
1 cup fresh bread crumbs
2 T. butter

MORNAY SAUCE:

1 T. finely chopped onion
3 T. butter
¼ cup flour
2 cups milk, scalded
2 egg yolks
½ cup whipping cream; or
  ¼ cup cream and ¼ cup
  white wine
2 T. freshly grated
  Parmesan cheese
2 T. grated Gruyere
  cheese
2 T. butter
¼ tsp. salt
White pepper to taste

Medium-Dry White

Flatten chicken breasts between sheets of waxed paper to about ⅛ inch thick. Top each half with a thin slice of prosciutto and Swiss cheese. Roll up breasts tightly, fold in sides. Dredge in flour, shaking off excess. Dip in egg beaten with milk; coat with bread crumbs. Saute on all sides in butter until golden. Transfer to a lame proof baking dish. Bake at 350° for 15 minutes. Cover with Mornay Sauce; broil 3 to 4 inches from heat for 3 minutes, or until browned.

For sauce, in a saucepan saute onion in butter until soft. Add flour; mix well. Cook over low heat, stirring for 3 minutes. Stir in milk; cook, stirring constantly until mixture is thick and smooth. Simmer for 10 minutes. Lightly beat egg yolks with cream. Add a little of the hot sauce to yolks; return all to pan. Add Parmesan, Gruyere, and butter. Stir the sauce until the cheeses and butter are melted. Season with salt and pepper to taste. (To hold, cover sauce with a buttered round of waxed paper, touching sauce to keep the air out. Heat, stirring to serve.)

SWEET AND SOUR CHICKEN SAVOY   4-6 Servings
Authentic Cantonese taste

SAUCE:

2 T. peanut oil
¼ cup sugar
¼ cup vinegar
2 T. soy sauce
2 tsp. juice from
    maraschino cherries
¼ tsp. garlic powder
½ cup sweet pickle mix
    with juice to cover or
    subgum ginger
2 T. cornstarch
1 cup chicken broth
1 can (8 oz.) pineapple
    chunks, drained
1 can (11 oz.) lychee
    nuts, drained
½ cup sweet and sour
    cauliflower (optional)

CHICKEN:

2 T. sherry
1 T. honey
1 tsp. lemon juice
1 tsp. crushed fresh
    ginger
2 whole chicken breasts,
    skinned and deboned,
    cut in 2-inch cubes
½ cup flour
¼ cup cornstarch
¾ tsp. salt
½ tsp. garlic powder
2 eggs, beaten
½ cup milk
Peanut oil

Medium-Dry White

For sauce, heat oil to smoking. Mix sugar, vinegar, soy sauce, cherry juice, and garlic powder. Stir-fry pickles 30 seconds; add sugar mixture. Bring to boil and cook 2 minutes. Dissolve cornstarch in broth; add slowly to mixture. Cook and stir until thick. (May be made ahead to this point.) Just before serving, reheat and add pineapple, lychee nuts, and cauliflower. Heat through.

For chicken, mix sherry, honey, lemon juice, and ginger. Add chicken; marinate for 15 to 30 minutes. Mix flour, cornstarch, salt, and garlic powder. Add eggs and milk to make a smooth batter. Dip chicken in batter. Fry in peanut oil at 350° until light brown. Drain. To serve, place chicken on top of sauce; gently spoon small amount of sauce on chicken. Serve with steamed rice.

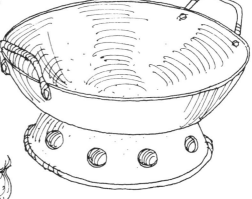

ENTREES: POULTRY

CHICKEN CURRY

6-8 Servings

2 whole chickens (about
3 lbs. each)
Water
4 T. salt
1 large onion, cut in
eighths
1 carrot, sliced
2 stalks celery, cut up
6 whole black
peppercorns
Bouquet garni (2 sprigs
parsley, 1 bay leaf, 1
tsp. thyme)

CURRY SAUCE:

3 T. butter
1 clove garlic, crushed
1 cup chopped onion
2 to 3 tsp. curry powder
1 cup pared chopped
apple
¼ cup unsifted all-
purpose flour
¼ tsp. ground cardamon
1 tsp. ginger
1 tsp. salt
¼ tsp. pepper
2 tsp. grated lime peel
2 T. fresh lime juice

Place chickens in a large pot and cover with water. Add salt, onion, carrot, celery, peppercorns, and bouquet garni; bring to a rolling boil. Skim; reduce heat to simmer. Cover and cook for 1 to 1¼ hours. Turn off heat and let stand until cool. Remove chickens and take meat from bones in large pieces. Strain liquid and remove fat; reserve 3 cups. (Any unused stock may be put into covered containers and frozen for future use.) For sauce, melt butter in large skillet. Saute garlic, onion, curry powder, and apple until onion is tender, about 5 minutes. Remove from heat and stir in flour, cardamon, ginger, salt, and pepper. Mix well. Gradually stir in reserved chicken stock. Add lime peel and lime juice. Bring to a boil, stirring. Reduce heat and simmer, covered, 20 minutes. Stir in cooked chicken and heat just to the boiling point. Serve with rice and condiments: chopped green pepper, chutney, whole salted peanuts, flaked coconut, mandarin oranges, raisins, pineapple chunks, and sliced green onions.

Ale

ENTREES: POULTRY

KOTOPITS (CHICKEN IN PHYLLO)

6-8 Servings

8 oz. frozen phyllo (10 to 12 sheets)
1 cup chopped celery
¾ cup chopped onion
½ cup butter (about)
2 cups chopped cooked chicken
2 T. chicken broth
2 T. chopped parsley
½ tsp. salt
½ tsp. grated nutmeg
⅛ tsp. pepper
1 egg, beaten
Hot cooked rice

LEMON-BECHAMEL SAUCE:

2 T. butter
2 T. flour
2 cups milk
1 tsp. salt
¼ tsp. white pepper
1 carrot, sliced
Bouquet garni: 2 sprigs parsley, 1 bay leaf, ¼ tsp. thyme, a small stalk celery
Fresh lemon juice

Medium-Dry White

Thaw phyllo. Cook celery and onion in 1 T. butter in covered skillet until tender. Add chicken and broth. Cook and stir, uncovered, until broth is absorbed. Stir in parsley, salt, nutmeg, and pepper. Remove from heat. Blend in egg; set aside. Melt remaining butter; brush over phyllo sheets. Make 3 stacks of phyllo, using 3 to 4 sheets for each. Spoon ⅓ of the chicken mixture over each stack to within 1 inch of edges. Roll as for jelly roll, starting at folded shorter side. Place, seam side down, on lightly buttered baking pan. Brush each roll with additional melted butter. Score each 3 or 4 times. Bake at 350° for 40 minutes, or until brown and crisp. Cut where scored. Arrange on platter with hot rice. Serve with Lemon-Bechamel sauce.

For sauce, melt butter, stir in flour; cook 2 to 3 minutes. Slowly add hot milk and cook over medium heat, stirring constantly until thickened. Add salt and pepper, carrot, and bouquet garni. Simmer slowly for 10 minutes. Add lemon juice to taste. Strain and serve.

ENTREES: POULTRY

CHICKEN WITH PEARS

8 Servings

2 frying chickens, cut up
1 cup coarse fresh bread crumbs
1 T. salt
½ tsp. pepper
½ cup oil
2 cans (16 oz. each) pear halves (8 halves)
4 tsp. cornstarch
1 T. dry mustard
2 T. lemon juice
2 T. soy sauce
1 tsp. grated lemon rind
¼ cup coarsely chopped peanuts

Medium-Dry White

Coat chicken with mixture of bread crumbs, salt, and pepper. Brown chicken on all sides in oil. Drain pears, reserving juice. Mix cornstarch with mustard in a heavy pan. Stir in 1 cup pear juice, lemon juice, soy sauce, and lemon rind. Cook, stirring constantly, until thickened. Place chicken in a large shallow roasting pan. Bake at 350° for 40 minutes, basting 2 or 3 times with sauce. Arrange pears around chicken; bake 10 minutes longer. Place chicken and pear halves on a heated platter. Blend drippings from roasting pan with sauce. To serve, dribble sauce over chicken. Sprinkle with peanuts.

TURKEY CASSEROLE AU GRATIN

8 Servings

Italian twist to turkey leftovers

1 cup chopped onion
1 large green pepper, seeded and chopped
6 T. butter
1 tsp. basil
1 can (28 oz.) tomatoes
5 to 6 cups cubed, cooked turkey
¼ tsp. salt
¼ tsp. seasoned pepper
1 pkg. (8 oz.) cream cheese
⅓ cup milk
½ cup grated Parmesan cheese

Medium-Dry White

Saute onion and green pepper in 2 T. butter until soft, about 5 minutes. Add basil and tomatoes, including juice. Cook rapidly, stirring until most of liquid has evaporated. Stir in turkey, salt, and pepper. Pour into shallow casserole. Mix cream cheese with remaining 4 T. butter until well blended. Gradually beat in milk until smooth. Spread over ingredients in casserole. Sprinkle with Parmesan cheese. Bake, uncovered, at 400° for 20 minutes, or until bubbly. Recipe may be doubled.

212

ENTREES: POULTRY

BREAST OF CAPON WITH ARTICHOKE HEARTS AND MUSHROOMS

8 Servings

4 large whole capon
   breasts (or chicken
   breasts), split
1 qt. water
2 stalks celery
1 small onion, quartered
Salt, white pepper
16 large mushrooms,
   sliced
2 T. butter
¼ onion, grated
Juice of 1 lemon
½ cup dry sherry
1 tsp. chicken stock base
⅛ tsp. dill
⅛ tsp. dry mustard
2 T. cornstarch
1 cup whipping cream
Seasoned salt, pepper
2 cans (14 oz. each)
   artichoke hearts,
   drained
Chopped parsley, chives,
   or paprika

Medium-Dry White

Put capon breasts, water, celery, onion, 2 tsp. salt, and ½ tsp. white pepper in a Dutch oven. Bring to a boil. Reduce heat, cover, and simmer for about 25 minutes, or until capon is tender. Strain broth; cool and reserve. Skin and bone breasts; chill. Cut each into thin slices.

Saute mushrooms in butter; add grated onion and lemon juice. Add 1½ cups strained broth, sherry, chicken stock base, dill, and dry mustard; simmer for 5 minutes. Mix cornstarch and cream; stir into simmering broth mixture. Continue stirring until thickened. Add seasoned salt and pepper to taste. (At this point sauce may be set aside; cover surface with buttered waxed paper. Gently reheat just before serving.) Add artichoke hearts and capon slices to sauce just long enough to heat through. Garnish with chopped parsley, chives, or paprika.

ENTREES: GAME

ROAST CORNISH HENS WITH PLUM SAUCE

Serve with wild rice and a green vegetable

4 Rock Cornish hens
Salt
Pepper
⅓ cup butter, melted
Plum sauce

Medium-Dry White

Sprinkle the body cavity of each hen with ¼ tsp. salt and a few grindings of pepper. Tie legs together. Arrange breast side up in shallow roasting pan and brush with melted butter. Roast uncovered, 15 minutes at 500°. Remove birds from oven and reduce temperature to 400°. Turn hens breast side down and pour ½ cup water over hens. Cover pan with foil and bake 30 minutes. May be prepared ahead to this point. Remove from oven and leave covered. When ready to serve: heat oven to 400°; uncover hens and turn breast side up. Baste with pan drippings and roast about 15 to 20 minutes until heated through, basting several times. Remove from oven and arrange on platter. Pour plum sauce over hens. Cornish hens are easily split in ½ after cooking and ½ is usually adequate for a light eater.

PLUM SAUCE

4 cups purple plums,
  quartered and pitted
2½ cups sugar
2 T. lemon juice
¼ tsp. cloves
¼ tsp. cinnamon
¼ tsp. allspice
¼ cup raspberry vinegar
  or red wine vinegar

Mix plums with sugar, lemon juice and spices. Put in shallow roasting pan and cover with aluminum foil. Bake mixture at 325° for 1 hour or until it begins to thicken. Pack in sterilized jars. Chill. Store in refrigerator. Remove hens from pan and degrease juices. Deglaze pan with raspberry vinegar and stir in 1 cup of plum mixture. Serve warm with hens.

ENTREES: GAME

PHEASANTS IN BRANDY AND CREAM   6 Servings

1 large onion, finely
   chopped
1 tsp. paprika
6 T. butter
3 pheasants, plucked,
   rinsed and trussed
½ cup brandy
2 cups chicken broth
1 tsp. salt
Freshly ground pepper
6 slices lean bacon
1 cup whipping cream
2 T. prepared horseradish

Saute onion and paprika in butter in large roasting pan. Add trussed pheasants. Saute over high heat until browned. Pour brandy over pheasants. Flame. Add broth and seasonings. Place bacon over birds. Roast uncovered, at 350° for 60 minutes, basting often. Transfer to platter. Skim fat from pan juices; stir cream and horseradish into juice, bring to a boil and reduce slightly. Serve sauce on the side. Serve with wild rice, salad, and poached peaches in raspberry sauce.

Full-Bodied Red

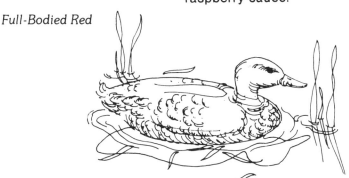

ROAST WILD DUCK   4 Servings

Equally good with goose

2 wild ducks
Oil or bacon grease
Salt
Pepper
2 small onions
1 medium apple
1 can (10½ oz.) beef
   consomme
⅔ cup sherry wine

Full-Bodied Red

Wash ducks thoroughly and pat dry. Rub ducks with oil inside and out. Salt and pepper inside and out and rub in. Place 1 small onion and ½ apple in each duck. Place in roaster, breast down. Add consomme and sherry. Cover. Roast at 350° for about 3 hours. Turn breast up last ½ hour. Remove cover. Add flour-water paste to juice in bottom of pan for gravy. Salt to taste. Cut through centers of ducks, lengthwise, with poultry shears. Serve ½ duck per person.

ENTREES: SEAFOOD

STEAMED SOLE WITH BLACK BEAN SAUCE

6-8 Servings

2 lbs. fillet of sole (or other thin fish fillets)
1 to 2 green onions with tops, minced
¼ cup soy sauce
2 T. fermented black beans, soaked (available from Chinese grocery)
1 T. oil (preferably sesame)
1 tsp. sugar
½ tsp. minced fresh ginger
½ tsp. salt
1 clove garlic, minced

Lay fish in steamer. Or, place fish on serving platter over boiling water in large pot; use metal percolator basket from coffee pot to support platter. Combine all other ingredients; spread over fish. Steam covered for 7 to 10 minutes. Fish and sauce can be wrapped in foil and cooked on grill. (Salmon steaks may be prepared in the same manner. Steam 15 to 20 minutes.)

Light Dry White

FLOUNDER MARGUERY

4 Servings

1 stalk celery, chopped
3 green onions with tops, minced
1 T. chopped parsley
1 clove garlic, pressed
5 T. butter
½ lb. shrimp, boiled and cleaned
½ cup chopped fresh mushrooms
3 T. flour
1½ cups milk
3 T. Sauterne wine
¼ tsp. nutmeg
Salt and pepper to taste
1 lb. fillet of flounder
1 tsp. grated Parmesan cheese

Saute celery, green onions, parsley and garlic in 2 T. butter until tender. Add cooked shrimp and mushrooms. Make a cream sauce by melting 3 T. butter, stir in flour. Add milk; cook, stirring constantly until thickened. Add wine, nutmeg, salt and pepper. Broil flounder; keep warm. Place flounder in ovenproof baking dish. Combine shrimp-mushroom mixture with cream sauce. Cover flounder with shrimp sauce. Sprinkle with grated Parmesan cheese. Run under broiler to brown.

Light Dry White

ENTREES: SEAFOOD

SPAGHETTI ALLA PUTTANESCA
6 Servings

Spicy and fiery

¼ cup olive oil
1 T. finely minced garlic
4 cups tomatoes, peeled and chopped (preferably fresh or imported canned Italian)
⅓ cup finely chopped parsley
2 T. finely chopped fresh basil or 1 tsp. dried basil
1 tsp. dried oregano
½ tsp. red pepper flakes or more to taste
2 T. drained capers
20 pitted imported olives, Italian or Greek
2 cans (2 oz. each) flat anchovies
24 littleneck clams, the smallest available
1 lb. spaghetti, cooked

Light-Bodied Red

Cook garlic in hot oil for about 30 seconds without browning. Add the tomatoes, 1 T. parsley, basil, oregano, red pepper flakes, capers, and olives. Cook over moderately high heat for about 25 minutes. Stir frequently. Drain the anchovies and chop coarsely. Wash the clams in cold water until clean. Add the anchovies and remaining parsley to sauce. Cook stirring for about 1 minute. Add the clams and cover. Cook for 5 minutes or until all the clams are opened. Serve hot with freshly cooked spaghetti.

ENTREES: SEAFOOD

PAELLA VALENCIANA

12 or more Servings

Truly a Spanish stew. You can add any vegetables, seafood, meats, or sausages you desire

3 whole chicken breasts
8 medium chorizos
  (Spanish sausages) or
  Polish sausage, in bite-
  sized pieces
½ cup olive oil
2 tomatoes, cut in eighths
1 cup each: chick peas,
  cut green beans, peas,
  fresh or canned
  mushrooms
2 cloves garlic, minced
3 pkgs. (6 oz. each)
  saffron rice
½ lb. or more shelled,
  cooked shrimp
1 dozen clams in shells
Salt to taste
Red and green pepper
  slices, artichoke
  hearts, lemon wedges
  for garnish

Bone chicken; cut into bite-sized pieces. Brown sausage and chicken in olive oil in paella pan or attractive Dutch oven. Remove. Add vegetables and garlic; brown and remove. Add rice, water and salt. Boil until done. Add chicken, sausage, vegetables, and cooked shrimp; reduce heat. Adjust seasonings. Place clams in salted water; bring to a boil. Remove when all clam shells have opened. Arrange around rim of paella. Garnish.

Light-Bodied Red

ENTREES: SEAFOOD

CLAMS AND LINGUINI

4-6 Servings

Truly outstanding!

24 cherrystone clams
4 cups water
Salt to taste
1 lb. linguini or other pasta
1 cup whipping cream
8 T. butter
1 T. finely chopped garlic
4 T. finely chopped parsley
3 T. finely chopped fresh basil
1 tsp. chopped fresh thyme leaves or ½ tsp. dried
Freshly ground pepper to taste
½ cup freshly grated Parmesan cheese

Open the clams. Drain and save both the clams and juice. You should have about 1½ cups of juice. Chop clams. Bring water and salt to a boil. Add the clam juice and linguini. While the linguini is cooking, heat the cream in a saucepan just to boiling. Meanwhile, heat 4 T. butter in another saucepan; add the clams, garlic, parsley, basil, thyme, and pepper. Do not add salt at this time. Add the cream. When the linguini is done, drain and place on a large hot platter. Immediately add the sauce and toss. Add the remaining butter, cheese and salt to taste. Serve hot.

Light Dry White

COQUILLES SAINT JACQUES AU VIN D'AIL

4 Servings

Scallops with garlic, wine and honey

1 lb. sea or bay scallops
¼ cup half and half
½ cup flour
½ cup baking powder
Dash white pepper
3 T. butter
3 T. oil
3 cloves garlic, minced
2 T. honey
¼ cup white wine

Light Dry White

Wash scallops several times in cold salted water until free of grit; drain on paper towels. If using sea scallops, cut into fourths. Toss scallops with half and half, then drain. Blot on paper towels. Coat in mixture of flour, baking powder, and pepper. Shake off excess flour. Heat butter, oil, and garlic. Add scallops. Brown on all sides. Spoon fat from pan. Combine honey with wine; pour over scallops. Bring to a boil; reduce heat and simmer 2 minutes. Arrange in 4 individual ramekins or shells. Serve with French bread, rice and salad.

VEGETABLES

ALIGOT

6 Servings

A specialty of Auvergne

2 lbs. potatoes, cooked
   and mashed
6 T. butter, melted
1 cup milk, heated
12 oz. cheese (Gruyere,
   Swiss, Cantal etc.),
   grated
1 clove garlic, mashed
Salt and pepper
1 slice bacon, cooked
   and fat reserved

Blend melted butter and milk into mashed potatoes. Put mixture in thick bottomed pan, stir over medium heat until it thickens and bubbles. Remove from heat. Add grated cheese. Stir with wooden spoon, scooping mixture from the bottom of the pan, letting it drop back. Do not let it burn. When mixture has the consistency of smooth stretched dough, add the garlic, salt and pepper and 1 T. fat reserved from bacon slice. Cooked, crumbled bacon may be sprinkled over top of dish. Serve with steak or roasts.

BEETS A LA FRAICHE

4 Servings

1 lb. fresh beets
Oil
3 T. butter
Salt and pepper to taste
½ cup creme fraiche

Place beets on baking sheet; brush with oil and bake at 375° for 45 minutes. Cool and peel; cut into thick slices. Simmer gently in saucepan with butter, salt and pepper. When hot, add creme fraiche; heat through and serve.

STIR-FRIED FRESH BROCCOLI IN LIGHT SOY SAUCE

4 Servings

2 medium stalks broccoli
1 T. light soy sauce
1 tsp. cornstarch
1 T. water
2 T. peanut oil
2 thin slices fresh ginger,
   peeled, minced

SAUCE:

1 tsp. dry sherry
½ tsp. salt
½ tsp. sugar
¼ cup broth or water

Wash broccoli. Cut into 2 parts: flower and stem. Each flower is cut into small lengthwise pieces. Peel tough outer skin from the large stems, then quarter each lengthwise. "Roll cut" each stem quarter. Combine the sauce ingredients. Mix light soy with the cornstarch and water. Heat oil in wok, sizzle ginger about 30 seconds. Add broccoli, stir-fry 2 minutes. Add the sauce; cover. Cook 1 minute. Remove cover, add cornstarch mixture, stir constantly for 30 seconds to thicken.

ACCOMPANIMENTS

RED CABBAGE

6 Servings

1 head red cabbage (3 lbs.)
⅓ cup sugar
⅓ cup water
½ cup red wine vinegar
Pinch of allspice
Salt to taste

Slice cabbage ¼ inch thick. Blanch in boiling water for 15 minutes. Drain. Do not be alarmed by blue color of cabbage; it will become red again when combined with vinegar mixture. Put sugar and water in pan. Over medium heat completely dissolve sugar by shaking pan — do not stir. When dissolved, bring to a boil and cover for 1 minute. Remove cover and continue cooking until sugar is caramelized to dark brown. Be careful not to burn it. Add vinegar to caramelized sugar and simmer over moderate heat 5 minutes. Place cabbage, vinegar-sugar mixture, allspice and salt in casserole. Mix thoroughly. Cover and bake at 350° for 45 to 60 minutes. Add water or beef broth if more liquid is needed during cooking. Adjust seasonings before serving.

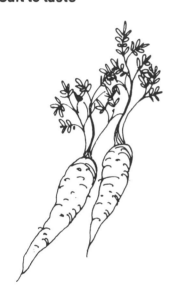

PARTY CARROT RING WITH BUTTERED GREEN BEANS

6-8 Servings

3 cups soft bread crumbs
1½ cups milk
5 eggs, beaten
1 pt. mashed cooked carrots
⅓ cup chopped celery
3 T. chopped, toasted, buttered almonds
1½ tsp. salt
¼ tsp. pepper
¼ tsp. marjoram
2 cups cut beans, cooked and buttered

Combine bread crumbs, milk, beaten eggs, carrots, celery, almonds, salt, pepper, marjoram. Pour into well-greased 1-qt. ring mold. Set in shallow pan of hot water. Bake at 350° for 1 hour. Let stand 5 minutes before loosening around edges. Then unmold onto warm platter. Fill center with hot buttered beans.

VEGETABLES

CARROTS FLAMBE

6 Servings

Elegant and so pretty

1½ lbs. carrots, peeled,
cut into 1-inch rounds
2 T. butter
¼ cup sugar
3 T. orange juice
1 tsp. grated orange rind
½ tsp. lemon juice
¼ tsp. ground ginger
2 T. orange-flavored
brandy

Steam carrots in small amount of water until tender. (Do not overcook.) Drain. Melt butter in skillet; stir in sugar, orange juice, orange rind, lemon juice, and ginger. Add carrots. Simmer until carrots are glazed. Heat orange-flavored brandy in a large ladle. Ignite and pour over carrots. Serve immediately.

RATATOUILLE CHINOISE

8-10 Servings

½ cup oil
1 medium head Chinese
cabbage, cut in 1-inch
slices
4 scraped carrots, thinly
sliced
1 pkg. (10 oz.) baby lima
beans, thawed
½ lb. fresh snow peas
1 large cucumber,
peeled, seeded and
coarsely sliced
½ lb. fresh mushrooms,
cut in ½
1 can (8 oz.) bamboo
shoots, drained and
sliced
1 T. soy sauce
2 cups chicken broth
2 T. sherry
2 tsp. sugar
1 tsp. salt
½ tsp. pepper
4 T. cornstarch
½ cup water

Heat oil in large skillet or wok. Saute vegetables over high heat. Start with cabbage, stirring 2 minutes; add carrots, stir 1 minute; add lima beans, stir 1 minute. Add snow peas, cucumber, mushrooms, and bamboo shoots; stir 1 more minute. Add soy sauce, broth, sherry, sugar, salt and pepper. Reduce to simmer; cover and cook 5 minutes. Dissolve cornstarch in water and add to vegetables. Stir several minutes until smooth and thick. May be served hot or cold.

ACCOMPANIMENTS

CHESTNUT PUREE

4-6 Servings

1 can (15¾ oz.) chestnut
   puree
½ cup whipping cream
3 T. butter
1 T. sugar
¼ tsp. nutmeg
Salt and pepper to taste

Combine all ingredients in top of double boiler; cover and heat through. You may reduce amount of cream if you wish a thicker consistency, or add beef or veal stock for a lighter one. Serve with game or fresh ham.

HONEY GLAZED CHESTNUTS

6 Servings

1 can (1 lb.) whole
   unsweetened chestnuts
4 T. honey

Drain chestnuts. Heat honey in heavy saucepan; add chestnuts stirring to coat well. Serve with roast pork, turkey or game.

CRANBERRY ICE

8 Servings

Makes a delightful accompaniment to turkey or other fowl

4 cups fresh cranberries
2 cups water
2½ cups sugar
Juice of 2 oranges
Juice of 1 lemon

Sort and wash cranberries. Cook cranberries in 2 cups water until the berries break up. Strain through a colander, using a potato masher to press berries through. Discard skins. Add remaining ingredients to berries. Heat until sugar dissolves. Cool. Freeze. Serve in individual bowls. Transfer to refrigerator 30 minutes before servings.

COINTREAU CRANBERRIES

4 Cups

Relish with zip

2 cups sugar
1½ cups water
½ cup orange or
   cranberry juice
1 lb. fresh cranberries
¼ cup Cointreau
Grated rind of 2 oranges
3 T. lemon juice
3 T. superfine sugar

In saucepan, combine sugar, water, and juice; boil for 5 minutes. Add cranberries; boil 6 minutes. Gently stir in remaining ingredients. Chill.

VEGETABLES

BAKED STUFFED ONIONS
8 Servings

8 medium to large onions
¼ cup butter
½ lb. good quality bulk
   sausage meat
1 ¼ cups bread crumbs
⅓ cup half and half
¼ cup chopped parsley
¼ tsp. thyme
Salt and pepper
1 cup beef broth
½ cup dry Madeira

Scoop out centers of onions leaving a shell ¼ inch thick. Chop centers. Blanch onion shells in boiling water 5 minutes. Drain and rinse with cold water. Saute chopped onion in ¼ cup melted butter until golden. Add sausage. Cook until all trace of pink is gone. Remove all fat from pan. Add bread crumbs which have been soaked in cream. Simmer for 5 minutes. Add parsley, thyme, salt and pepper. Season shells lightly with salt and pepper. Arrange in buttered baking pan. Fill with stuffing. Pour broth and Madeira over onions; dot each onion with butter and bring to a boil on top of stove. Bake at 350° for 45 minutes. Remove from oven and place onions in serving dish. Reduce liquid by ½ and pour over onions. Sprinkle with chopped parsley. Serve with turkey, game or beef.

POMMES DE TERRE DIJONNAISE
6 Servings

6 medium potatoes,
   pared, diced
2 T. oil
2 T. butter
Salt and pepper to taste
½ cup sour cream, at room
   temperature
1 tsp. Dijon mustard
⅓ cup chopped fresh
   parsley and chives
   combined

Fry raw potatoes in oil and butter until cooked and evenly browned. Add salt and pepper. Spread in a shallow 2-qt. baking dish. Bake at 350° for 15 minutes. Combine sour cream and mustard; spread over hot potatoes. Sprinkle with parsley and chives.

ACCOMPANIMENTS

SOUTHERN SWEET POTATOES   6-8 Servings
Simply scrumptious

¼ cup butter
¾ cup granulated sugar
¾ cup brown sugar
2 eggs
½ cup whipping cream
3 cups grated raw sweet
   potatoes

Cream butter and sugars. Add eggs. Beat until well blended. Combine egg mixture, cream, and sweet potatoes; mix. Pour in greased 2-qt. casserole. Bake uncovered at 350° for 1 hour.

BAKED OYSTERS AND SPINACH   4 Servings
Good first course or side dish

12 oz. oysters
Grated rind of 1 lemon
1 T. fresh lemon juice
4 or 5 slices bacon,
   partially cooked,
   chopped
1 pkg. (10 oz.) frozen
   spinach, cooked,
   drained, buttered
Salt, pepper
½ cup crushed saltines
Butter

Cut oysters in ½ if large; drain. Mix with lemon rind and juice. Place bacon in bottom of 1½-qt. casserole or 4 individual ramekins or shells. Add oysters, then spinach. Sprinkle with salt and pepper. Top with bread crumbs; dot with butter, salt and pepper. Bake at 350° for 30 minutes.

SAUERKRAUT RELISH   4-6 Servings
Good with brisket of beef

1 lb. sauerkraut
¼ cup coarsely grated
   carrot
1 T. minced onion
½ tsp. caraway seed
¼ cup vegetable oil
2 T. vinegar
1 tsp. sugar
½ tsp. salt

Combine sauerkraut, carrot, onion, and caraway seed. Combine oil, vinegar, sugar, and salt; add to sauerkraut mixture. Mix well, season with salt and pepper to taste; chill, covered, for 2 hours.

VEGETABLES

FRIED RICE

Leftovers the Oriental way

3 to 4 cups cooked rice
2 T. peanut oil
1 to 2 eggs, beaten
1 cup diced, cooked
chicken, pork, or shrimp
1 cup cooked baby peas
1 cup fresh bean sprouts
½ cup chopped green
onions with tops
1 T. bottled oyster sauce
1 T. soy sauce

Flake rice with fork. Heat oil in wok. Add rice; stir until heated. Make a well in center of rice; add egg. Cook, stirring egg constantly, until soft scrambled. Start incorporating rice, stirring in a circular fashion. One item at a time, stir in meat, peas, bean sprouts, and onions. Add oyster and soy sauces. Serve immediately.

WILD RICE AND SAUSAGE CASSEROLE 12-16 Servings

Great side dish for Cornish hens

2 cups uncooked wild
rice
1 lb. bulk pork sausage
1 lb. fresh mushrooms,
sliced
2 medium onions,
chopped
¼ cup flour
½ cup whipping cream
2½ cups chicken broth
⅛ tsp. each: oregano,
thyme, marjoram,
pepper
Salt to taste
½ cup slivered almonds,
toasted

Place rice in saucepan with 4 cups salted water. Cover and simmer 15 to 20 minutes. Drain. Cook sausage until brown; remove from pan and drain. Saute mushrooms and onions in fat remaining in pan; remove and drain. Pour off most of fat in pan. Stir in flour. Add cream; whisk until smooth. Add chicken broth. Cook, stirring constantly, until thickened. Season with oregano, thyme, marjoram, pepper, and salt to taste. Combine rice, sausage, mushrooms, onion, and sauce. Pour into 3-qt. casserole. Bake at 350° for 25 to 30 minutes. Sprinkle almonds over top.

ACCOMPANIMENTS

SPAGHETTI SQUASH

6 Servings

Different and delicious

1 medium spaghetti
  squash, about 2½ lbs.
2 T. butter
Freshly ground black
  pepper to taste

Pierce the squash all over with the tines of a fork. Place squash in a kettle; add cold water to cover. Bring to a boil and cook for 30 minutes. Place squash in the sink; slice it in ½ crosswise. Let drain. Using a heavy metal spoon, scrape the spaghetti-like strands into a bowl and serve tossed with butter and pepper. Or, squash may be served with a tomato sauce, sauteed mushrooms, Parmesan cheese, bits of ham, herbs, etc. Use in place of pasta with veal dishes.

NOTE: To cook in microwave, slice the squash in ½ lengthwise and scoop out seeds. Place cut side up in a pyrex dish in ½ inch of water and cover with plastic wrap. Microcook about 8 minutes until strands pull away from the sides of the squash.

DILLED SQUASH

8 Servings

4 acorn squash
1 medium onion, sliced
Butter
1 cup sour cream
½ tsp. salt
½ tsp. dill

Cut squash in ½; scoop out seeds. Place, cut side down, in baking pan with small amount of water. Bake at 400° for 45 minutes, or until tender. Cool. Scoop out cooked squash. Reserve shells. Saute onion in butter. Add sour cream, salt, and dill. Mix with cooked squash. Put back in shells. Bake at 375° for 10 to 15 minutes, or until heated through.

VEGETABLES

SWEET TURNIP CHIPS

8 Servings

Delicious with turkey

8 medium-sized white
   turnips
4 T. butter
2 cups chicken broth
1 T. sugar
½ tsp. salt
⅛ tsp. white pepper

Pare turnips and slice into ⅛-inch slices. Place turnips and rest of ingredients in saucepan, liquid should just cover turnips. Cook over high heat until almost all liquid has evaporated; turnips should be tender but not mushy. Put turnips in shallow, ovenproof dish. (May be held at this point.) Sprinkle turnips with a little sugar and bake at 325° for about 30 minutes.

YAMS AUX MARRONS FLAMBE

6 Servings

A delicacy from Martinique

3 yams, peeled
4 T. butter
¼ cup sugar
Grated peel of 2 limes
6 candied chestnuts
   (optional)
¼ cup Cognac or rum

Boil yams until tender but still firm. Slice lengthwise about ½ inch thick. Saute slices in butter over medium heat about 5 minutes. Arrange slices in ovenproof dish; sprinkle with sugar and grated lime peel. Cut chestnuts into quarters and place on top of yams. Put into 400° oven and bake several minutes until sugar has melted and top starts to brown. Watch carefully. Remove from oven. Heat Cognac and pour over yams. Flame. Delicious with game and turkey.

WALNUT SAUCE FOR VEGETABLES

About 1 Cup

Very easy and unusual

¾ cup minced green
   onions
2 T. minced parsley
3 T. cider vinegar
3 oz. coarsely chopped
   walnuts
½ cup vegetable oil
Salt and pepper
4 T. fresh dill, minced (for
   garnish)

Combine all ingredients except dill. Mix well. Pour over hot cooked vegetables and chill 2 hours. Bring to room temperature before serving. Garnish with fresh dill or parsley. May be used on beans, beets, zucchini, etc.

ACCOMPANIMENTS

RICE CHEESE CASSEROLE   8 Servings

4 cups cooked rice, wild
  or regular
2 cups grated Cheddar
  cheese (8 oz.)
¾ cup whole milk
½ cup freshly minced
  parsley
¼ cup butter, melted
2 eggs, slightly beaten
1 small onion, minced
½ tsp. salt

Mix all ingredients together in a buttered, 2-qt. casserole. Bake at 350° for 30 minutes.

BAKED RICE   10 Servings

Good with sweet and sour main dishes

½ cup butter
2 cups long grain rice
3 bouillon cubes (chicken
  or beef)
4 cups boiling water
3 T. soy sauce
½ cup slivered almonds
5 to 6 green onions, finely
  cut

Melt butter in large skillet. Add rice; cook and stir a few minutes. Dissolve bouillon cubes in water; add to rice. Cover and simmer 20 to 25 minutes, or until tender. Add soy sauce, almonds, and onions.

EASY POTATOES AU GRATIN   6 Servings

Great barbecue side dish

4 large potatoes, pared,
  cubed
1 small onion, quartered
½ medium green pepper,
  seeded, cut up
1 cup cubed Cheddar
  cheese
1 cup milk
3 eggs
2 T. soft butter
1½ tsp. salt
⅛ tsp. pepper

Combine ingredients. Process in batches in blender or food processor just until all potatoes are coarsely chopped. (Do not overprocess.) Pour into a greased 1½-qt. casserole. Bake at 350° for 1 hour.

VEGETABLES

CURRIED POTATOES

8-10 Servings

10 to 12 medium
   potatoes, peeled
1½ cups milk
⅓ cup grated sharp
   Cheddar cheese
¼ cup grated Swiss
   cheese
2 T. butter
1 T. chives
1 T. curry powder
1 tsp. salt
¾ tsp. tarragon
½ tsp. celery seed
½ tsp. white pepper
½ tsp. basil
¼ tsp. tumeric
⅓ cup minced onion
½ cup minced mushrooms
Paprika and parsley for
   garnish

Boil potatoes until firm-tender, about 20 minutes, and slice thinly. Set aside. Combine milk, cheeses, butter, spices and herbs in saucepan and simmer over very low heat. Stir often to blend and cook until smooth — about 15 minutes. Remove from heat, add onion and mushrooms. Place a layer of potatoes in bottom of a 3-qt. casserole, sprinkle with some salt and cover with a layer of sauce. Repeat layers ending with a layer of sauce. Bake at 350° for 20 to 25 minutes or until browned and bubbling. Sprinkle with paprika and chopped parsley.

SWISS GREEN BEANS

6-8 Servings

Buffet supper special

2 T. butter
2 T. flour
½ tsp. dill
½ tsp. salt
½ tsp. sugar
⅛ tsp. pepper
¾ cup milk
½ tsp. grated onion
½ cup sour cream
1¾ cups (7 oz.) shredded
   Swiss cheese
1 large bag (20 oz.)
   frozen French-style
   green beans, cooked,
   drained

Melt butter; blend in flour, salt, dill, sugar, and pepper. Cook, stirring until bubbly. Slowly add milk. Cook, stirring constantly until thickened. Remove from heat; stir in onion and sour cream. Combine sauce with cooked beans and 1½ cups shredded cheese. Pour into 2-qt. casserole; top with remaining ¼ cup cheese. Bake at 400° for 20 minutes. (May be made ahead, and refrigerated, and baked at 350° for 30 to 40 minutes.)

ACCOMPANIMENTS

MEATLESS LOAF

6 Servings

LOAF:

2 cups cooked brown rice
1½ cups grated Cheddar
 cheese
1 cup finely chopped
 carrots
½ cup chopped walnuts
 (optional)
½ cup plain yogurt
4 eggs, beaten
¼ cup chopped green
 onions with tops
2 T. chopped parsley
½ tsp. basil
½ tsp. salt

CHEESE SAUCE:

2 T. butter
2 T. flour
1½ cups milk
½ tsp. salt
1 cup grated Cheddar
 cheese

Combine all loaf ingredients, mix well. Spoon into greased 8x4-inch loaf pan. Place in a larger pan of hot water reaching to about 1 inch from top of loaf pan. Bake at 350° for 1 hour or until knife inserted in center comes out clean. Cool 10 minutes. Serve hot or cold with cheese sauce.

For sauce, melt butter and slowly stir in flour. Cook and stir for 1 minute. Add milk all at once. Whisk constantly until thickened and smooth. Stir in salt, then cheese. Blend thoroughly.

VEGETARIAN VERMICELLI

8 Servings

1 large bunch broccoli,
 cut into bite-sized
 pieces
1 box (16 oz.) vermicelli
¾ cup butter
1 cup whipping cream
1 cup grated Parmesan
 cheese
Garlic salt
Onion powder
Salt, pepper
1 can (28 oz.) tomatoes,
 drained, chopped

Cook broccoli and vermicelli together in water to cover until vermicelli is done and broccoli is still crunchy. Drain. Melt butter in large skillet; add vermicelli and broccoli. Toss. Stir in whipping cream and Parmesan cheese. Season to taste with garlic salt, onion powder, salt, and pepper. Add tomatoes; stir to heat through. Serve immediately.

SALADS, DRESSINGS & SAUCES

CAULIFLOWER SALAD

6-8 Servings

1 head fresh cauliflower
1 large bunch fresh
  broccoli
1 red onion, sliced thin
1 green pepper, diced
1 cup mayonnaise
1 tsp. dry mustard
½ cup sugar
½ cup vinegar
Salt
Pepper
1 jar (2 oz.) pimiento

Clean all vegetables and break into bite-sized pieces. Combine mayonnaise, mustard, sugar, vinegar, salt and pepper. Add to fresh vegetables and pimientos. Refrigerate, covered, overnight. Correct seasonings before serving.

CAULIFLOWER-PEA SALAD

6-8 Servings

Best with homemade mayonnaise

1 small head cauliflower,
  broken into small
  pieces
1 bag (20 oz.) frozen
  peas
6 to 8 stalks celery,
  chopped
6 green onions with tops,
  chopped
1 tsp. dill
Salt, pepper
Mayonnaise
Boston lettuce

Combine all ingredients except lettuce, using enough mayonnaise to bind. Toss lightly. Refrigerate overnight. Serve on lettuce.

HUNGARIAN SAUSAGE SALAD   4-6 Servings

5 T. salad oil
1½ T. cider vinegar
2 tsp. sugar
1 tsp. Dijon mustard
1 lb. smoked thuringer or
  kolbasi, cooked and
  thinly sliced
1 small red onion, thinly
  sliced
2 small dill pickles, thinly
  sliced
12 cherry tomatoes,
  halved
2 T. minced parsley
Salt and pepper to taste
Parsley

Combine oil, vinegar, sugar, and mustard; mix well. Combine sausage, onion, pickles, and tomatoes; toss lightly with dressing. Taste for seasoning. Sprinkle with parsley. Serve with rye or French bread.

CRAB-WILD RICE SALAD   4-6 Servings

Delicious main dish salad

1 pkg. (6 oz.) long-grain
  and wild rice mix
2 cans (7½ oz. each)
  crabmeat, drained,
  flaked and cartilage
  removed
1 T. lemon juice
¼ cup chopped green
  pepper
¼ cup chopped pimiento
2 T. minced parsley
½ cup mayonnaise
2 T. Russian salad
  dressing
½ tsp. salt
2 medium avocados,
  peeled and sliced

Cook rice according to package directions. Cool. Mix crab and lemon juice. Combine rice, crab, green pepper, pimiento, and parsley. Blend mayonnaise, Russian dressing, and salt; add to crab mixture. Toss lightly; chill. Serve with avocado slices.

SALADS, DRESSINGS & SAUCES

JAMBON EN GELEE

8 Cups

1 cup slivered cooked ham
1 T. minced shallots or white part of green onions
2 T. minced parsley
2 tsp. fresh tarragon or ½ tsp. dried tarragon
2 envelopes unflavored gelatin
1 cup boiling water
6 T. sugar
½ cup lemon juice
½ cup lime juice
1 cup crushed pineapple, drained
1 cup cottage cheese
1 cup salad dressing
2 T. prepared horseradish or to taste
1 tsp. Dijon mustard
Fresh pineapple chunks
Fresh parsley for garnish

Combine ham, shallots, parsley and tarragon with a few drops of lemon juice; cover and refrigerate. Soak gelatin in ¼ cup cold water for 5 minutes. Add boiling water, stirring until gelatin is completely dissolved. Stir in sugar. Dissolve sugar in mixture and add lemon and lime juices. Pour thin layer of gelatin mixture in bottom of 8-cup mold; allow to set. When set, drain any liquid from ham mixture and arrange over top of gelatin. Barely cover with more gelatin mixture. Refrigerate to set. Combine pineapple, cottage cheese, salad dressing, horseradish, and mustard. When ham mixture has jelled, stir remaining gelatin mixture into pineapple mixture, pour into mold. Refrigerate to set. When ready to serve, unmold and garnish with fresh pineapple chunks and fresh parsley.

Light Dry White

CURRIED TURKEY SALAD

4 Servings

3 cups diced turkey
1 cup diced celery
½ cup green grapes, halved
1½ cups mayonnaise
1 jar (9 oz.) chutney, chopped
3 T. curry powder
8 large lettuce leaves or 2 cantaloupes
1 pkg. (2 oz.) slivered almonds, toasted

Combine turkey, celery and grapes. Mix mayonnaise, chutney and curry powder; add to turkey and toss until mixed. Arrange on lettuce leaves or in fluted cantaloupe halves. Sprinkle with toasted almonds.

MUSTARD SAUCE

2 Cups

2 egg yolks
2 T. Dijon mustard
1 tsp. dry mustard
1 tsp. salt
Few grains cayenne
  pepper
2 tsp. tarragon vinegar
¾ cup vegetable oil
1 T. finely chopped
  shallots
1 T. sour cream
3 T. whipped cream

Place yolks and mustards in a mixing bowl. Add salt and cayenne. Beat until very thick. Beat in the vinegar very slowly. Then slowly beat in the vegetable oil, drop by drop, until the sauce thickens. Mix in rest of ingredients.

SESAME SEED DRESSING

8 Servings

½ cup oil
¼ cup wine vinegar
1½ T. sesame seeds,
  toasted in butter,
  drained
4 tsp. sugar
1 clove garlic, crushed
½ tsp. dry mustard
½ tsp. salt
2 oz. blue cheese,
  crumbled (or more)
½ lb. bacon, cooked,
  crumbled

Combine oil, vinegar, sesame seeds, sugar, and seasonings in a jar; shake well. Prepare enough salad greens to serve 8. Sprinkle with crumbled blue cheese and bacon. Toss dressing with salad and serve.

TURKEY GLAZE

Particularly good on microwave cooked poultry

½ cup butter
½ tsp. ground ginger
2 T. honey
2 T. brown sugar
2 T. water

Melt butter and add all other ingredients. Stir well. Remove fowl from microwave and brush on glaze. Then put fowl in regular oven at 400° for 10 to 15 minutes, depending on size. (Glaze may also be used for poultry done on the grill.)

DESSERTS & SWEETS

LUSCIOUS ORANGE BAKED ALASKA 12 Servings

Best ever

2 pts. vanilla or French
   vanilla ice cream (best
   quality, preferably hand
   packed)
½ pt. chocolate chip ice
   cream

ORANGE BUTTER:

6 T. butter
¾ cup sugar
⅓ cup orange juice
Grated rind of 2 oranges
2 tsp. grated lemon rind
2 T. lemon juice
¼ tsp. salt
2 eggs
2 egg yolks

MERINGUE:

5 egg whites
Dash cream of tartar
Pinch salt
⅔ cup granulated sugar
1 wooden cutting board
1 9-inch layer yellow
   cake

For orange butter, melt butter in top of a double boiler. Stir in rest of ingredients except eggs and egg yolks. Beat eggs with the egg yolks and add to butter mixture. Cook, over boiling water for 5 minutes beating constantly with a wire whisk until thick and smooth. Cool, stirring occasionally. Chill until ready to use.

For meringue, beat egg whites until frothy. Add cream of tartar and salt. Continue beating until soft peaks form. Gradually add sugar and beat until stiff peaks form.

To assemble Baked Alaska, center the yellow cake on the wooden board. Spread orange butter on just the top of the cake approximately ¼-inch thick. Put into freezer. Line a 1½-qt. mixing bowl with a couple of thicknesses of plastic wrap, layer the ice cream and orange butter as follows in the mixing bowl: First, ½ pt. of chocolate chip ice cream, next orange butter (enough to make a ¼-inch layer) then a little less than a pt. of vanilla ice cream, and then another ¼-inch layer of orange butter, and finally the rest of the vanilla ice cream which will be a little more than a pt. (You will end up with about ½ cup of orange butter which can be stored in the freezer for another use.) You should return the bowl to the freezer after each couple of layers to let the ice cream harden and to maintain the "layered look." When all the layering is done, let the bowl of ice cream and orange butter rest in the freezer about an hour. Remove the ice cream and cake from the freezer. Run warm water over the outside of the bowl. Turn the bowl upside down centered

DESSERTS & SWEETS

on the cake layer and unmold the ice cream. Carefully peel away the plastic wrap from the ice cream. Return to the freezer. Prepare the meringue. Remove ice cream from freezer. Working quickly, "ice" the Baked Alaska thoroughly with the meringue, covering every bit of ice cream and cake, especially around the bottom. There should be no gaps. When everything is covered use the spatula to make little swirls in the meringue. Brown the dessert in a preheated 500° oven for about 3 minutes or until nicely browned. Serve immediately, slicing with a long sharp knife.

NOTE: Make this dessert a week or so in advance of a party except for the addition of the meringue. Keep the Alaska stored covered until the day of the party. Early on that day, cover with the meringue and return the Alaska to the freezer uncovered until it's time to brown and serve.

DESSERTS & SWEETS

GATEAU FROMAGE DE NORMANDE   12 Servings

PASTRY SHELL:

¼ lb. butter
½ cup sugar
1 cup flour
Yolk of 1 egg

FILLING:

2 pkgs. (8 oz. each)
  cream cheese
1 cup sugar
½ cup whipping cream
½ cup sour cream
1 T. flour
2 egg yolks
1 tsp. vanilla
3 egg whites

For pastry, cream butter and sugar until fluffy; add flour and combine well. Mix in egg yolk and knead into pastry until completely absorbed. Take about ⅓ of pastry and pat on bottom of 9-inch spring-form pan. Bake at 425° about 8 minutes or until golden. Remove from oven and cool. When cool enough to handle, press remaining dough onto sides of pan. Set aside.

For filling, beat cream cheese and sugar until light and fluffy. Add whipping cream and sour cream; mix well. Stir in flour, egg yolks and vanilla. Beat egg whites until they form stiff peaks; fold into cheese mixture and pour into prepared pastry shell. Bake at 375° for 50 to 60 minutes. (It should puff up like a souffle and center should be moderately firm.) Leave cake in turned-off oven with door slightly ajar about 1 hour. Cake will fall and should be about level with top of pan. Best served warm topped with Sauteed Apples With Calvados.

SAUTEED APPLES WITH CALVADOS

2 medium, firm apples
2 T. butter
½ cup brown sugar
¼ tsp. allspice
1 tsp. lemon juice
¼ cup Calvados or apple-
  jack

Peel, core and thinly slice apples. Over moderate heat, melt butter, add brown sugar; stir until sugar dissolves. Add apples, allspice and lemon juice. Cook, stirring constantly until apples are tender but still hold their shape. Add Calvados, raise heat and cook until liquid evaporates.

DESSERTS & SWEETS

POACHED PEACHES IN RASPBERRY SAUCE

12 Servings

Delicious dessert after pheasant

8 T. butter
1 cup brown sugar
2 cups raspberries, pureed
Juice of 2 oranges
Grated rind of 1 orange
12 medium peaches, peeled and left whole
½ cup Grand Marnier, warmed

Caramelize 2 T. butter and brown sugar in blazer pan of a chafing dish. Stir in remaining butter, raspberry puree, orange juice and rind. Bring to a boil. Place peaches in pan. Reduce heat to simmer. Turn peaches constantly until heated through. May be made ahead to this point. Refrigerate.

To serve, bring to room temperature and reheat. Pour Grand Marnier over peaches and serve immediately.

PUMPKIN LOG

8-10 Servings

3 eggs
1 cup sugar
⅔ cup canned pumpkin
1 tsp. lemon juice
1 cup flour
1 tsp. baking powder
1 tsp. cinnamon
1 tsp. ginger
½ tsp. nutmeg
½ tsp. salt
1 cup chopped walnuts
Confectioners' sugar

FILLING:

6 oz. cream cheese
4 T. butter
½ tsp. vanilla

Beat eggs on high speed of mixer for 5 minutes. Gradually add sugar. Stir in pumpkin and lemon juice. Stir together flour, baking powder, and seasonings. Fold into pumpkin mixture. Spread in greased and floured jelly roll pan. Top with walnuts. Bake at 375° for 15 minutes. Turn out on towel sprinkled with some confectioners' sugar. Starting at the narrow end, roll damp towel and cake together. Let cool.

For filling, blend all ingredients until smooth. Unroll cake. Spread filling over cake. Roll without towel and chill.

DESSERTS & SWEETS

NICK'S MOCHA TORTE

Very special

CAKE:

1½ T. instant coffee
1 cup cold water
6 egg yolks
2 cups granulated sugar
2 cups flour
3 tsp. baking powder
¼ tsp. salt
1 tsp. vanilla
1 cup ground walnuts
6 egg whites

FILLING:

1½ cups butter, softened
3 cups confectioners'
  sugar, sifted
3 tsp. unsweetened
  cocoa
¾ tsp. instant coffee
3 T. Cointreau
3 T. orange juice

FROSTING:

6 cups confectioners'
  sugar, sifted
6 tsp. cocoa
1½ tsp. instant coffee
6 T. Cointreau
6 T. butter, melted
1½ tsp. vanilla
Walnut halves for garnish

Dissolve coffee in cold water. Beat egg yolks until light. Add granulated sugar in a thin stream. Beat until thick and lemon colored. Sift together the flour, baking powder, and salt. Gradually add the sifted ingredients to the egg mixture, alternating with the dissolved coffee. Add the vanilla and ground walnuts. Beat the egg whites until stiff but not dry. Fold into the batter. Pour into 3 buttered and floured 9-inch cake pans. Preheat oven to 325° and bake for 30 minutes. Cool 10 minutes before removing from pans. When layers are completely cool, cut in ½ horizontally to make a 6 layer torte. A serrated bread knife works well.

For filling, cream the butter and gradually add the sugar. Add remaining ingredients. Beat until very smooth. Spread between each layer of the torte.

For frosting, combine sugar, cocoa, and coffee. Add the liqueur, butter, and vanilla. Beat until smooth.

Frost top and sides of torte. A flat spatula, occasionally dipped in water, is the best tool. Garnish with walnut halves around top edge of torte.

DESSERTS & SWEETS

SORBET DE POIRE

1½ Pints

Pear sherbet

5 to 6 very ripe, peeled
   and cored fresh Bartlett
   pears
1 ⅓ cups sugar
2 T. lemon juice
1 T. egg white
4 T. good quality pear
   liqueur (optional)

Puree pears in food processor until no lumps remain. Gradually add sugar, processing several minutes. Sugar should be completely dissolved. Add lemon juice, egg white and liqueur. Process another minute. Put in covered freezer container and freeze about 2 hours. Remove from freezer and process 2 to 3 minutes. Taste and add more lemon juice and liqueur if desired. Freeze until ready to serve. To serve, place in crystal goblets and top each scoop with 1 T. pear liqueur.

BRITTLE ICE CREAM PIE

6-8 Servings

1¼ cups crushed
   gingersnaps
7 T. butter, melted
2 qts. vanilla ice cream,
   softened
1 pkg. Bits of Brittle,
   crushed (or 6 oz.
   Heath bars, crushed)
½ cup brown sugar
½ cup whipping cream
½ cup almonds, toasted
   brown
1 tsp. vanilla

Combine gingersnaps and 3 T. of melted butter. Press into 9-inch pie plate and freeze. Combine ice cream and Bits of Brittle. Mold onto gingersnap crust and freeze. For sauce, combine brown sugar, cream, and 4 T. butter. Bring to boil and stir. Remove from heat. Add almonds and vanilla. Serve warm sauce over individual slices of pie.

DESSERTS & SWEETS

SUPER APPLE CAKE

8-10 Servings

2 cups flour
2 cups sugar
2 tsp. baking powder
2 tsp. cinnamon
½ tsp. cloves
¼ tsp. ginger
¼ tsp. allspice
1 cup cooking oil
4 eggs
1 tsp. vanilla
½ cup raisins (optional)
¾ cup chopped nuts
4½ cups coarsely
shredded apples

Mix dry ingredients, excluding nuts and raisins. Add oil, eggs, and vanilla. Beat 3 minutes. Stir in raisins, nuts, and 4 cups of apples. Turn into greased 13 x 9-inch baking pan. Sprinkle with remaining apples, plus a little more sugar and cinnamon. Bake at 325° for 1 hour, or until done. Cake should be moist inside.

BUTTERSCOTCH CHEESECAKE

10-12 Servings

CRUST:

1 cup vanilla wafer
crumbs
3 T. confectioners' sugar
3 T. melted butter

FILLING:

1⅓ cups dark brown sugar
2 T. flour
3 pkgs. (8 oz. each)
cream cheese, softened
3 eggs
2 tsp. vanilla
½ cup finely chopped
pecans
Whole pecans for garnish
1 T. maple syrup
Sliced strawberries
(optional)

For crust, combine ingredients and pat into bottom of 9-inch spring-form pan. Bake at 350° for 10 minutes.

For filling, blend sugar and flour. Beat cream cheese until light and fluffy. Add sugar-flour mixture and continue beating. Add eggs 1 at a time, beating well after each addition. Then add vanilla and chopped nuts. Pour into crust and bake at 350° for 50 to 55 minutes. Cool as slowly as possible and then chill. Before serving, garnish edge with whole pecans and brush top with maple syrup. Serve with sliced strawberries if available.

DESSERTS & SWEETS

PRALINE PEAR TART

CORNMEAL PASTRY SHELL:

1 cup flour
½ cup cornmeal
½ tsp. salt
½ cup butter
¼ cup water
Sliced almonds (optional)

PEAR FILLING:

7 large, firm Bartlett pears, peeled, cored and quartered (3½ to 4 lbs.)
1 pkg. (2 oz.) sliced almonds (½ cup)
2 T. lemon juice
½ cup sugar
¼ cup cornstarch
¼ tsp. salt
3 T. butter
Nutmeg

PRALINE TOPPING:

¾ cup sugar
2 to 3 T. water
1 T. light corn syrup
1 pkg. (2 oz.) sliced almonds (½ cup)

GARNISH:

1 cup whipping cream, whipped

For pastry shell, combine flour, cornmeal and salt in a bowl. Cut in butter until mixture resembles coarse meal. Sprinkle with water; stir with fork until a ball is formed. Roll out dough to fit a 9-inch pie plate. Arrange pastry in pan. Tuck sliced almonds along the fluted edge, if desired. Refrigerate.

Arrange pears alternately with sliced almonds in the crust, mounding them somewhat higher in the center. Sprinkle with lemon juice. Combine sugar, cornstarch, and salt; sprinkle over all. Grate nutmeg over top and dot with butter. Bake at 350° for 1½ hours or until crust is brown and juices are bubbling.

For topping, combine ingredients and cook, without stirring, in a heavy pan over medium heat until mixture turns a delicate brown. Carefully stir with a metal spoon just enough to toast almonds on all sides. When dark brown (about 15 minutes), pour mixture into a well-oiled pan to cool and solidify. When cool, remove from pan and crush with a rolling pin or in a food processor. Sprinkle on top of warm pie. Serve each slice of pie with a dollop of whipped cream.

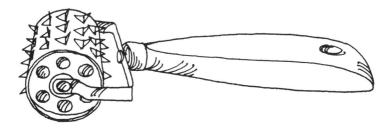

DESSERTS & SWEETS

LA CREMAILLERE A LA MACAROON   8-10 Servings

Scrumptious ending to any meal!

1 cup butter
3 cups confectioners' sugar
8 egg yolks
2 tsp. vanilla
½ cup dark rum
4 tsp. instant coffee
3 cups whipping cream
1 pkg. lady fingers
12 small macaroons (or 1 cup chopped candied fruit)
1 pkg. slivered almonds, toasted

Cream butter; add sugar, eggs and vanilla. Dissolve coffee in rum; add to butter mixture. Whip 2 cups of the cream. Fold into the mixture. Place ⅓ of mixture in bottom of 9 x 12 baking dish. Split and place lady fingers over mixture. Put another ⅓ of the mixture over lady fingers. Crumble macaroons over all. Top with remaining mixture. Freeze for 3 to 4 hours. Before serving, whip the remaining cup of cream and frost frozen dessert. Sprinkle with toasted almonds.

HEDGEHOG PUDDING   6-8 Servings

This hedgehog has almond quills!

¾ cup sugar

PUDDING:

6 egg whites
Pinch salt
6 T. sugar
½ cup slivered, toasted almonds

SAUCE:

1 cup whipping cream
6 egg yolks, beaten

To caramelize souffle dish, put ¾ cup sugar in skillet. Heat on medium high until sugar melts and turns golden brown. Immediately turn into buttered 1½-qt. souffle dish coating bottom and sides. Set aside.

For pudding, beat whites with salt to soft peaks. Gradually add sugar and beat to stiff peaks. Pour into caramelized souffle dish. Steam in a covered saucepan of hot water for 1½ hours on top of stove. The water must not boil. When done, turn pudding out onto shallow dish. Stick almonds all over it and serve with sauce. For sauce, heat cream just to boiling. Slowly whisk in egg yolks. Serve pudding and sauce warm or cold.

DESSERTS & SWEETS

APRICOT UPSIDE-DOWN CHOCOLATE CAKE

8 Servings

¼ cup butter
½ cup packed brown sugar
1 can (1 lb.) apricot halves
2 T. apricot syrup
⅔ cup flaked coconut
6 T. unsalted butter
1 cup granulated sugar
2 eggs
4 oz. sweet chocolate, melted
1 tsp. vanilla
1½ cups cake flour
½ tsp. baking soda
½ tsp. baking powder
½ tsp. salt
¾ cup buttermilk or soured milk

CHOCOLATE-CINNAMON WHIPPED CREAM:

1 cup whipping cream
¼ cup grated sweet chocolate
1 tsp. cinnamon

Melt ¼ cup butter. Spread in 8-inch square baking dish. Sprinkle with ½ cup brown sugar. Drain apricots, reserving 2 T. of syrup. Arrange apricots, cut side up, on brown sugar. Sprinkle with coconut and reserved apricot syrup. Cream 6 T. butter and 1 cup granulated sugar. Add eggs; beat thoroughly. Add chocolate and vanilla. Combine dry ingredients; add to butter-sugar mixture alternately with buttermilk, beating well after each addition. Pour batter over fruit. Bake at 325° (350° with metal pan) for 45 to 50 minutes, or until done. Let stand 1 minute; turn upside-down onto serving platter. Serve warm or cool with whipped cream.

Whip cream. Fold in chocolate and cinnamon.

PLUM DUMP

6 Servings

A hearty Colonial dessert

24 Italian plums, pitted, quartered
¼ cup brown sugar
1 T. lemon juice
3 T. flour
½ tsp. cinnamon
1 cup sugar
1 cup flour
1 tsp. baking powder
½ tsp. salt
1 egg, well beaten
½ cup butter, melted

Line bottom of shallow 2-qt. ungreased baking dish with plums. Combine brown sugar, 3 T. flour, lemon juice, and cinnamon; mix with plums. Combine sugar, 1 cup flour, baking powder, salt, and egg; sprinkle evenly over plums. Drizzle butter over all. Bake at 375° for 45 minutes.

DESSERTS & SWEETS

ICELANDIC PEARS

4 Servings

2 cups Chablis wine
1 cup orange juice
1 T. grated orange rind
Pinch of salt
Small stick of cinnamon
Slices of lemon
1½ cups sugar
4 Bartlett or Anjou pears, peeled, cored and halved
3 T. cornstarch
1 pt. vanilla ice cream
4 tsp. grated or shaved semisweet chocolate

Combine wine, orange juice, rind, salt, cinnamon, lemon and sugar in large saucepan; add pears and simmer 45 minutes to 1 hour until pears are tender. Remove pears to bowl. Combine cornstarch in a little water and add to wine mixture. Cook, stirring constantly until thickened and clear. Pour over pears. Cool and refrigerate. When ready to serve, place a scoop of ice cream between 2 pear halves set in a deep cup or glass. Cover with wine sauce and sprinkle with shaved chocolate.

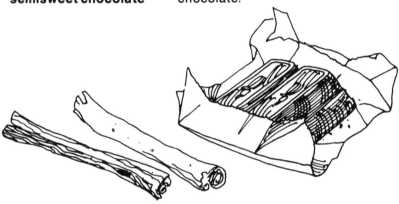

"CAT IN THE HAT" GERMAN PANCAKE

2 Servings

½ cup milk
2 eggs, beaten
1 tsp. sugar
½ cup flour
2 T. butter
Confectioners' sugar
Lemon wedges
Lingonberries

Combine the milk, eggs and sugar. Mix well. Slowly add the egg mixture to the flour. Stir until combined. Batter will be slightly lumpy. Melt butter in a 10-inch skillet. Pour batter into skillet when butter is sizzling hot. Immediately place skillet in a 425° oven. Bake for 10 minutes. Remove pancake from oven. Turn pancake over. Return to oven for 10 minutes or until it is well browned and puffy. Serve hot with confectioners' sugar, lemon wedges and lingonberries.

DESSERTS & SWEETS

CHEESE CUPCAKES

24 Servings

3 pkgs. (8 oz. each)
   cream cheese
1 cup sugar
5 eggs
1½ tsp. vanilla
24 cupcake liners
24 vanilla wafers

TOPPING:

1 cup sour cream
½ cup sugar
½ tsp. vanilla

Beat cream cheese and sugar until light and fluffy. Add eggs, 1 at a time, beating well after each addition. Add vanilla. Line cupcake tins with paper liners. Place a vanilla wafer on the bottom of each. Fill each ¾ full with cheese mixture. Bake 20 minutes at 375°. They won't be brown. Cool 5 minutes. Centers will sink. Combine topping ingredients and fill centers of cupcakes. Bake 5 minutes more. Cool. If desired, top with fresh fruit: strawberries, blueberries, grapes, etc.

CHOCOLATE TORTE

10-12 Servings

TORTE:

⅔ cup milk
1¼ tsp. vanilla
1¼ cups flour
1¼ tsp. baking powder
¼ tsp. salt
4 eggs
1½ cups sugar

FILLING:

3 cups confectioners'
   sugar, sifted
1 egg
½ cup unsweetened
   cocoa
½ tsp. vanilla
¾ cup sweet butter

FROSTING:

6 oz. semisweet
   chocolate pieces
1 T. butter
2 T. sour cream
Chopped nuts

For torte, scald milk. Add vanilla and set aside. Sift flour, baking powder, and salt; set aside. Beat eggs until light and fluffy; gradually add sugar. Add flour mixture alternately with milk. Pour into 2 well-greased and floured 9-inch pans with removable bottoms. Bake at 350° for 30 to 35 minutes or until cake pulls away from sides of pan. Cool and remove from pans. Cut layers horizontally in ½ and spread filling between each layer and on sides. Cover top with frosting and sides of cake with chopped nuts.

For filling, beat 1 cup of sugar with the egg. Add the rest of the sugar, cocoa, and vanilla. Gradually add butter and beat until fluffy.

For frosting, melt chocolate with butter over low heat. Remove from heat and add sour cream. Frost top of cake immediately. Frosting will be difficult to work with as it cools.

DESSERTS & SWEETS

LEMON GLAZED CHEESECAKE

9-inch graham cracker
    crust

FILLING:

3 pkgs. (8 oz. each)
    cream cheese
¾ cup sugar
3 eggs
¼ cup lemon juice
2 tsp. lemon rind
2 tsp. vanilla

TOPPING:

2 cups sour cream
3 T. sugar
1 tsp. vanilla

GLAZE:

½ cup sugar
1½ T. cornstarch
¼ tsp. salt
¾ cup water
⅓ cup lemon juice
1 egg yolk
1 T. butter
1 tsp. lemon rind

For filling, mix with blender or processor. Pour into crust and bake 20 minutes at 350°. Mix ingredients for topping and spread over cake. Bake 10 minutes more. (Start spreading around the edges, then move towards the center.) Combine ingredients for glaze except butter and lemon rind. Stir over heat until boiling and thickened. Add butter and lemon rind. Cool slightly and spread on cake. Refrigerate.

RICH CHOCOLATE CAKE WITH CUSTARD-LIKE CENTER

16 Servings

Divine!

1 cup butter
8 oz. semisweet
    chocolate
5 eggs
1¼ cups sugar
1¼ cups flour
Dash of salt

Melt butter and chocolate together. Beat eggs and sugar until light yellow; add chocolate mixture. Mix in flour and salt. Turn into well-greased, lightly floured 9½ to 10-inch tube pan. Bake at 425° for 20 minutes. Cake will not be firm on inside. Cool and unmold. Sprinkle with confectioners' sugar.

DESSERTS & SWEETS

BLACK BOTTOM PIE

8 Servings

CRUST:

16 to 18 graham
crackers, crushed
6 T. or more butter,
melted

FILLING:

1 T. unflavored gelatin
¼ cup cold water
1½ T. cornstarch
1 cup sugar
2 cups milk, scalded
4 egg yolks, beaten
2 tsp. vanilla
4 egg whites
½ tsp. cream of tartar
2 squares (2 oz.)
unsweetened
chocolate, melted
Whipped cream
Shaved chocolate

Mix crumbs and butter. Press into a 9-inch pie pan. Bake 10 minutes at 300°. Set aside. For filling, soften gelatin in water. Combine cornstarch and ½ cup sugar. In top of double boiler, add scalded milk slowly to beaten egg yolks. Add cornstarch and sugar. Cook over simmering water until mixture coats a spoon (about 20 minutes). Remove from heat. Add melted chocolate to 1 cup of custard mixture. Beat with rotary beater. When cool, add 1 tsp. vanilla. Pour into cooled crust. Chill. Blend gelatin into remaining hot custard. Cool, but do not let stiffen. Set aside. Beat egg whites with cream of tartar; slowly add ½ cup sugar. Continue beating until stiff. Add 1 tsp. vanilla and fold mixture into remaining custard mixture. Place on top of firm chocolate layer. Chill. Before serving, cover with freshly whipped cream and shaved chocolate.

CREME DE CAMEMBERT

4-6 Servings

A dessert served with French bread and red wine

1 wheel (8 oz.) very ripe
camembert cheese
Dry white wine
⅓ cup unsalted butter
1 cup toasted bread
crumbs

Choose a ripe camembert; scrape off skin carefully. Place cheese in bowl. Cover with wine and let sit for 12 hours. Drain and dry cheese. Cream thoroughly with butter and reshape into original form. Coat cheese with bread crumbs, covering entire surface. Chill well before serving. Fresh pears are a good accompaniment.

DESSERTS & SWEETS

PUMPKIN ICE CREAM PIE
6-8 Servings

2 pts. butter pecan ice cream
1¼ cups canned pumpkin
¾ cup firmly packed brown sugar
½ tsp. salt
1 tsp. vanilla
½ tsp. ginger
¾ tsp. cinnamon
¼ tsp. nutmeg
Dash ground cloves
1 cup whipping cream
2 T. brown sugar
2 T. butter
¼ cup chopped pecans

Spoon 1 pt. ice cream into 9-inch pie plate. Spoon remaining pt. petal-like around edges to make shell. Freeze. Mix pumpkin, ¾ cup brown sugar, salt, vanilla and spices. Measure 1 T. whipping cream in small saucepan and set aside. Whip remaining cream until stiff; fold into pumpkin mixture. Spoon into ice cream shell. Return to freezer. Combine 2 T. brown sugar and butter with cream. Heat to boiling; cook 1 minute, stirring constantly. Remove from heat and stir in pecans. Cool. Sprinkle over pie. Freeze 3 hours or more. Let stand 15 minutes before serving.

CHOCOLATE-ORANGE TARTS
30 Tiny Tarts

Nice for a tea party

PASTRY:

1⅓ cups flour
½ cup confectioners' sugar
¼ cup granulated sugar
½ cup butter
1 egg yolk
1 tsp. vanilla

FILLING:

4 oz. sweet baking chocolate
2 T. butter
¼ cup sugar
½ tsp. vanilla
⅓ cup orange marmalade

For pastry, combine flour and sugars. Add butter, egg yolk, and vanilla. Mix until blended. Press into tiny muffin molds, using 1 heaping tsp. pastry for each. Bake at 450° for 8 minutes, or until lightly browned. Cool. For filling, melt chocolate and butter; add sugar and vanilla. Cool slightly. Into each tart shell place ½ to 1 tsp. orange marmalade; add about 1 tsp. chocolate mixture. Tarts will keep about 2 weeks or can be frozen.

DESSERTS & SWEETS

CHERRY-APPLE PIE

6-8 Servings

PASTRY:

⅔ cup lard
2 cups flour
1 tsp. salt
2 to 4 T. ice water

FILLING:

1 lb. can (1⅔ cups) red pie cherries, well drained
4 cups sliced tart apples (about 4)
1 cup sugar
¼ cup flour
⅛ tsp. salt
½ tsp. cinnamon
2 T. butter

Using pastry blender or two forks, cut lard into flour and salt until mixture resembles coarse meal. Sprinkle water over dry ingredients. Press dough with knife until dough just holds together. Divide pastry into 2 parts. Use lightly floured pastry cloth and sock for easy rolling.

Roll dough lightly from center to edges to form circle ⅓-inch thick. Fit lower crust into 9-inch pie pan. Cut off pastry to allow a ½-inch overhang.

Roll out second ball of pastry. With knife or pastry wheel, cut strips ½-inch wide. Cover pie with strips. Starting at center, fold back every other strip and weave additional strips diagonally across pie, under and over until top is covered. Press ends of strips to rim, fold the overhanging crust from lower crust up and over and crimp edge.

For filling, distribute cherries evenly over bottom crust. Add apples. Sprinkle sugar, flour, salt, and cinnamon evenly over fruit. Dot with butter. Fit on lattice top crust as described above, trim and crimp edges. Bake at 425° for 35 minutes or until crust is browned. (Plain top crust may be used instead of lattice; but cut several gashes in top of crust to allow steam to escape.)

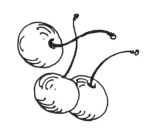

DESSERTS & SWEETS

BLACK WALNUT PUMPKIN CHIFFON PIE   8 Servings

1 baked 9-inch pastry
   shell
2 tsp. unflavored gelatin
¼ cup cold water
3 eggs, separated
1 cup sugar
1¼ cups cooked pumpkin
½ cup milk
½ tsp. salt
½ tsp. cinnamon
¼ tsp. nutmeg
½ tsp. ginger
½ cup black walnut
   meats, roughly chopped
Whipping cream, whipped

Sprinkle gelatin over ¼ cup cold water and let it soften for about 5 minutes. Beat egg yolks slightly. Add ½ cup sugar, pumpkin, milk, and spices. Cook over low heat, stirring constantly for 5 minutes. Remove pumpkin mixture from heat. Add softened gelatin. Stir until dissolved. Add nuts. Cook until slightly thickened. Beat egg whites until foamy. Add remaining sugar 1 T. at a time, continue beating until smooth and shiny. Fold into cooled pumpkin mixture. Pour into pastry shell. Chill until firm. Serve with whipped cream.

GREEN TOMATO PIE   6-8 Servings

Pastry for double crust pie
8 medium, green
   tomatoes
1 T. salt
1 cup sugar
2 T. flour
1 cup soft fresh bread
   crumbs
½ tsp. cinnamon
2 T. cider vinegar
2 T. butter, cut into bits

Core and cut tomatoes crosswise into ¼-inch slices. Sprinkle salt over tomatoes and stir gently. Set aside for 15 minutes. Drain on paper towels. Pat dry. Combine sugar, flour, bread crumbs, and cinnamon; mix. Add tomatoes and toss. Arrange in pastry shell. Sprinkle cider vinegar over and dot with butter. Top with crust. Bake at 375° for 45 minutes. Serve warm or at room temperature.

DESSERTS & SWEETS

APRICOT MERINGUE SQUARES
24 Squares

BASE:

1 cup butter
⅓ cup sugar
5 egg yolks
1 T. vanilla
1½ cups flour
1 cup apricot jam
1 to 2 T. apricot brandy or
  kirsch

MERINGUE:

5 egg whites
Dash salt
1 cup sugar
1 tsp. vanilla
2 cups chopped walnuts
  or pecans
Confectioners' sugar

For base, cream butter and sugar. Beat in egg yolks 1 at a time. Add vanilla. Stir in flour ½ cup at a time. Pat into greased 15 x 10-inch jelly roll pan. Combine jam and brandy; spread over batter. For meringue, beat egg whites with salt until foamy. Gradually add sugar. Beat until stiff peaks form. Beat in vanilla. Fold in nuts. Spread over jam. Bake at 350° for 40 minutes. Cool. Sprinkle with confectioners' sugar. Cut in 2½-inch squares.

ORANGE-CARROT COOKIES
3 Dozen

ICING:

3 T. orange juice
1 T. lemon juice
¾ lb. confectioners' sugar
Grated rind of 1 orange
Grated rind of 1 lemon

DOUGH:

1 cup sugar
¾ cup shortening
1 egg
2 cups flour
1 tsp. baking soda
½ tsp. salt
1 tsp. vanilla
1 cup cooked mashed
  carrots
1 cup walnuts, chopped

Make icing first; beat all ingredients thoroughly. To make cookie dough, cream sugar and shortening; beat in egg. Add remaining ingredients except nuts. Beat well. Stir in nuts. Drop by teaspoonful onto greased cookie sheets. Bake at 375° for 15 minutes. Ice cookies immediately, while hot.

DESSERTS & SWEETS

COCONUT THINS   15 Dozen

2 cups sugar
3 cups flour, sifted
1 tsp. baking soda
½ tsp. salt
1 cup margarine
1 cup butter
1 tsp. vanilla
1 cup extra thinly
   shredded coconut

Mix dry ingredients. Add shortening and vanilla. Stir in coconut. Knead until well combined. Roll into cylinders 2 inches in diameter. Refrigerate in waxed paper overnight. Slice thin. Bake at 350° on ungreased cookie sheets until light brown, 10 to 13 minutes.

FROSTED GINGER CREAM COOKIES   6 Dozen

½ cup shortening
1 cup sugar
1 egg
1 cup molasses
4 cups flour
½ tsp. salt
2 tsp. soda
2 tsp. ginger
1 tsp. cinnamon
1 tsp. cloves
1 tsp. nutmeg
1 cup hot water

Cream shortening and sugar. Add egg and molasses. Sift together dry ingredients and add alternately with water. Drop by teaspoonsful on greased cookie sheet. Bake at 400° for 8 minutes. Make a basic confectioners' icing with some grated lemon rind added, if desired. Frost cookies when cool.

YUMMY DATE-NUT COOKIES   3 Dozen

½ cup butter
½ cup brown sugar
1 cup honey
2 eggs
1½ cups whole wheat
   flour
½ tsp. cinnamon
½ tsp. baking powder
¾ cup raisins
¾ cup chopped walnuts
25 dates, cut into
   quarters

Cream butter; add brown sugar and ½ cup of honey. Add eggs. Gradually add flour, cinnamon and baking powder. Add raisins, nuts and dates. Drop batter from tsp. onto greased cookie sheets. Bake at 325° for 12 to 14 minutes. After cookies are done and still warm, drizzle remaining honey over top.

254

JAMS, JELLIES

CRANBERRY-APPLE JELLY
6 Jars (8 oz. Each)

A tasty, festive gift

2 cups cranberry juice
1½ cups apple juice
6 whole cloves
2 sticks cinnamon, broken
1 box (1¾ oz.) powdered fruit pectin
4 cups sugar

Combine cranberry juice, apple juice, cloves, and cinnamon. Simmer over low heat for 5 minutes. Stir in pectin and bring to a full boil, stirring constantly. Stir in sugar and return to a full rolling boil, stirring constantly. Skim off foam and remove spices. Spoon into hot sterilized jars.

SPICED ORANGE SLICES
Six 8 oz. Jars

8 oranges, peeled
5 cups sugar
1¼ cups white vinegar
1½ cups water
10 whole cloves
2 sticks cinnamon

Slice oranges about ½ inch thick. Remove seeds. Cover with water; simmer slowly in covered pan until tender, about 30 to 40 minutes. Drain. Boil sugar, vinegar, water and spices for 5 minutes. Add oranges. Simmer 1 hour until slices are well glazed. Pack carefully in sterilized jars; fill with syrup and seal.

JIFFY PEACH CHUTNEY

1 can (29 oz.) cling peach slices
½ cup pitted prunes
¾ cup brown sugar, packed
½ cup vinegar
½ cup chopped onion
½ cup dark raisins
¼ cup chopped preserved or fresh ginger
1 tsp. chili powder
½ tsp. dry mustard
½ tsp. curry powder
⅛ tsp. garlic powder

Drain syrup from peaches into a saucepan. Add sugar, vinegar, onion, raisins, and spices; simmer 30 minutes. Chop prunes. Add peaches and prunes to mixture and simmer 15 minutes longer. Keeps in refrigerator for as long as it lasts.

WINTER MENUS

COOKIE EXCHANGE
Ask each guest to bring 6 dozen of a different variety

Hot Spiced Christmas Punch
Potted Shrimp   Rillettes
Wasps' Nests
Desert Sands
Spitzbuben
Cherry Coconut Bars
Butter Stars
Meltaways

MANGIARE!

Italian Roast Peppers with Italian Bread
Lasagna
Lemon Veal or Chicken
Mixed Green Salad
Vinaigrette Dressing
Lemon and Orange Ice
Crisp and Nutty Sugar Cookies
Expresso

BRIDGE NIGHT SUPPER

Cheese Ball Deluxe
Stuffed Peppers
Rice
Swedish Rye Bread
Graham Cracker Cake

WINTER MENUS

RÉVEILLON

Caviar Mousse
Filet De Boeuf Alsacienne with Sauce Perigueux
Braised Endive
White and Green Salad
Cheese
(Brillat-Savarin, Boursault, or Brie)
Chestnut-Chocolate Loaf
French Roast Coffee

FIRESIDE DINNER

Hot Spiced Kir
Party Fondue
Food Processor French Bread
Tossed Green Salad
with
Herbed Salad Dressing
Orange Liqueur Cake

SKATING PARTY

Hot Brandied Chocolate
Ham and Swiss Toast
Crunchy Salad
Peppermint Freeze with Delicious Chocolate Sauce

BEVERAGES

HOT SPICED CHRISTMAS PUNCH   1 Quart; 8 Servings

Serve with homemade Christmas cookies

2 cups apple juice or
   cider
2 cups cranberry juice
1 stick cinnamon
6 whole cloves
1 orange, juiced and
   strained
2 T. brown sugar
Orange slices

Combine all ingredients, except orange slices. Heat slowly until hot and spicy, about 15 minutes. Serve very hot in punch cups or small mugs. Garnish with orange slices.

HOT BRANDIED CHOCOLATE   4 Servings

2 T. unsweetened cocoa
2 T. sugar
2 T. water
2 T. semisweet chocolate
   pieces
2 cups milk
6 oz. Cognac or rum

Combine cocoa, sugar, and water in saucepan. Stir over medium heat until sugar is dissolved; add chocolate pieces and stir until melted. Stir in milk and simmer, stirring occasionally until hot. Pour into cups and add 1½ oz. of Cognac or rum to each. May be topped with whipped cream and shaved chocolate.

CRANBERRY EGGNOG   14-16 Servings

6 eggs, beaten
1 pt. whipping cream,
   whipped
¾ cup sugar
2 pts. cranberry juice
Whole cranberries for
   garnish

Combine eggs and whipped cream. Fold in sugar. Stir in cranberry juice. Serve in punch cups and garnish each with a whole cranberry.

GRANDMA'S GROG   1 Serving

Sure cure for what ails you!

4 oz. water
¼ cup sugar
2 oz. lemon juice
2 oz. bourbon

Put water, sugar, and lemon juice in small saucepan. Bring to a boil. Simmer until sugar is dissolved. Pour into cup and add bourbon. Drink hot.

BEVERAGES

HARVARD MILK PUNCH

25 Servings

2 qts. milk
1 pt. coffee ice cream
16 oz. bourbon
8 oz. rum
Sugar to taste
Nutmeg

Blend ice cream and milk until smooth. Add liquors. Punch should be a pale cream color with a smooth taste, not raw or strong. Add sugar to taste. Sprinkle with nutmeg.

HOT SPICED KIR

4 Servings

2 cups white wine
⅓ cup creme de cassis
4 strips lemon peel
4 whole allspice
2 (3 inch long) cinnamon sticks
Thin lemon slices for garnish

Combine all ingredients except lemon slices in a stainless steel or enameled saucepan; simmer for 10 minutes. Pour into warmed wine glasses and garnish with a thin lemon slice.

SANTA SLING

1 Gallon

Best made in January for the following Christmas

2 whole cloves
4 apples (Winesap or Stayman)
1 qt. rye whiskey
8 oz. brandy
8 oz. peach brandy
8 oz. Jamaican rum
½ cup plus 1½ T. sugar
½ cup water

Insert 1 clove into each of 2 apples. Place in ovenproof dish with about 1 inch of boiling water and bake at 400° for 25 minutes. Put apples in a well-glazed stone jar. Pour liquors over apples. Dissolve sugar in water and stir into liquor mixture. Cover tightly and seal with tape. Set aside. When ready to serve, add 1 part water to 4 parts liquor. Serve over ice.

APPETIZERS

CHEESE BALL DELUXE

4 Pound Cheese Ball

Perfect for a holiday open house

6 pkgs. (8 oz. each)
   cream cheese
½ lb. Roquefort or blue
   cheese
½ lb. sharp Cheddar
   cheese
½ cup minced chives or
   green onions
1 garlic clove, minced
2 to 3 T. each of any 6 of
   the following: red
   caviar, black caviar,
   chopped green olives,
   chopped black olives,
   chopped parsley,
   chopped capers,
   chopped pimiento,
   diced cooked bacon
Parsley sprigs

Place 2 pkgs. cream cheese in food processor with Roquefort; process until blended. Remove to plate. Place 2 pkgs. cream cheese and Cheddar cheese in processor; blend and remove to plate. Place remaining cream cheese in food processor with chives and garlic; blend and remove to plate. Shape all mixtures into huge ball. Do not blend; just pile together and shape. Make marks on ball indicating 6 pie-shaped divisions. Decorate each division with one of the chopped toppings. Place parsley sprigs on top and around base of ball. If desired, cover whole ball with combination of chopped parsley and olives; decorate with strips of pimiento.

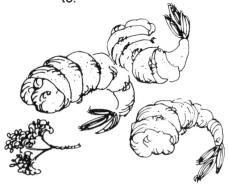

POTTED SHRIMP

1 Cup

1 cup butter
½ lb. tiny raw shrimp (or
   chopped shrimp)
1 tsp. paprika
¼ tsp. salt
⅛ tsp. mace
⅛ tsp. allspice
Few grindings pepper
2 T. lemon juice

Clarify butter. Heat 3 T. clarified butter in skillet; add shrimp and seasonings. Cook 2 minutes over high heat. Add lemon juice. Place shrimp in small crock, pressing down lightly. Spoon remaining butter over shrimp; cover and refrigerate. Use as a cocktail spread, or serve small portions on a lettuce leaf as an appetizer.

HORS D'OEUVRES

RILLETTES

A delicious, inexpensive pate

1½ lbs. lean pork, diced
small (shoulder or end
of rib)
1 cup pork fat, diced
small
2 tsp. salt
Freshly ground pepper
¼ tsp. nutmeg
¼ tsp. ground cloves
1 tsp. thyme
1 bay leaf
1 cup boiling water or to
cover

Mix meat and fat with salt, pepper, spices, and herbs. Cover with boiling water. Place in 325° oven. Cook 4 to 5 hours until meat is fork tender, stirring occasionally. Remove meat and fat. Set in colander to drain, reserving liquid. Remove bay leaf and beat meat with a fork gradually mixing in enough reserved hot fat to form smooth paste, reserving 1 cup of the liquid fat. Pack the rillettes into small jars or crocks. Pour reserved fat over to about a depth of ½ inch. They should be served cold with French bread and cornichons. Rillettes may be frozen; defrost well before using.

BAJA DIP

5 Cups

Spicy and good

1 pkg. (8 oz.) cream
cheese
1 cup sour cream
1 can (10 oz.) bean dip
1 to 2 T. chili powder
10 drops hot pepper
sauce
2 T. parsley
½ cup chives (or 2 oz.
pkg. frozen)
6 oz. grated Cheddar
cheese
6 oz. grated Monterey
Jack cheese

Mix all ingredients except the grated cheeses. Put into buttered 1-qt. casserole. Top with grated cheeses. Bake at 350° for about 20 minutes, or until the cheese bubbles. (Before serving, you may have to skim off a little of the extra oil from the cheeses.) Use as a dip with corn chips.

APPETIZERS

ARTICHOKE "QUI VIVE"

4-5 Dozen

1 can (15 oz.) artichokes
(not marinated)
1 cup mayonnaise
1 cup grated Parmesan
cheese
1 clove garlic, minced
½ tsp. seasoned salt
1½ loaves party rye bread

Rinse and drain artichokes. Chop into small pieces. Mix with mayonnaise, Parmesan cheese, garlic, and seasoned salt. Spread on party rye slices. Broil for 3 to 5 minutes, or until bubbly and brown. Mixture may also be put into 3-cup ovenproof dish and baked at 375° for 15 minutes or until browned and bubbling. Serve as spread with small rye rounds.

CAVIAR MOUSSE

1 Pint

8 T. unsalted butter
1 can (7 oz.) water-
packed tuna
1 T. chopped green onion
tops
1 jar (6 oz.) herring
tidbits in wine, drained
1 jar (4 oz.) black caviar
¼ tsp. garlic powder
½ tsp. sugar
1 jar (4 oz.) red caviar
(salmon or whitefish is
fine)

Melt butter and pour into blender. Add tuna and blend until it is the consistency of paste. Add green onions, herring, 1 heaping T. black caviar, garlic powder, and sugar. Blend until there are no perceptible lumps. It should be the consistency of whipped cream. Pack mixture into 1-pt. mold (a small bread pan is good) and refrigerate. When ready to serve, unmold by running a knife dipped in hot water around the edges. Spread sides with remaining black caviar. Spread top with red caviar. Serve with small pumpernickel or rye bread rounds. This may be prepared up to an hour before serving. Molded mousse may be frozen and defrosted a few hours at room temperature before serving. Leftovers may be kept tightly wrapped in plastic for several weeks in refrigerator.

HORS D'OEUVRES

SMOKED OYSTER ROLL

For smoked oyster lovers!

2 pkgs. (8 oz. each)
  cream cheese
2 to 3 T. mayonnaise
2 tsp. Worcestershire
  sauce
½ medium onion, grated
1 clove garlic, minced
2 cans (3.6 oz. each)
  smoked oysters,
  chopped
Parsley
Toast rounds

Mix cream cheese, mayonnaise, and seasonings. Spread out flat on a piece of foil. Spread chopped oysters over cream mixture. Roll up carefully using a spatula. Chill at least 24 hours. Do not freeze. Garnish with parsley. Slice and serve on toast rounds.

ITALIAN ROAST PEPPERS   6 Servings

6 sweet peppers, red or
  green or a combination
  of both
Salt and pepper to taste
2 tsp. finely chopped
  garlic
2 T. capers
1 T. finely chopped
  parsley
⅓ cup olive oil
1 can (2 oz.) anchovies

Place peppers under a preheated broiler close to the heat and let them roast, turning them frequently, until they are lightly charred and wrinkled all over. Immediately drop them into a brown paper bag and close bag tightly. When cool, remove peppers and, using fingers and a paring knife, pull and scrape away the skin. Cut off and discard the cores. Split peppers and seed. Cut into strips about ½-inch wide. Arrange the strips over the bottom of a serving dish. Sprinkle evenly with salt, pepper, garlic, capers and parsley. Pour oil over all. Chill. Drain anchovies and arrange over peppers. Serve at room temperature with crusty French bread. For a variation, omit capers and anchovies and stir in 2 to 3 T. oregano.

APPETIZERS

CHEESE AND LIVER PATE

20 Servings

BASIC GELATIN:

2 T. unflavored gelatin
4 chicken bouillon cubes
1½ cups water

TOMATO GLAZE:

¼ cup of basic gelatin
¼ cup V-8 juice

CHEESE LAYER:

1 cup shredded brick
  cheese
1 T. crumbled blue
  cheese
¼ cup sour cream
½ cup of basic gelatin
2 T. chopped celery
1 T. chopped green
  pepper

PATE LAYER:

2 T. butter
½ cup chopped fresh
  mushrooms
¼ lb. liver sausage
2 tsp. lemon juice
4 tsp. brandy
⅓ cup chopped pecans

For basic gelatin, heat gelatin and bouillon cubes in water. Stir until dissolved.

For tomato glaze, combine and pour into oiled 4½-cup mold. Chill just until set.

For cheese layer, beat cheeses and sour cream. Add gelatin. Fold in celery and pepper. Spoon over tomato layer. Chill until set.

For pate layer, cook mushrooms in butter until tender. Mix with sausage and lemon juice. Blend in remaining basic gelatin and brandy. Fold in nuts. Spoon over cheese layer. Chill until firm. Unmold and serve with crackers.

CRABMEAT MUSHROOM TRIANGLES   3 Dozen

1 can (7½ oz.) crabmeat
   (or frozen)
1½ cups chopped fresh
   mushrooms
½ cup finely chopped
   celery
¼ cup sliced green onion
2 T. butter
1 T. flour
½ tsp. salt
½ cup half and half
1 T. lemon juice
6 sheets phyllo dough
½ cup butter, melted

Drain and flake crabmeat, removing any cartilage. Cook mushrooms, celery, and onion in 2 T. butter over moderate heat until moisture is evaporated. Stir in flour and salt. Add half and half; cook until thickened. Remove from heat; add crab and lemon juice. Refrigerate until ready to use.

To assemble, lay out sheet of dough and brush lightly with melted butter. Cut crosswise into 6 strips about 3 inches wide. Place a scant T. of crabmeat mixture on bottom of each strip. Fold in triangles like folding a flag. Repeat procedure for rest of phyllo sheets. Place on an ungreased baking sheet. Brush lightly with melted butter. Bake at 375° for 10 to 12 minutes or until lightly browned and puffed. Serve hot.

NEW YEAR'S MUSHROOMS

Serve as first course or on lettuce as a salad

1 lb. fresh mushrooms,
   cleaned and sliced
4 cups water
2 T. lemon juice
½ cup sour cream
1 tsp. salt
2 T. grated onion
2 dashes pepper

Boil the mushrooms for 2 minutes in water to which lemon juice has been added. Remove mushrooms; dry on paper towels. Combine remaining ingredients and toss with mushrooms. Refrigerate overnight.

APPETIZERS

OYSTER AND ARTICHOKE CASSEROLE   6 Servings
Outstanding first course

3 green onions with tops, minced
1 clove garlic, minced
¼ lb. mushrooms, sliced
¼ cup butter
1 can (10½ oz.) cream of mushroom soup
2 T. minced parsley
½ cup Italian bread crumbs
1 pt. oysters (about 2 dozen), drained
Juice of ¼ lemon
Worcestershire and hot pepper sauce to taste
1 can (15 oz.) artichoke hearts, not marinated, drained

Saute green onions, garlic, and mushrooms in butter. Add undiluted soup, mushrooms, parsley, and bread crumbs, reserving enough bread crumbs to sprinkle over top. Next add oysters, lemon juice, Worcestershire, and hot pepper sauce. If mixture is too thick, thin it with a little more lemon juice. Fold in artichoke hearts. Place in a small casserole dish; top with reserved bread crumbs. Bake at 350° for 30 minutes.

DOUBLE LIVER PATE
Even if you don't like liver, you'll love this!

½ lb. chicken liver
¼ cup butter
1 T. Worcestershire sauce
1 tsp. salt
1 tsp. paprika
½ tsp. curry powder
¼ tsp. pepper
½ lb. liver sausage, diced
1 pkg. (8 oz.) cream cheese, diced
1 cup whipping cream

Saute chicken liver in butter 5 to 7 minutes. Drain and save drippings. Finely chop liver; cool. Combine drippings, liver, and seasonings; beat until smooth. Add liver sausage and cream cheese alternately with cream, beating until smooth and blended. Line 1½-qt. bowl loosely with plastic wrap. Spoon mixture into bowl, cover with plastic wrap and refrigerate overnight. Unmold and serve with French bread. Pate can also be served in a crock.

HORS D'OEUVRES

STUFFED BRUSSELS SPROUTS   Makes 16-20

1 lb. fresh Brussels
   sprouts, small to
   medium sized
2 T. salt
¼ cup red wine vinegar
2 tsp. sugar
1 tsp. salt
Few grindings black
   pepper

Cut stems and remove any discolored outer leaves from Brussels sprouts. Bring 2-qts. water to a boil and add 2 T. salt. Put Brussels sprouts into water. Let sprouts cook for about 10 to 15 minutes or until tender-crisp. Drain well and place in vinegar, sugar, salt and pepper. Remove from marinade. Drain well and pat dry. Slit Brussels sprouts lengthwise, but do not cut through. Using a knife, fill each sprout with enough Roquefort mixture so that sides hold firm. Do not overfill. Refrigerate covered until ready to serve.

DEVILED ROQUEFORT   ¾ Cup

Also makes a wonderful dip for beef fondue

¼ lb. Roquefort or blue
   cheese
4 T. butter
1 large clove garlic,
   minced
1 T. Dijon mustard
2 drops bitters

Put cheese and butter in food processor. Process until completely combined and smooth. Add garlic, mustard and bitters. Process several seconds more. Will keep for several weeks in refrigerator in tightly covered container.

SALAMI   Makes 4

4 lbs. ground beef
3 T. dry red wine
1 tsp. garlic powder
2 T. mustard seed
1 T. basil
1 T. oregano
1 tsp. onion powder
⅔ cup Parmesan cheese
¼ cup curing salt
   (available through
   butchers)

Mix all ingredients well, making sure there are no air pockets. Cover and chill in refrigerator 24 hours. Make 4 logs and wrap in nylon netting. Tie at both ends with string. Bake 4 hours at 225° in a broiler pan. Pat dry with paper toweling. Keeps in refrigerator in aluminum foil for 3 weeks or can be frozen up to 6 months.

SOUPS

RICH MUSHROOM SOUP   5 Cups

½ lb. fresh mushrooms,
  thinly sliced
¼ cup butter
¾ cup finely chopped
  parsley
1 can (10½ oz.) beef
  broth
1 cup half and half
2 egg yolks
1 cup sour cream
Salt to taste
Dash of white pepper
½ cup whipping cream,
  whipped

Saute mushrooms in butter until lightly browned. Add parsley; saute a few minutes more. Add beef broth and half and half; simmer for 3 minutes. Beat egg yolks with ¾ cup sour cream. Stir in some of the hot soup, then return all to pan. Remove from heat. Add salt to taste and dash of white pepper. Fold remaining ¼ cup sour cream into whipped cream. Heat soup almost to boiling (do not boil) and pour into individual heatproof bowls. Spoon whipped cream mixture onto soup. Set under broiler until topping browns. Serve at once.

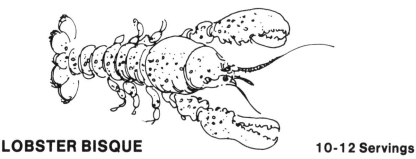

LOBSTER BISQUE   10-12 Servings

Elegant and delicious

2 cans (48 oz. each)
  chicken broth (9 cups)
1 bottle (8 oz.) clam juice
1 stalk celery
1 carrot, chopped
1 bay leaf
Fish trimmings (optional),
  non-oily
½ cup vermouth
9 T. sweet butter
9 T. flour
1 cup cream (whipping or
  half and half)
1 can (8 oz.) frozen
  lobster meat, thawed
  and soaked in ¼ cup
  sherry or Madeira wine

Simmer first 7 ingredients for 30 minutes. Strain. Work the butter and flour together. Slowly whisk a small amount of broth into butter-flour mixture. Whisk this gradually into the rest of broth. Simmer. Add cream. Add lobster meat at the last minute after bisque thickens to prevent toughening. May be kept warm in double boiler. Do not boil after adding lobster. Stock may be frozen and lobster added upon defrosting.

SEAFOOD GUMBO   10 Servings

Freezes and reheats nicely

1 cup shortening
1½ cups flour
3 qts. water or fish stock
1 can (16 oz.) tomatoes,
  with juice
1 large green pepper,
  diced
2 pkgs. frozen sliced okra
  (10 oz. each), thawed
2 large onions, diced
2 bunches green onions,
  chopped
1 cup diced celery
3 garlic cloves, minced or
  put through garlic press
1 bay leaf
1 T. dried parsley
½ tsp. thyme
Hot pepper sauce,
  cayenne pepper, salt
  and pepper to taste
¼ cup butter
3 lbs. shrimp, shelled and
  deveined
1½ pts. oysters
1 lb. crab or crayfish
1½ cups cooked rice

Make a roux by melting shortening and adding flour, stirring constantly over medium heat. Cook until dark brown. Be careful not to burn or scorch. Add water and tomatoes; bring to a boil, simmer. Meanwhile prepare the vegetables. In separate pan, saute green peppers, okra, onions, green onions, and celery until soft, but not brown in ¼ cup butter. Add to roux. Add seasonings and simmer 30 minutes more. Add more water if you desire a thinner consistency. Add shrimp, oysters and crabs or crayfish. Simmer 30 minutes more. Check seasoning. To serve, place 2 T. of cooked rice in each soup plate or bowl. Pour gumbo over the rice.

BREADS

CAUCASIC CHEESE BREAD

A Russian bread almost hearty enough to be a meal

2 pkgs. active dry yeast
½ tsp. plus 1 T. sugar
1 cup lukewarm milk
3½ to 4 cups flour
2 tsp. salt
8 T. butter, softened

FILLING:

2 lbs. grated Muenster
  cheese
1½ T. butter, softened
1 egg

Sprinkle yeast and ½ tsp. sugar over ½ cup of the milk. Dissolve and let stand until mixture is foamy, about 5 to 8 minutes. Pour 3 cups flour in bowl. Make a well in the center and add remaining ½ cup milk, yeast, sugar, salt and butter. Beat flour into ingredients until smooth. Place on board and knead 10 minutes. Place in buttered bowl, cover with a damp cloth. Let rise until doubled, 45 minutes to 1 hour. Punch down and let rise another 30 to 40 minutes.

While dough rises, make filling by combining cheese, butter and egg. Puree in food processor or food mill. Set aside.

Punch down dough. Roll on floured surface into a circle 22 inches in diameter. Place in 9-inch round tin. Let dough drop over edges. Fill with cheese mixture. Fold dough around cheese mixture, pleating dough like a pinwheel. Gather ends of dough that meet in center and twist into a knot. Let rest 15 minutes. Bake at 375° for 1 hour or until brown. Turn out and cool 15 minutes on a rack.

HERB MELBA TOAST

1 loaf thinly sliced day-
  old white bread
½ cup butter, softened
1 T. minced parsley
1 small clove garlic,
  mashed
¼ tsp. basil
¼ tsp. oregano
Freshly ground black
  pepper to taste
1 tsp. sesame seeds

Take crusts off bread. Cut into any desired shape. Mix butter and remaining ingredients. Spread butter liberally into bread and all the way to edges. Bake on unrimmed cookie sheet at 325° for about 15 minutes or until nicely browned and crispy. The bread should be crisp throughout. Keeps well in a closed container. Serve with soups or salads.

BREADS

SWEDISH RYE BREAD   2 Loaves
The secret is the molasses

1 pkg. dry yeast
¼ cup warm water (100 to 105°)
2 cups milk
⅓ cup butter
¼ cup molasses
¼ cup brown sugar
1 tsp. salt
2 cups rye flour
1 tsp. caraway seeds
4 cups sifted all-purpose flour

Sprinkle yeast on water. Let stand 5 minutes to dissolve. Scald milk; add butter, molasses, brown sugar, salt and rye flour. Beat until smooth. When lukewarm, add caraway seeds and yeast. Add white flour gradually to make a stiff dough. Knead until smooth and elastic, about 8 to 10 minutes. Cover and let rise in warm place until almost double in bulk (1 to 2 hours). Toss on a lightly floured board and divide into 2 equal parts. Form each into a rough loaf. Cut a small hole in center. Place on buttered cookie sheet. Prick with fork. Cover and let rise until double in bulk. Bake at 375° for 35 minutes. Brush with warm water when ½ baked and again when removed from oven. May be formed in traditional loaf size.

APRICOT BRANDY BREAD   2 Loaves
Great party or brunch bread

½ cup butter
2 cups sugar
2 eggs
½ cup apricot brandy
1 jar (16 oz.) chunky applesauce
2½ cups sifted flour
½ tsp. baking powder
2 tsp. baking soda
½ tsp. salt
1½ cups dried apricots, chopped
½ cup chopped pecans

Cream butter and sugar. Add eggs and beat until fluffy. Add applesauce and brandy. Sift flour, baking powder, baking soda and salt together. Add dry ingredients to creamed mixture. Add chopped apricots and pecans. Bake in 2 buttered, paper-lined loaf pans (9½ x 5½ x 3 inch) at 350° for 50 to 60 minutes.

BREADS

FOOD PROCESSOR FRENCH BREAD   2 Loaves

1½ cups warm water
1½ pkgs. active dry yeast
1 tsp. sugar
3½ cups flour
2 tsp. salt
1 tsp. sugar
Flour

Combine ½ cup warm water, yeast, and 1 tsp. sugar in small bowl; let stand until yeast is dissolved and mixture is foamy, about 5 minutes. Combine flour, salt, remaining sugar and yeast mixture in work bowl of food processor. With machine running, slowly begin adding 1 cup warm water. A soft ball should form in several seconds; if not, add a little more warm water. Let machine run 15 to 20 seconds, adding more flour if dough seems too soft. Transfer dough to lightly floured board. Knead with a little additional flour for several turns. Divide dough in ½ and shape into 2 cylinders 8 to 10-inches long. Transfer to greased baguette pans. Cut 3 or 4 diagonal slashes in top of each loaf with tip of knife or single-edged razor blade. Cover and let rise in warm place until doubled, about 45 minutes to 1 hour. Place oven racks in middle and lower quarters of oven and begin preheating to 450°. Center shallow pan of water on lower rack. When dough has doubled, place on middle rack directly above water and bake 10 minutes. Reduce heat to 400° and continue baking an additional 15 minutes, or until loaves are golden brown and have a hollow sound when tapped with the fingers. Remove bread from pans. For a crisp crust, return to oven for 5 minutes. Cool. If made the day before serving, wrap in foil. Freeze. Reheat, frozen, at 350° for 15 to 20 minutes.

BREADS

QUICK ORANGE BISCUIT RING   8 Servings

1 large orange
¾ cup sugar
6 T. butter, melted
2 pkgs. canned biscuits

Combine grated rind of orange and sugar in a small bowl. In another bowl, mix melted butter and juice of the orange. Dip each biscuit in butter mixture and then sugar mixture. Stand on end in a ring mold or angel food cake pan, side by side. Pour remaining butter and sugar over all. Bake at 350° for 40 minutes. To serve, invert on tray or pretty plate.

NO-KNEAD WHOLE WHEAT BREAD   2 Loaves

3 cups all-purpose flour
2 cups warm water
2 T. sugar
1 pkg. dry yeast
2 tsp. salt
½ cup hot water
½ cup brown sugar
3 T. melted shortening
3 cups whole wheat flour

Combine flour, warm water, sugar, dry yeast and salt. Beat until very smooth. Cover and let rise in warm place until light and bubbly, about 20 to 30 minutes. Mix hot water with brown sugar and melted shortening. Cool to lukewarm. Add to sponge, then add whole wheat flour. Mix until smooth but do not knead. Place dough in 2 greased loaf pans and let rise until doubled in bulk, about 1 hour. Bake at 350° for 50 minutes. This is a firm, heavy bread. You may want to try using 2 pkgs. of dry yeast.

APPLE OATMEAL PUDDING   4 Servings

An excellent breakfast dish

2 cups milk
2 T. brown sugar
1 T. butter
¼ tsp. salt
¼ tsp. cinnamon
1 cup rolled oats
1 cup diced, peeled
  apples
½ cup raisins
1 T. brown sugar

Combine first 5 ingredients in pan. Scald. Add oats, apples, and raisins; heat until bubbles appear at edge of pan. Turn into greased 1½-qt. casserole. Bake at 350° for 30 minutes. After first 15 minutes, stir and add 1 T. brown sugar.

LUNCHEON DISHES

TUNA IN LEMON CREAM SAUCE   6 Servings

SAUCE:

1 T. butter
1½ T. flour
¼ tsp. salt
Dash nutmeg
1 cup half and half
1 egg yolk, beaten
1 T. lemon juice

FISH:

½ cup chopped parsley
½ cup chopped green
  onions
¼ cup diced celery
1 clove garlic, minced
4 T. butter, melted
1½ cups sliced fresh
  mushrooms
2 cans (6½ oz. each)
  chunk light tuna,
  drained
1 cup shredded Swiss
  cheese

Light Dry White

For sauce, melt butter over medium heat. Blend in flour, salt, and nutmeg. Gradually add half and half, stirring constantly until thickened. Remove from heat. Stir small amount of hot sauce into egg yolk. Add this mixture back to rest of hot sauce, stirring briskly. Add lemon juice. Set aside.

For fish mixture, saute parsley, green onions, celery, and garlic in butter until onion is golden. Add mushrooms; stir over medium heat 2 to 3 minutes. Stir in lemon cream sauce. Gently fold in tuna. Spoon into individual ramekins or a shallow baking dish. Sprinkle cheese on top. Broil until cheese is browned.

NO-CRUST SPINACH QUICHE   8 Servings

1 carton (16 oz.) small-
  curd cottage cheese
1 pkg. (10 oz.) frozen
  chopped spinach,
  thawed
1½ cups cubed sharp
  Cheddar cheese (small
  cubes)
3 eggs, beaten
¼ cup butter, melted
3 T. flour
1 T. onion flakes
1 T. lemon juice
1 tsp. salt
½ tsp. minced fresh garlic

Light Dry White

Mix ingredients thoroughly. Turn into buttered 9-inch quiche or pie pan. Bake at 325° for 1¼ hours, or until set and nicely browned.

LUNCHEON DISHES

SEAFOOD STRUDEL

4 Rolls

8 T. butter
3 T. flour
1 cup scalded milk
½ cup grated Gruyere
  cheese
3 T. whipping cream
¼ tsp. dry mustard
½ lb. mushrooms, sliced
1½ lbs. shrimp, cooked
1 pkg. (6 oz.) frozen
  crabmeat, thawed and
  drained
12 phyllo leaves
¾ to 1 cup butter, melted
1 cup dry fresh bread
  crumbs

CHEESE SAUCE:

2 T. butter
2 T. flour
¼ tsp. salt
⅛ tsp. pepper
1 cup milk
¼ cup grated Gruyere
  cheese

Light Dry White

Melt 6 T. butter; stir in flour. Cook 3 minutes. Remove from heat; add milk, stirring constantly. Simmer for 5 minutes. Stir in cheese, cream and mustard. Cook, stirring, until cheese melts. Cool. Saute mushrooms in 2 T. butter; combine with shrimp and crabmeat. Add to sauce.

Work with 3 phyllo leaves at a time. Brush 1 with melted butter, then sprinkle entire surface with 1 T. bread crumbs. Place another leaf on top of crumbs; butter that leaf and sprinkle with bread crumbs. Put third leaf on top and just butter. Spread about 1¼ cups of seafood mixture in a strip along 1 of the short edges of the stack of phyllo. Roll up jelly-roll fashion. Place on cookie sheet; brush surface with butter. Repeat entire procedure to make 3 more rolls. May be made ahead to this point. To serve, bake at 350° for 40 to 50 minutes. Serve with cheese sauce.

For cheese sauce, melt butter in a saucepan. Stir in flour; cook 3 minutes. Remove from heat. Add salt and pepper; stir in milk. Return to heat; bring to a boil. Cook, stirring constantly for 1 minute. Add cheese; continue stirring until cheese is melted.

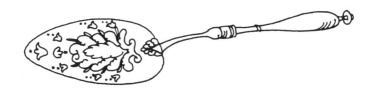

LUNCHEON DISHES

MEDITERRANEAN LINGUINI

6 Servings

1 lb. bacon
4 cloves garlic, minced
1½ cups pitted black
  olives
1 can (14 oz.) minced
  clams with juice
½ cup butter, melted
1 pkg. (12 oz.) linguini,
  cooked and drained
1 can (7 oz.) tuna, packed
  in water
½ cup chopped parsley
Lemon wedges

Fry bacon until crisp. Remove from pan, crumble, and set aside. Pour off all but ¼ cup of bacon drippings. Add garlic, olives, clams, and juice to bacon drippings; simmer 5 minutes. Add melted butter. Place the hot, cooked linguini in a 3-qt. warmed casserole. Pour mixture over. Break up pieces of tuna and sprinkle over. Sprinkle with crumbled bacon and parsley. Serve with lemon wedges.

Light Dry White

HAM AND SWISS TOAST

6 Servings

Late supper, brunch or apres ski

1½ lbs. fresh mushrooms
1 medium (3 oz.) onion,
  chopped
1 cup butter
½ cup dry white wine
¼ tsp. dried chervil
1 pt. half and half
¾ cup flour
Salt and pepper
Fresh lemon juice
6 slices toast, buttered
12 thin slices ham
12 thin slices Swiss
  cheese

Light Dry White

Clean, wash and slice mushrooms. Saute onion in ½ cup butter until limp. Add mushrooms, wine and chervil. Cover and cook over medium heat 10 to 15 minutes. Remove mushrooms and onions from pan. Reduce liquid to about ½. Add half and half. Thicken with remaining ½ cup soft butter blended with flour. Cook slowly 5 minutes. Mix in mushrooms and onions. Season to taste with salt, pepper and fresh lemon juice. Place buttered toast in a glass baking dish; do not overlap. Place 6 thin slices of ham on top of toast. Spoon creamed mushrooms on top of ham. Cover with another 6 slices of ham. Cover each with 2 slices of Swiss cheese. Lightly dust top with paprika. Bake at 375° for 20 minutes, or until heated through and cheese melts.

LUNCHEON DISHES

HAM AND BROCCOLI CASSEROLE   4 Servings

1 pkg. (6 oz.) seasoned
   long grain and wild rice
1 pkg. (10 oz.) frozen
   chopped broccoli
2 cups ham, cubed
1 cup sharp Cheddar
   cheese, cut in ½-inch
   cubes
1 can (10½ oz.)
   condensed cream of
   celery soup
1 cup mayonnaise
2 tsp. prepared mustard
1 tsp. curry powder
¼ cup grated Parmesan
   cheese

Cook rice and broccoli according to package directions. Spread rice in bottom of a buttered 13 x 9 x 2-inch casserole. Top with broccoli, then ham, and cheese. Blend soup with mayonnaise, mustard and curry. Pour soup mixture over casserole. Sprinkle with Parmesan cheese. Bake at 350° for 30 to 45 minutes.

Light-Bodied Red

MEATLESS NO-FAT SPAGHETTI SAUCE   6 Servings

1 medium onion, chopped
1 lb. mushrooms,
   chopped
1 clove garlic, minced
½ green pepper, chopped
2 cans (28 oz. each)
   Italian plum tomatoes,
   finely chopped
½ tsp. basil
¼ tsp. thyme
½ tsp. Italian spices
1 T. parsley
1 bay leaf
1 can (6 oz.) tomato
   paste
Salt and pepper to taste

Boil 4 oz. water in large saucepan. Add onion, mushrooms, garlic, and green pepper; cook over medium heat until tender. Add plum tomatoes and spices. Simmer 1 hour. Add tomato paste. Simmer 20 to 30 minutes longer. Salt and pepper to taste. Serve over high protein pasta.

Light-Bodied Red

LUNCHEON DISHES

GERMAN OMELET

4-6 Servings

¼ cup butter
2 cups cubed uncooked potatoes (frozen hash browns may be used)
¼ cup chopped onion
1 cup cubed ham
¼ cup chopped fresh parsley
6 eggs
¾ tsp. salt
Dash pepper
2 T. half and half
¾ cup shredded Monterey Jack cheese

Medium-Dry White

Melt butter in 9 to 10-inch frying pan. Add potatoes and onions. Cover and cook over medium heat. Brown evenly for about 20 minutes, or until potatoes are tender and golden. Add ham and cook a few minutes. Sprinkle with parsley. Reduce heat. Beat eggs, salt, pepper, and half and half until blended. Pour egg mixture over potatoes and ham. Cover and cook until eggs are set, about 10 minutes. Occasionally slip spatula around edge of pan to allow egg mixture to run down into potatoes. Sprinkle cheese over top and cover until cheese melts. Garnish with fresh parsley. Cut in wedges to serve.

EGGS SAVOYARDE

4 Servings

Something different for a weekend breakfast or brunch

Butter, garlic
3 medium potatoes (1 lb.), thinly sliced
Salt, pepper
1 cup half and half (about)
4 eggs
2 T. grated Parmesan cheese
2 T. grated Gruyere cheese

Rub a 1½-qt. casserole with butter and cut garlic. Add potatoes, sprinkling with salt and pepper to taste. Pour in just enough half and half to reach top of potatoes. Bake, uncovered, at 350° for 30 to 45 minutes, or until tender. Poach eggs in salted water with a little vinegar for 3 to 5 minutes, or to desired firmness. Remove with slotted spoon; place on top of potatoes. Sprinkle with cheese. Broil about 1 minute to melt.

LUNCHEON DISHES

CHILI CHEESE QUICHE   6 Servings

¼ cup flour
½ tsp. baking powder
½ lb. Monterey Jack
   cheese, grated
5 eggs, beaten
1 can (4 oz.) chili
   peppers, diced
½ pt. cottage cheese
¼ cup butter, melted and
   cooled
Dash salt
½ lb. cooked seasoned
   pork sausage (optional)
1 9-inch unbaked pastry
   shell

Medium-Dry White

Combine flour and baking powder; toss with grated cheese. Add eggs, chili peppers, cottage cheese, butter, and salt. Blend well. Arrange cooked sausage in bottom of pastry shell, if desired. Pour egg mixture into pastry shell and bake at 400° for 10 minutes. Reduce heat to 350° for 35 to 40 minutes.

BÖREK (CHEESE FILLED PASTRY)   12 Servings

1 lb. phyllo pastry (20
   sheets)
1½ cups butter, melted
2 eggs, beaten
2 lbs. large curd cottage
   cheese
2 T. parsley
¾ lb. grated Muenster
   cheese

Light Dry White

Butter a 12 X 15-inch baking pan. Lay 1 sheet phyllo in bottom; spread with about 1 T. melted butter. Repeat with next 9 sheets. Combine eggs, cottage cheese, and parsley. Pour over phyllo. Sprinkle with Muenster cheese. Top with last 10 sheets of phyllo, spreading butter between each sheet. Cut into 12 squares before baking. Bake at 350° for ½ hour, or until light brown. May be frozen, cooked or uncooked.

ENTREES: MEAT

FILET de BOEUF ALSACIENNE WITH SAUCE PERIGUEUX

6-8 Servings

An elegant party dish featuring presliced tenderloin in a delicious short-cut puff pastry

1 beef tenderloin (about 3½ lbs.)
⅓ cup oil
1 small onion, sliced
1 carrot, sliced
1 stalk celery, chopped
¼ tsp. thyme
6 whole peppercorns
3 whole cloves
1 bay leaf
1 clove garlic, chopped
1 tsp. salt
1 cup dry white vermouth
⅓ cup Cognac or brandy
6 to 8 thin slices Westphalian or Virginia ham
4 to 6 T. pate de foie gras
½ cup strong beef broth, reduced to 3 to 4 T.
Suet from tenderloin
2 truffles or Chinese mushrooms, chopped

Place tenderloin in non-metal baking dish. Put oil, vegetables, spices, herbs, and garlic in heavy saucepan; cover and simmer about 10 minutes, or until vegetables are tender. Sprinkle salt over tenderloin; cover with cooked vegetable mixture. Pour on vermouth and Cognac; cover and marinate in refrigerator at least 24 hours, turning and basting several times. Before baking, drain and reserve marinade; dry tenderloin thoroughly. Make 6 to 8 evenly spaced slices in tenderloin, about ¾ of way through. Spread each ham slice with about 1 tsp. foie gras; insert into cuts. Put last slice on 1 end. Reshape tenderloin; cover with suet and tie. Roast at 425° for 25 minutes. Remove from oven; brush on reduced beef broth; cool at least 30 minutes. (May be done ahead, refrigerated, and brought to room temperature before final cooking.)

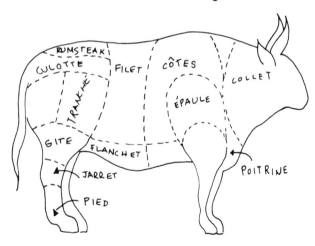

282

PUFF PASTRY:

1 ½ cups all-purpose flour
½ cup cake flour
¾ tsp. salt
3 sticks unsalted butter, chilled
½ cup ice water (about)

PERIGUEUX SAUCE:

2 cups beef broth
1 T. tomato paste
Reserved marinade
2 T. cornstarch
¼ cup Madeira wine
1 to 2 chopped truffles or Chinese mushrooms, chopped and soaked in 2 T. Madeira
1 T. butter

Full-Bodied Red

For pastry, mix flours and salt in large bowl. Dice butter into ¼ to ½-inch pieces and add to flour. Blend together rapidly until it forms 1-inch flakes. (Do not use food processor.) Blend in just enough water so dough masses together. Turn dough onto lightly floured board; roll into 12 x 14-inch rectangle. Sprinkle top lightly with more flour; fold in thirds as an envelope. Repeat rolling and folding 3 more times. By fourth time, pastry should acquire a definite shape. Wrap in plastic; refrigerate 1 hour. Roll and fold 2 more times. Refrigerate 30 minutes before baking. (It may be tightly wrapped and frozen for several months at this point.)

For final baking, spread remaining foie gras on tenderloin; roll in chopped truffles. Put meat on a rack in well-greased shallow baking dish. Roll out rectangle of pastry large enough to cover top and sides of meat. Untie meat. Lay pastry over meat; tuck in around bottom. Make several holes in top of pastry for steam to escape. Use extra pastry to make decorations. Brush top with glaze of 1 egg yolk mixed with 1 T. water; affix decorations and brush with glaze again. Bake at 425° for 20 minutes, or until pastry has started to brown. Lower oven to 375° and bake another 20 minutes. Let rest for 20 minutes before serving.

For sauce, boil beef broth, tomato paste, and reserved marinade until it reduces by ½. Skim off fat, strain, and adjust seasonings. Add cornstarch dissolved in Madeira, truffles and their juices (or Chinese mushrooms), and cook, stirring, until thickened. Swirl in butter. To serve, cut through existing slices; pass sauce. Accompany with braised celery or endive.

ENTREES: MEAT

RAGOUT DE BOEUF AU VIN ROUGE   8-10 Servings

Beef stew in red wine

3 lbs. boneless lean beef,
  cut in 1-inch cubes
Seasoned flour
6 T. butter
¼ cup brandy
1 large onion, chopped
1 lb. carrots, sliced
1 T. minced parsley
1 T. minced chives
  (optional)
1 clove garlic, minced
1 tsp. salt
½ tsp. thyme
½ tsp. marjoram
¼ tsp. freshly ground
  pepper
1 T. currant jelly
Dry red wine
½ lb. fresh mushrooms,
  sliced
Cornstarch

Full-Bodied Red

Coat beef with seasoned flour. Melt butter in large skillet. Brown meat on all sides. Reduce heat. Warm brandy in ladle; ignite and pour over beef. When flames die, remove meat and set aside. To fat in the skillet, add onion, carrots, seasonings, and jelly. Brown the vegetables slightly over low heat, stirring constantly. Add reserved beef. Sprinkle 2 T. flour over all. Stir well to mix. Add enough wine to cover. Cover and simmer slowly about 2 to 2½ hours, or until meat is tender. Add mushrooms during last 15 minutes. To thicken, stir in cornstarch mixed with a little water, allowing 1 T. for each 1 cup liquid. Cook and stir until thickened. Serve with rice or noodles.

SWEDISH POT ROAST   6-8 Servings

1 beef round-bone pot
  roast (3 to 4 lbs.)
6 T. butter
1½ cups chopped onion
2 cloves garlic, mashed
¼ cup red wine vinegar
2 to 3 T. honey
1 to 2 T. anchovy paste
4 sprigs parsley, minced
2 bay leaves
¾ tsp. pepper
1½ to 2 cans (10½ oz.
  each) beef broth
Flour

Medium-Bodied Red

Using large heavy skillet, sear meat on both sides in butter. Remove meat. Saute onion and garlic in same skillet, adding more butter if needed. Stir in vinegar, honey, and seasonings. Add broth and water. Heat to boiling. Add meat. Cover and bake at 325° for 2½ to 3 hours, or until tender. Transfer meat to platter. Remove bay leaves. Thicken liquid with flour for gravy.

ENTREES: MEAT

NORWEGIAN SAILOR'S BEEF

6-8 Servings

Hearty winter dish

2 lbs. boneless beef
  chuck
¼ cup red wine vinegar
1 T. olive oil
1 large clove garlic,
  minced
2 tsp. salt
1 tsp. dried thyme
Few grindings pepper
2 T. butter
2 large onions, sliced
2 tsp. prepared mustard
8 medium potatoes,
  peeled, thinly sliced
1 can (12 oz.) beer
¼ cup freshly grated
  Swiss cheese or
  Parmesan cheese
Fresh parsley

Medium-Bodied Red

Put meat in glass bowl. Combine vinegar, oil, garlic, salt, thyme, and pepper. Pour over meat. Cover and marinate in refrigerator overnight. Drain marinade. Cut meat into serving pieces and pound to ¼-inch thickness. Season with salt and pepper. Brown in skillet in butter; set aside. Brown onions in same skillet adding more butter if needed. Stir in mustard. In large casserole, alternate layers of meat, onion, and potatoes; sprinkle each potato layer with salt and pepper. End with a layer of potatoes. Pour ¼ cup water into skillet; heat to boiling, scraping brown bits from pan. Pour over casserole; add beer. Bring to simmer on top of stove; cover and bake in a 350° oven for 1 hour or until meat is almost tender. (May be done ahead to this point.) To finish, spoon off some of accumulated fat, sprinkle with cheese and baste with several spoonsful of liquid. Return to simmer and put in 425° oven and bake 20 to 30 minutes or until potatoes are browned and sauce is reduced. Sprinkle with parsley; serve from casserole.

ENTREES: MEAT

BAKED STEAK WITH BURGUNDY MUSHROOMS

8 Servings

Sunday supper special

1 beef sirloin steak, cut 2 inches thick (3½ lbs.)
1 T. oil
2 T. butter
½ tsp. salt
¾ tsp. thyme
1 clove garlic, minced
¼ lb. fresh or 1 can (3 oz.) mushrooms
½ cup Burgundy
2 T. chopped parsley

Brown steak in ovenproof skillet in oil 5 minutes on each side. Pour off fat. Spread steak with 1 T. butter; sprinkle with salt, thyme, and garlic. Bake, uncovered, at 375° for 25 minutes. Remove steak and keep warm. Add mushrooms to skillet; saute 3 minutes. Add wine and bring to a boil, stirring. Remove from heat; stir in remaining 1 T. butter and parsley. Serve sauce over meat.

Medium-Bodied Red

CHILI CON CARNE

4 Quarts

½ lb. dried pinto beans
5 cups canned tomatoes, chopped
1 green pepper, chopped
1½ T. oil
¼ cup butter
1½ lbs. onions, chopped
2 cloves garlic, crushed
½ cup chopped parsley
2½ lbs. ground chuck, cooked and drained
1 lb. ground lean pork, cooked and drained
⅓ cup chili powder
Scant 1 T. salt
1½ tsp. pepper
1½ tsp. ground cumin
1½ tsp. MSG

Wash beans and soak overnight. Simmer in fresh water to cover until tender (1 to 2 hours), drain. Add tomatoes and simmer 5 minutes. Set aside. Saute green pepper in oil for about 5 minutes. Add butter and onions. Cook until tender. Stir frequently. Add garlic and parsley. Add cooked meat to onion mixture. Stir in chili powder. Cook for 10 minutes. Combine meat with beans. Season with salt, pepper, cumin, and MSG. Simmer, covered, for 1 hour. Refrigerate at this point or freeze. To serve, simmer another 30 minutes. Skim fat if necessary. Serve with grated Cheddar cheese, chopped onions, crushed corn chips, crushed red peppers, and sour cream.

Beer

ENTREES: MEAT

VEAL RODNEY

6 Servings

1½ lbs. veal cutlets, cut in
  2 x ½-inch pieces
Salt and pepper
2 T. oil
8 T. butter
½ lb. fresh mushrooms,
  sliced
4 whole green onions,
  finely chopped
1 shallot, minced
2 T. chopped parsley
½ cup dry vermouth or
  Madeira
½ cup whipping cream
¼ cup flour
1 clove garlic, minced
3 beef bouillon cubes
1 cup boiling water
1 T. tomato paste or
  catsup (optional)

Medium-Bodied Red

Season veal with salt and pepper. Put oil and 4 T. butter in skillet. When it begins to foam, quickly saute veal pieces for about 2 minutes, stirring constantly. Transfer veal to shallow casserole. Saute mushrooms, green onions, shallot, and parsley in 2 T. more butter about 3 minutes. Add vermouth and bring to a boil. Add cream; again bring to boil, boiling 1 minute. Set aside. In a second pan, melt 2 T. butter; add flour; stir over medium heat 2 to 3 minutes. Add garlic. Dissolve bouillon cubes in boiling water. Stir in tomato paste. Gradually stir into flour-butter mixture. Cook, stirring constantly, until thickened. Add mushroom sauce. Pour sauce over veal. Cover and bake at 350° for 30 minutes, or until bubbling. Flavor improves if made the day ahead and refrigerated; to serve, return to room temperature and cook as above. Serve over rice and with green vegetable or salad.

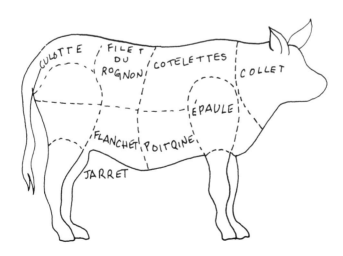

ENTREES: MEAT

LASAGNA

This one has sausage and meatballs on the side

SAUCE:

3 T. olive oil
1 to 2 cloves garlic, cut into fourths
2 cans (6 oz. each) tomato paste
1½ cups water
1 can (28 oz.) Italian plum tomatoes, finely chopped
2 cups water
1½ tsp. oregano
2 T. freshly chopped parsley
Salt and pepper to taste

SAUSAGE:

1 lb. mild Italian sausage, cut into 3-inch pieces

MEATBALLS:

2 lbs. ground beef
1½ tsp. salt
3 T. grated Parmesan cheese
2 eggs
⅛ tsp. garlic powder
1 6-inch piece very dry French or Italian bread

RICOTTA:

2½ lbs. ricotta cheese
2 eggs
½ tsp. parsley
1 T. grated Romano cheese
½ tsp. salt
Pepper to taste
1 pkg. (1 lb.) lasagna noodles, cooked according to package directions
1 to 2 Scamorza cheeses, sliced

Sauce: Saute garlic in oil until brown. Discard garlic, add tomato paste and fry several minutes. Add 1½ cups water. Stir and cook 10 minutes. Add tomatoes to sauce. Stir in 2 cups water and add oregano and parsley. Season with salt and pepper. Simmer 40 minutes.

Sausage: While sauce is cooking, place sausage in frying pan and cook over medium heat until lightly browned. Poke sausage several times to drain grease. Remove sausage and drain, then add to sauce and simmer for 1 hour.

Meatballs: Soak bread in water until soft. Squeeze out, shred into small pieces and combine with rest of ingredients. Form into meatballs and fry until browned. Add meatballs to sauce and cook 45 minutes.

Ricotta: Mix ricotta ingredients together in a large bowl.

Assembly: Remove sausage and meatballs from sauce and set aside. Put several spoonsful of sauce into a 13 x 9-inch pan, enough to cover the bottom. Use only several spoonsful of sauce per layer. Do not use all of sauce in assembling the lasagna. Add a layer of noodles, ricotta, sauce, noodles, Scamorza, sauce, noodles, etc. Plan on 2 layers of ricotta and 2 layers of Scamorza. End up with noodles, Scamorza, and sprinkle with a little Parmesan cheese. Bake at 300° for 45 minutes. Cut into squares. Serve with extra sauce, Parmesan cheese, meatballs, and sausage on the side.

ENTREES: MEAT

PORK SATE

Indonesian dish

2 T. peanut oil
1 T. curry powder
¼ cup soy sauce
¼ cup creamy peanut
  butter
¼ cup finely chopped
  peanuts
1 T. light brown sugar
2 T. lime juice
½ tsp. crushed red pepper
  (optional)
1 clove garlic, crushed
1 lb. boneless pork loin,
  cut into 1-inch cubes
3 cups hot cooked rice

PEANUT SAUCE:

2 T. peanut oil
¼ cup chopped green
  onions
½ cup ground peanuts
2 cups chicken broth
1 T. light brown sugar
1 tsp. lime juice
¼ tsp. ground ginger
⅛ tsp. chili powder
1 T. cornstarch

Light-Bodied Red

Mix peanut oil and curry powder in a small saucepan; simmer over low heat 2 minutes. Gradually blend soy sauce into peanut butter; stir in peanuts, curry mixture, brown sugar, lime juice, red pepper and garlic. Add pork cubes; toss well to coat all sides. Cover tightly and chill at least 4 hours or overnight.

Thread marinated pork cubes onto skewers (you may add mushrooms, green pepper, red onion and cherry tomatoes, if desired). Broil slowly about 6 inches from heat source or grill over hot coals, turning often until pork is tender and cooked, about 8 to 10 minutes. Serve with hot cooked rice and peanut sauce.

Just before cooking pork, prepare sauce. Heat oil in saucepan; add onions, saute until tender. Stir in peanuts, chicken broth, brown sugar, lime juice, ground ginger and chili powder. Cook over medium high heat, stirring constantly until mixture comes to a boil. Reduce heat, simmer uncovered for 15 minutes. Mix 1 T. water and cornstarch; blend into hot sauce. Cook and stir until thickened and translucent. Keep warm until ready to serve.

ENTREES: MEAT

PARTY FONDUE

Delicious and fun — a new twist for fondue

1 lb. pork tenderloin
1 lb. boneless chicken
   breasts
1 lb. boneless sirloin
1 head cabbage,
   separated into leaves
½ lb. fresh spinach
16 to 20 pearl onions,
   blanched
1 pt. cherry tomatoes
½ lb. mushrooms, halved
   if large
3 fresh zucchini, cut in
   chunks
3 green peppers, cut in
   squares
Cooking oil
Choice of sauces:
   hollandaise, curry, chili,
   sweet and sour,
   chutney

Full-Flavored Dry White

Cut pork, chicken, and beef in bite-sized pieces. Prepare vegetables of your choice. Heat oil in fondue pot. Wrap meats with cabbage or spinach, adding a vegetable or 2. Place on fondue forks. Cook in oil in traditional manner. (Wooden skewers may hold more. A skewer of all vegetables is also delicious.) Serve with choice of several sauces.

NOTE: Herbed fondue oil is a nice variation. Add to oil: 1 sprig fresh thyme, 1 sprig fresh rosemary, 1 bay leaf, and 1 whole clove of unpeeled garlic.

ENTREES: MEAT

COTES DE PORC A L'AUVERGNATE   8 Servings

1 head cabbage (3 lbs.),
  chopped
1 medium onion, chopped
1 clove garlic, minced
3 T. butter
½ tsp. salt
Dash of pepper
8 center-cut pork chops,
  ¾ inch thick
½ cup dry white wine
1 cup whipping cream,
  scalded
1 bay leaf
4 T. freshly grated
  Parmesan cheese
2 T. dry bread crumbs

Light Dry or Medium-Dry White

Cook cabbage in boiling salted water for 5 minutes; drain. In large skillet, saute onion and garlic in 2 T. of butter. Stir in cabbage, salt, and pepper. Cook, stirring frequently, until moisture is evaporated. Remove from skillet. Brown pork chops in skillet in 1 T. butter; set aside. Pour off fat from skillet leaving only a thin film on bottom. Deglaze skillet with wine. Continue cooking until wine is reduced to ¼ cup. Stir into cabbage. Spread ⅓ of cabbage in large casserole at least 4 inches deep. Lay 4 pork chops on top in a single layer. Add another ⅓ of cabbage, then 4 more chops. Add remaining cabbage. Casserole should be firmly packed. Pour scalded cream over top; insert bay leaf in center. Cover and bake at 350° for 1½ hours. Remove bay leaf, season to taste. Mix cheese and crumbs; sprinkle over casserole. Bake, uncovered, for 30 minutes more, or until top is browned and crusty.

BERINGILA (EGGPLANT AND HAM)   6 Servings

2 medium or 4 small
  eggplants
1 onion, chopped
3 T. oil
2 cups cooked ham,
  chopped
¼ to ½ cup white wine
2 tomatoes, chopped
Parmesan cheese

Medium-Dry White

Peel eggplants; slice, sprinkle with salt. Let stand 15 minutes. Saute onion in 1 T. oil. Add ham and wine. Cook until wine has nearly evaporated. Add tomatoes. Cook 10 minutes. Pat eggplant dry and flour. Fry in 2 T. oil. Drain on paper towels. Layer eggplant and ham mixture in greased casserole. Top with grated cheese. Bake at 350° for 30 minutes.

ENTREES: MEAT

STUFFED PEPPERS

6 medium green or red
  sweet peppers
½ cup chopped onion
1 small clove garlic,
  crushed
1 lb. pork sausage
2 cups cooked rice
3 T. chopped parsley
Few grindings black
  pepper
¾ cup beef broth
¾ cup soft bread crumbs
3 T. oil

TOMATO SAUCE:

1 small onion, minced
3 T. butter or bacon fat
2 T. flour
1 can (16 oz.) tomatoes,
  drained and chopped
1 cup beef broth
1 small clove garlic,
  crushed
1 tsp. dried thyme
1 tsp. sugar
Salt and pepper to taste

Cut off tops of peppers; remove seeds and pith. Parboil in salted, boiling water. Remove from water and drain upside down. Cook onion, garlic and sausage until sausage browns; add rice, parsley, black pepper and broth. Salt to taste and stuff into peppers. Mix bread crumbs with oil and sprinkle on top of peppers. Place peppers in ovenproof dish and pour in about ¾ cup water or beef broth. Bake at 350° for 40 to 50 minutes or until crumbs are brown. For sauce, saute onion in butter until golden. Stir in flour and cook 3 minutes. Add tomatoes and broth, beating until smooth. Add garlic, thyme, sugar and salt and pepper to taste. Cover and simmer slowly for 20 minutes. When ready to serve, remove peppers to serving dish and spoon on some of the tomato sauce. Pass remaining sauce.

Medium-Bodied Red

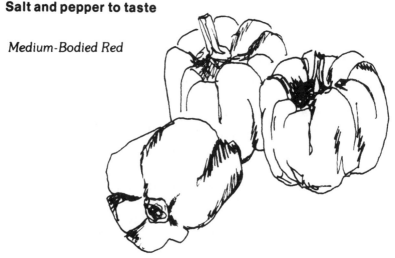

CHICAGO-STYLE PIZZA

4 Servings; 2 Slices Each

Chicago is famous for its wonderful, thick, gooey, deep-dish pizzas. The special method was developed by Uno's Pizzeria in the 1950's

CRUST:

1 pkg. dry yeast
1¼ cups warm water
1 T. sugar
1½ tsp. salt
¼ cup oil
3 cups flour
2 T. cornmeal

SAUCE AND TOPPING:

1 can (28 oz.) Italian pear tomatoes, well drained and chopped
1 T. oregano
1 tsp. sugar
1 lb. mozzarella or Scamorza cheese, thinly sliced
1 lb. mild Italian sausage, broken up, cooked and drained
½ cup grated Parmesan cheese

Light-Bodied Red

For crust, dissolve yeast in water. Add sugar, salt, and 2 T. oil. Stir in flour to make a soft dough. Turn out onto well-floured board. Knead about 3 minutes. Put in greased bowl; cover and let rise in warm place until doubled in bulk, about 1½ hours.

For sauce, combine tomatoes, oregano, and sugar. Set aside.

Brush a 14-inch, deep-dish pizza pan with 2 T. oil; sprinkle with cornmeal. Punch dough down; press in bottom of pan. Let rise about 30 minutes. Arrange cheese over dough. Place sausage over cheese. Spread with tomato sauce. Sprinkle with Parmesan cheese. Place pizza in a 500° oven. Immediately reduce heat to 450° and bake 20 to 25 minutes or until cheese is melted and crust is golden.

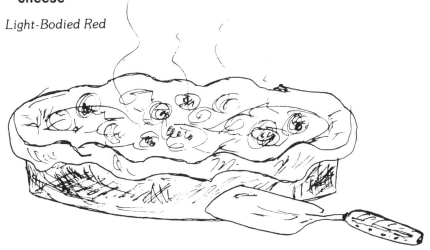

ENTREES: MEAT

CABBAGE AND SAUSAGE CASSEROLE   4 Servings

1 cabbage (2 lbs.),
   quartered
1½ tsp. ground cumin
1 lb. bulk sausage
½ cup diced onion
2 eggs, lightly beaten
1 T. minced parsley
¼ tsp. dried thyme
⅛ tsp. ground allspice
6 oz. boiled ham, cut in
   ¼-inch cubes
3 T. butter
2 large tart apples,
   peeled and cored
1 cup half and half

Light-Bodied Red

Boil cabbage in salted water to cover 15 minutes or until tender. Drain, core, and separate leaves. Dry on paper towels and sprinkle with salt, pepper, and 1 tsp. cumin. Saute sausage, breaking it into small pieces with onion until onion is golden. Pour off fat. Transfer sausage to bowl; stir in eggs, parsley, thyme, and allspice. Saute ham in 1 T. butter until lightly browned. Chop apples into ¼-inch cubes. Combine cream and ½ tsp. cumin. Place ⅓ of cabbage in lightly buttered 2-qt. casserole. Sprinkle on some of cream mixture. Add ½ of the sausage mixture, apples, and ham, sprinkling each layer with some of the cream mixture and salt and pepper. Repeat, ending with a layer of cabbage. Dot with 2 T. butter and bake covered at 400° for 30 minutes. Reduce heat to 350° and bake 1¼ hours. Remove cover and bake 15 minutes longer. Let stand 5 minutes before serving.

ENTREES: POULTRY

STUFFED CHICKEN BREASTS SUPREME · 4 Servings

2 large whole chicken
  breasts, split
½ lb. fresh mushrooms,
  finely chopped
¼ cup finely chopped
  onion
3 T. butter
¼ cup Sauterne
½ tsp. salt
¼ tsp. sage
⅛ tsp. pepper
2 T. flour (about)
2 T. chopped parsley
4 thin slices boiled ham
  (4-inches square)
1 egg
1 T. milk
¾ cup soft bread crumbs
2 T. vegetable oil

CREAMY WINE SAUCE:

2 T. butter
2 T. flour
1 T. minced parsley
1 chicken bouillon cube
¼ tsp. onion powder
¼ tsp. salt
Dash nutmeg
Dash white pepper
1 cup half and half
¼ cup Chablis or
  Sauterne wine

Light Dry White

Remove bones and skin from chicken breasts. Pound out thin between 2 sheets of waxed paper. Saute mushrooms and onion in 1 T. butter. Add Sauterne, salt, sage, pepper, and 1 tsp. flour. Cook and stir until thickened. Stir in parsley. Place a rounded T. of mushroom mixture on each slice of ham; fold corners over to cover it. Invert onto centers of chicken breasts; fold chicken over ham to cover. Fasten with picks. Chill. Shortly before serving, dust with remaining flour. Beat egg with milk; dip floured rolls in egg, then in crumbs. Heat remaining 2 T. butter with oil; brown chicken rolls slowly on all sides turning carefully with 2 spatulas. Bake at 350° for about 20 minutes, or until cooked through. Remove picks and serve with sauce.

For sauce, melt butter; stir in flour. Add parsley, bouillon cube, onion powder, salt, nutmeg, and white pepper. Gradually add 1 cup half and half and ¼ cup white wine. Cook, stirring constantly, until thickened.

ENTREES: POULTRY

CHINESE CHICKEN AND VEGETABLES
4 Servings

½ oz. Chinese dried black mushrooms
1 lb. boneless chicken breasts
1½ cups sliced bok choy
4 oz. canned water chestnuts, sliced
1 T. light (thin) soy sauce
1 T. cooking rice wine (or sherry)
½ tsp. salt
1 T. cornstarch
3 T. water
2 T. peanut oil
2 cloves garlic, minced
4 oz. canned bamboo shoots, drained
8 oz. fresh bean sprouts
4 oz. fresh pea pods

Medium-Dry White

Place dried mushrooms in bowl and add water to cover. Soak for 30 to 40 minutes, until spongy but not soggy. Discard water. Cut chicken into 1-inch pieces. Slice bok choy and water chestnuts. Cut ends off pea pods; remove fibers down each back. In small bowl, mix soy sauce, rice wine, and salt. In another small bowl, mix cornstarch and water. Remove and discard stems from rehydrated mushrooms. Heat oil in wok to highest temperature. Add garlic; stir-fry. Add chicken; stir about 2 minutes. Add mushrooms and soy sauce solution, stirring after each. Then cover and cook 1½ minutes. Add remaining vegetables, except pea pods; stir. Add cornstarch solution and pea pods. Stir gently and serve immediately with rice.

POULET COCOTTE
4 Servings

2 to 3 lbs. chicken, cut into serving pieces
2 to 4 T. bacon fat
2 cloves garlic
24 small whole onions
2 large potatoes, cut into small cubes
½ lb. mushrooms, cut in ½ if large
2 pork sausages or knockwurst, cut in 2-inch pieces
2 T. flour
1 cup water
Bouquet garni: 2 sprigs parsley, ¼ tsp. thyme, and 1 clove garlic

Full-Flavored Dry White

Brown chicken in bacon fat. Place in casserole. Brown garlic, onions, potatoes, and mushrooms; remove to casserole. Lightly brown sausage. Drain about 2 T. fat from the skillet. Stir in 2 T. flour. Deglaze skillet with 1 cup water. Pour sauce on top of chicken mixture and add more water or chicken broth to almost cover. Add bouquet garni. Cover casserole and cook in 325° oven about 1½ hours or until tender.

ENTREES: POULTRY

CHICKEN BREASTS WITH CRABMEAT SAUCE

6-8 Servings

Very different and very good

3 to 4 large, whole
   chicken breasts, split,
   boned, skinned
Fresh lemon juice
Salt, pepper
¼ cup butter

CRABMEAT SAUCE:

2 T. butter
2 T. flour
¼ tsp. salt
Dash white pepper
1 cup whipping cream
2 T. dry sherry
1 egg yolk, slightly
   beaten
½ tsp. tarragon or to taste
1 pkg. (6 oz.) frozen
   crabmeat, thawed,
   sliced

Medium-Dry White

Flatten breasts slightly. Sprinkle with lemon juice, salt, and pepper. Melt butter in large shallow baking dish. Add chicken; turn to coat. Cover with foil. Bake at 400° for about 15 minutes, or until just barely done.

To prepare sauce, melt butter. Stir in flour, salt, and pepper. Gradually stir in cream. Add sherry. Cook, stirring constantly, until thickened. Add a little hot sauce to egg yolk. Return to pan. Add tarragon, then crabmeat. Pour off juices from chicken. Spoon sauce over chicken breasts. Broil until delicately browned.

ENTREES: SEAFOOD

FISH FONDUE BOURGUIGNONNE

6 Servings

1 lb. raw medium shrimp,
  peeled and deveined
1 lb. raw swordfish
  steaks, cut into 1-inch
  pieces
Vegetable oil
Clarified butter
Sauce remoulade
Sashimi sauce
Dill sauce

Light Dry White

Arrange the shrimp and swordfish on a large serving platter garnished with sprays of watercress and parsley. Set up your buffet table in advance with a heatproof tray holding the fondue set or chafing dish, the fish platter, and another tray holding the sauces and fondue forks. Use equal portions of clarified butter and oil to fill the fondue pot to 1½-inch depth. Heat oil and butter in a saucepan over burner until sizzling hot. Pour into fondue pot and place over alcohol burner. When ready to serve, each guest spears a fish piece with a fondue fork and cooks it in the hot fat until done. This only takes a minute or so. Serve cooked fish with sauce remoulade, sashimi sauce or dill sauce.

SAUCE REMOULADE

1 Cup

1 cup mayonnaise
1 hard-cooked egg,
  chopped
2 T. hot prepared mustard
  or 1 tsp. dry mustard
1 clove garlic, minced
1 tsp. dried tarragon
1 tsp. anchovy paste
1 tsp. capers

Blend ingredients together well.

SASHIMI SAUCE

1 Cup

1 cup Japanese soy
  sauce
½ tsp. dry mustard
1 T. salad oil
1 T. grated, peeled fresh
  ginger

Blend ingredients together well.

ENTREES: SEAFOOD

DILL SAUCE

1 Cup

1 cup sour cream
1 T. minced parsley
1 T. lemon juice
1 tsp. chopped chives
1 tsp. grated onion
Chopped fresh or dried
  dill to taste

Blend together well.

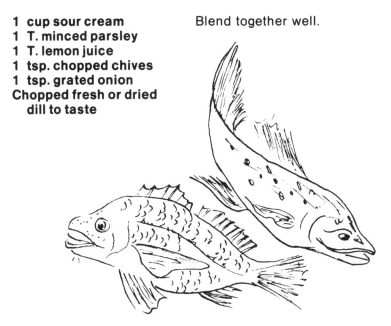

SWEET AND SOUR FISH

4-6 Servings

Impressive Chinese dish

1 whole fish (2 lbs.),
  cleaned and scaled
1 T. rice wine
1 T. soy sauce
1 tsp. lemon juice
Salt and pepper

SAUCE:

1 cup cider vinegar
1 cup brown sugar
2 T. cornstarch
1 tsp. minced fresh
  ginger
1 green onion, minced
½ cup chopped green
  pepper
½ cup chopped tomatoes

Slash fish diagonally at 1-inch intervals on both sides. Rub inside and out with wine, soy sauce, lemon juice, salt and pepper. Set aside for 30 minutes. Meanwhile, the sauce, mix together first 3 ingredients and set aside. Stir-fry rest of ingredients in a little hot oil for 2 minutes; add reserved vinegar mixture. Bring to a boil; reduce heat. Keep warm. Blot fish dry. Roll in enough cornstarch to coat. Heat enough oil to fry fish. Baste fish frequently, turning once. When golden brown, remove and arrange on platter. Cover with sauce and serve immediately.

Light Dry White

ENTREES: SEAFOOD

MUSHROOM STUFFED SOLE

4 Servings

4 fillets of sole (about 1½ lbs.)
¼ cup butter
¼ lb. fresh mushrooms, finely chopped
1½ cups fine fresh bread crumbs
3 T. lemon juice
2 T. minced parsley
Salt, pepper
2 egg yolks, slightly beaten
¼ cup dry white wine
Parsley sprigs
Lemon wedges
Hollandaise sauce

Light Dry White

Thaw fish, if frozen. Saute mushrooms in 3 T. butter; stir in bread crumbs, 2 T. lemon juice, parsley, ½ tsp. salt, and dash pepper. Blend in egg yolks. (Food processor can be useful.) Brush fillets with 1 T. lemon juice; sprinkle with salt and pepper. Spoon stuffing onto largest ½ of each fillet. Fold over other ½. Fasten with wooden picks. Place in buttered 2-qt. shallow baking dish. Dot with butter. Pour in wine; cover with foil. Bake at 350° for 20 to 30 minutes, or until fish flakes easily with fork. Garnish with parsley and lemon wedges. Serve with hollandaise sauce prepared from a favorite recipe.

LOBSTER THERMIDOR

6 Appetizer Servings

½ lb. fresh mushrooms, sliced
6 T. butter
Dash paprika
⅛ tsp. dry mustard
1 T. minced parsley
½ cup sherry
2 T. flour
1 cup whipping cream
½ tsp. salt
Dash pepper
1 lobster (1 to 1½ lbs.) boiled, meat removed and cubed
2 T. grated Parmesan cheese

Light Dry White

Saute mushrooms in 3 T. butter. Add paprika, mustard, parsley, and sherry. Heat to boiling. Melt remaining butter; blend in flour. Stir in cream; cook until thickened, stirring constantly. Season with salt and pepper. Add mushroom mixture and lobster meat to cream sauce; blend. Fill seafood shells or ramekins; sprinkle with cheese. Bake at 450° for 10 minutes. Serve hot.

ENTREES: SEAFOOD

FISH PARMESAN

4 Servings

1 lb. fillets of sole or
   flounder
1 cup sour cream
¼ cup Parmesan cheese
2 T. lemon juice
1 T. grated onion
½ T. salt
Dash hot pepper sauce
Parsley

Light Dry White

Place fillets in single layer in a well-greased baking dish. Combine remaining ingredients. Spread over fish fillets. Sprinkle with paprika. Bake at 350° for 20 to 25 minutes. Sprinkle with parsley.

POUVRE HOMME

3-4 Servings

Delicious with grilled or stuffed tomatoes

1 lb. potatoes
1 large onion, thinly
   sliced
1 lb. fresh cod fillets
4 T. milk
4 oz. grated Cheddar
   cheese
Salt, pepper
1 bay leaf

Light Dry White

Peel and slice potatoes. Place a layer of fish in greased casserole. Season with salt and pepper. Cover with onions and potatoes. Continue layering, finishing with potatoes. Add bay leaf where it can be removed before serving. Pour milk over; sprinkle with cheese and a few butter bits. Bake at 350° for 30 to 40 minutes until potatoes are done. May add more milk if needed.

WHITEFISH IN TOMATO SAUCE

4 Servings

Tasty and gorgeous

1 can (16 oz.) stewed
   tomatoes
1 tsp. oregano
½ tsp. garlic salt
Dash pepper
2 lbs. whitefish or halibut
   fillets
½ cup grated Parmesan
   cheese
Chopped parsley
Lemon wedges

Light Dry White

Mash tomatoes in saucepan; add oregano, garlic salt, and pepper. Simmer 15 minutes. Preheat broiler 10 minutes. Brush fillets with vegetable oil and place skin side up on broiler pan. Broil on bottom shelf about 8 minutes. Do not turn until done. Skin will char. Place on platter, fleshy side up and spoon sauce over. Sprinkle with cheese and parsley; garnish with lemon wedges.

VEGETABLES

BEANS A LA CREME

6 Servings

Not for the calorie counter

1½ lbs. young string
   beans left whole
4 qts. boiling water
2 T. salt
1 cup whipping cream
Salt and pepper to taste
⅓ cup freshly grated
   Parmesan cheese

Put beans in boiling salted water. After water returns to boil, cook about 7 minutes. Drain and rinse with cold water. Place in shallow casserole; cover with cream, salt and pepper to taste. Place in 450° oven until top begins to brown, about 15 to 20 minutes. Sprinkle with cheese and return to oven for about 10 minutes.

BROCCOLI PUFF

8-10 Servings

6 eggs
6 T. flour
1½ lbs. small-curd
   cottage cheese
½ lb. Cheddar cheese,
   shredded
1 pkg. (10 oz.) frozen
   chopped broccoli,
   thawed, drained (not
   cooked)
½ cup butter, melted
2 green onions with tops,
   minced

Have ingredients at room temperature. Combine ingredients in large mixing bowl, beat until well blended. Pour into greased 9 x 13-inch pan. Bake at 350° for 1 hour, or until knife comes out clean. Allow to rest 10 minutes before cutting and serving. Can be made the night before.

BROCCOLI AND BACON

8-10 Servings

2 to 3 lbs. fresh broccoli
7 to 8 slices bacon, cut
   into 1 to 2-inch pieces
MSG
Salt
Bottled oyster sauce

Cut tops of broccoli into pieces a little larger than bite-sized. Cut peeled stalks on bias, fairly thin.

Put broccoli in boiling water. Bring to a boil and simmer for about 2 minutes. Immediately rinse in cold water.

Saute bacon until crisp. Remove bacon; pour off some fat. Add broccoli to hot fat. Sprinkle with MSG and salt. Add 3 to 4 T. oyster sauce and 4 to 5 T. water. Let liquid come to a boil, stirring while cooking, until tender-crisp — not soft. Turn into serving dish and top with crisp bacon.

ACCOMPANIMENTS

CABBAGE AU GRATIN

6 Servings

1 head cabbage (3 lbs.) cut into wedges
½ lb. bacon, diced
1 large onion, chopped
Salt and pepper
1 cup medium white sauce
½ cup buttered bread crumbs
½ cup grated Cheddar cheese

Cook cabbage by steaming until tender. Drain and chop. Cook bacon until crisp. Remove from pan and drain. Saute onion in bacon drippings until golden. Place cabbage, bacon and onion in greased baking dish. Pour white sauce over cabbage. Top with crumbs and cheese. Bake at 350° for 15 to 20 minutes.

HOLIDAY VEGETABLES

12 Servings

1 medium head cauliflower (about 2 lbs.)
1 bunch broccoli (about 1½ lbs.), cut in flowerettes
1 pt. cherry tomatoes (15 to 20)

MORNAY SAUCE:

¼ cup butter
¼ cup flour
2 cups chicken broth
¼ cup grated Swiss cheese
¼ cup grated Parmesan cheese
Pinch each of nutmeg, salt, pepper

Steam cauliflower head in covered pan until fork tender. At the same time, steam broccoli flowerettes in covered pan until fork tender. Saute cherry tomatoes in butter, but do not allow to become mushy. For sauce: melt butter; whisk in flour. Cook for 2 minutes; do not let brown. Whisk in chicken broth. Cook, stirring constantly, until thickened and smooth. Add cheeses slowly; heat until melted. Add seasonings. In ovenproof casserole, spoon a layer of sauce across bottom. Place cauliflower in center; surround with broccoli and tomatoes. Pour another layer of sauce over cauliflower only; place under broiler to lightly brown cheese. Serve with extra sauce on the side.

VEGETABLES

CHOUX ROUGES AUX POMMES   4-6 Servings
A Flemish dish

1 head red cabbage (2 lbs.)
5 large crabapples
2 T. butter
Salt and pepper
3 whole cloves
1 tsp. cornstarch
1 T. cider vinegar
2 T. currant jelly

Trim, wash and chop cabbage. Peel, core and quarter apples. Put cabbage, apples, butter, salt, pepper and cloves in large heavy pot, cover with water. Cover and simmer 2½ hours. Dissolve cornstarch in vinegar; stir in currant jelly. Pour off excess liquid from cabbage and stir in currant jelly mixture. Stir over medium heat until slightly thickened. Serve.

BRAISED ENDIVE   6 Servings
Elegant with beef tenderloin

12 Belgian endive, trimmed and washed
½ cup veal or beef broth
1 T. lemon juice
4 T. butter
1 tsp. salt
¾ cup whipping cream
Parsley for garnish

Arrange endive in 1 layer in well buttered shallow ovenproof casserole. Add beef broth, lemon juice, butter and salt. Cover and bring to a boil on top of stove; reduce heat and simmer 20 minutes until tender and liquid is reduced by ½. Bake at 325° in lower part of oven for 1 hour. Remove from oven and place endive in skillet and cover with about ½ cup whipping cream. Simmer slowly, basting occasionally for about 15 minutes. Remove endive to serving dish and add remaining cream to skillet. Stir until smooth; season to taste with salt, white pepper and lemon juice. Pour sauce over endive; garnish with parsley.

ACCOMPANIMENTS

LEEKS IN ARMAGNAC

6-8 Servings

Vegetable or first course

12 leeks
3 T. olive oil
1 T. salt
¼ tsp. dried thyme
⅓ cup chicken broth
¼ cup Armagnac or
 brandy
Juice of ½ lemon
1 T. minced parsley
Salt and pepper to taste

Cut leeks in ½ lengthwise; soak in cold water. Clean thoroughly. Drain and cut in ½ crosswise. Brown in olive oil over medium heat for 7 to 10 minutes. Add salt, thyme, broth and Armagnac. Stir, cooking over medium high heat for 10 minutes. Reduce to simmer, cover and cook until tender, about 10 to 15 minutes. Add lemon juice, correct seasonings. Heat 1 minute more; serve sprinkled with parsley. For an hors d'oeuvres, transfer to shallow dish; stir in a mixture of 1 T. lemon juice and 3 T. olive oil. Cover and chill thoroughly. Serve chilled.

BRAISED MUSHROOMS AND LEEKS

4-6 Servings

1 lb. fresh mushrooms,
 cleaned and quartered
4 leeks, well cleaned,
 patted dry and thinly
 sliced
¼ cup butter
1 T. flour
½ tsp. brown sugar
1 cup chicken broth
Salt and pepper

Saute mushrooms and leeks in butter in heavy skillet until leeks are softened. Sprinkle with flour and brown sugar, stirring constantly; reduce heat to simmer. Add chicken broth, cook and stir until slightly thickened. Season with salt and pepper to taste.

ONIONS IN MADEIRA

6-8 Servings

4 T. butter
4 large Spanish onions,
 peeled, sliced ¼ inch
 thick
⅔ cup Madeira wine
1 T. chopped parsley
Salt and pepper to taste

Melt butter in heavy skillet. Add onions, toss until golden but not soft. Add ½ cup of Madeira. Cover. Raise heat and cook until tender. Remove cover and reduce liquid to glaze. Stir in remaining Madeira and parsley. Season to taste.

VEGETABLES

SESAME PARSNIPS

8-10 Servings

2 lbs. parsnips, peeled,
  cut into pieces
½ cup butter
¼ tsp. ground cardamon
Salt to taste
½ cup fresh white bread
  crumbs
1 T. sesame seeds, lightly
  toasted
1 T. melted butter

Boil parsnips in water to cover until tender. Cool slightly. Puree in blender or food processor with ½ cup butter, cardamon, and salt. Place in buttered 1½-qt. casserole dish. Mix bread crumbs, sesame seeds, and melted butter; sprinkle over parsnips. Bake at 400° for 20 to 25 minutes.

CREAMY SPINACH ON ARTICHOKE BOTTOMS

8 Servings

8 fresh artichoke bottoms
  or 1 can (8 oz.)
  artichoke bottoms
1 pkg. (10 oz.) frozen
  creamed spinach,
  thawed
12 mushrooms, sliced,
  sauteed
½ cup sour cream
½ cup mayonnaise
2 T. lemon juice

Drain artichoke bottoms. Fill with creamed spinach. Cover with sauteed mushrooms. Place on baking sheet. Combine sour cream, mayonnaise, and lemon juice. Pour over artichokes. Bake at 375° for 15 minutes, or until heated through.

NUTMEG SQUASH PUDDING

4-6 Servings

1 lb. fresh orange winter
  squash, peeled and
  cubed, or 1 pkg. (10
  oz.) frozen mashed
  squash, thawed
2 eggs
¼ cup brown sugar
2 T. melted butter
1½ tsp. lemon juice
1 tsp. nutmeg
1 tsp. salt
Cinnamon
1 cup milk
¼ cup chopped walnuts

If using fresh squash, boil in salted water until tender; mash. In medium bowl, beat eggs slightly. Add squash, sugar, butter, lemon juice, nutmeg, salt, cinnamon, and milk. Beat until smooth. Pour into buttered 1-qt. casserole. Set in large pan with 1 inch of water. Bake at 350° for 50 minutes or until knife comes out clean. Sprinkle nuts over hot pudding. May be frozen.

ACCOMPANIMENTS

RISOTTO ALLA MILANESE
6-8 Servings

4 cups beef broth
2 cups uncooked long-grain rice
⅛ tsp. saffron
1 tsp. beef extract
4 T. butter
½ to 1 cup grated Parmesan cheese

Heat broth to boiling point. Place rice, saffron, and beef extract in top of double boiler; stir in hot beef broth. Put over boiling water, reduce heat to simmer and steam for 30 minutes or until all liquid is absorbed. Remove from heat. Stir in butter and cheese. Salt to taste. Serve immediately. Pass extra grated cheese.

HEALTHFUL RICE
4-6 Servings

½ cup dried black beans, cooked
1½ cups brown rice
3 to 3½ cups water
1 T. butter
1 tsp. salt
1 large onion
3 cloves garlic, minced
12 oz. Monterey Jack cheese, shredded
8 oz. ricotta cheese, thinned slightly with a little milk
½ cup grated Cheddar cheese

Soak beans overnight according to package directions or bring to boil in water; cover and let stand for 2 hours. Simmer partly covered for another 2 hours. (Can use pressure cooker instead; 15 lbs. pressure for 25 to 35 minutes.) Drain. Meanwhile, cook rice, water, butter, and salt in covered pan for 45 to 60 minutes or until done. (Brown rice will not get soft like white rice.) Mix rice, beans, onion, and garlic. Layer alternately in a greased casserole with Monterey Jack cheese and ricotta. End with rice mixture. Bake at 350° for 30 minutes. During last few minutes, sprinkle with Cheddar.

RICE-STUFFED BAKED TOMATOES
8 Servings

8 large tomatoes
6 slices bacon
3 cups chopped onion
1 cup chopped fresh mushrooms
1½ to 2 cups cooked wild rice; or 1 pkg. long grain and wild rice, prepared according to package directions
Salt, pepper to taste

Slice off tops of tomatoes and scoop out centers. Drain. Fry bacon until crisp. Drain and crumble. Cook onions and mushrooms in bacon fat until soft, but not browned. Add rice and bacon. Season to taste. Stuff tomatoes, heaping generously. Place in shallow pan. Bake at 350° for 20 minutes, or until heated through.

VEGETABLES

WILD RICE SOUFFLE

6 Servings

2 T. butter
3 T. flour
¾ cup milk
5 egg yolks, slightly
beaten
½ tsp. salt
¼ tsp. white pepper
2 cups shredded Swiss
cheese
1 cup cooked wild rice
2 T. freshly grated
Parmesan cheese
5 egg whites, room
temperature

Heat butter until foaming. Whisk in flour, 1 T. at a time. Whisk milk in gradually. Cook over low heat, stirring constantly until thickened. Blend ¼ cup of hot sauce into egg yolks. Return to saucepan. Cook and stir over low heat until mixture is quite hot, about 5 minutes. Add salt and pepper. Stir in Swiss cheese until almost melted. Stir in wild rice. Generously butter a 1-qt. souffle dish. Dust with grated Parmesan. Beat egg whites until stiff, but not dry. Fold rice into whites. Bake at 375° for about 30 minutes or until puffed and browned. Serve immediately.

BROWN AND WHITE RICE CASSEROLE

8 Servings

6 slices bacon, chopped
4 green onions, chopped
½ lb. fresh mushrooms,
sliced
Butter
¼ cup slivered almonds
¾ cup white rice
¾ cup brown rice
¼ tsp. each: salt, pepper,
thyme, marjoram
3¼ cups beef broth
Parmesan cheese

Cook bacon until crisp; drain. Discard bacon drippings. In same pan, saute green onions and mushrooms in 2 T. butter until limp; set aside. In same pan, saute almonds, brown rice and white rice in 3 T. butter until golden brown, stirring frequently. Turn into 2-qt. casserole along with bacon and seasonings. (This much may be done ahead and kept at room temperature.) Just before baking, pour in beef broth; stir well and cover. Bake at 350° for 40 minutes. Stir in mushroom-onion mixture. Adjust seasonings. Dot with butter and sprinkle with Parmesan cheese. Bake 10 minutes more, covered.

ACCOMPANIMENTS

RICE A L'INDIENNE

6 Servings

Excellent with curry

2 cups uncooked rice
¼ cup chopped onion
2 T. butter
1 tsp. salt
5 whole peppercorns
5 whole cloves
Cinnamon stick, 1 inch
    long
1 small bay leaf
Grated rind of 1 orange
2 cups hot chicken broth

Place all ingredients in top of double boiler. Steam over simmering water for 30 minutes or until all liquid is absorbed. Fluff with fork. Turn into covered dish. Serve.

SPICY BUTTERNUT SQUASH

4 Servings

2 medium butternut
    squash
½ cup butter
¼ tsp. allspice
½ cup brown sugar
1 tsp. cinnamon
¼ tsp. nutmeg
4 T. maple syrup

Halve squash; scoop out seeds and membranes. Dot with butter. Blend spices and sugar. Sprinkle in cavities. Put 1 T. syrup in each ½. Bake at 350° for 50 minutes or until squash is very tender. Colorful filled with cooked peas just before serving.

WINE-GLAZED YAMS

6 Servings

6 medium yams
1½ cups sugar
½ cup red wine
¼ cup light raisins
¼ cup pecan halves
2 T. butter
Dash cinnamon
Salt to taste

Cook yams until tender. Peel; quarter. In heavy skillet, cook sugar, stirring constantly, until caramelized. Slowly stir in wine. Add remaining ingredients, stirring until butter melts. Place yams in shallow baking dish. Pour wine sauce over yams. Bake at 350° for 20 to 25 minutes, basting once or twice.

SALADS, DRESSINGS & SAUCES

WHITE AND GREEN SALAD
6 Servings

Simple, elegant winter salad

3 stalks celery
½ cup salad oil
3 T. lemon juice
3 T. tarragon vinegar
2 T. sugar
1 tsp. minced onion
1 tsp. salt
½ tsp. oregano
Dash pepper
1 can (8 oz.) hearts of
  palm, cut into sections
1 can (8 oz.) white
  asparagus, cut into
  sections
1 can (8 oz.) celery
  hearts, cut up
1 avocado, cut up
1 head Boston lettuce

Clean celery; cut off tops and bottoms. Finely chop. (If desired, use food processor or blender.) Add oil, lemon juice, vinegar, sugar, onion, oregano, salt, and pepper; blend. Pour over hearts of palm, asparagus, celery hearts and avocado. Marinate several hours. Serve on lettuce leaves.

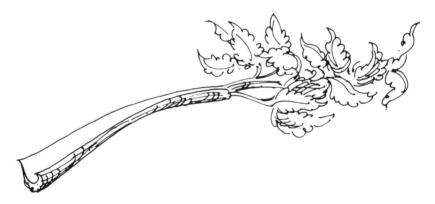

CHEESE SALAD
4 Servings

½ lb. Swiss or Gruyere
  cheese, cut into thin
  strips
½ cup sour cream
1 T. chopped chives
1½ tsp. dry mustard
1 tsp. grated horseradish
Salt
Pepper

Mix all together and serve at room temperature on bed of lettuce.

SALADS, DRESSINGS & SAUCES

SPECIAL SALAD　　　　　　　8 Servings

CARAMELIZED ALMONDS:

½ cup sliced blanched almonds
½ cup sugar

DRESSING:

1 tsp. salt
Dash pepper
4 T. sugar
2 T. parsley
4 T. vinegar
½ cup salad oil
Dash hot pepper sauce

SALAD:

1 head romaine lettuce
2 cups chopped celery
4 chopped green onions
1 can (15 oz.) mandarin oranges

To caramelize almonds, cook over medium heat, stirring occasionally until sugar melts and sticks to nuts. Remove immediately from heat and cool in pan. Break into pieces. (Can be done ahead.)

Combine all dressing ingredients; shake until well mixed; chill.

Just before serving, assemble salad; toss with dressing and sprinkle ½ cup almonds on top.

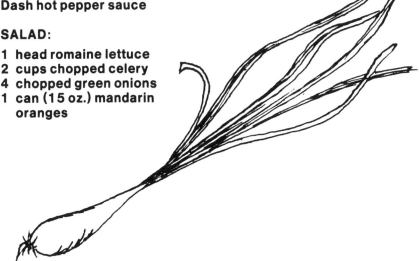

GRAPEFRUIT-SHRIMP COCKTAIL　　6 Servings

Good combination

½ cup mayonnaise
2 T. milk
2 tsp. lemon or lime juice
⅛ tsp. garlic powder
1 T. minced chives
¼ tsp. salt
1 lb. cooked shrimp
3 grapefruit

Mix all sauce ingredients. Add shrimp. Cover; refrigerate at least 1 hour. Cut grapefruit in ½. Remove membrane and every other section. Fill each space with 1 shrimp. Pour remaining sauce over top.

SALADS, DRESSINGS & SAUCES

CHRISTMAS RIBBON RING   12 Servings
Lovely made in Christmas tree mold

1 pkg. (3 oz.) strawberry
   gelatin
2 T. sugar
1 can (1 lb.) whole
   cranberry sauce
1 pkg. (3 oz.) lemon
   gelatin
1 pkg. (8 oz.) cream
   cheese, softened
1 can (8½ oz.) crushed
   pineapple, undrained
¼ cup chopped salted
   pecans or walnuts
1 pkg. (3 oz.) lime gelatin
1 can (1 lb.) grapefruit
   sections
1 avocado, sliced

Cranberry layer: Dissolve strawberry gelatin and sugar in 1¼ cups boiling water. Add cranberry sauce, mixing well. Chill until partially set. Pour into 8-cup ring mold. Chill until almost firm.

Cheese layer: Dissolve lemon gelatin in 1¼ cups boiling water. Add cream cheese, beating smooth with electric beater. Add pineapple with syrup. Chill until partially set. Stir in nuts. Spoon over cranberry layer in mold. Chill until almost firm.

Grapefruit layer: Top cheese layer with grapefruit sections and avocado slices. Dissolve lime gelatin in 1¼ cups boiling water and then add grapefruit syrup. Chill until partially set. Pour over cheese layer. Chill overnight and unmold.

SPICED ORANGE-APRICOT ASPIC   12 Servings

1½ cups canned apricot
   nectar
½ cup vinegar
1 cup sugar
14 whole cloves
2 sticks cinnamon
14 dried apricots, diced
Boiling water
1 pkg. (3 oz.) orange
   gelatin
1 envelope unflavored
   gelatin

Bring first 5 ingredients to a boil, add apricots and simmer 10 minutes. Remove cloves and cinnamon sticks. Drain juice from pan. Add enough hot water to juice to make 4 cups; add packet of orange gelatin plus unflavored gelatin. Mix with apricots and chill in an 8-cup greased mold.

SALADS, DRESSINGS & SAUCES

FROZEN SPICED PEACH SALAD

10-12 Servings

Tasty with souffles

1 jar (30 oz.) spiced
  peaches
1 pkg. (3 oz.) cream
  cheese
¼ cup sugar
1 T. lemon juice
1 cup miniature
  marshmallows
½ cup chopped pecans
⅔ cup evaporated milk,
  frozen until crystals
  form on edges

Drain and chop peaches, reserving ½ cup liquid. Beat cheese and sugar until smooth. Beat in liquid and lemon juice. Fold in peaches, marshmallows and pecans. Whip evaporated milk until stiff. Fold into cheese mixture. Pour in 11 x 7-inch pan. Freeze. Cut into squares and serve on lettuce leaves.

CRUNCHY SALAD

10-12 Servings

2 heads (10 oz. each)
  iceberg lettuce,
  chopped
3 stalks celery, cut into
  medium pieces
½ cup chopped salted
  peanuts
2 packages (8 oz. each)
  dried beef, cut up
1 cup blue cheese salad
  dressing
4 to 6 slices bacon, fried,
  drained and crumbled

Mix all ingredients except bacon. Arrange in salad bowl and top with bacon.

SALADS, DRESSINGS & SAUCES

BULGUR SALAD

6 Servings

1 cup fine bulgur
3 medium tomatoes, chopped
1 cup chopped parsley
1 cup finely chopped onion
⅓ cup lemon juice
2 tsp. salt
⅓ cup olive oil
1 T. dried mint
Lettuce

Soak bulgur in cold water for 10 minutes. Drain in cheesecloth. Squeeze out excess water. Put into bowl; add tomatoes, parsley, onion, lemon juice, and salt. Toss with fork. Just before serving, add oil and mint. Serve on bed of lettuce.

HERBED SALAD DRESSING

1 Cup

½ cup salad oil
½ cup red wine vinegar
1 small clove garlic, minced
1 T. sugar
2 tsp. salt
1 tsp. dry mustard
½ tsp. pepper
½ tsp. paprika
½ tsp. mixed herbs (parsley, thyme, marjoram, coriander, etc.)
¼ tsp. curry powder

Place all ingredients in covered jar; shake well and refrigerate. Chill at least 2 hours before using.

CHEESE SAUCE FOR VEGETABLES

¼ cup butter
1 carton (4 oz.) whipped cream cheese with chives
Dash salt, pepper

Mix ingredients together. Place in microwave on low for 40 seconds.

SALADS, DRESSINGS & SAUCES

MARCHAND DE VIN SAUCE

¾ cup butter
½ cup finely chopped
  onion
½ cup minced ham
⅓ cup chopped
  mushrooms
⅓ cup finely chopped
  shallots
2 cloves garlic, minced
2 T. flour
½ tsp. salt
⅛ tsp. pepper
Dash cayenne pepper
¾ cup beef broth
½ cup red wine

In a skillet, melt butter; lightly saute onion, ham, mushrooms, shallots, and garlic until onion is golden brown. Add flour, salt, pepper, and cayenne. Brown well for about 10 minutes. Blend in broth and wine. Cook, stirring constantly, until thickened. Reduce heat; simmer for about 45 minutes.

MUSHROOM SAUCE
2½ Cups

3 T. butter
½ lb. mushrooms, sliced
1 medium onion, sliced
1 stalk celery with leaves,
  coarsely chopped
1 tsp. salt
1 tsp. Worcestershire
  sauce
1 T. dry sherry
1 cup whipping cream
½ cup milk

Melt butter and saute vegetables until tender. Place in blender or food processor; add salt, Worcestershire sauce, sherry, and cream. Cover and puree 30 seconds. Pour into saucepan; add milk and heat through. Do not boil; serve hot.

RED WINE SAUCE
2 Cups

6 T. butter
6 green onions, minced
¾ cup dry red wine
1½ cups brown sauce or
  canned beef gravy
1 T. lemon juice

Heat 4 T. of butter until hot but not smoking. Slowly cook green onions until wilted. Add wine. Simmer uncovered until liquid is reduced to ¼ cup. Add brown sauce and lemon juice and heat. Add remaining butter, bit by bit, swirling it in by rotating the pan gently.

DESSERTS & SWEETS

THE 8th DEADLY SIN

8-10 Servings

For chocoholics!

1 lb. dark sweet
  chocolate
5 oz. sweet butter
4 large eggs
1 T. sugar
1 T. flour
2 cups whipping cream
1 T. confectioners' sugar
1 tsp. vanilla
Chocolate curls, for
  garnish
8 oz. frozen raspberries,
  pureed, and strained

Line an 8-inch cake pan with buttered and floured waxed paper. In the top of a double boiler, melt chocolate and butter until shiny and smooth. Set aside. In another double boiler, whisk egg and sugar over simmering water until sugar is dissolved and mixture is barely warm. Remove from heat and beat with electric mixer at highest speed, until eggs are the consistency of lightly whipped cream (about 8 minutes). Carefully fold in flour and gently, but thoroughly fold in chocolate mixture. Pour into prepared pan and bake at 425° for 15 minutes. Remove from oven and cool. (It will be soft in center and crusty on top.) Place cake in its pan in freezer overnight.

On day of serving, remove cake from freezer. Quickly spin pan over a burner set on high and turn cake out onto a flat platter. Remove waxed paper. Whip cream with confectioners' sugar and vanilla until stiff. Pile ¾ of whipping cream in center of cake in a mound. Decorate with chocolate curls, then pipe rosettes with remaining cream around edges. Refrigerate until 5 minutes before serving. Pass raspberry puree separately.

WALNUT BRANDY SAUCE

2 Cups

1 cup packed brown
  sugar
¼ cup butter
¼ cup whipping cream
2 T. light corn syrup
¼ cup brandy
¼ cup lightly toasted
  chopped walnuts

In saucepan combine sugar, butter, cream, and corn syrup; heat to boiling, stirring constantly. Reduce heat to low; cook, stirring, for 5 minutes. Add brandy and walnuts; simmer 1 minute. Serve warm over ice cream.

DESSERTS & SWEETS

CHOCOLATE CREPES WITH FUDGE SAUCE 6 Servings

CHOCOLATE CREPES:

6 T. flour
2 T. unsweetened cocoa
¼ tsp. salt
2 eggs
2 egg yolks
1 T. sugar
¼ cup vegetable oil
⅓ cup milk

FILLING:

2 cups whipping cream
¼ cup confectioners'
   sugar
3 T. instant coffee

**CHOCOLATE FUDGE
SAUCE:**

½ cup unsweetened
   cocoa
1 cup sugar
1 cup light corn syrup
½ cup half and half
3 T. butter
¼ tsp. salt
1 tsp. vanilla

For crepes, combine flour, cocoa, salt, eggs, egg yolks, sugar, oil, and milk in a blender or food processor. Blend until smooth. Let the batter rest for 1 hour in refrigerator. Cook crepes 1 at a time in a seasoned 5-inch crepe pan. Makes 12 crepes.

For filling, whisk cream in large bowl over ice. When cream mounds softly, add confectioners' sugar and coffee. Continue whisking until cream forms peaks. Place a big spoonful of cream mixture on each crepe and roll up. Arrange 2 rolled crepes on each of 6 plates. Top with fudge sauce.

For fudge sauce, place all ingredients except vanilla in a small saucepan; bring to a boil for 5 minutes. Remove from heat and stir in vanilla. Makes almost 2 cups.

GRAHAM CRACKER CAKE   8 Servings

A deliciously rich cake

½ cup butter
1 cup sugar
3 eggs, separated
1 tsp. vanilla
1 cup graham cracker
   crumbs
½ cup flour
2 tsp. baking powder
1 cup milk
Butter cream frosting
Chopped pecans

Cream butter and sugar until light and fluffy. Beat in egg yolks, 1 at a time. Add vanilla. Mix dry ingredients together; add alternately with milk. Beat egg whites until stiff; fold into batter. Turn into a greased 8-inch square baking pan. Bake at 350° for 20 to 25 minutes. Frost with butter cream frosting; sprinkle with chopped pecans.

DESSERTS & SWEETS

ORANGE LIQUEUR CAKE
12-14 Servings

Make this the day before serving

TORTE:

⅔ cup milk
1¼ tsp. vanilla
1¼ cups flour
¼ tsp. salt
1¼ tsp. baking powder
4 eggs
1½ cups sugar

SYRUP:

½ cup sugar
½ cup water
¼ cup Grand Marnier or other orange liqueur or rum

FILLING:

3 eggs, separated
½ cup sugar
1 T. cornstarch
Dash salt
1 cup orange juice
5 tsp. lemon juice

FROSTING:

½ pt. whipping cream
Sugar to taste
2 T. Grand Marnier or rum
Orange segments, fresh or canned for garnish

For torte, heat milk until bubbles form on sides of pot. Add vanilla to milk, set aside. Combine flour, salt, and baking powder. Beat eggs until light and fluffy. Gradually add sugar. Blend in flour mixture alternately with milk mixture. Pour batter into 2 well-buttered and floured 9-inch spring-form pans. Bake at 350° for 30 to 35 minutes or until cake pulls away from sides of pan. Let cool about 10 minutes. Remove from pans.

For syrup, boil sugar and water about 5 minutes. Remove from heat and add Grand Marnier. Pour over warm layers. Cake may be wrapped well and frozen at this point.

For filling, beat egg whites until stiff, but not dry. In top of double boiler mix together sugar, cornstarch, and salt. Stir in orange juice, lemon juice, and slightly beaten egg yolks. Cook over hot water, stirring constantly until thickened. Remove from heat. Fold egg whites into orange sauce.

To assemble cake, cut each cake layer in ½ horizontally. Spread warm filling between layers. Smooth excess over top and sides. Refrigerate. This should be done the day before serving. Several hours before serving time, whip cream; sweeten to taste. Add Grand Marnier. Frost top and sides of cake. Garnish with orange segments (marinated in a little Grand Marnier, if desired). Refrigerate until serving.

DESSERTS & SWEETS

FLORIDA ORANGE PIE

8 Servings

MERINGUE SHELL:

4 egg whites
¼ tsp. cream of tartar
1 cup sugar
⅓ cup finely crushed
  walnuts (optional)

FILLING:

4 egg yolks
½ cup sugar
3 T. grated orange rind
2 T. lemon juice
⅛ tsp. salt
2 oranges, cut in ½ with
  sections scooped out,
  drained and chopped
1 pt. whipping cream

For meringue shell, beat egg whites with cream of tartar until foamy; gradually add sugar and continue beating until very stiff peaks are formed. Spread over bottom and up sides of greased 9-inch pie plate, making bottom ¼ inch thick and sides 1 inch thick. Sprinkle edge with crushed nuts, if desired. Bake at 275° for 1 hour, or until crisp to touch. Cool. For filling, beat egg yolks slightly in top of double boiler. Add sugar, orange rind, lemon juice, and salt. Cook over boiling water, stirring constantly until thickened, about 8 minutes. Fold in orange sections; cool. Whip 1 cup cream; fold into filling. Pour into shell; chill 12 hours. Before serving, whip remaining 1 cup cream; spoon on pie.

POIRES NOIRES

6 Servings

Bittersweet chocolate coated pears

1 cup sugar
4 cups water
Juice of 1 lemon
2 cinnamon sticks
4 whole cloves
6 firm pears, Anjou or
  Comice, with stems
  intact
6 oz. semisweet
  chocolate
4 T. unsalted butter,
  softened
Holly leaves with berries
  or fresh mint

Dissolve sugar in water. Add lemon juice and spices. Simmer for 10 to 15 minutes, tightly covered. Peel pears carefully, leaving stem intact, and cut a slice off bottoms so they will stand upright. Poach pears in the gently boiling syrup until tender, about 35 to 40 minutes. Cool pears in syrup and chill overnight. Melt chocolate in top of double boiler. Add butter; stir until melted and mixture is smooth. Remove pears from syrup and dry gently with paper towel. Dip pears in chocolate to coat evenly. Lift pears to drain off excess chocolate; arrange on a serving plate. Decorate top of each pear with a sprig of holly or fresh mint. Pears will keep under refrigeration without weeping for at least 24 hours, sometimes even 2 days.

319

DESSERTS & SWEETS

PRUNE AND ARMAGNAC ICE CREAM   1 Quart

1 lb. dried, pitted prunes
Armagnac or brandy
1 qt. milk
8 egg yolks
1 to 1¼ cups sugar

Two weeks in advance, place prunes in a large crock. Add Armagnac to cover. Cover crock. Set aside in a cool place to macerate. Loosely pack prunes into a 1-cup measure. Fill the remainder of cup with Armagnac; set aside. Scald milk; set aside. Whisk egg yolks over low heat in a large saucepan until warm. Continue whisking, adding sugar gradually. When sugar has been added and has begun to dissolve, remove from heat. Whisk in hot milk. Return to low heat. Stir constantly until custard is thick enough to coat a spoon heavily. Remove from heat. Cool for at least 2 hours. Beat vigorously with a whisk or an electric beater. Strain custard mixture into an ice cream dasher. Follow the manufacturer's directions for freezing. When ice cream is just beginning to set, drop in prunes 1 at a time (while machine is in operation) and drizzle in Armagnac. Continue freezing until ice cream is firm. Serve topped with a prune and drizzled with Armagnac.

PEPPERMINT FREEZE   4 Servings

Use up those leftover candy canes

6 candy canes, about 8 oz.
1 cup milk (or enough to cover canes)
2 cups whipping cream, whipped

Pound candy canes and soak in milk, mix with whipped cream and freeze in shallow pan or 4 sherbet glasses. Stir every ½ hour to keep from separating. May be served in chocolate cups garnished with crushed candy canes.

DESSERTS & SWEETS

CHESTNUT-CHOCOLATE LOAF 12-16 Servings

Very rich — a chocolate lover's delight

1 cup butter
1 can (15 oz.)
 unsweetened chestnut
 puree
1 cup sugar
8 oz. unsweetened
 chocolate, melted,
 cooled
2 to 3 T. brandy
1 tsp. vanilla
½ cup slivered almonds,
 toasted
Confectioners' sugar
1 cup whipping cream,
 whipped, sweetened

Cream butter until light and fluffy. Add chestnut puree 1 T. at a time. Gradually beat in sugar, then cooled chocolate, brandy, and vanilla. Stir in almonds. Pack into an oiled and waxed paper-lined 9 x 5-inch loaf pan or a small mold. Refrigerate overnight or up to 2 days. To serve, turn out onto platter. Sift confectioners' sugar over cake. Cut into very thin slices. Serve with whipped cream. You may wish to pipe some whipped cream decoratively over cake.

BRANDIED ORANGE SHELLS 8 Servings

Pretty and elegant for company

4 very large navel
 oranges
3 to 4 cups water
2 cups sugar
Sugar for coating
2 cups brandy
½ gallon vanilla ice cream
8 candied lemon leaves
 or mint leaves
 (optional)

Cut oranges in ½ crosswise. In saucepan just large enough to hold oranges, combine water and sugar. Heat until sugar is dissolved. Add oranges. If needed, add more water just to cover oranges. Simmer gently for 20 to 30 minutes, or until very tender. Allow to stand overnight to absorb as much syrup as possible. Add brandy. Place oranges and brandy-syrup in covered jars or plastic containers. Refrigerate at least 3 days or up to 3 months until ready to use. Carefully scoop out pulp; do not puncture shells. Puree pulp in blender or food processor, adding enough brandy syrup to make proper sauce consistency. Dry shells well. Coat several times with sugar; place cut side down to dry between coatings. Fill cups with ice cream. Top with pureed pulp. If desired, garnish with lemon or mint leaves. Brandied orange shells may be eaten.

321

DESSERTS & SWEETS

LEMON AND ORANGE ICE

4 Servings

Tart, Italian ice

2 cups cold water
½ cup granulated sugar
1 tsp. grated lemon rind
½ cup fresh lemon juice
1 cup fresh orange juice
6 T. Grand Marnier or orange liqueur

Boil water, sugar, and lemon rind together about 5 minutes. Cool. Add lemon and orange juices; mix well. Freeze about 1½ hours. Add 2 T. of liqueur to lemon mixture and beat until all ice crystals have been broken down. This may be done in blender or food processor. Return to freezer. ½ hour before serving, remove from freezer and let soften in refrigerator. Spoon into 4 wine glasses and pour 1 T. of liqueur over each serving.

BRANDY ICE

6-8 Servings

An easy, spectacular dessert

1 qt. good quality vanilla ice cream, softened
¼ cup or more creme de cacao
2 T. brandy
6 to 8 sugar cubes
Lemon extract

Stir together ice cream, creme de cacao and brandy. Refreeze. Place ice cream in individual dishes. Soak sugar cubes briefly in lemon extract. Place 1 on top of each serving and light. Serve at once.

RAISIN CREAM PIE

8 Servings

Very rich

1 cup raisins
1 cup sour cream
1 cup sugar
2 eggs, slightly beaten
½ tsp. cinnamon
¼ tsp. ground cloves
¼ tsp. salt
1 T. butter
1 pkg. (3 oz.) cream cheese, softened
½ cup sifted confectioners' sugar
1 cup whipping cream
1 baked 9-inch pastry shell

Chop raisins; add sour cream, sugar, eggs, spices and salt. Bring to boil. Reduce heat and cook until thickened, stirring constantly. Add butter. Cool completely. Beat cream cheese and confectioners' sugar together. Whip cream and fold into cheese mixture. Spread ½ of cheese mixture into a baked 9-inch pastry shell. Add raisin mixture and top with remaining cheese mixture. Chill.

DESSERTS & SWEETS

WASPS NESTS
About 100

½ cup sugar
¼ cup water
½ lb. blanched almonds, slivered
3 egg whites
2 cups confectioners' sugar
8 oz. semisweet chocolate, grated

Boil sugar and water together until syrup spins a thread (240° on candy thermometer). Stir in almonds. Beat egg whites until stiff, adding confectioners' sugar by the spoonful. Fold almond mixture and chocolate into egg whites. Drop dough by the ½ tsp. on buttered and floured cookie sheet. Bake at 300° until dry, about 25 minutes. Let stand 10 minutes; remove from pan.

CURRANT COOKIES
2 Dozen

3 T. currants
4 tsp. dark rum
⅓ cup sugar
¼ cup butter, softened
1 egg
Pinch of salt
1 tsp. grated lemon rind
½ cup plus 2 T. sifted flour

Macerate currants in rum for 30 minutes. Drain and reserve liquid. Beat sugar and butter until light and fluffy. Add egg, reserved rum, salt and lemon rind, beating well. Fold in flour and currants. Drop by teaspoons on greased baking sheets, 2 inches apart. Flatten with spoon dipped in cold water. Bake at 350° for 8 to 10 minutes or until edges are browned. Let cool for 2 minutes and remove to rack. Cool completely.

CRISP AND NUTTY SUGAR COOKIES
6 Dozen

1 cup butter
2 cups dark brown sugar
1 cup granulated sugar
3 eggs, slightly beaten
1 tsp. vanilla
1 tsp. cinnamon
4 cups flour
1 tsp. soda
2 cups chopped pecans

Cream butter and sugars together. Stir in eggs and vanilla. Stir in dry ingredients. Fold in nuts. Separate dough into 4 equal parts. Roll each into a log shape of equal thickness on a floured board. Wrap each "log" in foil or waxed paper. Chill for 12 to 24 hours. Rolls may also be frozen. Slice thinly and bake on cookie sheets at 350° for 10 to 12 minutes or until light brown.

DESSERTS & SWEETS

SPITZBUBEN
About 12 Dozen

A traditional Bavarian Christmas cookie

1 cup butter
1 cup sugar
1 tsp. vanilla
2 cups flour
1 cup almonds, finely ground
1 cup raspberry jelly
1 cup confectioners' sugar (about)

Cream butter and sugar thoroughly. Add vanilla. Stir in flour and almonds. Roll on well-floured board to ⅛-inch thickness. Cut with decorative 1-inch cutter. Place on cookie sheet. Bake at 300° until cookies just begin to turn golden, about 15 minutes. Cool on rack. Put two cookies together with jelly. Dust with confectioners' sugar.

BUTTER STARS
3 Dozen

DOUGH:

1 cup butter
6 T. confectioners' sugar
1 egg yolk
3 cups flour
1 T. sherry

ICING:

1 egg white
½ cup sugar
1 tsp. almond extract

Cream butter and sugar. Add egg yolk, flour and sherry. Mix thoroughly. Chill dough ½ hour. Roll dough ½ inch thick and cut out with star cutter.

For icing, beat egg white until stiff, but not dry. Fold in sugar and extract. Put a spoonful on each cookie. Bake 30 minutes at 325°.

GINGERSNAPS
5 Dozen

¾ cup shortening
1 cup brown sugar
1 egg
¼ cup molasses
2 cups sifted flour
2 tsp. baking soda
1 tsp. ginger
1 tsp. ground cloves
1 tsp. cinnamon
¼ tsp. salt

In a large bowl, cream shortening and sugar together. Beat in egg, then molasses. Sift together dry ingredients; gradually add to sugar mixture. Blend well. Cover with plastic wrap; chill. Form dough into small balls. Roll in granulated sugar. Place 2 inches apart on greased cookie sheets. Flatten balls of dough with glass tumbler. Bake at 350° for 12 to 15 minutes, or until crisp. Cool on wire racks.

DESSERTS & SWEETS

DESERT SANDS

10 Dozen

Very elegant

COOKIES:

1 cup butter
⅞ cup sugar
1 tsp. ammonium carbonate (from pharmacy)
1 T. water
1 tsp. vanilla (from pharmacy)
2½ cups sifted flour
Pinch of salt

DIPPING CHOCOLATE:

6 oz. semisweet chocolate
4 T. butter
1 tsp. vanilla
Pinch of salt

Melt butter and brown slightly. Put in bowl; add sugar. Set bowl over pan of ice cubes. Cream until cold, light and fluffy. Crush ammonium carbonate with mortar and pestle. Dissolve in water. Stir ammonium carbonate and vanilla into butter. Add flour and salt; beat well. Using a demitasse spoon, make almond-shaped cookies. Place on buttered baking sheet. Bake at 300° about 15 minutes. Watch carefully.

To make dipping chocolate, melt chocolate and butter over simmering water. Add vanilla and salt. Stir gently to smooth. Dip 1 end of cooled cookie into melted chocolate. Place on waxed paper and refrigerate a few minutes to cool.

NUTMEG SQUARES

12 Squares

Delicate brunch or dessert bar

1 cup sugar
½ cup shortening
1 egg, beaten
1¼ cups flour
½ tsp. salt
½ tsp. baking powder
1¼ tsp. nutmeg
½ cup buttermilk
½ tsp. baking soda dissolved in 1 T. hot water
1 tsp. vanilla
1 to 2 T. sugar
¾ cup raisins (about)

Cream sugar and shortening. Beat in egg. Add flour, salt, baking powder and nutmeg. Stir in buttermilk, dissolved baking soda and vanilla. Spread in buttered 8½ x 13½-inch pan. Sprinkle liberally with sugar and raisins. Bake 20 minutes at 400° until golden brown. Do not overbake. Cut into bars.

DESSERTS & SWEETS

NOISETTES DES CHOCOLATS   6 Dozen

4 squares (4 oz.)
   unsweetened
   chocolate, melted
2 cups sugar
4 eggs
½ cup cooking oil
2 tsp. vanilla
2 cups flour
2 tsp. baking powder
½ tsp. salt
Confectioners' sugar

Mix chocolate and sugar well. Add eggs, 1 at a time, beating thoroughly. Beat in oil and vanilla. Mix together dry ingredients. Add to chocolate mixture; mix well. Chill in refrigerator overnight. Shape into walnut-sized balls and roll in confectioners' sugar. Place on well-greased cookie sheets, 2 inches apart. Bake at 350° for 10 minutes.

CHERRY-COCONUT BARS   16 2-inch Squares

Easy and delicious

1¼ cups sifted flour
½ cup butter, melted
3 T. confectioners' sugar
2 eggs, slightly beaten
1 cup granulated sugar
½ tsp. baking powder
¼ tsp. salt
1 tsp. vanilla
¾ cup chopped nuts
½ cup coconut
½ cup maraschino
   cherries, quartered

Cream 1 cup of flour with butter and confectioners' sugar. Spread in an 8-inch square pan. Bake 20 to 25 minutes at 350°. Combine remaining ingredients. Spread over top of baked pastry. Bake an additional 25 minutes at 350°. Cool before cutting into bars. Recipe may be doubled. At Christmas time use both red and green maraschino cherries for a festive touch.

DELICIOUS CHOCOLATE SAUCE   3 Cups

Especially good served warm over peppermint ice cream

4 oz. unsweetened
   chocolate
½ cup butter
⅓ cup unsweetened
   cocoa
1½ cups sugar
½ pt. whipping cream
2 tsp. vanilla

Melt chocolate in double boiler; add butter, cocoa and sugar. Cook for 45 minutes, stirring often. Add cream and cook 10 minutes longer, stirring constantly. Slowly add vanilla. It may appear to curdle when cream is added, but will become smooth as stirred. Can be kept several weeks in refrigerator.

DESSERTS & SWEETS

NORWEGIAN LEMON BARS
24 Bars

Very rich

1½ cups flour
¾ cup butter
2 eggs
½ cup coconut
½ cup chopped pecans
1½ cups brown sugar, packed
¼ tsp. baking powder
2 T. flour
Dash of salt
1½ cups confectioners' sugar
1 T. butter
Juice and rind of 1 lemon

Mix flour and butter together. Pat into 8-inch square baking pan. Bake at 350° for about 20 minutes or until browned. Mix the eggs, coconut, pecans, brown sugar, baking powder, flour and salt. Pour over pastry; bake for 30 minutes more. Combine confectioners' sugar, butter, juice and rind of lemon. Spread over top of cooled bars. Refrigerate. To serve, cut chilled bars into small squares.

CHOCOLATE BALLS
30 Balls

A nice addition to your Christmas cookie platter. Children can make these

4 oz. semisweet chocolate pieces
1 T. butter
1 egg
1 tsp. vanilla
Pinch of salt
1½ cups confectioners' sugar
Finely chopped walnuts

In the top of a double boiler, melt chocolate with butter. In a small bowl, beat egg with vanilla and a pinch of salt until foamy. Add confectioners' sugar and the egg mixture alternately to the chocolate. Transfer the mixture to a bowl. Chill, covered, for 1 to 2 hours or until firm enough to shape. Pinch off pieces of chocolate mixture. Form into 1-inch balls and roll in chopped nuts. Arrange balls on waxed paper. Chill.

PEANUT BUTTER SAUCE
2 Cups

Yummy on chocolate ice cream

1 cup brown sugar
6 T. cream or milk
1 T. butter
4 T. peanut butter (crunchy or smooth)

Mix first 3 ingredients. Stir over low heat until boiling. Continue cooking for 4 minutes. Remove from heat and add peanut butter. Serve warm. Keep covered in refrigerator.

DESSERTS & SWEETS

GALACTOBOURIKO

SYRUP:

3 cups water
3 cups sugar
½ slice lemon
1 tsp. rose water or 1 jigger brandy

FILLING:

8 cups milk
8 eggs
2½ cups sugar
¾ cup farina
4 T. unsalted butter
2 tsp. vanilla

PASTRY:

½ lb. phyllo dough
½ cup melted, clarified, unsalted butter

For syrup, combine ingredients and bring to boiling point. Simmer 20 minutes. Cool.

For filling, scald milk. Set aside. Beat eggs in a saucepan; add sugar and beat. Add ½ of farina and mix well. Add hot milk gradually; then remaining farina. Cook on low heat until it begins to thicken. Continue cooking a few minutes longer. Cool to lukewarm. Stir in butter and vanilla. Stir from time to time.

Butter a 12 x 8-inch pan. Butter each phyllo sheet and place ½ of the sheets on the bottom of the pan. Build up sides to fold over filling. Pour in filling. Cover with all but 3 buttered phyllo sheets. Fold over sides then cover with remaining 3 sheets. Brush with butter. Cut the top at 1½-inch intervals. Stop at filling. Bake at 350° for 45 minutes. Remove from oven and immediately pour cold syrup over the galactobouriko. Cool to room temperature.

VIENNESE PRUNES

1 Pound

1 lb. pitted prunes
White wine to cover prunes
Whole blanched almonds
1 cup flour
⅛ tsp. salt
1 cup grated sweet chocolate

Soak prunes overnight in wine. Drain, reserving wine. Simmer prunes in water to cover for 30 minutes. Drain. Fill each prune with 1 whole almond. Chill. Combine flour, salt and 1 cup of reserved wine. Beat until smooth. Dip prunes in batter; fry in hot oil at 390° until golden. Drain on paper towels. Roll in chocolate and serve immediately.

DESSERTS & SWEETS

PLUM PUDDING

10 Servings

This uses plums

½ cup flour
½ tsp. soda
1 tsp. cinnamon
½ tsp. ground cloves
¼ tsp. salt
⅓ cup fine dry fresh bread
    crumbs
½ cup butter
¾ cup brown sugar
3 eggs
1 can (1 lb. 14 oz.) purple
    plums, drained, pitted,
    and chopped
1 T. grated orange rind
1 pkg. (8 oz.) chopped
    pitted dates
1½ cups seedless raisins
1 cup currants
1 cup chopped pecans

RUM HARD SAUCE:

½ cup butter
1½ cups sifted
    confectioners' sugar
2 T. light rum

Grease an 8-cup mold or 2 smaller molds. Dust evenly with some sugar; tap out any excess. Combine flour, soda, spices, and salt in a small bowl; stir in bread crumbs and set aside. Cream butter and sugar until light and fluffy. Add eggs 1 at a time. Stir in plums and orange rind. Stir in flour mixture until blended. Add rest of fruit and pecans. Spoon into prepared mold. Cover with lid of mold or 2 pieces of waxed paper, covered with tin foil and held in place with a double rubber band. Place on a rack in a kettle or steamer; pour in boiling water until ½ of the pudding mold is covered. Cover tightly. Steam 4½ hours for large mold or 3 hours for smaller molds. (Keep water boiling gently throughout cooking time.) Cool pudding in mold for 10 minutes. Unmold. May be served immediately or wrapped in foil and reheated in oven or steamer. This pudding freezes well. Thaw before heating to serve. Serve warm with Rum Hard Sauce.

For sauce, combine all ingredients until light and fluffy.

CANDIES & GIFTS

APRICOT FRUITCAKE
4 Cakes

An elegant Christmas hostess gift

2 cups butter, softened
2¼ cups firmly packed
  light brown sugar
1 cup honey
10 eggs
4 cups sifted flour
2 tsp. cinnamon
2 tsp. baking powder
1 tsp. ground allspice
¾ tsp. salt
3 lbs. dried apricots,
  sliced
2 lbs. pecan halves
1½ lbs. pitted dates,
  sliced
1 lb. golden raisins
1 cup apricot nectar
½ cup half and half
2 T. fresh lemon juice
1 cup brandy
¼ cup orange-flavored
  liqueur

Cream butter, sugar and honey. Add eggs, 1 at a time, beating well after each addition. Sift flour, cinnamon, baking powder, allspice and salt. Stir ½ of the flour mixture into sugar mixture. Dredge apricots, pecans, dates and raisins in remaining flour. Combine nectar, half and half, and lemon juice; add to batter. Fold in apricot mixture. Pour into 4 buttered and floured 9½ x 5-inch loaf pans. Bake at 250° for 2½ to 3 hours or until tester comes out clean. Cool in pans. Combine brandy and liqueur. Sprinkle over cakes; let stand 1 hour. Wrap tightly in foil. Refrigerate at least 1 week.

PECAN CARAMELS
About 3 Pounds

May be frozen or doubled

1 cup butter
2 cups sugar
1 cup white corn syrup
1 can (14 oz.) sweetened
  condensed milk
⅛ tsp. salt
1 T. vanilla
1 cup pecan halves

Line bottom of buttered 9-inch square pan with pecan halves. In heavy pan, melt butter. Add sugar, corn syrup, sweetened condensed milk, and salt. Bring to boil, stirring constantly. Lower heat and cook to 242° on candy thermometer (16 to 18 minutes). Remove from heat; add vanilla. Pour over pecan halves; cool completely. Slip out of pan and cut into squares. Wrap in plastic or waxed paper.

CANDIES & GIFTS

GRAHAM CRACKER GINGERBREAD HOUSE   1 House

Easy and fun for children

1 paper milk carton
   (gallon size)
1 square (6 inches)
   cardboard
3 to 4 cups basic white
   icing, homemade or
   canned
1 pkg. (16 oz.) graham
   crackers
Pastry bag with decorator
   tip
1 pkg. (12 oz.) Graham
   Crackos cereal
1 bag (10½ oz.) miniature
   marshmallows
8 candy canes (2-inch
   size)
Ribbon candy (optional)
1 bottle (2 oz.) colored
   sprinkles

Prepare milk carton by cutting in ½ horizontally; reserve top ½. Remove handle and staple opening closed. Glue top ½ to cardboard square. Spread icing over entire carton and arrange graham crackers on top and sides. Using pastry bag with decorator tip, draw a door and windows with icing. Cover all seams and edges on sides of house with Graham Crackos. Use generous amounts of icing when applying cereal. Cover roof with marshmallows. Pipe icing along eaves of house. Place 2 candy canes at each corner. Ribbon candy may be placed on either side of candy canes. Place additional marshmallows around base; add sprinkles if desired. Icing may be tinted with vegetable colors to pipe wreaths and Christmas trees on door and sides of house.

CANDIES & GIFTS

BARBECUED PECANS

4 Cups

4 T. melted butter
¼ cup Worcestershire
sauce
1 T. catsup
⅛ tsp. hot pepper sauce
4 cups pecans
Salt (optional)

Mix first 4 ingredients; stir in pecans, and mix well. Spread pecans evenly over a shallow baking pan. Bake at 300° about 30 minutes, stirring often. Sprinkle with salt, if desired, and cool.

BISCUIT DU CHIEN

At Least 200 Biscuits

For the dog in your life

1 pkg. dry yeast
⅓ cup warm water
3½ cups all-purpose flour
2 cups whole wheat flour
2 cups oatmeal
1 cup rye flour
1 cup cornmeal
½ cup nonfat dry milk
4 tsp. salt
1 pt. chicken or beef
broth
1 egg
1 T. milk

Dissolve yeast in warm water. Mix all dry ingredients; pour into yeast mixture and broth. Knead on floured board for about 3 minutes, forming a stiff dough. Divide dough into 2 portions. Roll out each portion about ¼-inch thick. Shape into bones or cut with cookie cutters. Place on greased cookie sheet; brush with glaze made by mixing egg with 1 T. milk. Bake at 300° for 45 minutes. Turn off heat and leave in oven overnight.

BUTTERY PECAN BRITTLE

2½ Pounds

2 cups sugar
1 cup light corn syrup
½ cup water
1 cup butter
3 cups pecans
1½ tsp. baking soda

In a 3-qt. saucepan, combine sugar, corn syrup, and water. Cook and stir until sugar dissolves. Bring to boiling point; blend in butter. Stir frequently until mixture reaches syrup stage (230°). Add nuts when temperature reaches soft crack stage (280°); stir constantly until mixture reaches hard crack stage (305°). Remove from heat. Quickly stir in soda, mixing thoroughly. Pour into two 15½ x 10½-inch buttered jelly roll pans. As candy cools, stretch it thin by lifting and pulling from edges with two forks. Loosen from pans as soon as possible. Turn candy over. Break into pieces.

CANDIES & GIFTS

BRANDIED PEANUTS

Delicious gift, can't have too many

3 cups salted Spanish
  peanuts
1 cup confectioners'
  sugar
2 T. peanut oil
1 T. whipping cream
3 T. brandy

Heat peanuts on a cookie sheet for 10 minutes at 350°. Mix rest of ingredients in large bowl until smooth. Stir hot peanuts into mixture. When thoroughly covered with mixture, spread on waxed paper and let cool. Store in airtight containers.

BEST-EVER TOFFEE   About 1 Pound

1 lb. milk chocolate
1 cup butter
3 T. water
1 cup sugar
2 cups whole pecans
1 T. vanilla (Mexican
  vanilla, if possible)

Grate chocolate into 9 x 12-inch cake pan. Reserve ½ of grated chocolate for topping. Melt butter, water, and sugar slowly in heavy saucepan. Cook until mixture becomes a medium golden color and thick (hard-crack stage, 285°-290° on candy thermometer) stirring constantly with a wooden spoon. Remove from heat. Add pecans and vanilla. Mix well. Quickly pour into pan containing ½ of grated chocolate. Spread with spatula. Sprinkle reserved chocolate on top. Cool and refrigerate. Remove from refrigerator. Push candy out of pan. Place in plastic bag and pound with mallet to break into smaller pieces. Freezes well.

DEVILED NUTS   1 Pound

3 T. butter
1 lb. peanuts (or mixture
  of almonds, cashews,
  peanuts)
Dash of Worcestershire
  sauce
1½ tsp. salt
¼ tsp. cayenne pepper
⅛ tsp. chili pepper
⅛ tsp. ground cumin
⅛ tsp. paprika

Melt butter over low heat; add nuts. Cook, stirring constantly, about 3 to 5 minutes, or until golden brown. Remove from heat; stir in Worcestershire sauce. Using slotted spoon remove nuts; drain on paper towels. Put in paper bag with spices; shake well. Cool. Store in airtight container.

CANDIES & GIFTS

GAZEBO FUDGE

5 Pounds

Can't fail

½ cup butter
1 can (13 oz.) evaporated milk
2 lbs. sugar
½ lb. miniature marshmallows
2 oz. unsweetened chocolate
1 pkg. (12 oz.) semisweet chocolate pieces
3 pkgs. (4 oz. each) sweet baking chocolate, broken up
1 T. vanilla
2 cups chopped pecans (optional)

Combine butter, milk, and sugar in large pan. Stir until sugar dissolves. Bring to a boil. Cover and boil 5 minutes. Turn off heat. Add marshmallows. Stir until melted. Add chocolates, 1 type at a time, stirring until melted. Add vanilla and nuts. Pour into buttered 15½ x 10½ x 1-inch jelly roll pan. Cool several hours, then cut.

BRANDIED APRICOT TRUFFLES

3 Dozen

½ cup apricot preserves
2 T. apricot brandy
8 oz. semisweet chocolate
2 T. unsalted butter
Sifted confectioners' sugar

Blend apricot preserves with brandy. Puree in blender. Melt chocolate with butter in double boiler. Stir until smooth. Transfer the mixture to medium bowl and cool to room temperature. Add apricot puree; blend well by hand. Refrigerate covered until firm, about 4 hours. Scrape spoon across surface of mixture and quickly press into balls. Refrigerate uncovered until cold (1 hour). Roll in confectioners' sugar. Best when stored in refrigerator.

SUGARED WALNUTS

12 Servings

Nice Christmas gift!

1 can (28 oz.) walnuts
½ cup sugar
Salad oil
⅛ tsp. salt

Boil 1½ qts. water and add walnuts. Boil 1 minute. Rinse under hot water; drain well. Toss nuts in sugar until coated. Heat 1 inch salad oil to 350°; add ½ of the nuts and fry until golden. With slotted spoon, place nuts in sieve to drain. Toss lightly with salt. Cool on waxed paper. Repeat with remaining nuts.

CANDIES & GIFTS

CHOCOLATE TRUFFLES

About 3 Dozen

Easy and just the right touch to end a special dinner

¼ cup strong coffee (or 1
   T. instant coffee
   dissolved in ¼ cup
   boiling water)
7 oz. semisweet baking
   chocolate
2 oz. unsweetened
   chocolate
¾ cup chilled unsalted
   butter, cut into thin
   slices
¼ cup brandy or orange
   liqueur
¾ cup unsweetened
   cocoa

Break up chocolate and stir into the hot coffee. Soften in top of double boiler. Beat with electric mixer until smooth and creamy. Remove from hot water and beat another minute to cool. Gradually beat chilled butter into chocolate with mixer. When smooth, beat in liqueur by dribbles. Chill for 2 hours or until firm. When firm roll into small balls. Then roll in unsweetened cocoa.

CARAMEL POPCORN

2½ Quarts

3 T. corn oil
½ cup yellow hull-less
   popcorn
½ cup butter
1 cup firmly packed light
   brown sugar
¼ cup light corn syrup
½ tsp. salt
½ tsp. vanilla
¼ tsp. baking soda

Preheat oven to 250°. Pour corn oil into a 4 to 5-qt. skillet. Place over medium-high heat and add 1 kernel of popcorn. When the kernel pops, add popcorn. Place cover on kettle leaving small air space at edge of cover. Shake frequently until popping stops. Remove pot from heat. Measure 2½ qts. of popped corn and place in large roasting pan. Put in oven to keep warm. Melt butter in 2-qt. saucepan. Stir in sugar, syrup, and salt. Bring mixture to a boil and boil 5 minutes. Remove from heat. Stir in vanilla and baking soda. Pour over warm popcorn, mixing well. Separate pieces and place in a single layer on two large baking sheets. Bake at 250° for 1 hour. Cool completely. Store in airtight container.

1447

CATERERS

ALLEN CATERING

Elegant Cold Summer Buffet for 12
(Prepare day before)

Fresh Fruit Kabobs
Boneless Barbecued Chicken Breasts
Sliced Beef Tenderloin with Sauce Bearnaise
Chilled Rice Salad
Marinated Fresh Vegetables
Petite Dinner Rolls   Butter
Assorted Miniature Pastries

CHILLED RICE SALAD

1½ T. olive oil
1½ tsp. curry powder
1 oz. chicken base paste
3½ cups water
1½ cups chopped celery
1½ cups uncooked rice
¾ cup slivered almonds
½ cup mayonnaise
Salt and pepper to taste

In a saucepan, heat oil and curry powder about 1 minute. Add chicken base, water, celery and rice. Heat to boiling. Lower heat, cover and simmer 20 minutes or until rice is tender. Chill at least 6 hours. Stir in almonds, mayonnaise, salt and pepper. Garnish with parsley and cherry tomatoes.

MARINATED VEGETABLES

1 qt. oil and vinegar salad dressing
1 T. oregano
1 pt. cherry tomatoes
1 can (12 to 14 count) artichoke hearts
1 large zucchini, sliced
¾ lb. fresh mushrooms
1 small head cauliflower broken into bite-sized clusters
24 ripe olives

Combine dressing with oregano. Place tomatoes, artichoke hearts, zucchini, mushrooms and cauliflower in ceramic dish. Pour dressing on top and marinate overnight. Arrange vegetables on platter lined with lettuce leaves. Use black olives to separate vegetables.

338

CATERERS

FRESH FRUIT KABOBS

1 fresh pineapple
1 cantaloupe
1 honeydew melon
1 pt. strawberries

Clean and cube pineapple, cantaloupe and honeydew. Store in separate containers in refrigerator. To serve, clean strawberries and arrange on 6-inch wooden skewers alternating the different fruits.

BARBECUED BONELESS CHICKEN BREASTS

6 whole chicken breasts,
    split, boned, unskinned
Salt and pepper to taste
Barbecue sauce
Lettuce
Parsley

Arrange chicken breasts in roasting pan. Season lightly with salt and pepper. Baste with your favorite barbecue sauce. Bake in 350° oven for 50 minutes or until done, basting occasionally with additional barbecue sauce. Cool breasts on wire rack. Arrange on platter lined with lettuce leaves. Garnish with parsley. Return to refrigerator until ready to serve.

COLD BEEF TENDERLOIN

4½ to 5 lb. trimmed
    tenderloin
Salt and pepper to taste

Place tenderloin in roasting pan and season with salt and pepper or favorite seasoned salt. Roast in 400° oven for 25 to 35 minutes for rare, 120° on meat thermometer. Remove from oven and cool. Chill in refrigerator. Just before serving, slice meat and arrange on wooden board or other attractive platter.

CATERERS

CHEF RONALDO

Informal "After the Game" Supper for 20

French Hobo Sandwich
Sauteed Mushrooms with Madeira Sauce
Rice Salad Au Vinaigrette
Cream of Avocado Soup
French Fried Straw Potatoes
Crepes Fitzgerald
Cappuccino

FRENCH HOBO SANDWICH   20 Servings

20 French rolls, about 5 inches long
14 lbs. tenderloin, pretrimmed weight
1 lb. butter
3 lbs. large mushroom caps

MADEIRA WINE SAUCE:

1 large onion, finely diced
¼ cup parsley, finely minced
8 oz. mushroom stems, finely diced
½ tsp. crushed garlic
4 T. butter
½ cup Madeira wine
40 oz. canned beef broth
3 oz. tomato paste
8 T. butter
8 T. flour
Salt and pepper to taste

Split French rolls lengthwise. Trim and cut tenderloin into 2-oz. pieces. Saute in butter until desired doneness. Saute mushroom caps in butter. For the wine sauce, saute the onion, parsley, mushroom stems and garlic in butter for approximately 5 minutes, add Madeira wine. Cover saucepan and reduce liquid down approximately by ½. Add beef broth and about 2½ cups water. Add tomato paste. Simmer for 1 hour. Make a roux by melting 8 T. butter in a saute pan. When it begins to foam, add flour and stir into a paste. Cook carefully for about 3 minutes, stirring occasionally. Add the roux carefully into the simmering stock and beat with a French whip until a medium thick sauce is obtained. Open French rolls, place 4 pieces of sauteed meat inside. Garnish with mushrooms and top with Madeira sauce.

CATERERS

CREAM OF AVOCADO SOUP

4 cans potato soup
40 oz. half and half
3 ripe avocados

Prepare soup as per label instructions diluting with half and half. Cool. Puree the avocados in a blender. Add to soup. Mix thoroughly and chill in refrigerator until ready to serve.

FRENCH FRIED STRAW POTATOES

10 lbs. potatoes, peeled
Cooking oil

Julienne the potatoes in a food processor by using the shredding attachment and soak in ice water for about 30 minutes. Strain potatoes. Pat dry with paper towels. Carefully French fry in a pot of cooking oil heated to between 350° and 375°. Salt and serve immediately. If necessary, you can store the potatoes in a warm oven for a few minutes.

CREPES FITZGERALD   40 Servings

8 oz. flour
16 oz. milk
6 eggs
Pinch salt
2 oz. butter

Mix flour, milk, eggs and salt in a bowl to a heavy cream consistency. Strain. Then add butter. Pour batter into a 5 to 6-inch crepe pan and fry. Put crepes aside.

CHEESE FILLING

60 oz. cream cheese
20 oz. sour cream
Sugar and vanilla to taste
Fresh or frozen
**   strawberries**

Beat cream cheese in a mixer; add sugar and vanilla. Fold in sour cream. Chill mixture. Lay crepes flat on table. Spread cheese mixture evenly onto each crepe. Roll into cigar shape. Top with fresh or frozen strawberries. Allow 2 crepes per person.

CATERERS

MITCHELL COBEY

French picnic for 4

Pate Au Poivre with Cornichons
Ratatouille
Sausage Salad
Assorted Cheeses
(St. Christopher, Petite Cabrette, Belles des Champs, Carroll Gratte,
Paille, Pierre Robert)
Baguettes or Petits Pains
Oranges Orientales
California Chardonnay

PATE AU POIVRE

3 lbs. pork, ground
1⅓ lbs. pork fat, ground
6 to 8 slices fat
2 T. salt
1 T. thyme
¼ tsp. pate spice
⅛ tsp. pepper
2 cloves garlic, minced
¼ cup white wine
4 eggs
2 T. green peppercorns
2 T. pink peppercorns
Black peppercorns,
  crushed

Combine meat and ground fat. Line terrine with fat slices. Add all remaining ingredients except black peppercorns to pork and mix well. Fill terrine with mixture and pack down firmly. Scatter crushed black peppercorns on top and press into meat. Place terrine in a pan that will hold enough water to come ½ way up sides of terrine. Bake uncovered for 3 hours at 350°. Cool. Weight down; refrigerate overnight.

SAUSAGE SALAD

1 lb. string beans
½ lb. Gruyere cheese
¼ lb. Genoa salami
Sherry wine vinegar sauce

Cut tips off beans and drop into large pot of salted, boiling water. Cook until just tender. Rinse under cold water. Drain. Cut cheese into bite-sized cubes. Slice salami into ½-inch strips. Mix with sherry wine vinegar sauce.

CATERERS

SHERRY WINE VINEGAR SAUCE

3 T. Dijon mustard
⅓ cup sherry wine vinegar
Dash of salt and pepper
¾ cup vegetable oil

Place mustard, vinegar, salt and pepper in food processor. While machine is running, slowly add vegetable oil.

RATATOUILLE

Use equal amounts of onion, zucchini, eggplant and ½ that amount of sweet red pepper. Slice onions and peppers and saute with fresh garlic to taste. When softened place mixture in baking dish. Cut zucchini into chunks and saute briefly. Add to baking dish. Slice eggplant and cut each slice into strips. Saute in oil until slightly softened. Add to baking dish. Sprinkle with salt, pepper, thyme, 2 bay leaves and ½ cup tomato puree. Bake at 400° for 30 minutes.

ORANGES ORIENTALES

4 large oranges
3 cups sugar
1 cup water
¼ cup Cointreau
1½ tsp. Grenadine

Peel rind only from oranges. Julienne and put in saucepan with water to cover. Bring to a boil; drain and rinse in cold water. Place rind in saucepan with sugar and water. Dissolve sugar over low heat and then boil over medium heat for 10 minutes. Cool. Add Cointreau and Grenadine. Peel pith from oranges. Slice horizontally. Place orange slices in deep serving dish; cover with syrup. Chill.

CATERERS

COLONIAL CATERERS

New Orleans Party for 25

Crabmeat Canapes	Oysters Rockefeller
Baked Shrimp	Quiche Lorraine

Cream of Artichoke Soup
Mixed Green Salad with Avocado and Bacon
Jambalaya
Ham Steak Hawaiian with Sweet Potatoes and Sauce a la Germaine
Corn Bread

Peach Flambe	Beignets
Chardonnay	French Market Coffee

CRABMEAT CANAPE   28 Servings

4 shallots, finely chopped
¼ cup olive oil
6 oz. medium cream
   sauce
1 lb. crabmeat
2 oz. white wine
Salt and pepper
2 tsp. parsley, chopped
7 slices toast, trimmed,
   cut in triangles

Saute shallots in oil. Blend in cream sauce, add crabmeat and wine. Season to taste. Cook about 8 minutes, sprinkle with parsley. Allow to cool. Spread on toast and bake in a moderate oven for 5 minutes. Serve immediately.

CREAM OF ARTICHOKE SOUP   25 Servings

2 cups shallots, chopped
1 bunch celery, chopped
4 carrots, chopped
4 bay leaves
Pinch of thyme
1 cup butter
4 qts. chicken consomme
4 egg yolks, slightly
   beaten
4 cups artichoke hearts,
   sliced
4 cups whipping cream
Salt and pepper

Saute shallots, celery, carrots, bay leaves, and thyme in butter. Add consomme and simmer for 10 to 15 minutes. Whisk small amount of consomme into beaten yolks. Pour yolk mixture into consomme in a slow, steady stream, beating constantly. Do not boil. Add artichoke hearts. Mix with cream. Season to taste.

CATERERS

OYSTERS ROCKEFELLER
Serves 25

8 oz. bacon, finely
   chopped
6 cloves garlic, chopped
¼ lb. butter
1 bunch green onions,
   finely chopped
6 cups canned or cooked
   spinach with juice,
   chopped
1 bunch parsley, finely
   chopped
1 T. celery salt
¼ tsp. cayenne pepper
1 cup oyster liquid
4 oz. absinthe or Pernod
Salt to taste
Bread crumbs
6 dozen oysters,
   shucked, reserve shells
Rock salt

Brown bacon; add garlic and nearly brown. Add butter and green onions. Cook a few minutes; add spinach and all other ingredients except bread crumbs and oysters. Thicken with crumbs. Simmer 10 minutes. Half fill 12 piepans with rock salt. Arrange 6 oyster shells in each piepan. Place 1 room temperature oyster in each shell. Top with sauce. Put under broiler 6 inches from flame until heated through and browned on top.

JAMBALAYA
25-30 Servings

2 onions, chopped
½ cup butter
4 cans (1 lb. each)
   tomatoes
2 cans (6 oz. each)
   tomato paste
12 cloves garlic, chopped
8 stalks celery, chopped
1 green pepper, chopped
4 tsp. parsley, chopped
1 tsp. thyme
3 whole cloves
1 lb. ham, diced
8 lbs. shrimp, peeled and
   boiled
3 cups cooked rice
Salt, pepper and cayenne

Saute onions in butter for 5 minutes. Add tomatoes, tomato paste and cook 5 minutes, stirring constantly. Add garlic, celery, green pepper, parsley, thyme and cloves. Cook 30 minutes, stirring frequently. Stir in ham and cook for 5 minutes. Stir in shrimp and cook 5 minutes. Stir in rice, season to taste and simmer 30 minutes, stirring often.

CATERERS

HAM STEAK HAWAIIAN WITH CHAMPAGNE
SAUCE A LA GERMAINE
25 Servings

25 small ham steaks
25 sweet potatoes,
   boiled, peeled and
   halved
2 cups flour
1 cup oil
25 slices pineapple
25 maraschino cherries

CHAMPAGNE SAUCE:

6 white onions, finely
   chopped
1 cup olive oil
1½ cups flour
3 T. dry mustard
Pinch of salt
2 bottles Champagne
2 cups sugar

Broil ham steaks. Roll sweet potato halves in flour and fry in oil. Top each ham steak with a lightly broiled pineapple slice with a cherry in the center. Arrange on an ovenproof platter surrounded by sweet potatoes. For the sauce, saute onion in oil. Stir in flour; add mustard and salt, then Champagne. Pour sauce in the platter with ham steaks and sweet potatoes. Sprinkle sugar over ham and potatoes and run platter under low flame until well heated.

PEACH FLAMBE

2 qts. vanilla ice cream
8 macaroons, crushed
25 peach halves
4 lumps sugar
4 oz. rum

Place 1 scoop of ice cream in a dish. Sprinkle macaroon crumbs over ice cream. Dice peach halves and put in a chafing dish with lumps of sugar and rum. Ignite. While burning, pour over ice cream.

BEIGNETS

½ lb. butter
2 cups water
4 T. sugar
2 cups flour
4 eggs
2 egg yolks
Cooking oil
Confectioners' sugar

In a heavy bottomed pot, bring butter, water and sugar to a boil. Add flour all at once and stir vigorously over fire until mixture leaves the sides of the pot. Place mixture in a bowl and cool slightly. Add eggs and egg yolks 1 at a time and beat thoroughly after each addition. Spoon mixture in the size of a small egg into 375° fat; fry until brown. Sprinkle with confectioners' sugar.

FOODSTUFFS

Foodstuffs' One O'Clock Brunch For 8

Champagne Fruit Compote
Poached Salmon with Cucumber-Dill Sauce
Spinach Tart
Cognac French Toast
Croissants   Homemade Strawberry Jam
Fresh Roasted Mocha-Java Coffee
Champagne

CHAMPAGNE FRUIT COMPOTE

2 bananas, peeled and
  sliced
2 pts. strawberries,
  halved
2 cups fresh pineapple,
  diced
1 green apple, cored and
  diced
2 temple oranges, peeled,
  sliced and quartered
4 kiwis, sliced
¼ cup Cognac
¼ cup Grand Marnier
Split of Champagne

Place fruits in crystal bowl with Cognac and Grand Marnier. Chill. When ready to serve pour Champagne over fruit. Serve immediately.

COGNAC FRENCH TOAST

3 loaves FOODSTUFFS'
  baguettes or other
  suitable baguettes
½ cup sugar
2 cups Cognac
2 cups water
12 large eggs
½ cup milk
2 tsp. vanilla
½ tsp. salt

Cut baguettes into 1½-inch slices. Dissolve sugar in Cognac and water. Dip bread slices in mixture. Place on cookie sheet; refrigerate overnight. When ready to cook, combine eggs, milk, vanilla and salt. Dip slices in mixture. Place on clean buttered cookie sheet. Bake in 350° oven for 10 minutes on each side or until golden brown.

CATERERS

POACHED SALMON

Allow ½ to ¾ lb. per person. Clean but do not scale. Leave head attached; remove gills. Wrap fish in several layers of damp cheesecloth. Lay on rack or several layers of foil so fish may be lifted out of pan easily. Place fish in pan and set on top of stove. Add as many qts. of water needed to cover fish 2 inches. Add 1 T. salt and 1½ T. wine vinegar for every 2 qts. water. You may prepare the fish to this stage and allow to sit until ready to cook. For a 5 to 10 lb. fish: bring water to 185°, about 45 minutes. Water will move slightly but not bubble. This will keep flesh firm. Maintain water temperature at 185° for an additional 45 minutes. Lower heat and allow temperature to reach 140°, about 45 minutes. To serve hot, allow to remain at 140° before removing from pan. To serve cold, cool several hours in liquid before removing it. Then serve or place in refrigerator still wrapped in cheesecloth. To prepare for serving, remove from liquid; drain and place on tray. Cut cheesecloth and remove gently taking care not to flake body. Remove any bones jutting from fins into flesh. Remove jawbones attached to body at neck end of fish. To serve flat, peel off skin on upper side and gently scrape off brown to expose pink meat. Carefully slide onto serving platter.

SPINACH TART

1 10-inch pastry shell
1 small onion, chopped
2 cloves garlic, minced
1 pkg. (10 oz.) spinach, thawed and squeezed dry
1 lb. ricotta cheese
3 T. flour
1 cup grated Gruyere cheese
4 large eggs
½ tsp. salt
⅛ tsp. ground black pepper
⅛ tsp. ground nutmeg
½ tsp. basil
2 cups creme fraiche

Saute onion and garlic in 1 T. butter. Drain. Line unbaked shell with spinach, ricotta, onion and garlic. Mix flour with Gruyere and place on top of spinach. Beat eggs. Add salt, pepper, nutmeg and basil. Pour into shell and top with creme fraiche. Bake in 375° oven for 40 minutes or until set.

CATERERS

GAPER'S CATERERS

Holiday Menu for 8

Beignets Au Fromage
Gingered Pear Wedges with Prosciutto
Cream of Pumpkin Soup
Celeriac Salad on Romaine Leaves
Imperial Turkey
Thanksgiving Dressing
Cranberry and Kumquat Relish
Orange Yams
Puree of Peas in Artichoke Bottoms
Cold Lemon Souffle decorated with Whipped Cream Rosettes
and
Bittersweet Chocolate Curls
French Roast Coffee

BEIGNETS AU FROMAGE   36 Servings

1 lb. natural Gruyere
  cheese
¾ cup flour
¼ tsp. salt
1 egg, beaten
1 T. salad oil
½ cup beer, at room
  temperature
1 egg white, stiffly beaten
Fat for deep frying

Cut cheese in small cubes. Sift ½ cup flour with the salt; stir in oil and egg. Add beer gradually, stirring until the mixture is smooth. Let stand for 1 hour. Fold in egg white. Lightly dredge the cubes of cheese in the remaining flour and coat with the batter. Brown in deep fat at 375°. Drain on absorbent paper. Serve piping hot.

GINGERED PEAR WEDGES
AND PROSCIUTTO   24 Pieces

3 large fresh Bartlett
  pears
1 T. freshly grated ginger
6 slices prosciutto

Slice each pear into 8 wedges and sprinkle with ginger. Slice prosciutto and wrap around each gingered pear wedge.

CATERERS

CREAM OF PUMPKIN SOUP

6-8 Servings

3 T. butter
4 green onions, chopped
1 medium onion, sliced
1½ lbs. pumpkin, diced (2 lbs. canned pumpkin)
4 cups chicken broth
½ tsp. salt
½ tsp. white pepper
1 cup half and half
1 T. butter
Chopped parsley and croutons

Melt 2 T. butter in a large saucepan. Add chopped green onions and saute until almost soft. Remove from pan. Saute onion until brown (a well-browned onion imports a nutty taste to the soup). Add pumpkin, chicken broth, salt and pepper. Bring to a boil and simmer until pumpkin is soft. Puree the soup in a blender or food processor. Correct seasonings. Add half and half and butter. Heat the soup to the boiling point and serve garnished with chopped parsley and croutons. (For a different touch add curry powder or nutmeg to taste.)

CELERIAC SALAD

3 large celeriac
Herb French dressing
Romaine leaves
2 eggs, hard cooked

Blanch celeriac in boiling salted water to cover for 5 minutes; drain. Cool the root and cut into fine julienne strips. Toss the celeriac gently with dressing. Arrange Romaine leaves on individual salad plates. Fill leaves with celeriac and garnish with 2 chopped yolks and white of 1 hard-cooked egg.

PUREE OF PEAS IN ARTICHOKE BOTTOMS

6 Servings

1 tsp. sugar
1 cup boiling water
2 pkgs. (10 oz. each) frozen peas
4 T. unsalted butter
6 artichoke bottoms
Butter

Add sugar to boiling water. Add peas and cook 3 to 4 minutes. Drain. Reserve cooking liquid. Place peas in blender or food processor. Add 4 T. butter and puree, using the reserved cooking liquid as needed to make the mixture completely smooth but not watery. Heat artichoke bottoms thoroughly in hot butter in frying pan. Mound puree on artichoke bottoms and serve.

CATERERS

THANKSGIVING DRESSING   Enough for a 15-lb. Turkey

3 pkgs. (6 oz. each) wild
   and long grain rice
6 cups chicken broth
3 T. butter
3 T. lemon juice
1½ tsp. tarragon
¼ cup butter
1 lb. mushrooms, sliced
1 large onion, minced
1 green pepper, chopped
1 tsp. sauce Diable
½ cup dry sherry
½ cup parsley, minced
1 cup toasted hazelnuts,
   pecans or walnuts,
   coarsely chopped
Salt and pepper

Place rice, chicken broth and 3 T. butter in a 6-qt. saucepan or Dutch oven. Cover tightly and bring to a boil. Simmer gently for 20 minutes. Remove cover and simmer 10 more minutes or until rice has absorbed broth. Add lemon juice and tarragon. Stir with a large fork. This will keep rice grains separate. Melt remaining butter in 10-inch skillet and saute mushrooms, onions, and green pepper until soft. Add sauce Diable and sherry; cook 2 minutes. Remove from heat. Combine vegetables with rice, using 2 forks. Toss in parsley and nuts. Season with salt and pepper.

CRANBERRY AND KUMQUAT RELISH

4 cups fresh cranberries
2 cups kumquats
2½ cups sugar or to taste

Grind cranberries with kumquats. Blend in sugar. Chill relish thoroughly.

ORANGE YAMS   6-8 Servings

2 lbs. purple yams
½ cup butter
2 T. sugar
2 T. orange juice
2 tsp. grated orange rind

Cook purple yams in simmering salted water for 25 to 30 minutes, or until they are tender. Cool yams, peel and cut into thick slices. Arrange slices in a buttered glass baking dish. Cream together butter, sugar, orange juice and grated orange rind. Cover the yams with the sauce. Bake at 375° until they are nicely glazed.

CATERERS

GEORGE JEWELL

English Picnic for 6

Breast of Chicken on Bed of Fresh Mint with Thin Lemon Twist
Tabouli
Avocado Mousse Centered with Escabeche of Jumbo Shrimp
Snow Pea Salad with Sesame Dressing
Sour Dough Bread   Whipped Butter
Country Cheese with Fresh Berries

BREAST OF CHICKEN WITH LEMON AND MINT

8 whole chicken breasts,
  halved
1 whole lemon
⅓ cup flour
1½ tsp. salt
½ tsp. paprika
4 T. salad oil
2 T. brown sugar
1 lemon, thinly sliced
1 cup chicken broth
2 sprigs fresh mint

Wash chicken and drain on paper towels. Grate peel of whole lemon. Reserve. Cut lemon in ½ and squeeze juice over chicken, rubbing juice into each piece. Place chicken, flour, salt and paprika in paper bag and shake to coat well. Brown chicken slowly in oil. Arrange in 2-qt. casserole. Sprinkle grated lemon peel over chicken. Add brown sugar and sliced lemon. Pour on broth; top with mint. Cover and bake in 375° oven until chicken is tender, about 30 to 40 minutes. Remove mint before serving. Cool to room temperature.

AVOCADO MOUSSE WITH SHRIMP ESCABECHE

1 medium avocado,
  peeled and diced
1 T. lemon juice
1 cup sour cream
1 tsp. sugar
¼ tsp. salt
½ tsp. onion salt
Few grains of cayenne
½ cup mayonnaise
1 envelope unflavored
  gelatin
½ cup cold water

Soften gelatin in water; dissolve over low heat. Place all ingredients in blender. Blend until smooth, about 1 minute, stopping blender to stir down once if necessary. Pour into lightly oiled 3-cup ring mold. Cover with foil and chill until firm. Unmold on serving platter and fill center with Escabeche of shrimp.

SHRIMP ESCABECHE

1 cup chopped onions
3 cloves garlic, pressed
⅔ cup olive oil
2 lbs. shrimp, uncooked
½ cup lemon juice
1½ tsp. salt
Pinch of black pepper
¼ tsp. dry mustard
2 pickled jalapeno
   peppers, seeded and
   minced
1 cup chopped green
   onions

Saute onion and garlic in ⅓ cup of oil until onion is transparent. Add shrimp and cook until shrimp is pink. Remove from heat and cool. Mix remaining ingredients and add to shrimp. Marinate covered in refrigerator for 24 hours; baste several times.

TABOULI

1 cup cracked wheat
½ cup minced onion
½ cup plus 2 T. olive oil
2 cups chicken broth
2 lemons
½ tsp. salt
½ tsp. pepper
2 T. freshly chopped mint
¾ cup finely chopped
   tomatoes, skinned and
   seeded
¾ cup finely chopped
   cucumbers, peeled and
   seeded
¾ cup finely chopped
   green pepper, seeded
1 clove garlic, minced

Soak cracked wheat in water to cover for 2 to 3 hours. Drain. Saute minced onions in 2 T. olive oil until translucent. Add wheat and broth. Simmer covered for about 15 minutes or until water is absorbed. Cool. Add remaining olive oil and juice of 2 lemons to moisten. Season to taste with salt and pepper. Add mint, tomatoes, cucumbers, peppers and garlic. Marinate at least 2 hours or overnight.

CATERERS

INGRID

Dinner with Ingrid

Gravad Lax with Sauce Piquante
Breast of Mermaid with Bearnaise
Fresh Artichokes   Fresh Asparagus   Fresh Baby Carrots
Fried Cheese with Black Currant Sauce

GRAVAD LAX   25 Servings

Select an absolutely fresh 5 lb. salmon. Scale, cut in ½ lengthwise
and fillet. Place ½ of salmon, skin side down on bed of fresh dill. Mix
1 cup salt with 1 cup sugar. Pour ½ of salt mixture on pink flesh of
salmon. Add a thick layer of fresh dill; add remaining salt mixture.
Place the other ½ of salmon, flesh side down on top. Weight down
with heavy wooden cutting board. Refrigerate 24 hours. To serve,
place fillets skin side down on cutting board. With a very sharp knife,
make paper thin slices starting at larger end and cutting horizontally
towards the tail. Will keep 10 days to 2 weeks under refrigeration.

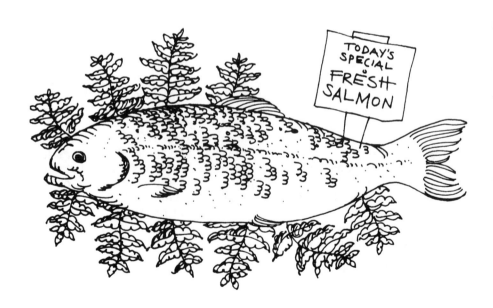

SAUCE PIQUANTE

½ cup Coleman's dry
    mustard
½ cup brown sugar
¼ cup vinegar
½ cup olive oil

Thoroughly blend dry mustard, sugar and vinegar. Stir in olive oil and mix well. This sauce is very hot so serve sparingly.

BREAST OF MERMAID

Allow ½ skinned and boned chicken breast per person. Pound chicken until very thin. Salt and pepper sparingly. Place in refrigerator for 2 hours. Dip each piece of chicken into well-beaten egg and well-crushed packaged herbed poultry dressing. Saute quickly in unsalted butter until lightly browned. Garnish each ½ breast with 2 small pieces of Alaskan king crab. Nap with sauce bearnaise. Serve with an abundance of fresh vegetables.

FRIED CAMEMBERT WITH BLACK CURRANT SAUCE

Allow 2 oz. camembert cheese per person. Cut cheese into serving wedges. Dip wedges into well-beaten egg and bread crumbs. Chill for several hours. Heat oil to 350°. Fry cheese wedges until lightly browned. To make sauce combine one 12 oz. jar of black currant jam with ¼ cup brandy. Pour sauce over hot cheese.

CATERERS

THE MIXING BOWL

An Indoor Shore Dinner for 4

Moules Ravigote
Landlubbers Clambake

MOULES RAVIGOTE

MAYONNAISE:

2 egg yolks
1 T. wine vinegar
1½ tsp. dry mustard
1 tsp. salt
⅛ tsp. ground white pepper
1 cup vegetable oil
2 T. fresh strained lemon juice
1 tsp. finely chopped garlic

MOULES:

6 dozen large mussels in their shells
2 hard-cooked eggs, finely chopped
¼ cup capers, drained and rinsed
¼ cup finely cut fresh chives
¼ cup finely chopped fresh parsley

Drop egg yolks into warm, dry mixing bowl. Beat vigorously for about 2 minutes, until thickened. Stir in vinegar, mustard, salt and white pepper. Beat in ½ cup of oil, ½ tsp. at a time. Make sure each addition is absorbed before adding more. It should now be the consistency of thick cream. Pour in remaining oil in slow, steady stream, beating constantly. Stir in lemon juice and garlic. Taste for seasoning. Refrigerate until ready to use. Scrub mussels thoroughly under cold running water. Use a stiff brush or steel mesh scouring pad. With sharp knife pull black hairlike tufts off shells and discard. Combine mussels and 1 cup of water in a heavy 4 to 6-qt. casserole. Bring to boil over high heat. Cover tightly; reduce heat to low and steam mussels 10 minutes. Turn once or twice to cook evenly. When steamed all mussels should be open; discard ones that are closed. Using tongs, transfer mussels to a large platter. Remove and discard shells. Chop mussels coarsely; cool to room temperature. In a large bowl, combine mussels, eggs, capers, chives, and parsley. Toss gently but thoroughly. Add mayonnaise and coat well.

LANDLUBBERS CLAMBAKE

Damp seaweed or corn
husks, celery, lettuce or
spinach leaves
(seaweed may be
obtained from a
seafood specialty
house)
1 qt. water
4 lobsters (1¼ to 1½ lbs.
each)
4 ears of corn with husks
on
4 dozen soft shell clams
1 potato
1½ lbs. butter, melted
Preheated bowls for
melted butter
Salt
Peppermill
4 soup bowls for clams
4 serving platters (for
everything else)
4 nutcrackers
Large white paper dinner
napkins
Paper bibs

Cover the bottom of a large pot with 3 to 4 inches of damp seaweed. Add 1 qt. of water and turn up heat until water boils. Place lobsters, head down in pot and cover them with a layer of seaweed. Add foil-wrapped corn and cover with another layer of seaweed. Place clams on top of corn and cover with seaweed. Place potato on top and cover pot. The potato is your thermometer. When potato is tender, about 1 hour, the clambake is ready. Turn off heat. Lift clams from pot with ladle and put into soup bowls, retaining as much juice as possible. Using tongs, remove corn and lobsters to platter. Serve with bowls of melted butter.

CATERERS

NORTH SHORE CATERING OF LAKE FOREST

Summer Poolside Barbecue for 30

Gazpacho Soup
Baby Back Ribs
Corn in the Husk
Cucumber Mousse with Mint Sauce
Fruit Kabobs

"QUICK" GAZPACHO SOUP   30 Servings

5 cups cucumbers,
  peeled, seeded, diced
2½ cups diced celery
2½ cups diced onion
2½ cups diced green
  pepper
3 fresh tomatoes
¼ cup chopped parsley
⅛ cup olive oil
1 T. lemon juice
1 T. Worcestershire
1 tsp. salt
1 T. wine vinegar
¼ tsp. hot pepper sauce
2 cans (46 oz. each)
  tomato juice
Dash garlic powder

Finely dice cucumbers, celery, onion, green pepper and tomatoes. Add remaining ingredients and chill for 24 hours before serving. Serve cold in plastic mugs.

CORN IN THE HUSK   30 Servings

30 ears of corn
1 lb. butter, melted

Soak corn in water for about 30 minutes prior to placing on the grill. Place on outer edge of grill for about 10 to 15 minutes. Peel back husk; use as handle; dip in butter.

BABY BACK RIBS

30 Servings

30 slabs of baby back ribs
Barbecue sauce

Grill slabs and apply generous amounts of your favorite barbecue sauce. For best results, parboil or pre-bake prior to barbecuing. This can be done a day ahead.

CUCUMBER MOUSSE

30 Servings

8 cucumbers, peeled and
seeded
½ cup onion
1 cup celery
1½ cups reserved onion
and celery liquid
1 T. lemon juice
1 tsp. Worcestershire
Dash hot pepper sauce
and garlic powder
1 tsp. salt
1 cup minced, fresh
parsley
1 qt. chicken broth
3 T. unflavored gelatin
1½ cups sour cream
1½ cups mayonnaise
½ cup chopped green
onions

Grind cucumbers, onion and celery. Reserve liquid. Combine reserved liquid, lemon juice, Worcestershire, hot pepper sauce, garlic powder, salt, parsley, chicken broth and gelatin. Bring to a boil. Allow to reach room temperature. Combine remaining ingredients, pour into oiled molds. Refrigerate. Serve with mint sauce.

MINT SAUCE

1 pt. sour cream
¼ cup mayonnaise
1 T. fresh mint, minced

For sauce, combine all ingredients.

CATERERS

OUT-TO-LUNCH

All American New Year's Day Celebration for 25

Curried Almonds
Oven Baked "Out to Lunch" Chili
Cranberry and Corn Meal Muffins
Pea Pod and Avocado Salad
Celery Seed Dressing
Rice Custard Pudding with Raspberry Puree
California Champagne   Domestic Beer

CURRIED ALMONDS   25 Servings

3 lbs. shelled almonds
3 cloves garlic
1½ cups olive oil
3 tsp. curry powder
Salt to taste

Place blanched almonds in a flat baking pan with the garlic, olive oil and curry powder. Shake well to coat the almonds. Roast at 350° for 25 to 35 minutes or until the almonds are crisp and lightly browned. Sprinkle with salt and add more curry powder, if necessary. Drain on paper towel.

Recipe works well with cashews or Brazil nuts, or any combination.

CRANBERRY AND CORNMEAL MUFFINS   4 Dozen

3 cups flour
3 cups yellow cornmeal
6 T. sugar
4 T. baking powder
2 tsp. salt
6 eggs, lightly beaten
3 cups milk
⅔ cup vegetable oil
1 cup finely chopped
  cooked smoked ham or
  bacon
2 T. chopped chives
3 cups fresh cranberries,
  rinsed and drained

Combine flour, cornmeal, sugar, baking powder and salt in bowl. Beat the eggs into the milk and oil. Add to dry ingredients. Stir to moisten. Add the ham, chives, and cranberries. Mix. Spoon into well-greased muffin tins. Bake at 425° for 15 to 20 minutes, or until done. Serve warm.

CATERERS

OVEN-BAKED "OUT TO LUNCH" CHILI   25 Servings

10 lbs. coarsely ground
   beef
2 large onions, chopped
   medium fine
2 T. mixed Italian herbs
8 T. chili powder
2 tsp. cayenne pepper
2 tsp. garlic powder
3 T. Lawry's seasoned
   salt
1 T. coarsely ground
   black pepper
1 tsp. salt
5 cans (10¾ oz. each)
   tomato puree
2 cans (28 oz. each)
   whole tomatoes
4 cans (15 oz. each)
   kidney beans

Preheat oven to 500°. Combine ground beef and onion. Place in large roasting pan. Put in oven for 5 minutes. After 5 minutes, stir mixture thoroughly. Return to oven. Keep checking and stirring mixture at 5 minute intervals until meat mixture is thoroughly browned and all fat has been rendered. Remove browned meat mixture from oven and pour off all fat. Reduce oven temperature to 325°. Add to meat mixture all remaining ingredients except kidney beans. Cover pan with foil or tightly fitting cover and return to oven. Bake at 325° for 2 hours.

Remove cover, add kidney beans, stir to distribute, cover. Return to oven and bake 1 additional hour. Transfer chili to large serving crock with ladle. When serving surround crock with small bowls filled with chopped onions, sour cream, and grated Cheddar cheese.

PEA POD AND AVOCADO SALAD   25 Servings

3 lbs. fresh pea pods,
   blanched
4 avocados, peeled and
   sliced
4 large heads romaine
   lettuce, rinsed and
   dried
2 large bunches
   watercress
1 lb. bean sprouts
6 oz. alfalfa sprouts
12 radishes, thinly sliced

Blanch pea pods by dropping pods into rapidly boiling water for 1 minute; drain. Immediately submerge in ice water. Rub peeled avocado with lemon juice to avoid discoloration. Tear lettuce into bite-sized pieces and put into large salad bowl. Add all remaining ingredients and toss lightly. Add Celery Seed dressing and quickly toss again.

CATERERS

CELERY SEED DRESSING

¼ cup whole celery seeds
¾ cup sugar
¼ tsp. black pepper
¼ tsp. paprika
¼ tsp. dry mustard
1 tsp. salt
1 T. lemon juice
⅓ cup tarragon vinegar
1 cup vegetable oil

In large mixing bowl, add all ingredients except oil. Beat with wire whisk until completely blended. Add oil and beat until incorporated. Chill. Stir well before using.

RICE CUSTARD PUDDING   25 Servings

3 cups uncooked white
   rice (not instant)
3½ qts. whole milk
1 cup butter
16 large eggs
2⅔ cups sugar
1 tsp. ground nutmeg
4 tsp. vanilla extract
2 cups light seedless
   raisins
Equal amounts of
   cinnamon and sugar,
   mixed, for topping

Grease a 20 x 12-inch baking pan. Cook rice, following directions on label of package. Pour into buttered baking dish. Scald milk with butter. Separately, in mixing bowl, beat eggs slightly with sugar, nutmeg and vanilla extract. Gradually stir this mixture into scalded milk mixture. Arrange raisins over rice in baking dish. Strain egg mixture over rice and sprinkle with cinnamon-sugar. Place baking dish in shallow pan of hot water in oven. Bake at 325° for 1 hour, until almost set but soft in center. As mixture cools, custard will set. Serve with Raspberry Puree.

RASPBERRY PUREE

2 pkgs. frozen
   raspberries
¼ cup Cointreau

Blend above in blender on high for 1 minute. Strain through fine sieve into bowl to remove seeds. Serve chilled on Rice Custard Pudding.

PEPPERCORNS

JAMOCA WALNUT MOUSSE

36 Servings

2¼ cups plus 2 T. sugar
½ tsp. salt
7 T. instant coffee
2½ tsp. vanilla
4 envelopes unflavored
   gelatin
5 cups milk
2 T. Kahlua
12 large egg yolks
10 large egg whites
5 cups whipping cream
1 cup chopped walnuts
1½ cups rich chocolate
   sauce

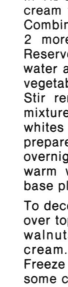

Combine 1¼ cups sugar, salt, coffee vanilla, gelatin and milk in 3-qt. saucepan. Beat Kahlua and 12 egg yolks until smooth. Combine egg yolk and gelatin mixture in saucepan. Whisk continuously over medium heat until mixture thickens slightly, about 10 to 15 minutes. Cool until partly congealed. In 4½-qt. mixing bowl, whip 10 egg whites until frothy. Slowly add 1 cup plus 2 T. sugar, whipping to soft peak stage. Reserve. In 4½-qt. mixing bowl whip 2 cups of cream to thick, custard consistency. Combine cream with egg whites. Whip 2 more cups of cream until stiff. Reserve. Rinse 4½-qt. bowl with cold water and coat with thin layer of vegetable oil. Reserve 2 T. walnuts. Stir remaining walnuts into gelatin mixture. Fold gelatin mixture into egg whites and whipped cream. Pour into prepared bowl, cover and refrigerate overnight. To unmold, dip briefly in warm water and invert on a metal base placed on wire rack.

To decorate: drizzle chocolate sauce over top and sprinkle with remaining walnuts. Whip remaining cup of cream. Pipe rosettes on mousse. Freeze until ready to serve. Ladle some chocolate sauce on each serving.

CATERERS

Allen Catering
322 Skokie Boulevard
Northbrook, Illinois

Chef Ronaldo
65 East Palatine Road
Prospect Heights, Illinois

Mitchell Cobey, Cuisine
100 East Walton
Chicago, Illinois

Colonial Caterers
223 South Main Street
Naperville, Illinois

Foodstuffs, Inc.
338 Park Avenue
Glencoe, Illinois

Gaper's Caterers
16 West Washington Street
Chicago, Illinois

Ingrid's
902 Asbury Avenue
Evanston, Illinois

George Jewell
1110 West Belmont Avenue
Chicago, Illinois

The Mixing Bowl, Ltd.
1341 North Sedgwick Street
Chicago, Illinois

**North Shore Catering of
   Lake Forest**
419 West Washington Street
Lake Bluff, Illinois

Out to Lunch, Inc.
200 East Chestnut Street
Chicago, Illinois

Peppercorns Catering, Ltd.
564 West Main Street
Lake Zurich, Illinois

VARIATIONS OF MY FAVORITE RECIPES

VARIATIONS OF MY FAVORITE RECIPES

VARIATIONS OF MY FAVORITE RECIPES

VARIATIONS OF MY FAVORITE RECIPES

CATEGORY INDEX

CATEGORY INDEX

CATEGORY INDEX

CATEGORY INDEX

CATEGORY INDEX

373

CATEGORY INDEX

CATEGORY INDEX

INDEX

INDEX

INDEX

INDEX

INDEX

INDEX

INDEX

INDEX

INDEX

INDEX

INDEX

INDEX

SOUPCON II COMMITTEE

Editor-in-Chief	Patricia Michael Ballot
Managing Editor	Joanne Bennett Pelletiere
Copy Editor	Ellen Stokes Honig
Art Director	Mary Lois Scofield Hakewill
Food Editors	Roberta Hankes Olshansky Catherine Marx Schwartz Annette Ashlock Stover
Associate Editors	Joan Potter Bergman Diane Nicholson Dean Judy Kennedy Elias Nancy Monek Gaynor Ann Self Lee Heidi Brumbaugh Mangel Hope McCulloch Martin Katharine Hellman Morris
Business Manager	Lolly Magnuson Siemon
Production Manager	Victoria Relfe Hamilton
Production Assistants	Sharon Luschen Keller Barbara Valicenti Sharon Weir Zalesky
Catering Editor	Susan Melinette Riding
Wine Editor	Melanie M. Brunner
Wine Consultant	George J. Schaefer

Order Information

To order a Soupçon II cookbook,
please contact The Junior League of Chicago
by phone, mail or e-mail at the following:

The Junior League of Chicago
attn: Cookbook Committee Chair
1447 North Astor Street
Chicago, Illinois 60610

312-664-4462 ext. 109
E-mail: jlcsoupcon2@yahoo.com

Web site: www.jlchicago.org

Please include your name, address,
phone, e-mail address and the number of
books for your order.

Thank you for supporting the mission of
The Junior League of Chicago!